INSURANCE LAW
AND
PRACTICE IN NIGERIA

INSURANCE LAW
and
PRACTICE IN NIGERIA

by

J.O IRUKWU,
MBA., Ph.D., ACII., FIIN., FCI., Arb, FBIM
of Lincoln's Inn, Barrister; Solicitor and Advocate of the
Supreme Court of Nigeria; President, Nigerian Insurance
Law Association; Visiting Professor, West African
College of Insurance and Risk Management, Monrovia,
Liberia; President, Faculty of Risk Management
(FARIM)

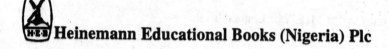 Heinemann Educational Books (Nigeria) Plc

HEINEMANN EDUCATIONAL BOOKS (NIGERIA) PLC
Head Office: 1 Ighodaro Road, Jericho, PMB 5205, Ibadan
Phone: (02) 2412268, 2410943; *Fax:* (02) 2411089, 2413237.

Area Offices and Branches
Abeokuta. Akure. Bauchi. Benin City. Calabar. Enugu. Ibadan
Ikeja. Ilorin. Jos. Kano. Katsina. Maiduguri. Makurdi. Minna
Owerri. Port Harcourt. Sokoto. Uyo. Yola. Zaria

© J.O. Irukwu 1967, 1991
Published with the cooperation of Franklin Book
Programmes 1967
Second Edition 1971
Reprinted 1972
Third Edition 1978
Reprinted 1981
First published in this Revised Edition by
Heinemann Educational Books (Nigeria) Plc 1991
Reprinted 1999

ISBN 978 129 498 1

Printed by Pat-Mag Press Limited Ibadan

FOREWORD TO THE FIRST EDITION

Modern Insurance was almost unknown in this country until the early part of this century; it is therefore understandable that there is hardly any literature on the subject which makes any special reference to the practice of insurance in this country. As far as I know, this book is the first of its kind, and the author's attempt to cover some of the many facets of the practice of Insurance Business in Nigeria is indeed commendable. Personally, I have derived considerable pleasure from a perusal of the contents and I am indeed very pleased to have both the opportunity and privilege of writing this foreword. Insurance is a complex business and to the layman, it offers an avalanche of pitfalls and this is why a book such as this which attempts to explain in a practical manner its many ramifications must be commended. Both the practising lawyer and the Nigerian professional Insurer will find a great deal that is of value in the sections dealing with the history of the Insurance Industry and the substantive law applicable to it.

The ordinary citizen will find the sections dealing with Insurable interest, Brokers, Contributions, Warranty and the Doctrine of Proximate Cause very useful. It is well known that failure to appreciate the true meaning of the subject of Contribution in Insurance business as well as the doctrine of proximate cause of any loss suffered by the insured quite often leads to endless controversy between the insurer and the insured. Some of the sections dealing with very important aspects of Insurance in this book such as Endorsements on Insurance Policies, Re-insurance, and General Claims Procedure, although useful, deserve more attention in the interest of the layman or the ordinary citizen who is compelled by provisions of many local statutes to take out insurance policies in regard to some aspects of his business and to whom this book is primarily addressed.

In Part 2, Chapter V, under the subject of 'Insurable Interest' the author ventures to submit that among Nigerians there exist some cultural or ethnic groups who may legitimately be considered to have an 'Insurable interest', in the lives of its members, to the extent of the burial and other expenses that would be incurred at the death of such members. However, it is well known that the right which is required to support an Insurable interest must be a right (not a moral obligation or claim) which the law recognises as valid and subsisting. No doubt, the issue will some day engage the attention of the Nigerian Courts of law and interesting questions as to the time of existence of such Insurable interests will arise.

On the whole, the author attempts in rational and coherent form to state the principles and practice of Insurance law in Nigeria; he has in his effort to present the principles of the Insurance law in ordinary simple language avoided the use of archaic expressions which in the past have confounded the layman and, in many ways, bedeviled the progress in this country of Insurance Industry.

Finally, the language of the preface has encouraged my hope that the effort and labour of the author deserve the support of the legal profession in this country.

C. Idigbe,
Chief Justice,
Mid-western Nigeria.

Chief Justice's Chambers,
High Court of Justice,
Benin City,
Mid-western Nigeria.

PREFACE TO THE THIRD EDITION

It is now ten years since the first edition of this book was published. During this period, there has been a lot of changes and developments in the business of insurance and the general legal position has also altered considerably. A new edition of the book has become necessary as a result of the continued demand for the book and in particular, due to the changes in the law arising from the provisions of the Insurance Decree 1976 which came into force on the 1st December 1976. Other legislations that have led to changes in the law and practice of insurance in Nigeria include the Insurance Regulations 1977 and Decree No. 49 of 1977 establishing the Nigeria Reinsurance Corporation. All the changes in the law contained in these enactments have been reflected in this edition.

In the current edition some chapters have been rewritten and three new chapters have been added. A new chapter X which discusses the general principles of reinsurance has been added to this edition. This chapter also covers the different types of reinsurance treaties and facilities available in the Nigerian market. The whole of chapter XIII which dealt with the subject of governmental control has been deleted and replaced by a new chapter XIV entitled "Governmental Control and State intervention in Insurance." This chapter gives reasons for governmental control and discusses the extent of governmental control in Nigeria, including details of the conditions for carrying on insurance business in Nigeria, and the conditions to be fulfilled by an applicant for registration as an insurer. It also lists the conditions under which the Director of Insurance may cancel the registration of a registered insurer. The chapter also covers in some detail the provisions of the Insurance Decree 1976 and the various changes introduced by that decree. It also discusses the newly created office of Director of Insurance and the extent of the authority of the Director as conferred on him by the decree. It concludes with an examination of Decree No. 49 of 1977 establishing the Nigeria Reinsurance Corporation, identifying the duties and functions of the Corporation.

The last chapter, which is completely new, deals with the subject of the future of insurance and the insurance industry in Nigeria. It examines the various classes of insurance and predicts the likely trend

vii

and the pattern of their future development. The chapter also examines the future of the insurance industry itself, the role of the insurance manager and the qualities and essential tools that the insurance manager of the future must possess if he is to cope successfully with the challenges of the future. If also discusses the importance of records and statistics in the future development of insurance in Nigeria. The chapter emphasised the need for a code of conduct for insurance practitioners in line with the existing code of conduct for members of the Insurance Institute of Nigeria. The full text of the Institute's Code of Conduct is published as an appendix to this edition.

At the time when the second edition of this book was published in 1971, the economy of Nigeria was just picking up after the setback caused by the Nigerian Civil War. Since then, the Nigerian economy has grown tremendously, and so has the insurance industry. Any progress in the national economy is generally reflected in the insurance industry. When the first edition of the book was published in 1967, the total annual premium income of all the Nigerian insurance companies was less than £9,000,000. When the second edition was published in 1971, the gross national premium income of all the insurance companies in the country had risen to approximately ₦100,000,000. The estimated gross annual premium income of the market for 1977 is approximately ₦250,000,000. This is clearly an indication that Nigerians are becoming more insurance conscious and that the Nigerian insurance industry is responding adequately to the needs of our economy. This remarkable development in the insurance industry places certain responsibilities on all insurance practitioners, and it is in response to this duty that this book has been written and up-dated.

In view of the fact that this book has become a useful source of reference for students of insurance generally, the busy legal practitioner, and all others interested in insurance law and practice in Nigeria, I have found it necessary to bring into this volume all the relevant legislations and regulations touching upon the business of insurance in Nigeria in the form of appendices to this volume. These include the Insurance Decree 1976, Insurance Regulations 1977, the Nigeria Reinsurance Corporation Decree 1977, the National Insurance Corporation of Nigeria Decree 1969 and the Marine Insurance Act, 1961. Also included in the list of appendices is a comprehensive list of all the approved insurers and a list of registered insurance brokers as at the date of publication, and the code of conduct for members of the Insurance Institute of Nigeria.

As stated in earlier editions, the purpose of this publication has always been to promote insurance education. It is also my wish that the book will assist in ensuring a better understanding of the purpose of insurance and its role in the development of the national economy. I do hope that this edition will achieve these objectives.

I wish to thank all those who have played a part in seeing to the publication of this edition.

Lagos, October, 1977.   J. O. I.

ix

PREFACE TO THE SECOND EDITION

This book was written in 1966 and published at the beginning of 1967. Since then there have been a lot of changes and developments in the business of insurance in Nigeria. Two factors have made a new edition of the book necessary: first, the changes and developments in the business of insurance in Nigeria during the period 1966 to date, and secondly the increasing popularity of the book.

In this edition some chapters have been re-written, and two new chapters have been added. The new Chapter 12 entitled: "DISCHARGE OF LIABILITIES UNDER LIFE POLICIES" deals with the subject of Surrender Values of Life policies—a subject that became very topical following the lapsing or surrendering of a number of life policies at the end of the Nigerian Civil War. Another interesting point touched upon in this chapter is the question of a possible 'Breach by the life office' where the insurer decides to cease underwriting life business in Nigeria but the insured is still willing and able to keep his policy alive by paying his premiums—what is an adequate compensation to the policyholder in such a case? This and other related questions are answered in this chapter.

The new chapter 13 deals with the subject of GOVERNMENTAL CONTROL OF INSURANCE—a subject which was never touched upon in the first edition. The chapter states the reasons for Governmental Control and the methods by which this control is exercised in Nigeria. The Insurance Companies Act, 1961, and some of its provisions are discussed in this chapter. This chapter concludes with a list of suggested Reforms such as The Rehabilitation of Insurance Companies; Wide Distribution of Shareownership; Criminal Prosecution of Defaulting Directors and Periodical Examination of Insurance Companies to ensure their stability. It is hoped that these reforms, if effected, would be both in the national interest and in the interest of the insuring community.

The insurance Companies Act, 1961, provided for the Registration of Insurance Companies as distinct from incorporation. This section of the Act had not been enforced at the time the first edition of this book appeared in 1967. The subject of Registration and the conditions to be fulfilled before registration are contained in chapter 13.

The Nigerian economy has grown tremendously during the past decade and so has the insurance industry and from all indications, this trend is continuing. At the time the first edition of this book was published early in 1967, there were just over thirty insurance companies operating in the country with a total annual premium income of just under £9,000,000. Today, there are now about seventy registered insurance companies with an estimated annual premium income of about £50,000,000 at the end of 1970—the estimated figure for 1971 is expected to be in the region of £60,000,000. This clearly confirms two things:

(a) that the economy of Nigeria is growing daily, and
(b) that as the economy grows so does the need for insurance protection.

The primary purpose of this publication has always been to promote insurance education and to eliminate misunderstandings between the insurer and the insuring community. It is hoped that the present edition will foster this objective.

I wish to thank various friends who have read sections of this book and have made many helpful suggestions; and in particular, Mr. William Shand, Life Assurance expert of the Swiss Reinsurance Company. My thanks are also due to the book reviewers and critics especially to Messrs Fola Sasegbon and C. O. Akpamgbo—both distinguished Lawyers whose constructive criticisms of the first edition compelled me to add an index of cases and a chapter on War damages and the insurance of War risks to the present text.

J. O. I.

Lagos,
October, 1971.

PREFACE TO FIRST EDITION

The subject of insurance and the law governing its operation in Nigeria is one that should be of interest to all; but in writing this book I have in mind, and I am constantly addressing myself to five classes of readers.

First, the layman, who provides the premiums out of which the funds (and therefore the security) of the industry is built; and who, therefore, ought to have an elementary knowledge of the law governing the business in Nigeria, and particularly in so far as it bears on his legal rights and obligations in the transaction. Second, the students in High Schools and the Universities taking formal courses on the subject of insurance. Third, the insurance official, especially the insurance claims official, who ought to be conscious of his dual responsibilities: on the one hand as a trustee of the insurance fund for 'the benefit of the insuring community as a whole, and on the other as a prudent business-man providing a service which should be run on a sound commercial basis, with a view to ensuring that the business remains economically viable, and that a cordial relationship is maintained between the insurer and the insured. Fourth, the foreign investor or non-Nigerian entrepreneur wishing to acquire a working knowledge of the basic principles and the law governing the busniess of insurance in Nigeria. This class of reader, no matter the nature of his business, would inevitably participate in some form of insurance, such as Workmen's Compensation insurance, Motor insurance, or Fire insurance on his property. Fifth, the busy general legal practitioner who is likely, now and then, to be required to refresh his mind, at short notice on some aspects of the actual operation of insurance law in Nigeria; and who would therefore welcome a concise and handy source of reference on the subject.

In his famous book, 'The Principles of Moral and Political Philosophy' [1], Dr. William Paley remarked that "when a writer offers a book to the reading public, upon a subject on which the public are already in possession of many others, he is bound by a kind of

1 ('*The Principles of Moral and Political Philosophy*' *by Dr. William Paley*, D.D., 13th Edition, Volume 1, 1801).

literary justice to inform his readers, distinctly and specifically, what it is he professes to supply, and what he expects to improve". My answer to Dr. Paley as to what I propose to supply, and may-be improve, is simple.

Although a lot of literature has been published in various countries on the subject of insurance and insurance law, this, as far as I know, is the first book that is written specifically from a background of the practice of insurance in Nigeria. My only excuse for writing it is my conviction that this study will help fill a gap that definitely exists at present in Nigerian insurance law literature, and might also act as a spur to other Nigerian writers on this subject.

In stating the general principles, I make no claim to originality. In many respects, and as befits a student of an immense subject, I have drawn from existing literature on the subject in the established markets of the world, but my practical sources have been my intimate and personal contact with the insurance industry in both Nigeria and the United Kingdom. In appropriate cases, I have had to refer to American law and practice on the subject.

Like lawyers, auditors, and tax collectors, insurance Companies are often the subject of angry and bitter criticism by some members of the public. Quite often one hears complaints like this one: "these insurance companies, they are all alike—clever rogues, that's what they are. They charge you a premium to insure something, and when you make a claim, they point out some flimsy condition hidden away in tiny print on the back of the policy, to prove that you are not covered". These criticisms of insurance Companies may or may not be justified, but one of the aims of this book is to help clear up such misunderstandings, which, in many cases may be due to a lack of understanding of the basic principles and objects of insurance.

The subject of insurance covers an extensive, complex and highly technical field of endeavour. Its many branches are highly specialised, and no one person can successfully master all its branches. In fact in order to acquire a sound knowledge of any one of the main departments of the business, one must undergo a fairly long period of training in both the theory and the practice of insurance. In this Country, at the present time, the standard professional examinations in insurance are the examinations of the Chartered Insurance Institute, London; the basic professional qualifications being the Associateship of the Chartered Insurance Institute (A.C.I.I.) diploma which is normally obtained within three years.

This is followed by the Fellowship (F.C.I.I.). In each case, a candidate may specialize in any branch of his choice. Some Universities and Colleges offer courses on insurance. The main branches of insurance are: Marine Insurance, Fire Insurance, Life Assurance, and Accident Insurance. Each branch is further divided into sub-classes or sections. For example, in what is called the Accident Department of an Insurance Company, officials may be called upon to specialize in and handle any of the following sub-classes: Employer's Liability and Workmen's Compensation, Public Liability, Personal Accident, Burglary, Fidelity Guarantee, and Motor insurance. Despite the numerous specialist branches, of which the above are a few, the fundamental principles are virtually the same in all classes of insurance.

The aim of this book is to state the principles and the practice of insurance in Nigeria, and the legal position at the time of going to Press. The current Nigerian statutes touching upon the business of insurance, and a list of the insurance companies together with most of the leading intermediaries (the brokers) are attached as appendices.

It is hoped that the legal position has been stated up to the 31st January, 1967.

J. O. I.

Lagos,
January, 1967.

xiv

ACKNOWLEDGEMENTS

I would like to express my gratitude to the following for their assistance; my friend, John A. Allison, A.C.I.I., for reading the script at its early stages and making very useful suggestions on the technical aspect; my cousin, Dr. A. U. Ogan, B.SC., PH.D., who also read through the manuscript and made very valuable suggestions from the intelligent layman's viewpoint; Messrs W. T. Greig (Insurance) Limited, West African Provincial Insurance Company Limited, Provincial Insurance Company Limited, and Messrs. Franklin Book Programmes for their kind co-operation; my office typists who helped in typing the script, and a host of other individuals and institutions who assisted me in many respects and whose names I cannot enumerate here.

I would like to record my gratitude to the many authorities whose works I have been privileged to consult. I am indebted to the various Publishers for any references to these works, and if I have overlooked anyone's rights, I ask for forgiveness.

Finally, I acknowledge my indebtedness to all those who made the writing of this book possible: my Family— both the "immediate" and the 'extended'; my teachers, tutors and lecturers, both in this Country and in the United Kingdom; and those students preparing for the C.I.I. examinations who attended my lectures from 1962 to 1966 (under the auspices of the Insurance Institute of Nigeria) and whose intelligent and searching questions led me into converting my lecture notes to what has now turned out to be a book on the Principles of Insurance Law and Practice.

Jo Ogbonnaya Irukwu.

TABLE OF CASES

CONTENTS

xix

xxi

CHAPTER I.

INTRODUCTION AND HISTORICAL BACKGROUND

General Historical Developments:
Nigerian Historical Background

General Historical Development:

Although insurance is comparatively new in Nigeria, the practice of insurance has been in existence for a very long time in Europe. There is abundant evidence that insurance business was fairly well established during the time of Shakespeare. In 1601 during the reign of Elizabeth I, an Act was passed by the British Parliament, which set up a Court of Arbitration for the settlement of disputes on marine insurance policies. The preamble to this Act shows that the practice of insurance was then of long standing. In view of the fact that the preamble to this Act has been almost universally acclaimed as a classical exposition of the theory and purpose of insurance, it is reproduced below:

"Whereas it hath been time out of mind an usage amongst merchants, both of this realm and of foreign nations, when they make any great adventure (especially into remote parts), to give some consideration of money to other persons (which commonly are in no small number) to have from them assurance made of their goods, merchandises, ships and things adventured, or some part thereof, at such rates and in such sort as the parties assurers and the parties assured can agree, which course of dealing is commonly termed a policy of assurance; by means of which policies of assurance it cometh to pass upon the loss or perishing of any ship, there followeth not the undoing of any man, but the loss lighteth rather easily upon many, than heavily upon few, and rather upon them that adventure not, than those that do adventure, whereby all merchants, especially the younger sort, are allured to adventure more willingly and more freely. . . . . ."

At the time when this Act was passed, there were no insurance companies such as we have today. What existed then in this regard were merchants who were prepared to share in the underwriting of a risk on much the same lines as in the case of insurances underwritten at Lloyd's of London today. In addition to these merchants, there were the ancient guilds which provided some form of relief (a kind of mutual insurance) for their members in cases of loss by accidental fire.

Marine Insurance is probably the oldest branch of insurance. In his book on Insurance, Mr. Harold E. Raynes makes reference to a Marine policy (which is preserved at the Record Office in London) dated September 1547. This document was called a "bill of surance" and consisted of about fourteen lines written in Italian on a small sheet of paper. The sea journey insured against was from Cadiz to London. The history of marine insurance in continental Europe dates further back still. It is believed that the word policy was derived from the Italian word "polizz" and it was the Italian Merchants who introduced insurance into Britain. In fact, most of the earliest marine policies were written in Italian.

In terms of historical development, Marine Insurance was followed by fire insurance which increased in popularity after the Great Fire of London in 1666. After fire insurance, came life assurance which was introduced in 1750, and is now the largest branch. In more recent times the application and the extension of the insurance principle to all kinds of accidents and contingencies has resulted in numerous kinds of insurance. The result now is that almost every imaginable contingency is insurable, including the weather. A pregnant woman may, for instance, insure against the possibility of twin-birth, and even a prospective bride may take out an "engagement policy" against the possibility of a breach of promise!

Nigerian Historical Developments:

The concept of insurance in its modern form was introduced into Nigeria by the British. This, and the fact that until quite recently most of the leading insurance companies in Nigeria were either partly or wholly British-owned, has meant that the theory and practice of insurance in Nigeria has, to a large extent, followed the British pattern. Furthermore, this has given a British stamp to such aspects of Nigerian insurance practice as loss adjustments or claims settlement procedure, office routine and general insurance administration.

Long before the British arrived on the scene, there was a lot of organised trading activity in the territory now known as Nigeria, but there was no organised insurance business as we know it today. There existed, at that time, what might be described as crude or primitive forms of mutual and social insurance schemes. Apart from the 'extended family system', which was by its very nature, a social insurance scheme, there were the 'age-grade' associations and some clan unions which acted as mutual insurance societies to their members, on much the same lines as the English ancient guilds. The 'Age-grade' associations maintained funds built up by individual contributions from members. These funds were collected periodically almost in the same way as industrial life assurance premiums are collected. From the funds thus accummulated, funeral expenses for deceased members were met, and if a member of a particular 'age-grade' association died without making some material provision to tide over his dependents during the critical period immediately following his death, either the extended family, or the 'age-grade' association would take over the responsibility of maintaining the deceased member's dependents until they could stand on their feet.

Both the extended family system and the clan unions still exist in Nigeria today, but most of their insurance functions have been taken over by an organised insurance system. Similarly, the 'age-grade' system still plays an important role in some parts of the Country, especially in matters relating to rural development, but like the extended family system and the clan unions, they no longer render any noticeable insurance service to their members.

The Development of Modern Insurance Business in Nigeria:
Modern insurance business was introduced into Nigeria as late as the 20th Century. With the establishment of trading posts in Nigeria towards the end of the last century by many European trading companies, mostly British, these companies started effecting their insurances with established insurers on the London insurance market.

As time went on, some British insurers appointed agents to represent their interests in Nigeria. These agents were given powers of attorney to obtain insurance business, issue cover and service claims on behalf of their principals in London. Initially, the agents were mainly expatriate banks and traders, but later Nigerian traders and merchants were appointed agents. These agencies later gave way to full branch offices of the parent companies. Virtually, all British insurance Companies in Nigeria developed in this way. That is, first, a Nigeria-based agent is appointed to represent the principal in London, then the agent later gives way to a branch office of the parent Company in Lagos, with sub-offices throughout Nigeria. In the course of time (but not in all cases) a Nigerian Company is formed, with a Nigerian nationality, but closely linked with the parent company in Britain. For example, the Provincial Insurance Company Limited started business in Nigeria under the Chief Agency of a Nigerian merchant. As business progressed, a branch of the "Provincial' was set up in Nigeria. This branch office made reasonable progress and was later taken over by a Nigerian Company now known as the West African Provincial Insurance Company Limited, which itself was incorporated in 1958.

The first insurance Company to have a full branch office in Nigeria was the Royal Exchange Assurance in 1921, and until 1949, it remained the only Company fully established in the country. In 1949, three other companies were registered - the Norwich Union Fire Insurance Society, (now functioning as part of the Guinea Insurance Company Limited), the Tobacco Insurance Company Limited, and the Legal and General Assurance Society Limited. By 1987 there were 95 registered Insurance Companies in Nigeria.

A list of the insurance companies operating in Nigeria and the classes of business that they handle, appears as an appendix to this volume.

At the end of 1976, there were about 76 registered insurance companies in Nigeria. Following the enactment of the Insurance Decree 1976 which came into force òn the 1st December of that year, new and stringent rules and regulations were introduced aimed at ensuring that only financially strong and viable insurance companies operate in the country. The existing insurance companies were given six months to comply with the new regulations or forfeit their licence. As a result of this exercise by the 31st May when the notice expired, only 56 companies were registered. A list of these companies appears as an appendix to this book. Since then, and before going to press, 4 new companies have been registered and these new companies are also listed in the appendix.

CHAPTER II

THE THEORY AND PURPOSE OF INSURANCE

Every human being is faced with the possibility that one or more of the hazards which form part of life will sooner or later befall him and cause him some financial loss. According to that person's position in the community, the loss may be very small or very large. If a villager's hut is damaged by fire, he can replace it simply by gathering the necessary building materials from the forest outside his door. If however, a big modern factory is damaged by fire, the cost of repairs may be immense and would involve the purchase of machinery from abroad, the maintenance of personnel during repairs, loss of profits as a result of delays in production, compensation to injured employees, and other onerous responsibilities which the factory owner would be ill-prepared to meet at a time when his assets are in ruins as a result of the fire.

Some people may be lucky, and live all their lives without suffering any serious disaster or misfortune, but even these few lucky ones, cannot, at any one moment say with certainty, that misfortune will never fall on them. Quite apart from those financial disasters which may or may not happen, there are many hazards which are also entirely beyond human control. For example, the family breadwinner knows it is beyond his control to prevent death from coming his way. He knows he would die sooner or later, but he is uncertain as to when he would die. If he dies at an early age, his family would be left without someone to provide for them. Similary, the family would suffer some financial loss should the breadwinner lose his earning power as a result of an accident.

In addition to those losses just mentioned, there are several other losses which may arise as a result of damage or destruction of one's property. A landslide, an earthquake or a crashing aeroplane may destroy a person's house. A man's motor car which he has purchased with his life's savings may be wrecked in an accident, or might get stolen. A flood or thunderstorm might ruin a family's home. Rioters and strikers may wreck a person's house and other property. These and many others are the hazards which are inherent in life, and the fear of the disastrous financial losses that would follow if any of these happens has been responsible for the development of insurance.

The purpose of insurance is to compensate or indemnify the victim for his financial losses. Insurance neither eliminates the loss, nor does it undertake to stop the misfortune or disaster from happening. All it does is to help soften the blow from a purely economic viewpoint. Thus, the fact that the breadwinner has been wise enough to have taken out a life policy would not prevent him from dying in a motor accident but the proceeds of the life policy, which is payable to the dependents will help lighten their burden.

The Law of Averages: The theory of insurance derives from the law of averages. The system works on the assumption that only a small proportion of a large group will suffer losses from a given cause (the insured peril) within a specified period. On this assumption, a common fund is created into which the small contributions (premiums) of each member of the group are pooled, and out of this fund, the few who suffer losses are compensated. As was stated in the preamble to the English Act of 1601 mentioned earleir, the aim of all insurance transactions is to ensure that "THE LOSS LIGHTETH RATHER EASILY UPON MANY THAN HEAVILY UPON FEW".

How the Modern Insurance System Works:

In all classes of insurance, each member of the insurance group known as the insured, the assured, or the policy-holder, pays a relatively small sum of money into a common pool administered and controlled by the insurer, who, in Nigeria is usually an incorporated Insurance Company with limited liability. In return for the payment, which is called the premium, the insurer agrees to assume the insured's risks and undertakes to indemnify the insured for losses arising from specified perils insured against.

The terms of the insurance agreement are embodied in a document which is called the policy. When the insured suffers a loss that is insured against, the loss is reported to the insurance Company. The company investigates the claim, and if everything is in order it pays the sum it has agreed to pay.

In the early days. of mutual insurance, the insurer used to operate on the assumption that only a few of the risks it insured would materialise, and the mutual insurer would be left with some profit at the end of each insurance period. For example, assuming that about 2,000 persons are insured with Company XYZ Limited in any one year at an annual premium of ten pounds each. This would provide a total premium income of about twenty-thousand pounds. At the end of the insurance period only about fifty of this number suffer losses resulting in claims amounting to about ten thousand pounds. Making allowance for administrative costs, staff salaries, and other expenses, the Company should hope to make some profit from the operation.

Anybody familiar with the financial operations of a modern limited liability insurance company will have little difficulty in seeing that this illustration is an over-simplification of the matter. The modern insurer operates under a slightly more sophisticated system than the early mutual insurers. Unlike the mutual insurer, the modern proprietary company has both policy-holders and share-holders, and the interest of each group has to be protected. The modern insurer works on the assumption that the premiums recieved over his whole business will be sufficient to meet the claims arising, together with his working expenses and leave him a small profit. The assumption is based on the theory of probability and to safeguard policy-holders against the possibility of the total premium fund being exhausted by some catastrophic event producing a vast accummulation of claims amounting to more than the premium fund, the insurer is required by law to maintain a specific relationship between his assets and his premium income, that is, his liability assumed. (See Insurance Companies Act, 1961, Section 4 on "margin of solvency".)

Legal Definition of Insurance: All law lexicons define insurance as "a contract whereby a person called the insurer or assurer, agrees in consideration of money paid to him, called the premium, by another person, called the insured or assured, to indemnify the latter against loss resulting to him on the happening of certain events. The policy is the document in which is contained the terms of the contract......." (Osborne's Law Dictionary, 4th Edition P.178)

Slater's Mercantile Law (14th Edition by Lord Chorley and O. C. Giles) describes insurance as follows: "Insurance is the purchase of security. The assured, anxious to protect himself against a risk, purchases from the insurer the right to be indemnified if the risk should materialise. The purchase price which the assured pays the insurer is known as the premium - often an annual payment and the insurer's promise to pay if the event insured against occurs is embodied in what is called a policy".

The Difference between Insurance and Gambling: Most writers on the subject of insurance go to great length to prove to their readers that insurance is not gambling. The excuse being that the new-comer making his initial acquaintance with insurance is often struck by the similarity between insurance and gambling. It is submitted, that despite this apparent similarity between insurance and gambling, insurance is certainly not gambling, as the reader is bound to discover. The real point of difference between insurance and gambling is that insurance can only be granted where an INSURABLE INTEREST exists. The term insurable interest means that the insured must have an interest in the preservation of the thing to be insured, to the extent that he will suffer financially on the happening of the peril or event insured against. An insurance effected without an insurable interest would be gambling, or a mere wager; and such an "insurance contract" would be either illegal, void, or at least unenforceable at law.

In the early days of life assurance in Britain, this fundamental distinction between insurance and gambling was either not recognised or it was just ignored. In those days, it was quite common for people to insure the lives of politicians, public men and women, such as famous actors and actresses, and even notorious criminals in whom they had no insurable interest. This practice has since been abolished in the United Kingdom by the Life Assurance Act, 1774, and it is now settled law that all insurance contracts, in order to be valid, must have an insurable interest. (The subject of insurable interest is discussed at some length in a later Chapter).

The Primary and Secondary Functions of Insurance:
Insurance has been described as the "handmaiden of commerce and industry" and this is not an exaggeration. It is impossible to imagine how the modern industrial and commercial enterprise could function efficiently without some form of organised insurance service. The functions of insurance are two-fold - the Primary functions and the Secondary or subsidiary functions.

Primary Functions: The primary function of insurance, as we have seen, is to ensure that the financial losses of the individual are fairly and equitably distributed over the insured community.

The policy-holders or the insured community pay premiums into a common pool, out of which the unfortunate few who suffer losses are compensated.

Secondary Functions: In addition to the primary function of insurance, the insurance industry provides a number of secondary services which are of immense value to the community as a whole. By offering financial security to businessmen and industrialists, the insurance industry encourages and promotes commercial enterprises. The present large scale commercial and industrial activity in Nigeria has been made possible, to a large extent, by the existence of an organised insurance system. Many people hold the view that it is only those persons who actually suffer losses and are therefore indemnified by the insurer that benefit from insurance. This view is not correct. To a modern businessman or industrialist, the assurance that he would be indemnified in the event of a loss, is as valuable as an actual payment after a loss. The insurer's promise to the effect that he would indemnify him in the event of a loss, gives the businessman security and peace of mind and encourages him to venture and take risks without which there cannot be any substantial economic progress.

Some insurance undertakings provide loan schemes for buildings, at times on the security of a life policy. The large sums of money accummulated by insurers are invested in State approved securities, and this helps to provide the State with a steady flow of investment funds with which it can promote and develop local industries which are essential to the community. Such investments will eventually contribute profits to the National purse, as well as provide labour for the working population in a given area.

Finally, the insurance industry is an important employer of labour, and in this way contributes its share in helping to solve the problem of unemployment. At present there are well over twenty-five thousand persons employed in the insurance sector in Nigeria, either as officials, agents or canvassers.

THE SUBJECT - MATTER OF INSURANCE

The subject-matter of insurance may be some corporeal or material property of value, for example, a motor car or a house. Alternatively, it might be an event, the happening of which will create a legal liability, for example, the insurance effected by a doctor insuring himself against a possible claim by a patient for professional negligence. In marine insurance, the ship or the cargo it carries could be the subject-matter of the insurance. In a life policy, the life of the assured is, ofcourse, the subject-matter of the insurance. In all classes of insurance, whatever it is that is the subject-matter of the insurance is generally stated and described in the policy. Thus, in a motor policy, the motor vehicle which is insured is generally described in the policy schedule. The make, type, engine and chassis numbers, and the registration numbers of the insured vehicle are inserted in the policy for purposes of identification in the event of a claim. Similarly, in a fire policy covering a house, the building which is the subject-matter of the insurance is adequately described in the policy.

Distinction between the Subject-matter of the Insurance and the Interest of the insured in the Subject-matter. A distinction is made between the subject-matter of the insurance, and the interest of the insured in the subject-matter, which is often referred to as the SUBJECT-MATTER OF THE CONTRACT. This distinction is of great importance because it is now an established rule of insurance law that the insurance policy does not insure the subject-matter of the insurance, as such, but the interest of the policy-holder in it. Whilst the subject-matter of the insurance may be property, life or liability, the subject-matter of the contract is the financial interest or INSURABLE INTEREST of the policy-holder in the subject-matter of the insurance. For purposes of illustration, let us assume that Mr. Agi has just purchased a radiogram at twenty naira. He insures it against burglary with Company XYZ Limited for its full purchase value. In this example, the subject-matter of the insurance is the radiogram, but the subject-matter of the contract is Mr. Agi's pecuniary interest in the radiogram, in this case the sum of twenty naira. If whilst the policy is still in force (that is before the expiration of the insurance period which is usually twelve months) Mr. Agi sells the radiogram to Mr. Bawa, the insurance contract would terminate because the interest insured against has ceased to exist.

The authority for the proposition that the insurance policy does not cover the subject-matter of the insurance, but the insured's pecuniary interest in the thing or event insured against is the leading case of CASTELLAIN v. PRESTON (1883), II Q.B.D., 380. We reproduce below the relevant portion of the Court's judgment in this case:

"What is it that is insured in a fire policy? Not the bricks and materials used in building the house, but the interest of the insured in the subject-matter of the insurance"

Insurance Terminology:

(a) **Insurance or Assurance?** The layman making his first acquaintance with insurance terminology, soon begins to wonder why writers on the subject refer sometimes to "insurance" and at other times to "assurance". Furthermore, he might observe that some insurance companies use the word "assurance" as part of their name, for example, the Royal Exchange Assurance, New India Assurance Company, and Phoenix Assurance Company, while most others use the word "insurance", like the Universal Insurance Company and a host of others.

The legal position is that it is of no special significance which word is used. It has been suggested that the word "assurance" be used exclusively to describe that class of insurance in which the event insured against is certain to happen, sooner or later, and that the term "insurance" should refer only to that class where the risk insured against may or may not happen. An example of the first class is life assurance; death will occur someday; and an example of the second class is fire insurance, the fire may or may not occur. This suggestion has not yet been adopted by the insurance industry generally. As a general rule, both in Nigeria and in most parts of the United Kingdom, the word "assurance" is reserved for life assurance, and the word "insurance" for all other classes of insurance. For convenience, this book will adopt that practice.

(b) Moral and Physical Hazards:

Both moral and physical hazards refer to the special features of a risk proposed for insurance. Whenever a risk is proposed for insurance, the underwriting department of an insurance company has to scrutinize the proposal to ensure that both the moral and physical hazards presented by the risk are not abnormal. If both moral and physical hazards are good, the insurer will insure at the normal rate of premium, but if the risk proposed for insurance shows features of either a bad moral or physical hazard, the insurer would either decline to insure or insure at a loaded premium.

Difference between Moral and Physical Hazards: Whereas moral hazard refers to the personal character of the insured as such, physical hazard relates to the subject-matter of the inurance itself This can best be illustrated by means of examples.

Examples of Moral Hazard: As was stated above, moral hazard refers to the character and general disposition of the insured or the person wishing to effect an insurance. If the proposer is honest and very careful in the way in which he handles his affairs his moral hazard is said to be above-board, and such a person would attract a normal rate of premium. There are different degrees of a bad moral hazard ranging from a merely careless individual to a downright crook. For instance, a very careless but honest person is as much a bad moral hazard as the man who would deliberately prolong his period of disability after an accident in order to increase his claim on his personal accident policy. The worst example of a bad moral hazard is the person who would take out an insurance policy just for the purpose of making a profit by means of a false claim.

The attitude of insurers to the question of moral hazard varies depending on the type of insurance concerned. For example, an insurer would grant an "Act" only motor policy to almost anyone including a known criminal or a notoriously careless person, but before issuing an "all risks" policy which virtually covers losses from any cause, the insurer would have to be satisfied that the moral hazard is impeccable.

Examples of Physical Hazard: In a motor policy which insures against fire damage to the motor vehicle, an old motor car with rather faulty and defective electrical system susceptible to self-ignition is a bad physical hazard. Similarly, for purposes of a fire policy, a timber house with a thatched roof is a poor physical hazard. In a life policy a proposed life-assured who is suffering from cancer or some other deadly disease is a poor physical hazard. In a burglary policy, a jeweller's shop in the centre of a big city which is not adequately secured with locks, bolts and other burglar proofing is a bad physical hazard.

(c) **Third Party:** There are two parties to an insurance contract - the insurer and the insured. All others are strangers to the contract, and are referred to as third parties because they are not parties to the insurance contract between the insured and the insurer. For instance, the pedestrian who is knocked down by the insured in a motor accident is a third party and a stranger to the contract between the insurer and the insured. The Third Party motor policy is so called because it insures the insured or the policy holder against his legal liability to other members of the public who are not parties to the insurance contract and are therefore third parties.

Under the legal doctrine of the privity of contracts, only persons who are parties to a contract can derive any benefit from the contract, but there is a statutory exception to this common law rule. The Motor Vehicles (Third Party Insurance) Act empowers an injured third party, under certain conditions, to enforce his judgment directly against the insurer although he was not a party to the contract of insurance.

CHAPTER II

THE THEORY AND PURPOSE OF INSURANCE

Every human being is faced with the possibility that one or more of the hazards which form part of life will sooner or later befall him and cause him some financial loss. According to that person's position in the community, the loss may be very small or very large. If a villager's hut is damaged by fire, he can replace it simply by gathering the necessary building materials from the forest outside his door. If however, a big modern factory is damaged by fire, the cost of repairs may be immense and would involve the purchase of machinery from abroad, the maintenance of personnel during repairs, loss of profits as a result of delays in production, compensation to injured employees, and other onerous responsibilities which the factory owner would be ill-prepared to meet at a time when his assets are in ruins as a result of the fire.

Some people may be lucky, and live all their lives without suffering any serious disaster or misfortune, but even these few lucky ones, cannot, at any one moment say with certainty, that misfortune will never fall on them. Quite apart from those financial disasters which may or may not happen, there are many hazards which are also entirely beyond human control. For example, the family breadwinner knows it is beyond his control to prevent death from coming his way. He knows he would die sooner or later, but he is uncertain as to when he would die. If he dies at an early age, his family would be left without someone to provide for them. Similarly, the family would suffer some financial loss should the breadwinner lose his earning power as a result of an accident.

In addition to those losses just mentioned, there are several other losses which may arise as a result of damage or destruction of one's property. A landslide, an earthquake or a crashing aeroplane may destroy a person's house. A man's motor car which he has purchased with his life's savings may be wrecked in an accident, or might get stolen. A flood or thunderstorm might ruin a family's home. Rioters and strikers may wreck a person's house and other property. These and many others are the hazards which are inherent in life, and the

THE INSURERS. The general term insurer may apply to either an individual, a company or a society providing insurance cover. There are, in fact, three main kinds of insurers. They are, the Mutual Associations, the proprietary companies, and the private individual underwriters now found chiefly at the Corporation of Lloyd's in London. From the purely Nigerian point of view, there is in practice, only one class of insurer - the proprietary insurance company, usually with limited liabilities. Nevertheless, we will discuss here all the three different kinds of insurers.

Mutual Insurance Association: A mutual insurance Association is a kind of co-operative insurance organisation, and it is operated solely for the benefit of its members. Such an association has no share capital and no share-holders. Any profits left over after the losses and the expenses have been paid is distributed amongst the members, oftentimes in the form of a discount from the usual premium rates. Mutual insurance associations were the earliest forms of insurers. Under the scheme, members make contributions periodically to a common fund. Out of this common fund, the unfortunate members who suffer losses are compensated.

In continental Europe and in most of the American States a lot of insurance business is still transacted on mutual lines, but there is strictly no mutual insurance association in Nigeria today.

Proprietary Companies: These are limited liability companies formed in accordance with the provisions of the Companies Acts. The capital of he company is subscribed by the share-holders to form the nucleus of an insurance fund and to provide for the initial working expenses. This initial insurance fund provided by the share-holders or the proprietors of the company is augmented by the premiums paid by the members of the public who insure with the Company. Unlike the members of the mutual insurance association, the insured person in a proprietary company has no interest in the profits of the company and he cannot be called upon to make good or contribute towards any deficiency in the insurance fund should the company experience a bad year or a major disaster. The profits of the proprietary company belong to the share-holders, who subscribed its capital.

The only qualification to the statement that the share-holders, and not the policy-holders, have an exclusive right to the profits of this type of insurance company is in respect of life assurance.

Under most life assurance schemes, two kinds of policies are issued, (*a*) the participating or "with-profits" policy, and (*b*) the non-participating or "without-profits" policy. Although the with-profits policy-holders are not in quite the same legal position as the share-holders in the sense that they are not liable for the debts of the company, they have some interest in relation to the life fund income or life profits of the company, as any profits from the life account will be distributed between the with-profits policy-holders and the company's share-holders or proprietors in accordance with the conditions generally laid down in the Company's Articles of Association. A company may provide in its Articles of Association that one tenth of the life profits would be distributed amongst the share-holders, and the remaining nine-tenths amongst the participating or with-profits policy-holders.

Almost all the insurance business in Nigeia is effected through this class of insurer as the other classes are virtually non-existent. (See appendix for a list of insurers in Nigeria). Proprietary companies transact insurance business with the public generally, unlike the mutual associations which do business only with their members.

Lloyd's Underwriters:

This group of insurers are a hybrid kind and do not fall into any of the two main groups mentioned earlier. Lloyd's as an insurance institution, is an association of underwriters or insurers based at Lloyd's Corporation in the City of London. Legally, it is strictly a collection of private individual underwriters with each member being personally liable for the payment of his proportion of each loss.

A member of the public wishing to effect an insurance at Lloyd's cannot approach the insurer directly, he must go through a Lloyd's broker. The insurance when accepted is distributed amongst several individual underwriters in the particular group known as the "Syndicate", and each underwriter signs in the policy the percentage he has accepted. This percentage determines the premium he will get and his maximum liability in the event of a loss. As we have just pointed out, each underwriting member of Lloyd's is only liable for his proportion in the event of a loss, and the failure of one underwiriting member to pay his share of a loss would not increase the liability of others who underwrote the same policy. The profits go to each member proportionately, and the insured has no right to the profits.

Although Lloyd's had its beginnings late in the seventeenth century in a humble coffee house belonging to one Edward Lloyd, it has now become a most important international insurance "market place". Lloyd's as a Corporation, derives its legal force from an Act of the British Parliament, Lloyd's Act 1871.

The more unusual insurances, which may not be acceptable to the less venturesome insurers are effected at Lloyd's. Almost every contingency can be insured at Lloyd's, and some Nigerian insurances, especially, the more unusual lines, are placed at Lloyd's.

P.S. The word "underwriter" where it appears in this context, is used as referring to the underwriting member of Lloyd's, that is, the individual insurer, as distinct from the underwriting agent often described as underwriter, who is the official that represents each syndicate.

THE INSURANCE INTERMEDIARIES - The Brokers and the Agents.

An examination of the insurance market would be incomplete without some reference to the different insurance intermediaries or middle-men, notably, the insurance brokers and the agents. We will now examine briefly, the functions of the brokers and the agents, and their legal positions.

The Insurance Agents: With the exception of business placed at Lloyd's, which must be placed through a Lloyd's accredited broker, insurance business may be placed directly by members of the public, with the company of their choice, or alternatively, through an insurance broker or agent. It is entirely at the discretion of the proposer either to approach the company directly, or to do so through an agent or a broker.

An agent is a person employed to act for another, called his principal. Under Nigerian law, the recognised legal function of the agent is to bring his principal into contractual relations with a third party. Once he has done that, he normally drops out. Both the insurance broker and the insurance agent are agents in the eyes of the law. Provided the agent has acted properly and within the scope of his authority, the principal is legally liable for the acts of the agent.

The insurance agent may be a full-time agent (but this is rare), or a part-time agent, such as a bank manager, a Solicitor, an accountant, a motor garage proprietor or any one whose main line of business could accommodate his participation in insurance business as a side-line. The agent may be a cash agent or a credit agent. The practice in this country is generally to appoint the agent initially on a cash basis, and if he justifies it, to convert him subsequently to a credit agent. The credit agent, as a general rule, has wider powers, subject, of course, to the terms of his appointment. An insurance agent is not required or expected to possess a sound technical training or knowledge of the intricacies of the insurance business. This is the main difference between him and the broker.

Own Case Agent: Ordinarily, the function of the agent is to get business from proposers and pass it on to his principals in return for his agency commission. In addition there is another class of agent known as the "Own Case" agent, who may be an individual, a firm, or a company. He is so called because he receives commission on his own insurances only, and does not, normally, introduce outside business.

THE INSURANCE BROKERS

A prudent business man who is not familiar with the customs and technicalities of a market would employ an expert in that field to act for him in order to ensure that he gets a good bargain. The early European traders who found it a little difficult to understand the technical details of marine insurance business employed experts in this field to act for them. This marked the origin of the brokers. With the passage of time, these brokers extended their activities from marine insurance to all classes of insurance.

The insurance broker is a full-time insurance specialist of professional standing, or at least the law expects him so to be. Since the broker undertakes the responsibility of advising, recommending and arranging insurance cover, he is presumed in law to have the necessary professional and technical knowledge of the relevant class of insurance business. His primary function is to act for the insured in the handling of all his insurance problems.

A competent broker, as soon as he is appointed. will make a study of the insurance needs of his client, listing out the different kinds of insurance that should be effected, depending on the nature of his client's business. If the client is a business-man or an industrialist, he would then carry out a physical examination or survey of the client's business premises and draw up a list of the different projects. Where appropriate, he would make recommendations with a view to improving the physical hazard so as to obtain a low premium and good terms from the insurers. Having done this, he then places the insurance with the company or companies that he considers most suitable. The broker should always be in constant touch with the companies, and with the insurance market generally, so that he could advise his clients appropriately.

CLAIMS: If a claim arises, it is the duty of the broker to negotiate settlement with the insurers and their loss adjusters, and he must ensure that his client receives a fair settlement.

The strange thing about the institution of brokerage, is that for all this numerous services that the broker renders to his client, he is not entitled to demand or receive any payment from the insured. He is paid a commission based on a percentage of the premium by the company in which the business has been placed. The broker's commission rate, because of his greater responsibilities, is slightly higher than that paid to the ordinary insurance agent.

In spite of the fact that he is paid by the insurance company, the broker is not the agent of the company. He is the agent of the insured. This is the fundamental distinction between the agent and the broker. Whereas the broker is the agent of the insured by whom he is employed for the purpose of effecting the insurance, the agent is an agent of the insurer on whose behalf he acts, subject to the terms of his appointment. The authority for this principle is the English case of Rozanes v.Bowen, reported in *the Times* June 20, and November 14, 1928.

Because the broker is the agent of the insured, any material non-disclosure or any other misrepresentation of fact by him relating to an insurance, will operate against his client. Similarly, any knowledge or information communicated to the broker, but not passed on to the company, is not notice to the company. In the case of an insurance agent, the reverse is the case. The company is bound by the act of the agent provided he was acting within the terms of his appointment, and in the interest of the insurer at the material time.

We have seen that the broker is required to have a sound technical knowledge of the law and customs of the insurance business. Therefore, if he negligently gives faulty advice which causes damage to the insured or the proposer, he renders himself liable to be sued for damages in an action for professional negligence. The broker is presumed to hold himself out to the public as a person who possesses a sound technical knowledge of insurance and therefore, one prepared to give sound professional advice and arrange insurance cover in the most favourable manner for all those who instruct him to act for them. The agent is not presumed to hold himself out as an expert in the business, but merely as an intermediary.

Broker's Liability to the Insurers for Premium: Although the broker is the agent of the insured for purposes of effecting the insurance, and under the normal law of agency should drop out of the transaction after bringing his principal (the Insured) and the third party (the insurer), into contractual relations, the Courts in the Limited States of America have held in recent times that where proposals are submitted by the broker and policies are issued on credit and those policies are handed over to the broker to deliver to his clients and to collect the premiums, the broker becomes the agent of the insurer for the purpose of collecting the premiums, and is personally liable to the insurer for the premiums.

and is personally liable to the insurer for the premiums.

The custom of the trade in Nigeria, under these circumstances, is to hold the broker responsible to the insurers for the premiums. This point has been tested in the Nigerian courts and decided in favour of insurance companies. See the case of Niger Insurance Company Limited vs. I.O. Fasakin (carrying on business in the name of Resourceful Insurance Consultants) Lagos High Court (Suit No. LD/1215/83). Also see the case of Niger Insurance Company Limited vs. Fadon Brokers (Suit No. 1/606/85) where it was held that once the policies of insurance have been issued and there is no indication from the broker that such policies should be cancelled, it would be deemed that the premiums have become due and payable to the plaintiff. Failure by broker to return such policies or the premium due on them, will entitle the insurance company to debit the account of the defendant with the amounts due on such policies.

Insurance Agent is the agent of the proposer or Insured for purposes of Completion of Proposal Form: As has been stated above, the insurance agent, as opposed to the broker, is the agent of the insurer who appoints him, and provided he acts within the scope of his appointment and in accordance with the terms of his appointment, the insurer is liable for his acts, and his knowledge under these circumstances, is the knowledge of the insurer. The only important qualification to this (and this has led to several disputes in Nigeria recently) is where the proposer or the Insured has employed the Agent to complete the proposal form for him. If a proposer, employs an agent (as is quite often the case, especially with illiterate or semi-literate proposers) to complete the proposal form for him, the agent in completing the form is the agent of the proposer or the Insured. Therefore any misrepresentation contained therein or any breach of the principle of utmost good faith, for example, by the non-disclosure of a material fact, will be held against the Insured, who is responsible for the information contained in the proposal form.

CHAPTER IV.

KINDS OF INSURANCE

Writers on the subject of insurance have adopted several different methods of classification. Some have classified insurances according to their subject matter into the following categories: (a) those covering property, for example fire insurances on buildings and other property, or marine insurances on ship and cargo; (b) those covering liabilities, for example, the employer's liability to his workmen for injuries at work, or the liability of the motorist to other road users for damage to their property or injury to their person arising from the use of the insured vehicle; (c) those covering the person, for example, personal accident insurance granting benefits for accidental death or disablement, and all classes of life assurance; and (d) those covering other rights, interests or contingencies, such as the fidelity guarantee insurance under which the insurance company undertakes, in consideration of the premium, to indemnify the insured e.g. the employer against loss by reason of the fraud or dishonesty of persons holding positions of trust in the employer's business, such as cashiers or bank managers.

Others have adopted the alternative method of classifying insurances into two groups - those that are contracts of indemnity, and those that are not.

In practice, however, insurers themselves have divided up the business of insurance into four departments, namely, the Marine department, the Fire department, the Life department, and the Accident department. Most composite offices adopt this classification, and in each department there may be sub-divisions into sections. For example, the accident department would include sections dealing with Motor insurance, burglary insurance and personal accident insurance. We will adopt the practical classification of the industry, and in the following paragraphs will discuss briefly the more common kinds of insurance under each department.

MARINE INSURANCE

The marine department is concerned with the insurance of ship, freight and cargo against maritime risks. The ship, cargo, freight and profits are exposed to very many hazards during a voyage by sea, and the purpose of marine insurance is to protect the owner of the relevant interest against accidental losses arising from the materialisation of these sea perils. Marine insurance is an essential feature of modern international trade, and its main divisions are as follows:-

Ship Insurance: This is the insurance taken out by the ship owner to cover him against loss of the ship and its machinery by the operation of the perils of the sea. A ship insurance, like a motor insurance is generally issued for a twelve - month period.

Cargo Insurance: Cargo insurance refers to insurances in respect of goods, produce or merchandise carried by the ship.

Freight Insurance: Freight is the money paid to the ship-owner for the carriage of goods to their destination. It is only paid on delivery of the goods. If the ship is lost and the goods are therefore not delivered, there is no freight. Freight insurances are effected to cover the risk of loss of the freight in case the cargo is lost or is otherwise not delivered.

The shipowner may, in addition to the insurances mentioned above, take out a liability insurance to cover him against his legal liability to third parties, for example as a result of negligent collision at sea.

The Nigerian Marine Insurance Act of 1961 is an up-to-date codification of the law on this subject. The Act defines marine insurance as 'A contract whereby the insurer undertakes to indemnify the assured, in manner and to the extent thereby agreed, against marine losses, that is to say, the losses incident to marine adventure" (Section 3.)

FIRE INSURANCE

A fire policy covers the policyholder against loss of, or damage to the insured property, resulting from an accidental fire. The main risk insured against is fire, but in recent years the scope of insurance written in the fire department has extended a great deal. Many special perils, some quite unrelated to a fire, are covered on payment of an extra premium. The different kinds of insurance cover granted by the fire department can be grouped under four headings:-

(a) the ordinary fire insurance;

(b)   the Special Perils insurance;
(c)   Loss of Profits or Consequential Loss insurance; and
(d)   Combined or Comprehensive insurance.

The Ordinary Fire Policies: These are issued to indemnify the insured against accidental fire damage to the property covered under the policy, such property may be a building or the contents of a building. To constitute a fire within the meaning of a fire insurance policy, the fire must be accidental, (from the point of view of the insured), and there must be an actual ignition. Any damage arising as a direct consequence of the fire is covered, for example damage by smoke, or by water used in fighting the fire or damage by the fire brigade whilst fighting the fire. Generally, there are two kinds of fire policies, one type for private dwellings and their contents and the other for business premises and their contents. The cover granted by the private dwellings policy is wider.

Special Perils Insurance: The term special perils refers to those extra or additional perils which though they are insurable, are not covered by the ordinary fire policy. There is a long list of these perils which may be covered under a fire policy at an additional cost. The more common ones are, earthquake, Flood, Storm, Riots and Civil commotion, Strikers and malicious persons, and even damage resulting from the bursting or overflow of water tanks. If a fire policy is to be extended to include a special peril, an endorsement is issued extending the cover on the existing fire policy.

Loss of Profits Insurance: The ordinary fire policy covers the insured person against loss due to fire damage to his material property. The insurers will provide the money necessary to repair or reinstate the material damage. If it is a building they will provide the money to repair or reinstate and if it is property, such as machinery, the insurers will provide the money to repair the damage or to reinstate. Under the ordinary fire policy, the insurers are not liable to pay the policyholder for the loss of the profits that would normally have accrued to him had his business not been upset by the fire. Loss of profits or consequential losses are not covered by the ordinary standard fire policy.

In two reported cases, one English, the other Scottish, the courts held that the ordinary fire policy does not cover, "loss of profits or custom" In WRIGHT v. POLE (1834), 1 Ad. and El. 621, the plaintiff Wright had contended that, by insuring his interest in the

Ship Inn, he was entitled to recover under his fire policy, not only the amount of the fire damage, but also a further substantial amount for loss of custom or profits which he sustained while the damaged inn was being rebuilt. The court held that he was not so entitled. A similar decision was given in the case of Menzies v. North British and Mercantile Insurance Company (1847), 9 Dunl. (Ct. of Sess.) 694. These decisions emphasised the limitations of the cover granted by the ordinary fire policy, thus promoting the demand for loss of profits insurance, which, as the name suggests, insures against loss of profits.

Combined or Comprehensive Insurance: Comprehensive policies to cover private houses and household furniture and personal effects against a wide variety of risks are written in the fire department of most companies in this country. The contents cover differ. from the cover granted in respect of the building itself, but broadly speaking, both the contents and the buildings policy insure against damage resulting from the undermentioned perils:

(1) Fire, lightning, thunderbolt and explosion;
(2) Aircraft or articles dropped therefrom:
(3) Burglary and housebreaking;
(4) Earthquake, gale, hurricane, cyclone or windstorm;
(5) Impact with the insured building by a road vehicle;
(6) Flood including the overflow of the sea.

In addition to the perils listed above, the buildings policy also grants the houseowner some limited public liability cover against claims made on him as the owner of the house as a result of bodily injury to third parties or damage to their property. Similarly, the contents policy in addition to these perils also provides compensation to the estate of the policyholder in the event of his death resulting from violence by burglars or housebreakers or by fire. There is a wide variation in the scope of the cover granted by each company, and the policyholder must read through his policy to ascertain the extent of cover granted.

LIFE ASSURANCE

The primary purpose of life assurance is to insure against the loss of future income which may arise as a result of the premature death of the income producer. In recent years, however, there have been different adaptations of the idea to suit different needs, for example, most endowment assurances are mainly a device for saving up funds for the future use of the policyholder.

Though life assurance is comparatively new to Nigeria, it has been known to mankind since about the middle of the sixteenth century. Until as recently as twenty years ago it was thought by the insurance industry that conditions in tropical Africa were unsuited for underwriting life assurance business, because it was believed that the normal life expectancy of the average African would not justify a profitable life assurance programme. This myth has since been exploded and although no purely African or Nigerian mortality tables are available at the present time, the business of life assurance has been reasonably profitable in West Africa.

Life assurance business is divided into two main sections - Ordinary life assurance and industrial life assurance, the distinction being that in industrial life assurance the premiums are payable at more frequent intervals, for example, weekly or fortnightly and the sums assured are much smaller, whereas in ordinary life assurance the reverse is the case. Industrial life assurance is not very common in this country. Most of our discussions on life assurance will be in connection with ordinary life assurance which is the more common one.

There are many adaptations of the ordinary life assurance policies and many of these are available in the Nigerian insurance market. In spite of the many variations, there are in fact three fundamental types of life assurance and all the numerous adaptations are merely variations of these three main types. The three fundamental types are:-

(1)   The Term Assurance.

(2)   The Whole life Assurance.

(3)   The Endowment Assurance.

Term Assurance: The earliest kind of life assurance was a term assurance. This is an assurance for a fixed period in which the assurers in return for a premium undertake to pay the sum assured in the event of the life assured dying within the period or term stated in the policy. According to available records, the first such policy was issued in 1583 A.D. to Richard Martin on the life of William Gybbons at a premium of sixteen naira (₦16) per cent. The policy was effective from the 18th of June 1583 for a term of twelve months with a sum assured of ₦764 : 68k Unfortunately, the life assured died before the end of the term on the 9th of May, 1584, and the sixteen underwriters who subscribed to the policy had to pay up. In keeping with the religious fervour of that period, this early policy had ended in the following words: "God send the said William Gibbons health and long life."

Term assurances which run for only twelve months are not very common in this country today, but they may still be obtained, for example, a creditor may take out a short term policy on the life of his debtor until the debt has been paid or for a period when the debtor is making a hazardous journey. The more popular types of life assurance today are permanent contracts which remain in force throughout the duration of the contract provided the periodical payments are maintained. Both the whole life assurance and the endowment assurance are permanent contracts.

WHOLE LIFE ASSURANCE

The whole life assurance has been described as the "purest form" of life assurance. There is no element of investment. Under a whole life assurance contract, the assurers undertake to pay the sum assured whenever the person whose life is assured dies. In this case the question is not whether or not the sum assured will be paid, it is certain that it will be paid sooner or later, the only uncertainty is as regards the time when it will be paid.

Whole life policies are issued by all the life companies in this country, and they are most suited to the family man who wants to provide for his dependants in the event of his death. Premiums may be paid monthly, quarterly or annually In the early contracts the premiums were paid throughout the duration of the life of the life assured, but it is now possible to obtain a policy which would provide for premium payment to cease at a given age, say at fifty-five or sixty when the assured retires from service or ceases to earn any sizeable income.

ENDOWMENT ASSURANCE

An endowment assurance contract provides that the assurers will pay the sum assured when the life assured reaches a certain age or when he dies, whichever occurs first. For example, if Mr. A aged 20 years takes out a twenty years endowment policy for a sum assured of ₦4,000, he will get his ₦4,000 at the age of forty years if he survives to that age, but if he dies before attaining this age, say just before his 21st birthday, the money will go to his estate or personal representatives immediately. The term of years under the endowment schemes vary from ten years to forty years and the rate of premium payable is naturally higher for shorter periods. The few insurance conscious Nigerians seem to prefer the endowment assurance to the whole life policy. Perhaps this is understandable. In a whole life policy, the policyholder, who in virtually every case pays the premium, can never receive the policy proceeds since they are only payable on his death; but in an endowment assurance the life assured obtains the policy money if he survives until maturity date.

The endowment policy provides a saving for a given purpose and also offers protection for dependants in the event of the death of the life assured before maturity. It may also be used to make financial provision against old age when the ability to work and earn money would cease. An adaptation of this kind of insurance can be used to make provision for the education of children. Indeed, most of the children's assurances are a variation of the endowment assurance scheme.

MORTGAGE PROTECTION INSURANCE

A fourth type of title Assurance policy that is steadily gaining popularity is MORTGAGE PROTECTION ASSURANCE

Mortage Protection Assurance is a special form of life assurance contract designed to assist and encourage house ownership.

The contract provides for the payment of the balance of a building loan should the borrower/property owner die before the full repayment of the loan.

The policy is essentially a Term Assurance contract with the loan repayment period as the duration of the policy.

Mortgage Protection Assurance, may be arranged on a reducing term basis, i.e. the sum assured is reduced by the amount of the annual loan repayment. Alternatively, the policy may be for a fixed amount (the loan amount plus interest) with provision to pay the life assured the sum insured should the assured survive the term of the policy.

Mortgage Protection policies are usually assigned to particular creditors who provided the building loan and is a very useful tool in freeing the estate of a deceased debtor of any encumbrances on a property.

ACCIDENT INSURANCE

The scope of accident insurance is wide, and it is the youngest and most recent of the four main branches of insurance. It includes all types of insurance not covered by the Marine, Fire and Life departments, with the exception of National Insurance or Social Insurance, which, in countries where it exists, is handled by the state. In the United States, what we know in Nigeria and in Britain as Accident Insurance is called Casualty Insurance, but this is only a difference in name, the basic principles are, to a large extent similar. In the legal terminology of insurance, an accident is a mishap which is neither looked for nor designed by the insured. In the English case of FENTON v. THORLEY, (1903) A.C.p. 448 an accident in this context was defined as ".... an unlooked for mishap or an untoward event which is not expected or designed" (per Lord Macnaghten). The event may have been designed or intended by someone else, but provided it was accidental or unexpected by the victim, it is an accident from the point of view of the victim. Thus, for instance, a burglary carried out by another person is an accident from the victim's point of view.

Classification of Accident Insurance: Accident insurance may be classified into three groups:-

(*i*) Insurance of a person's legal liability arising from accidents, for example, public liability insurances;

(*ii*) Insurance of the person against accidental injury, death or sickness. An obvious example is personal accident insurance;

(*iii*) Insurance of property against accidental loss or damage, an example of which would be burglary insurance.

Some accident insurance policies are a combination of all these three classes. For instance, the private motor car comprehensive policy covers the car itself in respect of accidental damage or loss; the policy gives a limited personal accident cover in respect of the insured; and the liability of the insured for bodily injury to third parties and damage to their property is also covered.

An alternative method of classifying accident insurance is according to the class of business. The classes of accident insurance business are: Personal accident, Employer's liability and Workmen's Compensation, Public Liability, Burglary and "All Risks",

Motor Insurance, Fidelity Guarantee Insurance, Engineering Insurance and Aviation Insurance. We will discuss briefly the more important types of insurance handled by the accident department.

(a) **Personal Accident Insurance:** This kind of accident policy provides for the payment of specified sums in the event of accidents to the person insured. When the personal accident policy is extended to cover disablement arising from disease or sickness an agreed weekly payment is made to the insured during the period of the illness or disablement. Sickness insurance is yet quite rare in this country, but it is transacted on a large scale in most of Europe and America.

There is a wide variety of personal accident insurance schemes available, but the commonest type in this country is that in which the insured pays a premium of between N5 – N10 in return for a policy in which the insurance Company undertakes to pay N2,000 in the event of death resulting from an accident. For an additional premium of about 1 per cent the insured could secure cover in respect of weekly payments varying from about N10 to N20 during his period of confinement as a result of an accident.

(b) **Employer's Liability Insurance:** The purpose of employer's liability policy is to indemnify the employer in respect of his legal liability to his employees for occupational injury or disease. The common law and Workmen's Compensation Acts impose certain legal obligations on employers. Under the common law, the employer is liable for any negligent act of his which result in injury or damage to his employees and he is also vicariously liable for the negligent acts of his servants and other agents.

The Workmen's Compensation Decree of 1987 (which, for the main part, enacts the Workmen's Compensation Act of 1942) imposes strict liability (without fault or negligence) on all employers of labour. Under the Act, if a workman is killed or injured whilst acting within the course of his employment, the employer must pay compensation to the workman or his dependents in accordance with the provision of the Decree. Unlike the 1942 Act, this degree makes it compulsory for certain categories of employers (to be determined by the Minister) to take out an employer's liability or a Workmen's Compensation insurance policy to protect themselves against these risks. The Decree extends coverage to more workers and remove difficulties and delays in the administration of compensation.

(c) **Public Liability Insurance:** This kind of policy insures the policy holder against his legal liability to members of the public generally. The insurer in return for the premium paid undertakes to indemnify the insured against all claims made on him by third parties who suffer damage as a result of the insured's negligent or tortious acts.

Public liability insurance is more common in the more industrialised countries of the world. A few Policies are sold every year by the insurance companies in this country, but the idea of public liability insurance has not quite caught on. Most of the policies issued in this country today are in respect of petrol stations and large industrial undertakings. The policies are tailored to the needs of the insured. For example, a petrol seller would insure against damage to third party property or personal injury arising from say, an accidental fire and a hunter may insure against a straying bullet which might cause damage to a third party.

(d) **Burglary Insurance:** Burglary insurance policies provide cover against loss of or damage.to the insured property by burglary or housebreaking. In some cases the policy may be extended, on payment of an additional premium, to cover loss or damage due to a case of simple larceny.

Under the criminal law, burglary consists of "the act of breaking and entering at night the dwelling house of another with intent to commit a felony therein, or breaking out after having committed a felony" (Sec. 16, Larceny Act, 1916. See also Nigerian Criminal Code Sections 410, 411, and 412, at Cap. 42, Page 746 and 747 Volume 2, Laws of Nigeria, 1958.) The criminal law also recognises what is known as "Constructive breaking". A constructive breaking is where the criminal has gained entry into the premises by means of a trick or threat without any actual breaking. The standard burglary policy modifies the criminal law definition of burglary in order to avoid disputes owing to the subtleties of the criminal law definition. The operative clause of a typical burglary policy issued in this country would read something like this:

"........if at anytime during the period of insurance any of the property insured and described in the schedule ....shall be lost or destroyed by theft consequent upon ACTUAL FORCIBLE AND VIOLENT ENTRY of the premises containing the insured property.......... the Company shall, subject to the policy conditions, pay or indemnify the insured in respect of the stolen or damaged property". The policy wording has been slightly modified, but the essential point to note is that the burglary policy insists that there must be An ACTUAL FORCIBLE AND VIOLENT ENTRY of the premises the contents of which have been insured. Such a policy would not cover loses suffered as a result of a mere constructive breaking. For example, where the thief gains entry by pretending to the steward boy, that he is an employee of the National Electric Power Authority and had come to read the meter, this might be a case of constructive breaking and entering which would therefore constitute a burglary for purposes of the criminal law, but there would be no valid claim under a burglary policy as there was no actual forcible and violent entry. Two types of burglary policies are available. One on private dwellings, which insures the contents of private dwellings and flats, and the other on Business premises, factories, retail shops, warehouses, club houses and the like.

(e) **"All Risks" Insurance:** The "all risks" insurance is the most popular form of insurance cover available for valuables such as gold, jewellery, watches and cameras. The cover is very wide, that is why the policy is termed "all risks". It virtually covers accidental loss or damage of any kind, including loss or damage due to fire, theft or even if the article is simply lost or damaged. In an "all risks" policy, each item insured is specified and the value stated.

Before issuing this kind of policy insurers must satisfy themselves that the moral hazard of the proposer is good. The subject of moral hazard was discussed at great length in Chapter 2.

(*f*)   **Motor Insurance:**   In terms of premium income, motor insurance is the largest single section of the whole industry, but this does not imply that it is the most profitable as most of this vast premium is drained up by claims and management expenses. Motor insurance business is grouped into sections according to the type of vehicle as follows :-

Private Cars,
Commercial Vehicles
Agricultural and Forestry Vehicles
Vehicles of Special Construction, such as Mobile Cinemas and canteens,
Motor Trader's Vehicles, and
Motor Cycles.

The risks which a motor vehicle owner would like to insure against fall into two main groups, the first being the risk of damage to or destruction of the motor vehicle itself, and the second being the risk of being called upon to pay damages to third parties for injuries done to them or for damage to their property arising from the use of the motor vehicle. For all the different types of motor vehicles specified above, insurers offer alternative kinds of policies depending on the extent of cover required by the proposer. There are four such kinds of policies, namely: the full comprehensive policy, the third party fire and theft policy, the simple third party policy, and the "Act" liability policy. The features of these various types of motor policies are discussed in detail on page 130.

(*g*)   **Fidelity Guarantee Insurance:** Fidelity guarantee insurance has been devised to replace the ancient system of private suretyship, which has proved unsuitable for modern business trends. Until quite recently, a person seeking employment, especially where the position necessitated the handling of money, was required to produce private sureties or guarantors who would undertake to make good any loss arising from the dishonesty of the person guaranteed. This old system, (which to some extent still applies in this country) has been found most imperfect. The surety might die or get bankrupt, or a qualified and reliable applicant might lose the opportunity of securing a good employment if he fails to find willing sureties. These and other disadvantages of the old-fashioned system of private suretyship led to the development of the modern Fidelity guarantee insurance. The fidelity guarantee business is divided into four sections according to the kind of policy issued. The four kinds of guarantees are (a) Court bonds, (b) Government bonds, (c) Local Government Guarantees and (d) Commercial Fidelity guarantee insurances. Court bonds, government bonds and local government guarantees are not sold in large numbers in this country, but Commercial guarantees are fairly popular. Under a commercial guarantee policy an employer is given an indemnity against loss of money or stock by the fraud or default of his employees named in the policy, such employees may be cashiers, managers, storekeepers, salesmen, etc.

COURT AND GOVERNMENT BONDS;   Bonds are provided by insurance companies to meet Court or Government requirements for security in the case of persons appointed to fiduciary positions. Thus, receivers and managers appointed to the Courts may have to furnish bonds, as may administrators of estates of deceased persons or receivers in estates of mental patients.

Government bonds guarantee the performance of the duties of officials appointed by government departments in such matters as bankruptcy, deeds of arrangement, company liquidation, customs and excise arrangements to ensure the payment required on dutiable commodities, and many other cases where professional or commercial people are placed in a position of trust by government departments. Rates vary widely, and the contracts may be on a fixed or annual basis. The wording of the bond is usually prescribed by the Court or the department concerned.

LOCAL GOVERNMENT BONDS; Local authority bonds providing similar protection to commercial fidelity guarantee insurances go further by guaranteeing not only the honesty of the employee, but also the proper performance of the employee's duties. They can take the form of individual collective or blanket contracts.

(*h*) **Miscellaneous Classes of Insurance effected in the Accident Department:** In addition to the ones mentioned above, there are several other classes of insurance undertaken in the accident department. The more common ones are: (*a*) Engineering insurance, under which boilers, engines, electrical plants and lifts or elevators may be covered. (*b*) Goods-in-transit insurances, under which goods and other merchandise may be insured against loss or damage arising whilst the goods are being transported from one place to another, (*c*) Professional Indemnities, which *indemnifies* firms and professionals (such as doctors, lawyers, accountants, insurance brokers, architects, bankers and others) against their legal liabilities for professional negligence or other default, and (*d*) Livestock insurance which indemnifies the insured against loss of his animals by death arising from accident or disease. Others are Libel Insurance, Credit Insurance and Glass Insurance, but these are comparatively rare in this country at the present time.

(*i*) **Aviation Insurance:** Aviation insurance (that is, the insurance of aircraft, the cargo they carry, and the operators' legal liability for damage to third party property and injury to passengers) is generally handled in the accident department and it is a highly specialised line of business. A Comprehensive Aircraft Policy would cover,

(*a*) Loss of or damage to the aircraft both in the air and on the ground as a result of burglary, theft or other accidental loss or damage, such as a collision.

(*b*) Legal liability of the insured owner or the pilot for the death of or bodily injuries to third parties and ground damage to third party property.

(*c*) Legal liability of the insured or pilot in respect of death of, or bodily injuries to passengers. In addition to the comprehensive policy on the aircraft, the aircraft operator would require a Cargo Policy on "all risks" lines to cover cargo transported by the airline. Airport liability policies and products liability policies may also be taken out

NIGERIAN AVIATION POOL

The concept of pooling under an insurance or reinsurance pool involves an arrangement whereby a number of insurers or reinsurers agree to share premiums and losses in accordance with the terms indicated in the pooling agreement. Each member of the pool contributes to a particular class of insurance or particular class of risk resulting in a combination of their capacities in the pool.

Pools can be classified into Direct Insurance Pools or Reinsurance Pools. They may also be classified geographically either national, sub-regional or regional. Whatever the classification, all pooling arrangements help to increase the collective retention capacity of the members of the pool or the market they represent. Provided the pools are run profitably, they help in minimising the outflow of foreign exchange from the territories concerned since they increase the retention capacity of the relevant markets.

Most African and other third world countries suffer from an acute shortage of foreign exchange. Although the governments of these countries accept and recognise the international character of insurance and reinsurance, they maintain, as a matter of policy, that everything possible should be done to increase local retention capacity so as to reduce the outflow of money in hard currency for the purchase of reinsurance cover abroad. To this end, they support and encourage the establishment of insurance and reinsurance pools aimed at increasing local retention capacity.

It is in response to this policy that the Nigerian insurance industry, encouraged by the Nigeria Reinsurance Corporation, has established a number of insurance and reinsurance pools in this market in recent years. Such pools include the Third World Pool, the WAICA Reinsurance Pool, the Fire Pool, the Nigerian Motor Pool and the Nigerian Aviation Pool.

The Nigerian Aviation Pool started business in January 1984, taking over the insurance of small aircrafts including helicopters and their liabilities. During its first year of operation, the Pool wrote Hull risks on aircrafts with values not exceeding ₦1 million and liabilities not exceeding ₦1 million. The Pool made a total premium of ₦641,292.44 out of which ₦277,800.71 was distributed to members and ₦330,000 went into reserve for investment. In 1985, a total premium of ₦762,580.18 was earned and the distribution to members' account was ₦294,496.32. Since then, the capacity of the Pool has been increasing and on the whole it has been a very successful experiment resulting in a substantial increase in the local retention capacity and a general improvement in aviation insurance expertise as well as in the quality of service offered to the Pool's clients. It is worth mentioning that the Pool which started operations without any capital base in 1984 can now boast of several millions of naira investment in the national economy. All the other Pools have enjoyed more or less the same measure of success as the Aviation Pool, thus lending support to the pooling concept.

PART TWO

CHAPTER V

FUNDAMENTAL PRINCIPLES OF INSURANCE LAW & PRACTICE AS APPLICABLE TO NIGERIA.

Synopsis: Introduction - The Nature of the Insurance Policy—
Fundamental Principles:
Insurable Interest
Utmost Good faith
Indemnity
Subrogation
Contribution
Proximate Cause.

Introduction: Very few persons really take the trouble to read through their insurance policies in order to ascertain and note the terms and conditions of the insurance well in advance of a claim. Of the few who bother to read through the policies, only a small proportion actually understand them. The result is that when a claim arises and it is found that the particular loss is not covered by the terms of the insurance contract, there is always the tendency to blame it all on the insurance company. There might, of course, be some 'black sheep' amongst the insurers, but a lot of this unpleasantness is due to either a lack of understanding or a misunderstanding of the terms of insurance contracts generally.

The aim of the following chapters is to eliminate or at least to minimise such misunderstandings by stating the "rules of the game" for the benefit of the parties taking part in the transaction.

Insurance is a Contract: A contract is an agreement between two or more persons enforceable at law. As has been previously stated, the commonly accepted legal definition of insurance is that it is "a contract whereby a person called the insurer, agrees in consideration of money paid to him, called the premium, by another person, called the assured or insured, to indemnify the latter against loss resulting to him on the happening of certain events".

It follows from this definition, that an insurance being a contract. it must conform to the general rules of law relating to all contracts, in addition to those special rules of law that govern insurance transactions. For any form of contract to be valid, it must possess the following characteristics:

(1) There must be an agreement between two or more persons based upon an OFFER made by one party followed by an UNQUALIFIED ACCEPTANCE of that offer by another party.

(2) The contract must be for a lawful purpose and must be legal in its form. The parties must have intended to create legally binding obligations

(3) There must be either a valuable consideration or form. The term, valuable consideration, in this context means that each side must give something of value for the promise of the other. In an insurance contract, the consideration on the part of the insured is the premium he pays to the insurer, and the consideration on the part of the insurer is his promise to pay in the envent of a loss. A gratuitous promise is not a contract and cannot ordinarily be enforced in a court of law, because the prospective receiver or promisee has given no consideration. But such a promise can be enforced if there is form, that is, if the agreement is under seal and is signed, sealed and delivered.

(4) The parties to the contract must be legally capable of contracting. Generally speaking, infants and persons of unsound mind are not capable of contracting.

(5) There must be an agreement, based upon an equality of knowledge of all the material facts. There must be "CONSENSUS AD IDEM" which means that the minds of the parties must be in one accord. If the insured at the time of the negotiation thought he was buying a personal accident insurance, and the insurer thought he was selling a motor car insurance, there is no contract between the parties as their minds were not in one accord at the material time.

The Policy: The parties to an insurance contract are (*a*) the insurer (usually an insurance company) and (*b*) the insured or assured. In all classes of insurance, other than life, the insured is the person for whose benefit the policy is taken out. He takes the proceeds of the policy in the event of a claim. But in life assurance, there may be three parties to the contract, for example, when a creditor takes out a life policy on the life of his debtor or when a wife takes out a policy on the life of the husband. In these cases, the parties to the contract would be (*a*) the insurer, (*b*) the person whose life is insured, and (*c*) the assured or the beneficiary under the policy, in this example, the creditor or the wife.

The agreement between the parties to the contract is set out in the policy of insurance. The policy is the "evidence" of the insurance contract, under which, generally, the insurer in return for a monetary consideration, known as the premium, undertakes to indemnify the insured against any financial loss which he may suffer as a result of the happening of the event insured against. The liability of the insurer is usually limited to the amount stated in the policy, and this amount is known as the sum insured or sum assured in the case of a life or marine policy. Under no circumstance (in the absence of fraud) can the insurer be called upon to pay more than the sum assured.

Purpose of the insurance policy: By tradition and practice, the purpose of the insurance policy as evidence of the insurance contract is threefold. The first is to define the risk that is being transferred or insured against; (the word transferred has been used advisedly, because what happens in practice is that the insured, for his own peace of mind, transfers a risk which otherwise would have fallen on him to his insurers). The second is, to state the conditions and the terms of the contract, and the third, is, to make plain the procedure that will be followed in the event of a loss occurring. In practice the policy forms vary depending on the particular branch of insurance concerned, but generally speaking, the fundamental principles apply to all branches of insurance.

Fundamental Principles of Insurance: We have seen that insurance contracts, in addition to being subject to the general rules of law relating to contracts generally, are also subject to those special rules of law applicable to insurance transactions. These basic rules or fundamental principles are (*a*) Insurable Interest, (*b*) Utmost Good faith, (or in the U.S.A. the doctrine of Non-Concealment) (*c*) Indemnity, with the corrollaries of, (*d*) Subrogation and (*e*) Contribution, and (*f*) Proximate Cause. We will discuss these fundamental principles in some detail in the following chapters, but briefly, the absence of an insurable interest renders an insurance contract void and of no legal effect, and the validity of the contract depends on the existence of the utmost good faith at the time when the policy was taken out. The insurance contract is a contract of indemnity, which means that in the event of a loss, the amount recoverable by the insured will be limited to his (the insured's) interest in the subject-matter of the insurance. Both subrogation and contribution are corrollaries of the doctrine of indemnity and derive their legal force from the principle of indemnity.

INSURABLE INTEREST

The law requires that every person who takes out an insurance policy must have an insurable interest in the subject-matter of the insurance. If the insured has no insurable interest, the contract is invalid; it is a gambling or wagering contract and not an insurance contract. Insurable interest has been described as the legal right to insure, the implication being that its absence amounts to an absence of the legal right to insure. In order to constitute an insurable interest, the insured must be in some legally recognised relationship to what is insured whereby he will suffer some financial loss by the happening of the event insured against.

Insurable Interest defined: MACGILLIVRAY on Insurance Law, (Fifth Edition at p. 186) offers a "working definition" of insurable interest as follows:-

"Where the insurêd is so situated that the happening of the event on which the insurance money is to become payable would, as a proximate cause, involve the insured in the loss or diminution of any right recognised by law or in any legal liability there is an insurable interest in the happening of that event to the extent of the possible loss or liability".

The Marine Insurance Act of 1961 (one of the earliest insurance legislations passed by an independent Nigerian Parliament) defines insurable interest in the following words; Section 7 (1) and (2) ".......every person has an insurable interest who is interested in a marine adventure. In particular, a person is interested in a marine adventure where he stands in any legal or equitable relation to the adventure or to any insurable property at risk therein, in consequence of which he may benefit by the safety or due arrival of insurable property, or may be prejudiced by its loss, or damage thereto, or by the detention thereof, or may incur liability in respect thereof" Strictly, the definition of insurable interest as contained in the Marine Insurance Act, 1961, refers to what constitutes an insurable interest in a marine adventure, but the definition does indicate what would constitute an insurable interest in other insurance transactions. The requirement of insurable interest applies to all classes of insurance, whether the insurance is in respect of property, life, liability or contingency.

An equally enlightening definition of insurable interest is that given by the court in the leading English case of LUCENA v. CRAUFORD (1806), 2 Bos, & P.N.R. 269:

"A man is interested in a thing to whom advantage may arise or prejudice happen from the circumstances which may attend it. Interest does not necessarily imply a right to the whole, or a part of a thing, nor necessarily and exclusively that which may be the subject of privation, but the having some relation to, or concern in the subject of the insurance, which relation or concern by the happening of the perils insured against may be so affected as to produce a damage, detriment, or prejudice to the person insuring; and where a man is so circumstanced with respect to matters exposed to certain risks or dangers as to have a moral certainty of advantage or benefit, but for those risks or dangers, he may be said to be interested in the safety of the thing. To be interested in the preservation of a thing, is to be so circumstanced with respect to it as to have benefit from its existence, prejudice from its destruction. The property of a thing and the interest devisable from it may be very different; of the first, the price is generally the measure, but by interest in a thing every benefit or advantage arising out of or depending on such thing may be considered as being comprehended."

Essentials of Insurable Interest: Whenever an insurable interest exists, the following essential attributes must be present:

(a)   There must be property, life or limb, rights, interest or potential liability devolving upon the insured capable of being insured against.

(b)   Such property, life or limb, rights, interest or potential liability must be the subject-matter of the insurance; and

(c)   The insured or policyholder must bear some relationship, recognised by law, to the subject-matter whereby he would benefit by the safety of the property, life or limb, rights, interest or freedom from liability, and he would be prejudiced by any loss, injury or damage, or creation of liability.

The latest Nigerian statutory enactment on the status of the principle cf insurable interest in insurance law is contained in the Insurance (Special Provisions) Decree No.40 of 1988, which came into force on 12th October, 1988. The relevant section of that Decree reads as follows:

INSURABLE INTEREST IN LIFE OR OTHER INSURANCE

"3. (1)   Any insurance made by any person on the life of any other person or on any other event whatsoever shall be null and void where the person for whose benefits, or on whose   the account policy of insurance is made has no insurable interest in the insurance or where it is made by way of gaming or wagering.

(2)   A person shall be deemed to have an insurable interest in the life of any other person or in any other event where he stands in any legal relationship to that person or other event in consequence of which he may benefit by the safety of that person or event or be prejudiced by the death of that person or the loss from the occurrence of the event.

(3)   In this section, the expression "legal relationship" includes the relationship which exists between persons under Islamic law or Customary law where by one person assumes responsibility for the maintenance and care of the other."

This re-statement of the law under Decree No.40 of 1988 does not constitute any serious departure from the accepted definition of the scope and status of Insurable Interest in insurance law as generally accepted. It merely emphasizes the accepted principles discussed earlier to the effect that an insurance contract would not be valid in the absence of an insurable interest. Note, however, that the expression "legal relationship" has been widened to include relationships which exist under the Nigerian Customary law as well as Islamic law.

Examples of Insurable Interest: The most obvious example of an insurable interest is that of the absolute and unconditional owner of property, for example, the owner of a motor car or a house. Such an owner has an insurable interest to the extent of the cash value of the motor car or the house, and his is the simplest example of an insurable interest. There are several other types of insurable interest which are not so easy to identify. A mortgagee to whom property is mortgaged as security for a loan has an insurable interest to the extent of the mortgage debt, and so has the mortgagor, a trustee, a beneficiary and a bailee to whom property has been entrusted for a specific purpose.

An individual has an insurable interest in his own life to an unimited amount. A wife has an insurable interest in her husband's life, and on the authority of the English Court of Appeal decision in GRIFFITHS v. FLEMING (1909) 1 K.B. 805, it is now settled law that a husband has an insurable interest in the life of his wife. But a fiance has no insurable interest in the life of his intended bride and vice versa. A creditor has an insurable interest in the life of his debtor, but the debtor has no insurable interest on the life of his creditor. Insurance companies have interests in the lives and property insured with them and this entitles them to effect reinsurances to protect themselves against heavy losses.

There are several other examples of insurable interest, some of them peculiar to Nigerian law and custom. For instance, in parts of the country, some ethnic or Cultural groups (such as the Item Central Union in Bende Division) are bound by tradition to give a decent burial to their poorer members when they die, and to make some provisions to the dependants of the deceased to tide them over the difficult period. The Cultural or ethnic group therefore has an insurable interest in the lives of its members to the extent of the burial and other expenses that would be incurred at the death of each member. Both Dr. T. O. Elias in his book on the GROUNDWORK OF NIGERIAN LAW at Page 309 in the chapter on the Law of Personal Relations, and Miss Margaret M. Green in her book "IGBO VILLAGE AFFAIRS" (2nd Edition Frank Cass & Company Limited) referred to the "Age Groups" or the "Age-grade associations". These associations have certain legally recognised duties to their members, and it is submitted that they have an insurable interest in the lives of their members to the extent of such interests or duties. Like the cultural unions mentioned above, they too have to bury their deceased members; amongst other functions.

When must Insurable Interest Exist? This varies with the different branches of insurance. In life assurance, it is now settled law that there need not be insurable interest at the time of death or at the time the policy matures, but there must be insurable interest at the time the insurance contract is made. (DALBY v. THE INDIAN AND LONDON LIFE ASSURANCE CO. (1854) 15 C.B. 365). In Marine insuance, the rule is the reverse. Insurable interest must exist at the time of the loss. Section 8 (1) of the Marine Insurance Act 1961 provides that "The insured must be interested in the subject-matter insured at the time of the loss though he need not be interested when tne insurance is effected."

Fire and Accident Insurance: In fire and accident insurance the legal requirement is that there must be insurable interest both at the time the insurance contract is effected and at the time of the loss. But an accident or fire insurance effected to come into force at a later date would be valid provided an insurable interest exists at the time the policy takes effect. For example, if Mallam Adamu is to purchase a motor car on the 15th of September, he might call at an insurance office in July and have the car insured as from the 15th September. Provided the ownership in the car is vested in him on the 15th September when the policy comes into force the contract is valid as there was an insurable interest at the material time.

Utmost Good Faith: (or doctrine of Non-Concealment as in the U.S.A)
The second fundamental principle governing insurance transactions is that of utmost good faith. Under the general law of contract, the rule is that each party to the contract is entitled to make the best bargain he can, and as long as he does not make a false or fraudulent statement, he need not draw the attention of the other party to anything that might influence his judgment – the rule which applies is CAVEAT EMPTOR, which means, "Let the Buyer Beware." For example, if Mr. Agu goes to Mr. Bose, a motor car dealer, and purchases a second hand car for ₦3000, only to discover on his return home that the car is full of defects which Mr. Bose knew about but failed to disclose them, under the general law of contract the purchaser, Mr. Agu, has no right of action against the

seller, and Mr. Bose is entitled to keep the purchase price of three hundred pounds. The law requires the buyer to beware and to watch out for his own interest before entering into that sort of transaction. If he loses in the bargain, he only has himself to blame. (The story would, of course, have been different if the seller in this example had acted fraudulently or had given a warranty as to the absence of defects in the car, in this case he merely kept silent.) The reason for the "caveat emptor" rule is that goods can easily be inspected by an intending buyer, and if the prospective buyer is not satisfied with the condition of the goods, he can abandon the transaction. Insurance contracts are in a different category. The knowledge as regards the nature of the risk proposed for insurance is almost always exclusively possessed by one side. The proposer knows all about the risk at the time he is proposing for insurance, whilst the insurer knows nothing and has to rely on the proposer to supply him the information which would enable him assess the risk. In order to make insurance transactions fair for all the parties, the law has elevated insurance contracts to the status of contracts UBERRIMAE FIDEI, that is, contracts of the UTMOST GOOD FAITH. The practical effect of this principle of utmost good faith is that each party to the contract must not only refrain from actively misleading the other, but must DISCLOSE and not conceal any material information relating to the proposed insurance. The law requires the parties to disclose all material facts, and a material fact is one which would affect the mind of a prudent insurer, in deciding whether or not to accept the proposal, and on what terms he would accept. In the case of RIVAZ v. GERUSSI (1880), 6 Q.B.D. 222, a material fact in this context was defined as:

"a fact which would affect the judgment of a prudent and rational underwriter in considering whether he would enter into a contract at all or enter into it at one rate or another". And

Section 20, of the Marine Insurance Act, 1961, which to all intents and purposes, applies to all classes of insurance, defines a material fact in the following words-"every circumstance is material which would influence the judgment of a prudent insurer in fixing the premium, or determining whether he will take the risk."

The legal basis of the principle of utmost good faith and the duty of disclosure imposed by it was discussed at some length by the court in the leading case of CARTER v. BOEHM, (1766), 3 Burr 1905, and we reproduce below the relevant portion of the judgment of Lord Mansfield:

"Insurance is a contract upon speculation. The special facts upon which the contingent chance is to be computed lie most commonly in the knowledge of the Insured only; the underwriter trusts to his representations, and proceeds upon confidence that he does not keep back any circumstance in his knowledge to mislead the Underwriter into a belief that the circumstance does not exist, and to induce him to estimate the risk as if it did not exist. The keeping back of such a circumstance is a fraud, and therefore the policy is void. Although the suppression should happen through mistake, without any fraudulent intention, yet still the Underwriter is deceived, and the policy is void; because the risk run is really different from the risk understood and intended to be run at the time of the agreement. Good faith forbids either party, by concealing what he privately knows, to draw the other into a bargain from his ignorance of that fact and his believing the contrary."

The Marine Insurance Act, 1961, contains an up-to-date statement of the law on this point as it applies to Nigeria; and it is submitted that the Nigerian Courts would apply the provisions of this Act to all classes of insurance. The relevant sections of the Act state as follows: Section 19. "A contract of Marine Insurance is a contract based upon the utmost good faith, and, if the utmost good faith is not observed by either party, the contract may be avoided by the other party"

Section 20 (1)   "subject to the provision of this section, the assured shall disclose to the insurer, before the contract is concluded, every material circumstance which is known to the assured, and the assured shall be deemed to know every circumstance which, in the ordinary course of business, ought to be known by him. If the assured fails to make such disclosure, the insurer may avoid the contract."

Section 20 (2)   defines a material fact, and this has been reproduced above.

The Duty to disclose is only confined to known facts: The duty to disclose imposed by the law is confined to facts actually known to the party on whom the duty falls. Being a duty to disclose, that is to do a positive act, no one can be expected to disclose what he does not know. Therefore, if insurers wish to avoid the policy on the ground that there has been a non-disclosure of a material fact by the insured, they must show that the insured knew or ought to have known about the existence of the material fact. (Section 20, Marine Insurance Act). Thus, if the question-"Have you any disease?" - is inserted in a proposal form for a life policy, and the proposer gives the answer "No" believing that he is in perfect health, the insurers would not be allowed to repudiate liability under the contract if it later turns out that at the time of the proposal, the assured was suffering from tuberculosis, but of which he did not know about as it was at its early stages. (See Joel v. Law Union and Crown Insurance Company, (1908) 2. K.B. 863). But as soon as it is established that the insured knew or ought to have known the existence of the material fact, it is immaterial that he failed to make the disclosure owing to an inadvertence or because he did not consider the point material. Intention, innocent or otherwise is immaterial.

Contractual Extension of the Duty of Disclosure: We have seen that the duty to disclose material facts is confined to known facts as a person cannot reasonably be expected to disclose what he does not know. However, the Nigerian law allows freedom of contract, and as long as the terms of the contract are not illegal, the parties to the contract are free to restrict, extend or alter their legal rights as they see fit. Insurers have taken full advantage of this contractual freedom by extending the duty of disclosure imposed on the insured. In some modern insurance contracts, the insured virtually warrants the accuracy of the information supplied in the proposal form. To illustrate this point, we reproduce below the text of a typical declaration contained at the foot of proposal forms signed by the insured as forming the basis of the insurance contract:

"I, the undersigned, hereby warrant that the above statements and particulars are correct and true, and that I have not withheld any information which should be communicated to the insurance company and I hereby agree that this declaration shall be deemed to be of a promisory nature and effect, and shall be the basis of the contract."

The legal effect of this declaration in the proposal form is that if it turns out that the insured's answer to a question in the form is inaccurate, or if he fails to disclose a material fact which he never knew about, the insurance company would be entitled to avoid liability under the contract despite the fact that the insured acted honestly and in good faith in completing the proposal form. Thus if in such a proposal form the insured is asked - "Are you suffering from any disease"? and the insured answers "No", honestly believing that he is not suffering from any disease, if it turns out later that he was at the early stages of lung cancer at the material time, the company would be entitled to avoid the contract, as in this case it is immaterial that the insured did not know of his ill-health.

The practice of extending the duty of disclosure has been criticised as unfair to the insured, and the courts view the practice with disapproval and do everything in their power to lessen its effect on the insured, for example, by imposing a high burden of proof on the insurer who is relying on the declaration. Note the effect of Section 2 (1) of Decree No.40 of 1988 which stipulates that in a contract of insurance, a breach of a term whether called a warranty or a condition shall not give rise to any right by or afford a defence to the insurer against the insured unless the term is material and relevant to the risk or loss insured against.

Examples of Material Facts: All facts which tend to render a risk proposed for insurance greater than normal are material, and should be disclosed. This, however, is a general proposition, because the courts might hold that a fact, though it renders the risk greater than normal is not material in the particular context. Thus it has been held by an English Court that the fact of a motor car being garaged in a garage built with timber was not a material fact and therefore the failure to disclose this fact was not sufficient to justify repudiation of the contract by the aggrieved insurer. The policy concerned was a comprehensive motor car policy and the reason for the decision was that only a small part of the insurance premium relates to the fire risk. If the policy had been a fire policy, the decision would almost certainly have been different as the court would have held the fact material.

Facts which indicate that the proposer is in some respects abnormal are material. For instance, facts which show that the proposer has been refused insurance by other companies on account of his bad moral hazard, or in motor insurance, the fact that the proposer has had several previous convictions for motoring offences. Most of the questions asked in the proposal forms are material, and the insured should, in his own interest answer such questions truthfully.

Facts which the insured does not have to disclose: There are certain facts which the law regards as immaterial and no one can be penalized for failing to disclose them. All facts which lessen the risk proposed for insurance are not material. For instance, a proposer who has driven his car for twenty years without an accident need not disclose this fact in his motor proposal form.

Notorious facts or facts within the knowledge of everybody, such as the fact that Lagos is the capital of Nigeria or that doctors work in hospitals need not be disclosed. Similarly, facts which should be known by an insurer in the ordinary course of his business need not be disclosed. For example, you need not disclose to an insurance company that "mammy waggon" and "bolekaja" drivers are more prone to road accidents than priests, lawyers and insurance officials. These are facts which the insurer should have known in the normal course of his business. Also, matters of law need not be disclosed, because everybody is presumed to know the law.

Concealment or "Suppressio veri": A person may "truthfully" answer the questions in a proposal form and yet be in breach of the principle of utmost good faith as a result of a concealment or the suppression of the truth. This can best be illustrated by a reported English case. In this case, LONDON ASSURANCE V MANSELL (1879), 11 Ch.D. 363, the insurance company's proposal form (which was completed and signed by the proposer defendant Mr. Mansell) contained this question: "Has a proposal ever been made on your life at any other office or offices? If so, when? was it accepted at the ordinary premium, or at an increased premium, or declined? "To these questions, the insured answered as follows: "Insured now in two offices for ₦3,200, at ordinary premium rates. Policies effected last year." As a result of these answers the proposal was accepted by the insurance company. The truth, however, was that several insurance offices had declined to insure the life of the proposer. On these facts the court held that there had been a breach of the principle of utmost good faith by the insured on account of his concealment of material facts, and therefore the insurance company was entitled to avoid the contract. On the same facts, the company might have repudiated liability on the ground of misrepresentation or non-disclosure of material facts.

Misrepresentations: Innocent and Fraudulent: The subject of misrepresentations and their effect on contracts applies to all types of contracts and is not restricted to insurance contracts, but for convenience, we will discuss their legal effects briefly under this heading.

A representation is a statement by one of the parties, at the time of contracting, with the purpose of inducing the other party to enter into the contract. If such a statement is false, it is called a misrepresentation, and there are two types of misrepresentations - innocent and fraudulent.

Innocent Misrepresentation: An innocent misrepresentation is an inaccurate or false statement which the maker honestly believed to be true at the time he made it. If the innocent statement was actually material, that is, if it was the innocent misrepresentation that actually induced the other party to enter into the contract, and that party suffers damage by entering into the contract relying upon the misrepresentation, the contract is voidable at the option of the aggrieved person and he may take steps to rescind the contract.

Fraudulent Misrepresentation: This is a false statement which the maker knew to be untrue, or did not believe to be true, or one made recklessly without caring whether it is true or false. In the case of fraudulent misrepresentation, the aggrieved person, that is the person who has been induced by the fraudulent misrepresentation to enter into the contract, is entitled not only to rescind the contract, but he may also bring an action claiming damages for fraud or deceit.

What courses of action are open to an insurer where there has been a misrepresentation or a Breach of the duty of disclosure imposed by the principle of utmost good faith? We have seen that the breach of the duty of disclosure renders the insurance contract voidable at the option of the aggrieved person, usually the insurer. Similarly, a misrepresentation has the same effect, except that a fraudulent misrepresentation also entitles the aggrieved person to claim damages for deceit. In practice, however, there are three or four courses of action open to an insurer who has discovered a misrepresentation or a breach of the principle of utmost good faith:

(a) The insurer may repudiate liability.

(b) As the contract is only voidable and not void, the insurer may overlook the breach, and allow the contract to stand.

(c) The insurer may bring an action for delivery up and cancellation of the policy. This is the wisest course of action open to an insurer in respect of insurances on motor vehicles, in view of the provisions of the Road Traffic Acts and the Motor Vehicles (Third Party Insurance) Act, which compels an insurer, subject to certain conditions, to meet the claims of injured third parties despite the fact that there might have been a breach of duty on the part of the insured. Once the policy is delivered up and cancelled in response to an order of court, the liability of the insurer under these Acts would cease.

(d) Finally, if the policy has matured for payment, the insurer may refuse to make any payment and leave the insured to institute proceedings, which the insurer may answer by pleading the breach in defence.

The insurer must elect within a reasonable time which of these courses of action he will adopt. If he accepts a renewal premium after he became aware of a breach, he loses the right to repudiate and is deemed to have waived the breach. If the breach was innocent and unintentional, the insured is entitled to a refund of his premium if the insurer decides to rescind the contract.

The reader should note the effect of Insurance (Special Provisions) Decree No.40 of 1988 on the doctrine of Non-Disclosure as well as Warranties in insurance law. These provisions have had the effect of modifying the established common law rules on both subjects, and to that extent, qualifies the points made above.

On "Disclosure", the relevant section of this Decree reads as follows:-

Disclosure

(1) Where an insurer requires an insured to complete a proposal form or other application form for insurance, the form shall be drawn up in such manner as to elicit all such information as the insurer considers material in accepting the application for insurance of the risk; and any information not specifically requested shall be deemed not to be material.

(2) The proposal form or other application form for

insurance shall be printed in easily readable letters, and shall state, as a note in a conspicuous place on the front page, that "An insurance agent who assists an applicant to complete an application or proposal form insurance shall be deemed to have done so as the agent of the applicant".

(3)   A disclosure or representation made by the insured to the insurance agent shall be deemed to be disclosure or representation to the insurer, provided the agent is acting within his authority".

On "Warranties and Conditions", the relevant sections provide as follows:-

Warranty and Conditions

"2.   (1)   In a contract of insurance, a breach of a term whether called a warranty or a condition shall not give rise to any right by or afford a defence to the insurer against the insured unless the term is material and relevant to the risk or loss insured against.

(2)   Notwithstanding any provision in any written law or enactment to the contrary, where there is a breach of a term of a contract of insurance, the insurer shall not be entitled to repudiate the whole or any part of the contract or a claim brought on the grounds of the breach unless:-
(a) the breach amounts to a fraud; or
(b) it is a breach of a fundamental term (whether or not it is called a warranty) of the contract.

(3)   Where there is a breach of a material term of a contract of insured and the insured makes a claim against the insurer and the insurer is not entitled to repudiate the whole or any part of the contract, the insurer shall be liable to indemnify the insured only to the extent of the loss which would have been suffered if there was no breach of the term.

(4)   Nothing in this section shall prevent the insurer from repudiating a contract of insurance or grounds a breach of a material term before the occurrence of the risk or loss insured against".

CHAPTER VI

FUNDAMENTAL PRINCIPLES (*continued*)

Indemnity—Subrogation—Contribution.

INDEMNITY

It is a fundamental principle of insurance law that all insurance policies, except those of life and personal accident, are contracts of indemnity. When an insurance policy is said to be a contract of idemnity, it means that in the event of a loss arising from an insured peril the insured shall be placed in the same position that he occupied immediately before the happening of the event insured against. The insured is not allowed to recover more than his actual financial loss. In practice it is possible for an insured person to recover less than a complete indemnity, for instance, where he has under-insured, but it is illegal and against public policy for the insured to recover more than the amount of his actual financial loss. It is in the overall interest of the public that an insured should be forbidden from making a profit from what is, essentially, a misfortune. If the insured were allowed to gain by the loss or destruction of his insured property, he would be tempted to destroy it, and if the temptation to destroy is succumbed to, this would be injurious to the interest of the public generally.

The legal basis of this principle can best be illustrated with an example. If Mr. A, an unsrupulous man, were allowed to obtain more than indemnity, (that is more than his actual financial losses) he might build a small house for ₦20,000, walk into the office of a local insurance company and have that house insured for ₦40,000 against the risk of fire. As soon as the policy is issued, he then proceeds to set the house on fire secretly of course, and then claims the insurance moneys of ₦40,000 thus making a profit of nearly ₦13,600 from the fire. The fire in this example, might have spread and done considerable damage to adjoining property, and there might even have been loss of lives and personal injury, contrary to the general interests of the community. It is to guard against these evils, and to protect the interest of the community that the principle of indemnity was formulated.

The principle of indemnity was discussed by the court in the leading Engish case of CASTELLAIN v. PRESTON (1883) 11 Q.B.D. 380, C.A. As this case is considered the leading case on the subject, we reproduce below the following extract from the judgment which clearly defines the doctrine:

"The very foundation, in my opinion, of every rule which has been applied to insurance law is this, namely, that the contract of insurance contained in a marine or fire policy (and that equally applies to accident policies other than personal accident) is a contract of indemnity and of indemnity only, and that this contract means that the insured, in case of a loss against which the policy has been made, shall be fully indemnified, but shall never be more than fully indemnified. That is the fundamental principle of insurance law and if ever a proposition is brought forward which is at variance with it, that is to say, which either will prevent the insured from obtaining a full indemnity, or which will give the assured more than a full indemnity, that proposition must certainly be wrong"

How the Principle of Indemnity is Applied in Practice to the various Classes of Insurance

Motor Insurance: From the point of view of what constitutes an indemnity, motor insurance is the most controversial class of insurance in this country today, and most of the misunderstandings that arise relate to the "Own damage" section of the Comprehensive motor policy. In view of this fact, we are giving some priority to this class of business in our discussions on the practical application of the principle of indemnity.

Total Losses: Where there has been a total loss, that is, the insured vehicle has been damaged beyond economic repair or is completely wrecked, the insured will be paid the market value of the vehicle immediately before the accident. This is ofcourse, subject to the sum insured being adequate as the sum insured is the maximum liability of the insurer. Despite the fact that the sum assured or the sum insured is the maximum liability of the insurers in all cases, it does not follow that the insured will always be paid the full sum insured every time there is a total loss. Perhaps this point can best be explained by an example. Let us suppose that Mr. Bassey, on the 1st of April, buys a Volkswagen car for ₦8,000 and insures it comprehensively with Company XYZ Limited for that amount. Suppose also that two days after on the 3rd of April, the Nigerian Government reduces the tax on all small cars by one thousand naira, the dealers respond by reducing the selling price of Volkswagen Cars from Eight Thousand Naira to Seven Thousand Naira. On the 6th of April, Mr. Bassey's car is involved in accident and it becomes a complete wreck, and Mr. Bassey then puts in a claim with his insurance company.

Mr. Bassey will not be entitled to receive from the insurer the full sum of Eight Thousand Naira, as this will be more than an indemnity in view of the fall in the market value of the car immediately before the accident, in this case the sum of Seven Thousand Naira (as the car could not have depreciated to any noticeable extent in such a short time.) Once he is paid the sum of Seven Thousand Naira by his insurers, the latter are discharged from their liability to indemnify him.

Conversely, if instead of a reduction in import tax, the Government had increased the import tax on cars of that make by say, two thousand naira, thus raising the selling price of such cars to ten thousand naira. Mr. Bassey in our example, can only get the sum insured of eight thousand naira, which is the maximum liability of the insurers, although in this case, he would be getting less than an indemnity.

This example ignores the possibility of the policy being subject to an "excess". When a policy is said to be subject to an "excess", it means that the insured in his own insurer to the extent of the amount of the excess. For instance, if in this our example, Mr. Bassey's policy had been subject to a fifty naira excess, the insurer would have paid him the pre-accident market value of the car less the amount of the excess, that is, six thousand and fifty naira. In the event of a partial damage, if the cost of repairs is either less than or within the amount of the excess, no claim is made on the insurer, as the insurer's liability begins to run when the excess has been exhausted.

Partial Losses: In respect of accidental damage to the insured vehicle, the insurer indemnifies the insured by paying for the cost of repairing the damage. If the process of repairs results in "betterment", that is, if the vehicle is considerably improved, for example, where the whole body-work of an old car has been re-painted or where new tyres have been fitted to replace damaged and worn out tyres, the insured has a duty to contribute towards the cost of repairs proportionately because he is getting new for old.

Partial Losses Treated as a Constructive Total Loss:

In some cases, the damaged vehicle is still a repairable proposition, but because the estimated cost of repairs would exceed the market value of the vehicle after it has been repaired, the insurer might decide to deal with the claim as a constructive total loss. In that case, the insurer must indemnify the insured by paying him the pre-accident market value of the vehicle or the market value of a vehicle of similar make, type, age and condition.

Right to the Salvage: Whenever an insurer settles a claim either as a total loss or as a constructive total loss, and provided the insured has been fully indemnified, the insurer automatically becomes entitled to the salvage or remains of the insured vehicle, and they may deal with it as they see fit. It is not in keeping with the principle of indemnity for the insured to retain the salvage after he has been fully indemnified.

OTHER PROPERTY INSURANCES

The amount payable to the insured in respect of insurances on property would depend on whether the insured property is merely damaged or completely lost or destroyed. Where the property is lost, as in the case of an item insured under a burglary or an "All risks" policy, the amount payable to the insured is the market value of the lost property, but allowance must be made for normal wear and tear or depreciation in the value of the property since it was purchased. Similarly, where there has been an appreciation, that is, a rise in the value of the property, this must be taken into account in the settlement.

Buildings: For buildings damaged or destroyed, say by fire, the amount payable to the insured would be either the cost of repairing or reinstating the building to the same condition as it was immediately before the fire.

Goods or Merchandise: In the case of goods or merchandise in a trader's shop, for instance, where such goods are insured under a fire or burglary policy, the insured will be fully indemnified if he is paid the value of the goods to himself, that is, the wholesale price he paid to obtain the goods and not the selling price which he has fixed for the goods. The merchant's or the trader's anticipated profits is not covered under the ordinary policy. (Such contingencies may be insured against under a Loss of Profits Policy).

The reason for this basis of settlement is that if the insured is paid the wholesale price of the goods, he could have them replaced at the wholesale price without any extra cost to himself.

The Market Value Test: As a general rule, the test adopted in practice by most insurers as a guide in determining the amount that would suffice to indemnify the insured is the "market value" test. This, as we have seen, means that the insured is paid the market value of the lost or damaged property at the time and place of the event resulting in the loss or damage. This market value test is only a general proposition, to be used mainly as a guide. In some cases it might be found that the market price at the time and place of loss is not sufficient to indemnify the insured, and in such cases, suitable compromise settlements are effected. Certain policies do make special provisions as regards the basis of settlement in the event of a loss.

Whatever method of settlement is adopted, the ultimate intention should be to give the insured a perfect and complete indemnity, to which he is entitled, subject, ofcourse, to the sum insured being adequate; for, as in all cases, the maximum liability of the insurer is the sum insured. Thus, if Mr. Egbe buys a car for ₦1,8000 and insures it for ₦1,000 in order to take advantage of a reduction in premium, in the event of an accident resulting in the total destruction of the car, the maximum liability of the insurers would be ₦1,000 which is the sum insured. Having paid this amount to Mr. Egbe, the insurers are discharged from all liability under the insurance contract. The fact that Mr. Egbe would require the sum of ₦1,800 to give him a complete indemnity (in the sense of placing him in the same position that he occupied before the accident) is immaterial. Mr. Egbe has only himself to blame for underinsuring the car at the outset.

No Indemnity in respect of Sentimental Losses:

In all insurance policies which are contracts of indemnity, insurers are liable only for actual material losses which can be estimated in terms of hard cash. They cannot be called upon to pay for sentimental values as these cannot be assessed in terms of money. Therefore, if Mrs. A's wedding present (to which she attaches a high sentimental value) gets stolen or lost, all that she is entitled to get from her "all risks" insurers is the actual cash value. of the lost item. The fact that the lost item is worth a lot more than its actual cash value to the insured is of no consequence because no pecuniary value is attached to mere sentiment.

INDEMNITY IN RELATION TO MARINE INSURANCE

The "measure of indemnity" in a marine policy is governed to some extent by statute law. The indemnity provided by a marine insurance policy is not a perfect indemnity, and this is true both in Nigeria and in most of Europe and America, especially as the provisions of the Nigerian Marine Insurance Act. 1961, have followed established practice in the international markets.

In marine insurance, the practice is to use valued policies for both hull and cargo. This means that the value of both ship and cargo is fixed well in advance, usually at the time the insurance is effected, and in the event of a loss or destruction, the insured is paid this agreed value without any regard for wear and tear or depreciation. The Marine Insurance Act, 1961, confirms this practice in relation to marine policies effected in Nigeria. Section 68 (2) describes and defines the "measure of indemnity" as:

". . . . . the sum which the insured may recover in respect of a
loss on a policy by which he is insured, being in case of a valued
policy the full extent of the value fixed by the policy, and in the
case of an unvalued policy, the full extent of the insurable value"
(For a definition of insurable value, see section 18 of the Marine Insurance Act, 1961).

Unvalued policies are very rarely used in marine insurance in this country as the general practice is to issue agreed value policies as described above.

Personal Accident And Life Assurance Policies:

As we noted earlier, insurances of the person, that is, personal accident insurance and life assurance policies, are not contracts of indemnity. The law does not regard these classes of insurance as contracts of indemnity mainly because of the obvious difficulties that would arise in any attempt at fixing a monetary value on human life and limb. In relation to life assurance, the effect of this is that there is, legally, no limit to the number of life policies that a person may take out on his own life. Thus, provided Mr. Audu can afford to maintain the assurances, he is quite at liberty to assure his life for several millions of naira with virtually all the insurance companies in Nigeria, and each company must pay up its liability when the policy matures at the death of Mr. Audu. The only possible check against this type of over-insurance is the fact that premiums have to be paid, and the number of life policies that a person is able to maintain would be dependent on his financial position. Furthermore, insurance companies, in their proposal forms normally require a proposer to state what other policies are held. Therefore, whilst Mr. Audu is at liberty to assure his life for any amount, it is unlikely that he would find several million pounds of cover.

Although personal accident policies are not contracts of indemnity, the insurance industry in practice endeavours to apply the principle of indemnity in a limited sense to this class of insruance, mainly, in order to ensure that a person's personal accident benefits are related to his income. For example, most insurers insist that their consent must first be obtained before any additional personal accident insurance is effected by the policyholder, and they keep records which help to ensure that the amount payable at death, and the disablement benefits granted are dependent on the occupation of the insured and his financial position. For instance, no insurance company would issue a personal accident policy for ₦40,000 death benefit and ₦100 weekly disablement benefit to a clerk earning ₦700 a year.

The dangers of issuing out personal accident policies with benefits out of proportion to the insured's income can best be illustrated with an example. Assuming Mr. Imo, a clerk on a salary of ₦50 a month takes out a personal accident policy which allows him ₦100 a week during his period of disablement arising from an accident. In the event of an accident, Mr. Imo, knowing that he is much better off financially whilst the disablement lasts, might be tempted to prolong his period of disablement at the expense of his insurers, his employers and the nation in terms of loss of man-power.

Furthermore, there is also the possibility of such a policy-holder staging an accident in order to collect the insurance moneys.

Personal Accident Policies on the Life of Another:

Where an insurable interest exists, it is quite permissible for a person to take out a personal accident insurance on the life of another, for example, a creditor might effect a policy on the life of his debtor to the extent of the debt. It is submitted that this kind of policy is a contract of indemnity, as in the event of a claim arising, the amount recoverable is the actual financial loss sustained by the person who effected the insurance. This point is perhaps, only of academic interest, as insurers generally settle their personal accident claims by paying the amount and benefits specified in the policy without any further consideration of issues of indemnity.

Indemnity in Relation to Insurances of Liability and Interest:

Insurances in respect of liability and interest are contracts of indemnity. In the case of an insurance of liability, that is, where the insured has insured against his legal liability towards third parties, if a claim arises, the amount payable by the insurer is that amount that would suffice to indemnify the insured. Where the third-party claim had been settled by the insured, the insurer would indemnify the insured by reimbursing him the exact cost of settlement. And if the third party claim has been litigated up to judgment, the insurers would pay the amount awarded in the Court's judgment together with any costs and expenses incurred by the insured with the written consent of the insurer.

Most liability policies are subject to a limit of indemnity. If the third party claim exceeds the limit of indemnity, the policyholder will have to bear any amount in excess of the limit. Thus, if Mr. Agi, a petrol station owner, takes out a public liability policy which is subject to a limit of indemnity of ₦20,000 on any one claim, and his petrol station is negligently set on fire by one of his servants or employees, resulting in damage to a third party's property to the extent of ₦50,000, then, in the event of a claim by the third party, the insurers of Mr. Agi will pay up to their limit of ₦20,000, and the insured has to pay the balance of ₦30,000.

With regard to insurance of interest, for example, a commercial fidelity guarantee insurance where a servant or an employee of the insured has embezzled some money, the measure of indemnity would be the cash payment to the insured representing the exact amount misappropriated by the employee guaranteed. Thus, where the employee has embezzled the sum of ₦1,000, the insured will recover ₦1,000. The precise amount of the loss would be ascertained and certified by auditors from the insured's books of account.

Some Modifications of the Principle of Indemnity:

In recent times, the insurance industry has introduced certain modifications of the principle of indemnity. The most common, and perhaps the most controversial of these new devices is the VALUED POLICY or the agreed value policy.

A valued policy is one in which the value of the insured property is agreed upon between the parties at the time the insurance is effected. In the event of a claim arising, the insurer is bound to pay the agreed value, and is precluded from suggesting an amount less than the agreed value. It therefore follows that the measure of indemnity in a valued policy is not the market value of the insured property at the time and place of loss, but the value fixed at the inception of the policy. This value might even be greater than the actual cash value of the insured item at the time of the loss, in which case the insured would be getting more than a true indemnity.

The valued policy has been criticised as an unwarranted deviation from the well-established principle of indemnity. But the strongest argument in support of it is that it helps to eliminate misunderstandings between the insurer and the insured as regards the value of the thing insured especially wh·n a claim arises and the thing insured has ceased to exist. In pı ıctice, most insurers endeavour to keep within the principle of in emnity as much as possible, by ensuring that the agreed value represents the true value of the thing insured and that there is no over-valuation.

So long as the fundamental doctrine of the freedom of contracts is accepted by the Nigerian Legal system, there is no legal objection to the valued policy, as parties are free to contract as they see fit, and provided such a contract possesses all the attributes of a valid contract, it will be enforced by the Courts.

Where there has been a fraudulent or grossly excessive over-valuation of the insured item, the valued policy ceases to be an insurance contract, but a gambling transaction and would therefore be void and unenforceable.

In marine insurance it is the accepted international custom to use valued policies, and it is only in more recent times that the idea of the valued policy has spread to other property insurances. For example, valued policies are issued nowadays in respect of insurances on most works of art, such as paintings, sculptures and similar articles where difficulty might arise in determining the value of the insured property. Household goods and personal effects may be insured under this kind of policy, but it is not encouraged by the insurance industry. In motor insurance where the value of the motor vehicle has been agreed between the parties, the practice is to have this value revised at each renewal. In all cases, the agreed value is. only paid to the insured where there has been a total loss.

The Practical Methods of Providing Indemnity:

Hitherto, we have been discussing the principle of indemnity and its application to the various classes of insurance. We shall now discuss the practical methods by which indemnity is provided to the insured by the insurers.

In the absence of any provision in the policy to the contrary, the presumption is that the method of providing indemnity shall be by a cash payment. Most policies, however, give the insurer the option of paying cash, reinstating or replacing the lost or damaged property, or repairing the damage. From the foregoing, it follows that there are four possible methods by which the insurer can indemnify the insured, (a) by cash payment; (b) by replacent; (c) by reinstatement; and (d) by repairing. Whichever method is adopted, the aim should always be to provide a complete indemnity. But in order to obtain his indemnity, the insured must discharge his duty of proving his claim, that is, he must show that the loss or damage was caused by an insured peril, and that he has complied with the policy conditions. Having done this, the insurer must then discharge his obligations under the contract by indemnifying the insured in full, subject to the adequacy of the sum insured.

The Relationship between Indemnity and Insurable Interest

The insurance law principles of indemnity and insurable interest are very closely related, to the extent that one has been described as a corrollary of the other. Whenever an insurance contract is said to be one of strict indemnity, the insured will be indemnified only if he has an insurable interest in the subject-matter of the insurance contract. The insured's insurable interest must have a monetary value, and that monetary value is the limit of the amount recoverable by the insured in the event of a claim. Therefore the limit of the insured's indemnity is the extent of his insurable interest in the subject-matter of the insurance, because that is the amount that he requires to place him in the same financial position as he occupied immediately before the loss. Thus, where the insured has no insurable interest in the subject-matter of the policy, then there can be no indemnity as no loss has been sustained by the insured in respect of which he is to be indemnified. In short, the legal position is that where there is no insurable interest, there can be no indemnity.

Summary of the Consequences of the Principle of Indemnity:

In view of the importance of the subject, we will conclude our discussions by stating below, even at the risk of committing a repetition, the legal and practical consequences of the principle of indemnity, and these are:-

(1)   In the event of a loss, the amount that the insured will recover from his insurers will neither be more nor less than his actual financial loss.

(2)   If the thing insured is only partially destroyed or damaged, the insured can only claim the cost of repairing the damage and no more. If in the case of a partial loss, the insurers decide to treat the claim as a constructive total loss and pay the insured the full market value, he is bound to surrender the salvage of the property insured to the insurers. He cannot take a full indemnity and then retain the property insured.

(3)   The maxim is that "the insured must not take with both hands". This means that if the insured has been indemnified by his insurers to the full extent of his loss, he is bound to transfer to the insurers any rights which he may have against a third party in respect of the loss. The insured cannot receive an indemnity from a third-party, for instance, the primary tortfeasor, and then proceed to receive a further payment from his insurers. (This is the subject of Subrogation which is discussed in detail in this Chapter under the next heading).

(4) Where the insured has taken out more than one insurance policy in respect of the same interest, he is precluded from obtaining more than one complete indemnity. He is at liberty to decide which of his policies to claim from, but having obtained an indemnity from one, he is not allowed to obtain a further compensation from the second or subsequent insurance policies. (This is the subject of Contribution which is discussed at length later in this Chapter at p. 76).

(5) If the insured parts with or ceases to have any interest in the subject-matter of the insurance, then the insurance comes to an end. This is because the law holds the view that in the event of a loss or damage arising after the insured has sold or parted with the property insured, he cannot be said to have suffered any loss for which he is to be indemnified. Besides, the insurance contract is a personal contract in the sense that it is personal to the particular insured and the particular insurer. The case of ROGERSON v. SCOTTISH AUTOMOBILE AND GENERAL INSURANCE COMPANY (1931) 48 T.L.R. 17, clearly illustrates this point. In that case, a motor car was insured by the plaintiff-owner for twelve months. After driving the car for a few months, the insured exchanged the car for another one. The new car was involved in an accident and the insured put in a claim in respect of the damage to the new car, but the claim was rejected by the insurers on the ground that they did not insure the new car. The insured sued the insurers and the court held that the insurance company was not liable to meet a claim under the policy because the subject-matter of the insurance had been changed. The fact that the insurance policy still had many months to run was held immaterial. The author is unaware of any reported Nigerian case on the point, but it is pretty certain that the Nigerian courts would follow the reasoning in this English case, because it seems a logical consequence of the principle of indemnity as recognised in insurance law.

Similarly, if Mr. A., an Insured car owner sells the insured car before the expiry of the policy to Mr. B.. Mr. B. the new owner is not automatically covered under Mr. A's motor policy. Therefore if Mr. B. takes no steps to effect his own insurance on the car, he would be driving the car without insurance and thereby committing an offence contrary to the Road Traffic laws. In practice what happens in this country when there is a change of ownership is that the new owner approaches the insurance company of the previous owner to report the change of ownership. If the insurer is satisfied that there has been a genuine change of interest, it will obtain a completed proposal form from the new owner and provided he is a normal risk, an endorsement will be issued by the insurer noting the change of interest and substituting the name of the new owner for that of the previous insured.

SUBROGATION

The term Subrogation refers to the right of one person to stand in the place of another in order to avail himself of that others rights and remedies. It was defined in an American case as "the mode which equity adopts to compel the ultimate payment of a debt by one who in justice, equity and good conscience ought to pay it" (ARNOLD v. GREEN, 161 N.Y. 566).

From an insurance viewpoint, subrogation involves the substitution of the insurer who paid the loss in place of the insured to whom the payment was made, so that if there is any liability attaching to the person primarily responsible for the loss, the insurer may recoup or reimburse himself by claiming from the person primarily responsible for the loss. The doctrine of subrogation as it applies to insurance law and practice may also be expressed in another way. It is the right of the insurer who has granted an indemnity by paying the insured's claim, to receive the advantage of every right of the insured against third-parties which may reduce or extinguish the insurer's loss. Subrogation is a corrollary to the principle of indemnity and its purpose is to protect the more fundamental principle of indemnity by making it impossible for the insured to make a profit from his insured loss as would have been the case if he were allowed to collect his loss from his insurance company and then claim for the same loss from the third party responsible for the loss. In short, subrogation allows the insurer who has taken over the insured's losses to take over his remedies, if any Thus, for example, if a motor car owner who has insured his car against accidental damage suffers a loss as a result of collision caused by the carelessness of a third party, the car-owner has a choice of either recouping himself by claiming on his insurer or on the negligent third party. He has two distinct claims, one in tort against the third-party tortfeasor, and the other in contract against his insurers. It would be contrary to the principle of indemnity for the insured to recover in full from his insurers and to claim a further compensation from the negligent third party. In the circumstances, the insured car owner, if he is indemnified by his insurers must subrogate to them his rights against the third-party.

The principle of subrogation is an accepted rule of insurance law and practice in Nigeria, and was given statutory force by the Marine Insurance Act, 1961. Section 80 of this Act defines and describes the circumstances in which subrogation would arise as follows:-

Sec. 80 (1) "Where the insurer pays a total loss, either of the whole, or in the case of goods of any apportionable part, of the subject matter insured; he shall thereupon become entitled to take over the ineterest of the assured in whatever may remain of the subject-matter so paid for, and shall thereby be subrogated to all the rights and remedies of the assured in and in respect of that subject-matter as from the time of the casualty causing the loss.

(2) "Subject to the foregoing provisions, where the insurer pays for a partial loss, he shall acquire no title to the subject-matter insured, or such part of it as may remain, but shall thereupon be subrogated to all rights and remedies of the assured in and in respect of the subject-matter insured as from the time of the casualty causing the loss, in so far as the assured has been indemnified, according to this Act, by such payment for the loss".

Subrogation had its origin in English Common law, having been derived by the English courts from the Roman law. But today the principle of subrogation has become a settled rule of international insurance law and practice. It would be read into every insurance policy which is a contract of indemnity, and it is, therefore, not necessary to have it specifically stated in the policy. In practice, however, most insurance policies issued in this country have a subrogation clause, which has the effect of reminding the insured of its existence.

When does the insurer become entitled to exercise his *Subrogation Rights?* The legal position is that once a claim is settled and the insured is indemnified, the insurer automatically becomes entitled to exercise his subrogation rights, and the insured is bound in equity to lend his name to any proceedings which the insurer may wish to take against the wrongdoer. A recent decision has slightly qualified this general proposition. In this case (JOHN EDWARDS & COMPANY v. MOTOR UNION INSURANCE COMPANY, (1922) 2 K.B. 249; 38 T.L.R. 690). It was held that the right of an insured person to claim compensation from a third party in tort or contract is not in any way affected or diminished by the fact of his having received an indemnity from his insurers. Such an insured person having been indemnified by his insurers may still claim from the third party, but whatever money he recovers from the third party must be held by him in trust for the insurers to the extent of their outlay. In practice this is of little consequence as the money recovered by the insured from the third party will ultimately get to the insurers who have indemnified him This case also lays down the following important conditions that must exist before subrogation rights accrue to the insurer:

(a) There must have been a payment by the insurer under a contract of indemnity:

(b) Such payment must have been made in circumstances where there was a legal liability to pay. Thus, if there is no legal liability at all under a policy, any ex-gratia payment would not entitle the insurer to subrogation rights. Similarly, there would be no subrogation in respect of a loss which the insurers have not paid for.

Some reported cases on the Principle of Subrogation:

For purposes of further clarification and in order to further illustrate the legal basis of the principle of subrogation, we reproduce below extracts from judgments in a few leading cases on the subject.

(1) BURNAND V. RODOCANACHI (1882) 7 A.C. 333. This was a case before the English House of Lords, and below is an extract from the judgment of Lord Blackburn:

"The general rule of law (and it is obvious justice) is that when there is a contract of indemnity (it matters not whether it is a marine policy, or a policy against fire on land or any other contract of indemnity) and a loss happens, anything which reduces or diminishes that loss reduces or diminishes the amount which the indemnifier is bound to pay, and if the indemnifier has already paid it then if anything which diminishes the loss comes into the hands of the person to whom he has paid it, it becomes an equity that the person who has already paid the full indemnity is entitled to be recouped by having that amount back".

(2) CASTELLAIN v. PRESTON (1883) 11 Q.B.D. 380 (1) In this leading case, the court, in stating the effect of Subrogation, had this to say:-

"A person who wishes to recover for, and is paid by the insurers as for a total loss cannot take with both hands. If he has a means of diminishing the loss, the result of the use of those means belongs to the underwriters".

(3) ST. LOUIS, I.M. & S. RY. COMPANY v. COMMERCIAL UNION INSURANCE COMPANY, (139 U.S. 223, 235.) This was a case before the United States Supreme Court, and part of the judgment reads as follows:-

"In fire insurance, as in marine insurance, the insurer, upon paying to the insured the amount of a loss of the property insured, is doubtless subrogated in a corresponding amount to the insured's rights of action against any other person responsible for the loss. But the right of the insurer against such other person does not rest upon any relation of contract or of privity between them. It arises out of the nature of the contract of insurance as a contract of indemnity, and is derived from the insured alone, and can be enforced in his right only. By the strict rules of the common law, it must be asserted in the name of the insured. In a Court of equity or of admiralty, or under some state codes, it may be asserted by the insurer in his own name; but in any form of remedy the insurer can take nothing by subrogation, but the rights of the insured, and if the insured has no right of action none passes to the insurer."

EXAMPLES OF SUBROGATION

Motor Insurance: In thinking of an example of the practical operation of this principle, the one which immediately comes to mind is that of a motor car insured under a comprehensive policy which is damaged in a collision due to the negligence of another motorist. If the insured claims from his insurance company the cost of repairing his car, the insurance company upon indemnifying its insured under the comprehensive motor policy, is subrogated to the rights of the insured against the negligent third-party and will thus recover its outlays from the third-party. This is the commonest type of subrogation right exercised in Nigeria, other examples can be found from virtually all kinds of liability and property insurances, in circumstances where an insurer has settled a claim arising from the wrongful act of a third-party.

Workmen's Compensation and Employer's Liability Insurances: Subrogation rights may arise under a workmen's compensation insurance claim. The workmen's Compensation Acts (subject to certain conditions) require an employer to pay compensation to his employees killed or injured at work. Most wise employers in Nigeria effect a Workmen's Compensation insurance policy to cover themselves against their liabilities under the Act. An employer's insurer who has made some payment in circumstances where a third party was at fault, may recover from the negligent third party. For instance, in a recent unreported case (PUMP SERVICES (NIGERIA) LIMITED and another v. A.R.A. ONISIWO & ANOTHER SUIT NO. MIK. 357/63) the employer, Messrs. Pump Services had effected a Workmen's Compensation policy in respect of his liabilities under the Workmen's Compensation Acts to his employees. One day whilst the employees were engaged in the employer's business installing "cats eyes" along Ikorodu Road, the defendant's lorry negligently driven struck one of the workmen, killing him. The dependants of the workman claimed under the Workmen's Compensation Acts against the deceased's employers. The employers were indemnified by their insurer who in turn sued the owner and driver of the third party vehicle to recover their outlay. (This case is not being cited as an authority for any new legal principle, but merely to illustrate one of the circumstances under which Subrogation rights may arise in an insurance transaction. For Subrogation to arise, the insurance contract must be a contract of indemnity. Therefore, no

Subrogation rights would arise in respect of payments made under a personal accident policy.)

EXTENT OF SUBROGATION

In exercising his subrogation rights, the insurer is entitled to an amount equal to what he has paid to the insured, any recovery in excess of the insurers outlay must be handed over to the insured. For instance, Mr. Adam may buy a car for ₦1,000 and decide to underinsure the car for, say, ₦600. If the car is wrecked in an accident as a result of the negligence of a third party, Mr. Biko, all that Mr. Adam can claim from his insurers is the sum insured of ₦600. If the insurers in exercising their subrogation rights against Mr. Biko succeed in recovering the full value of the car, namely ₦1,000, they are only entitled to keep the sum of ₦600 and the balance of ₦400 must be handed over to Mr. Adam.

Modification of the Principle of Subrogation by a Policy Condition:

Under the general law, the right of subrogation is vested in the insurers after they have paid the claim made against them by the insured, not before. But in recent times, a practice has developed whereby a clause or condition embodied in almost all non-marine policies provides that the insurer may exercise his subrogation rights before payment has been made. The effect of this clause is to modify the common law doctrine of subrogation to the extent that the insurer may be subrogated to the insured's rights and remedies even before payment has been made. We reproduce below the exact wording of the subrogation clause contained in a fire policy issued by one of the leading insurance companies in Nigeria. This wording is typical and will be found in virtually all similar policies:

"The insured shall, at the expense of the company, do, and concur in doing, and permit to be done, all such acts and things as may be necessary or reasonably required by the company for the purpose of enforcing any rights and remedies, or of obtaining relief or indemnity from other parties to which the company shall or would become entitled or subrogated, upon its paying for or making good any loss or damage under this policy, whether such acts and things shall be or become necessary or required BEFORE or after his indemnification by the company".

There seems to be no legal objection to this contractual modification of the common law doctrine of subrogation, and it has now become a settled custom amongst insurers to include this clause in almost all fire and accident policies.

The reason for the subrogation clause becomes obvious when it is remembered that the insurer is subrogated only to the extent of the insured's legal rights and remedies against third parties. If the insured had no rights and remedies, the insurer would have none. Therefore, where the insured has waived or compromised his rights against a third party, this would affect the subrogation rights of the insurer. It follows that the purpose of the subrogation clause in these policies is to protect the interest of the insurer against any possible act of the insured which might otherwise prejudice the insurer's interest. Thus, by acquiring the right of subrogation before payment, the insurer is able to take effective measures to stop the insured from waiving his rights against the third party.

As far as policies of marine insurance are concerned, the right of subrogation arises only after payment has been made by the insurer, and it is most unusual to alter the legal position by means of a policy condition as in fire and accident policies. The Nigerian Marine Insurance Act 1961, is clear on this point. Section 80 of this Act expressly provides that the insurer shall become subrogated to the rights of the assured only after he has paid for a loss, either total or partial.

CONTRIBUTION

As far as it affects insurance law the term "Contribution" has been described as "the right of an insurer who has paid under a policy, to call upon other insurers equally or otherwise liable for the same loss to contribute to the payment". Contribution, as a legal doctrine, had its origin from the English Courts of Equity where it was first developed as a means of ensuring the equitable distribution of liability amongst joint debtors or joint wrongdoers. Thus, if Mr. 'A' and Mr. 'B' both motorists, by their collective acts of negligence cause damage to Mr. 'C's' property, both are jointly and severally liable to C and C may claim damages from either A or B or from both of them. If he claims in full from A, A having paid C in full is entitled to obtain contribution from B, the joint wrongdoer.

In insurance, contribution arises where there is double or multiple insurance in force covering the same subject-matter, the same interest, and the same peril. We have seen that the principle of indemnity forbids an insured person from recovering more than his actual loss. But nothing prevents a person from effecting two or more insurances in respect of the same interest, all that the law insists upon is that the sum total of his recoveries under all the policies must not exceed his actual financial loss. Thus for instance, Mr. 'A' may insure his car comprehensively with two companies, but in the event of a loss resulting in a claim, he can only recover the exact amount of his loss, that is a full indemnity, and no more, and he is free to claim in full from either company. The principle of contribution allows the insurer who has paid in full in these circumstances to recover a proportionate contribution from the other insurers.

Contribution, like the principle of subrogation, is a corollary to the principle of indemnity and only applies to insurance policies which are contracts of indemnity. It does not therefore apply to personal accident and life policies which are not contracts of indemnity. In the leading case of NORTH BRITISH & MERCANTILE INSURANCE COMPANY v. LIVERPOOL & LONDON & GLOBE INSURANCE COMPANY (1877) 5 Ch.D. 569, the subject of contribution was discussed at length. The following extract from the judgment explains the circumstances when contribution would arise: "Contribution exists where the thing done is done by the same persons against the same loss, and to prevent a man first of all recovering more than the whole loss, or, if he recovers the whole loss from one which he could have recovered from the other, then to make the parties contribute rateably. But that only applies where there is the same person insuring the same interest with more than one office"

Contribution defined in Marine Insurance Act, 1961: This Act defines the doctrine of contribution and explains the circumstances under which contribution rights would arise in the following words:-

Sec. 81 (1) "Where the assured is over-insured by double insurance, each insurer shall be bound, as between himself and other insurers, to contribute rateably to the loss in proportion to the amount for which he is liable under his contract".

(2) "If any insurer pays more than his proportion of the loss, he shall be entitled to maintain an action for contribution against the other insurers, and be entitled to the like remedies as a surety who has paid more than his proportion of the debt".

Sec. 33 of the same Act defines double insurance as follows:-

(1) "Where two or more policies are effected by or on behalf of the assured on the same adventure and interest or any part thereof, and the sums insured exceed the indemnity allowed by this Act, the assured is said to be over-insured by double insurance".

(2) "Where the assured is over-insured by double insurance—(a) the assured, unless the policy otherwise provides, may claim payment from the insurers in such order as he may think fit, provided that he shall not be entitled to receive any sum in excess of the indemnity allowed by this Act . . . ."

Essentials of Contribution: From the foregoing, it can be seen that certain conditions must be present before contribution arises. These conditions may be summarised as follows:-

(1) There must be at least two or more policies in force at the material time;

(2) Each of these policies must insure the same subject-matter and the same interest of the same insured;

(3) The policies concerned must cover the same peril that caused the loss: and

(4) all the insurances concerned must be contracts of indemnity. (North British & Merchantile Insurance Company v. Liverpool & London & Globe Insurance Company mentioned above).

Contractual Modification of the Principle of Contribution:

We have seen that one of the main purposes of the principle of contribution is to prevent the insured person who has more than one policy in respect of the same interest from recovering more than an indemnity. The law is not interested in the order in which he recovers his loss, provided he refrains from recovering more than his actual loss. Thus, at common law, if more than one policy is held in respect of the same interest, the insured can claim in full against one insurer only, if he so desires. The insurer who has paid in full will then have to take the trouble of obtaining a contribution to the loss from the other insurers. In order to guard against this, most non-marine policies issued in Nigeria contain a contribution condition or clause, which in effect provides that where two or more policies cover the same risk, the insured must claim under all the policies by recovering a pro-ratā proportion from each insurer.

The effect of this contribution condition is to modify the common law rule to the extent that the insured is deprived of the right or privilege of deciding the order in which to make his claim, that is, he is not allowed to claim in full from one of several insurers, but is compelled to claim a proportion from all the insurers. Below is the full wording of the contribution clause as contained in a Motor policy issued by one of the leading insurers in this Country. The wording of the clause is almost uniform amongst the insurance companies in Nigeria, and is similar to that contained in policies issued by the Tariff companies in the United Kingdom.

"If at the time any claim arises under this policy there is any other existing insurance covering the same loss, damage or liability the company shall not be liable to pay or contribute more than its rateable proportion of any loss damage compensation costs or expense." The English contribution clause, which is identical to the Nigerian one has been the subject of a judicial interpretation. The clause was examined with approval in the leading case of North British & Mercantile Insurance Company v. Liverpool & London & Globe Insurance Company (1877) 5 Ch.D. 569 in the following words:-

"Where there are several policies, and where there is, in point of fact, a double insurance, then in order to do away with the old practice of the insured recovering the whole amount from one of several insurance offices, and then the one from whom it was recovered being put to obtain contribution from the others, this clause (the contribution condition) was put in to say that the insured should, in the first instance proceed against the several insurance companies for the aliquot parts for which they are liable in consequence of that condition."

This extract from the court's judgement in the North British case also illustrates the distinction between the common law principle and the effect of the contractual modification by a policy condition. So far, there has been no reported Nigerian judicial pronouncement on the matter, but it is submitted that the Nigerian Courts, if confronted with a similar case, would uphold the judicial reasoning in the North British case.

The Practical Effect of the Contribution Condition: We have seen that the effect of the contribution clause is to compel the insured who has more than one policy to recover a pro-rata pro portion of his loss from each of the several insurers. The practical effect of this clause can best be illustrated with an example. A person insures his house against fire with two different insurance companies. With insurance company "A" he insures the house at ₦2,000, and with insurance company "B" he insures the same house at ₦4,000. Both policies cover the same risk, that is fire. Then a fire occurs resulting in damage to the building to the extent of ₦600. In accordance with the contribution condition attached to each policy, each insurer would bear its rateable proportion. The insured's claim against each company would be stated in the customary formula as follows :-

$$\frac{\text{Sum Insured with the individual Company}}{\text{Total Sum Insured}} \times \text{LOSS}$$

The liability of Company "A" in this example would be stated as follows :-

$$\frac{1000 \times 300}{3000} = ₦200$$

Similarly, the liability of Company "B" would be stated as follows :-

$$\frac{2000 \times 300}{3000} = ₦400.$$

In this example, the effect of the contribution clause is to make each company bear a rateable proportion of the loss. Thus, Company "A" pays one-third of the loss because its maximum liability is one-third of the total sum insured, and Company "B" pays two-thirds of the loss for the same reason. This is the way the insurance industry in Nigeria interpretes the term "rateable proportion."

To ensure the enforcement of the contribution condition, insurers, in their claim forms, which must be completed by the insured each time a claim arises, require the insured to disclose details of any other insurances held by him in respect of the same insured interest.

No Contribution where different Interests are Involved:

We have seen that contribution would not arise unless the interests in the property insured were the same. A situation may therefore arise in which two insurance companies may each have to pay for the same loss in respect of the same subject-matter in full because different interests are involved. For example, Chuku builds a house in Surulere. He borrows ₦4,000 from Abimbola to complete the building and pledges the house as security for the loan. Here there are two separate interests involved in the same subject-matter, which is the house. The two interests are (a) Chuku's interest as the "owner", and (b) Abimbola's interest as mortgagee. Each has an insurable interest and may insure the house against damage by fire. Assuming Chuku insures the house with Company "A" at its full value of ₦10,000, and Abimbola also insures the same house against fire with Company "B" for ₦4,000 the amount of his interest, in the event of a fire resulting in a total loss of the building, each insurer is liable to pay its own insured's claim. No contribution would arise because there are separate interests involved. Therefore, Chuku's insurers will pay him the sum of ₦10,000 to indemnify him for the loss, and Abimbola's insurers must pay him ₦4,000 to indemnify him for his own loss. This point is now only of academic interest, as in practice, where different interests are involved, as in this example, companies agree to apportion any loss rateably without regard to the rights and liabilities of the insured interest. This agreement is embodied in the English Fire Offices Committee Rule 12 and arose out of two cases in the late 19th Century involving a first and second mortgagee and Messrs. Hay of Glasgow.

Another meaning of the term Contribution: We have been discussing the legal doctrine of Contribution which is an important principle of insurance law. In the practice of insurance, the term "contribution" is occasionally used in another sense, and this must clearly be differentiated from the legal doctrine of Contribution. This secondary use of the word "contribution" can best be illustrated by an example. If, for example, the tyres of a motor car have been completely worn out at the time of an accident, and these tyres are replaced by new tyres, the insured is generally required to make a contribution towards the cost of the new tyres. This is because if he failed to contribute, he would be placed in a better position after an accident than he was before the accident. He would, in effect, be getting new tyres for old ones, and if he were allowed to get away without contributing towards the cost of the new tyres, this would be contrary to the principle of indemnity. Similarly, if a car got involved in an accident, and the whole body of the car had to be re-sprayed, the insured would, for the same reasons, be required to contribute towards the cost of the re-spray.

CHAPTER VII

FURTHER SPECIAL LEGAL FEATURES OF INSURANCE CONTRACTS

Proximate Cause—Simple Contracts—Assignment of policies—
Warranties and their importance in insurance law.

THE DOCTRINE OF PROXIMATE CAUSE

In the conduct of human affairs, every event that occurs is the effect of some cause. The event must have been preceded by some cause or happening. Thus, if a house is destroyed by fire, the cause of the fire may be a gas explosion or the house might have been set on fire by an angry mob of rioters or strikers. Whatever the cause of the fire, the effect produced by the fire, in this example the destruction of the house, is only the last link in the chain of causes and effect.

The doctrine of proximate cause is concerned with the rules which the insurance industry employs as a guide in determining whether or not a loss which is the subject of a claim was brought about by an insured peril. Thus, each time an accident occurs resulting in a loss which would form the subject of a claim, the cause of the loss must first be ascertained, that is, the proximate cause of the loss must be ascertained. If the proximate cause of the loss is an insured peril, then the insured can recover, but if on the other hand the proximate cause of the loss is an excepted peril or an uninsured peril, the insurers are not liable and the insured cannot recover in respect of his loss. The proximate cause of a loss may be an insured peril, or an excepted or an uninsured peril. In order to make the insurer liable to indemnify the insured, the loss must be a direct consequence of a peril insured against.

Proximate Cause defined: In the English case of PAWSEY v. SCOTTISH UNION & NATIONAL INSURANCE COMPANY (1908) reported in "The Times" of 17th October, 1908, proximate cause was defined as follows:-

"Proximate cause means the active efficient cause that sets in motion a train of events which brings about a result, without the intervention of any force started or working actively from a new or independent source."

The proximate cause is not necessarily the latest cause, but the DIRECT, DOMINANT, EFFECTIVE, AND EFFICIENT cause of the loss. In ascertaining the proximate cause of a loss, the courts have consistently declared that the guide is common sense, and causation is to be understood as the man in the street would understand it and not as a scientist or a metaphysician would. Thus, in the case of BECKER GRAY & COMPANY v. LONDON ASSURANCE CORPORATION, (1918) A.C. 101, Lord Summer in his judgement had this to say:-

" . . . . . Cause and effect are the same for underwriters as for other people. Proximate cause is not a device to avoid the trouble of discovering the real cause or the 'common-sense cause', and, though it has been and always should be rigorously applied in insurance cases, it helps the one side no oftener than it helps the other. I believe it to be nothing more nor less than the real meaning of the parties to a contract of insurance. . . . the causa proxima rule is not merely a rule of statute law, but is the meaning of the contract writ large."

Practical Application of the Principle of Proximate Cause:

Perhaps in theory, the doctrine of proximate cause and the rules applied in determining the proximate cause of a loss are clear. In practice, however, difficult cases do arise when it is not so easy to determine the proximate cause of a loss. If the loss is brought about by a single event, then no problem would arise, but quite often losses are caused by a series of events, one or more of which might be a peril or perils excepted by the terms of the relevant policy. In view of these difficult cases, certain rules have emerged which are used as a guide in determining the proximate cause of a loss. Briefly these guiding rules may be stated as follows:-

(1) If there is a single cause, and that single cause is an insured peril, then the proximate cause of the loss is an insured peril, and there is a valid claim under the policy.

(2) If there are several or concurrent causes and no excepted perils are involved, provided one of the causes is an insured peril, the loss is recoverable. If however, there are excepted

perils involved and it is not possible to separate the damage caused by the insured perils from that caused by the excepted perils, then the Insurers are not liable. But if it is possible to separate, insurers will be liable for that part of the loss caused by the insured peril, but not for that part caused by the excepted perils.

(3) If an excepted peril precedes the operation of the insured peril in such a way that it could reasonably be inferred that the insured peril was the natural consequence of the excepted peril, then the proximate cause of the loss is the excepted peril and insurers are not liable.

Excepted Perils: an insured peril is the risk or danger insured against, for instance, in a fire policy, fire is the insured peril. An excepted peril, on the other hand, is one specifically excluded by the wording of the policy. It differs from an uninsured peril which is not specially mentioned in the policy. For example, most comprehensive motor policies issued in Nigeria today specifically state (under the General Exceptions) that the Company shall not be liable in respect of damage to the insured vehicle caused by strikers and rioters. Thus, damage by strikers and rioters are excepted perils under the ordinary Nigerian motor policy and insurers are therefore not liable for damage arising from the operation of these perils.

The case of IN RE ETHERINTON AND THE LAN CASHIRE & YORKSHIRE ACCIDENT INSURANCE COM PANY (1909) throws some light on the practical application of the doctrine of proximate cause. The facts in this case are briefly as follows:-

The deceased had taken out a personal accident insurance policy from the insurers. The policy covered the deceased (or his dependents) against death or disability arising from accidents, but not as a result of sickness. The deceased went hunting and fell from his horse into a ditch. The accidental fall was not enough to kill him, but owing to the long exposure to the rain and cold, he caught pneumonia from which he died. The dependents of the deceased sought to claim from the insurers on the ground that the deceased had died as a result of injuries sustained as a result of the accidental fall. The insurers refused to pay on the ground that the proximate cause of the death was sickness that is pneumonia, and that the injury sustained from the fall was only a remote cause.

The Court held that the death was due to the accident and that the accident was the proximate cause of death. Part of the Courts judgement read as follows:-

"There is no pretence for treating the death as less due to the injury because one step in the train of circumstances which followed was that the insured had caught cold". The insurers had to pay the claim.

Marine Insurance Act, 1961 on Proximate Cause:

The only Nigerian statutory provision on Proximate cause is the Marine Insurance Act, 1961. In describing the losses covered and excluded under the Marine policy this Act provides that the insurer shall be liable for any loss proximately caused by a peril insured against, and then goes on to list out the excluded perils. The relevant sections read as follows:-

Sec. 56 (1) "Subject to the provisions of this Act and unless the policy otherwise provides, the insurer shall be liable for any loss proximately caused by a peril insured against, but, subject, as aforesaid, he shall not be liable for any loss which is not proximately caused by a peril insured against.

(2) In particular, -

(a) the Insurer shall not be liable for any loss attributable to the wilful misconduct of the assured, but, unless the policy otherwise provides, he shall be liable for any loss proximately caused by a peril insured against, even though the loss would not have happened but for the misconduct or negligence of the master or crew;

(b) unless the policy otherwise provides, the insurer on ship or goods shall not be liable for any loss proximately caused by delay, although the delay be caused by a peril insured against;

(c) unless the policy otherwise provides, the insurer shall not be liable for ordinary wear and tear, ordinary leakage and breakage, inherent vice or nature of the subject-matter insured, or for any loss proximately caused by rats or vermin, or for any injury to machinery not proximately caused by maritime perils."

THE INSURANCE POLICY AS A SIMPLE CONTRACT

Having stated the fundamental principles of insurance as they apply to Nigeria, we will now examine the legal nature of the insurance policy in the wider context of the general law of the land, especially in relation to that aspect of the law conveniently described as "Commercial law".

Insurance has been described as the purchase of security. This description suggests three things:-

(a)   That there is some kind of buying and selling involved in the transaction;

(b)   That there are two parties to the transaction; and (c) that for the transaction to be effective, there must be an agreement.

The policy is the document which evidences the contract effected by the parties. Being a contract, the rights and duties of the parties are governed by the general rules of law relating to contracts in addition to those special rules peculiar to insurance contracts which have been discussed in the preceding chapters.

Broadly, the law recognises two kinds of contracts, viz, Simple Contracts, and Speciality contracts otherwise known as contracts under seal. With the possible exception of Fidelity Guarantee policies, all insurance policies issued in Nigeria are simple contracts. We will therefore, examine the legal characteristic of all simple contracts.

Essentials of Simple Contracts: A contract has been defined as an agreement enforceable at law. An agreement to constitute a valid simple contract must posses the undermentioned essential attributes:-

(a)   There must be an offer by one party, followed by,

(b)   an Unqualified Acceptance of that offer by the other party;

(c)   There must be valuable consideration;

(d)   The parties must have capacity to enter into contracts;

(e)   There must be an intention on the part of the parties to create legal obligations; and there must be consensus ad idem.

(f)   The purpose of the contract must not be illegal.

We will now deal briefly with each of these essentials.

Offer and Acceptance: In general, the offer is usually made by the proposer when he completes a proposal form and hands it back to the insurance company's representative. The insurance company then accepts or rejects the offer depending on the information disclosed in the proposal form. This is only a general proposition as practice tends to vary from company to company and also depends on the branch of insurance concerned. For instance, in marine insurance no proposal form is used, and an offer may be made verbally over the counter or by telephone.

Acceptance: The validity of a contract depends on the unconditional acceptance of a prior offer made by the other party to the contract and this acceptance must be communicated to the offeror. Thus, if "A" offers to buy "B's" car for ₦400, there is an acceptance of "A's" offer if "B" agrees to sell at ₦400. If "B" in reply informs "A" that he will sell only at ₦500 there is a counter-offer by "B", which may be accepted or rejected by "A".

We have seen that insurance offers are generally made by the proposer when he completes the company's proposal forms. Insurers then read through the proposal form, and if they are satisfied on the information supplied in the form that the risk is insurable they communicate their acceptance to the proposer. The acceptance may be made orally or in writing.

In the life department, the normal practice is to address a formal letter of acceptance to the proposer advising him that his proposal has been accepted and that the company's liability would commence upon payment of the first premium within a certain number of days, usually between fourteen and thirty days. In marine insurance, the broker handling the business usually describes the risk on what is termed the "original slip". He then presents this slip to each underwriter or insurer he wishes to have on the schedule (this constitutes the offer). If the underwriter or insurer signs or initials the slip, this constitutes an acceptance and cover is effective from the agreed period.

Acceptance in respect of Motor Insurance: The Road Traffic Act which introduced limited compulsory third party insurance to this country, specifically stipulates that there is no insurance cover in compliance with the Act until a certificate of insurance, issued by an authorised insurer has been delivered to the insured. Therefore, in order to comply with the Act, the practice in the motor department is for insurers to indicate their acceptance by issuing a temporary cover note to the insured when his proposal is accepted. This cover note which embodies an insurance certificate in compliance with the Act is generally in force for the first thirty days whilst the full-year certificate is being prepared.

Consideration or Valuable Consideration:

The law requires that all simple contracts must be supported by consideration. This means that each party to the contract must give something valuable in return for the promise of the other. If "A" promises to "dash away" his gold wrist watch to "B" just because he likes "B" and "B" gives nothing in return for "A's" promise, there is no consideration on the part of "B" and should "A" change his mind, "B" cannot sue for breach of contract as there was never a contract between them. Consideration was defined in the case of CURRIE V. MISSA (1875) L.R. 10 Ex. 153 as follows:-

"A valueable consideration in the sense of the law may consist either in some right, interest, profit or benefit accruing to one party, or some forbearance, detriment, loss or responsibility given, suffered or undertaken by the other."

In insurance contracts, the consideration given by the insured is the premium he pays to the insurer, and the consideration given by the insurer to the insured is the promise to indemnify the insured in the event of a loss. The preamble to most policies issued in this country deals with the subject of the premium as consideration for the insurer's promise to pay in the event of a loss. The preamble in a private-car comprehensive policy would read as follows:-

"Whereas the Insured by a proposal and declaration dated as stated in the Schedule which shall be the basis of this contract and is deemed to be incorporated herein has applied to the Company for the insurance hereinafter contained AND HAS PAID OR AGREED TO PAY THE PREMIUM AS CONSIDERATION for such insurance in respect of accident loss or damage occuring during the period of insurance. . . . ."

The legal effect of this is that the liability of the insurer commences immediately acceptance is communicated to the insured and it is immaterial that the premium has not been paid. Therefore should Mr. Adu complete a proposal form of Company "B" for the insurance of his car and Company "B" accepts the proposal and issues its cover note, then if the car is wrecked in an accident shortly after, and before Mr. Adu has had time to pay the premium, the company must indemnify him, but they are entitled to sue for the unpaid premium.

Contractual Capacity:

The subject of contractual capacity is of little practical importance from our point of view, and we will therefore deal briefly with it. (For a more detailed study the reader is referred to any of the re- cognised works on the Law of Contract.) The general rule is that any person may enter into any form of contract provided such a contract is not illegal. But there are certain classes of persons whose rights to freedom of contracts have been curtailed by the law. The most important of these are infants, insane and drunken persons, and alien enemies. An alien enemy cannot make a binding contract during hostilities, and an infant stands in a privileged position in that he can repudiate almost all his contracts at will except those for necessaries. Similarly, a contract made by an insane or drunken person is binding on him only if the contract is for "necessaries" such as basic food or modest clothing, but all other contracts are voidable at the instance of the insane or drunken person if at the time the contract was purported to have been made the other party knew about the insanity or drunkenness. Luckily, insurers in this country rarely have occasion to do business with insane or drunken persons, but insurance policies are issued from time to time to in- fants, and although the matter has not yet been tested in the Nigerian Courts, it is submitted that the courts will uphold and enforce such contracts on the ground that they are for the infants benefit.

Intention to Create Legal Obligation & Consensus Ad Idem:

Since a contract is, by definition, an agreement enforceable at law between two or more parties, therefore to qualify as a valid con- tract, there must be a genuine agreement between the parties. There must be "Consensus ad idem", that is, there must be a meeting of the minds, and it must be clear from the nature of the transaction, that the parties intended to create legal obligation by their agree- ment.

Intention to Create Legal Obligations: If "A" invites "B", his friend to dinner, and "B" having accepted the invitation fails to turn up for the dinner, "A" cannot sue "B" successfully for breach of contract. This is because there was no intention on their part to create legally binding obligations by their agreement. By the very nature of all insurance transactions, it is certain that the parties to the insurance contract always intend to create legal obligations.

Legality of the Contract:

A contract which is illegal or a contract to do an illegal act is void and of no legal effect. The following are some examples of illegal contracts:

(a) Contracts to commit a criminal offence, for example an agreement to commit murder or arson;

(b) Agreements which by their nature are contrary to p ᵕlic policy. For example, an agreement between a landlord and an established prostitute whereby the landlord lets his house to the prostitute to be used by her in connection with her trade. (Pearce v. Brooks (1866) L.R. I Exch. 213). On the authority of Pearce V. Brooks, it is submitted that an insurance policy issued to a prostitute covering the car that she uses for her trade is illegal and therefore void.

The subject of illegality in the law of contract is quite wide and it is beyond the scope of this work to examine it in great detail. In addition to contracts which are void for illegality, there are other contracts, though not illegal, are void, for example, gambling and wagering transactions, and agreements in total restraint of marriage.

ASSIGNMENT

The term assignment means the transfer of property from one person to another. The law on the subject is a little complicated, and the procedure varies depending on whether the thing to be assigned is a chose in possession, that is, a tangible object such as a motor car, or a chose in action, that is an intangible right or interest in property, such as an interest in a life assurance policy. There is a further distinction between the assignment of a legal chose in action and the assignment of an equitable chose in action. Luckily, we need not concern ourselves with these complicated rules. For our purpose, assignment means the transfer of rights under an insurance contract from one person to another.

In insurance law and practice, a distinction is made between:

(a) the assignment of the policy, which is the transfer of rights under the insurance contract, and

(b) the assignment of the proceeds of the policy.

The latter does not affect the insurers and the insured is free to assign the proceeds of his polfcy to anybody he chooses. The insurance industry regards such an "assignement" as merely a direction to a debtor, (the insurer) to pay the debt to a person specified by the creditor (the insured). Thus, if Mr. Ade buys a car for ₦1,200 and insures the car with company XYZ Limited for the same amount and the car gets involved in an accident resulting in a total loss of the car, Mr. Ade may direct the insurance company to pay the proceeds of the policy to Mr. Udo a thifd party. Provided Mr. Ade, the insured, has executed a suitably worded discharge receipt to the insurance company, the company is bound to comply with his directions and will forward its cheque of ₦1,200 to the third party in this case Mr. Udo. This example is an assignment of the proceeds of the policy and does not in any way affect the rights and obligations of the parties to the insurance contract.

Assignment of the Policy: The assignment of rights under an insurance policy is a much more serious matter. This kind of assignment involves the transferring of the rights and liabilities of the insured under the policy to a third party.

Whether or not an insuranoe policy may be unilaterally assigned by the insured depends on whether or not the particular insurance contract is a personal contract. If the contract is a personal contract, the policy is not assignable, but if it is not a personal contract, the policy may be assigned at will. With the exception of marine insurance policies, all other property insurance policies are personal contracts. Life assurance policies and marine insurance policies are not personal contracts and are therefore freely assignable.

Assignment of Marine Insurance Policies: Section 51 of the Marine Insurance Act, 1961, specifically provides that marine insurance policies are assignable either before or after a loss and in such a case the beneficial interest would pass to the assignee who would then be entitled to sue in his own name. This section of the Act stipulates the procedure that may be followed in the event of an assignment.

Assignment of Life Policies: Life policies are assignable because the law regards them as reversionary interests, that is, interests in property the enjoyment of which is deferred to a future date. An assured may freely assign his interest in the life policy to anybody.

'Assignment' of all other Property Insurance Policies:
As stated above, all motor, fire, and other accident insurance policies in respect of property are personal contracts and are therefore not assignable. They can only be "assigned" with the consent of the insurer. What actually takes place is not an assignment, but the making of a new contract, a novation.

Personal Contract: These contracts are called personal contracts because they are personal to the parties concerned. The policy is personal to the particular insurer and the individual insured concerned, and it relates to the personal interest of the insured in the subject matter of the insurance. Therefore if the interest of the insured ceases to exist, the policy becomes ineffective and the parties are automatically discharged from their liabilities, and obligations under the contract. Thus, for example, Mr. "A" buys a motor car for ₦2,000 in January 1966 and insures it for that amount with insurance company "B" for a term of twelve months. If after six months Mr. "A" sells the car to Mr. "C", the interest of the insured Mr. "A" ceases when he sells the car and the insurance he effected on the car automatically ceases to be of any effect and would never pass to the new owner Mr. "C". It is a settled rule of insurance law that a policy-holder who sells or parts with an insured property cannot transfer or assign the insurance policy to a third party. Although there are no Nigerian reported cases dealing with this point, there are two old English authorities:

LYNCH v. DALZELL (1729) 4 Bro. P.C. 431 and SADLERS COMPANY v. BADCOCK (1743) 2 Atk. 554.

It is a common occurrence in Nigeria now, especially in motor insurance, for an insured owner to sell his motor vehicle before the expiration of the policy and to hand over the policy and insurance papers to the purchaser on the understanding that the buyer was buying both the motor vehicle and the unexpired term of the insurance. Such a purported "assignment" of the insurance policy is of no legal effect, and what it amounts to in fact is that the purchaser is driving his motor vehicle without insurance cover contrary to the provisions of the Road Traffic Acts. In such a situation, that is where there has been a change of interest, the insured should inform his insurance company that he has sold his motor vehicle, and if the buyer wishes to continue the insurance for the rest of the term, he should approach the insurer. The insurance company would then obtain a proposal form from him in order to check on his personal factors, such as accident record, state of health etc. If they are satisfied that the buyer is a normal risk, they would probably issue an endorsement to the policy of the previous insured, (the seller) noting a change of interest from the seller to the buyer, and the original insured drops out and is replaced by the purchaser who now becomes the insured or policy-holder.

Finally, a further reason why these property insurance policies are described as personal contracts is the fact that they involve some kind of mutual confidence. For instance, in deciding whether or not to accept the business the insurer has to take into consideration the personal attributes of the insured, such as his moral character and physical well-being. Thus, in a motor policy the terms and the premium would depend amongst other things, on the age of the proposer, his claims history and his general moral standing. These factors normally vary from person to person and the assignee might not be as good as the previous insured, or on the other hand he may be better.

WARRANTIES

Almost all insurance policies are subject to one kind of warranty or another (and it is very rare to have a policy which is not subject to a warranty). In view of this fact, warranties occupy an important position in insurance law.

The term warranty needs a special consideration because, unfortunately, it means one thing in the general law of contract and a different thing in insurance law and practice. Under the general law of contract, the terms of the contract are divided into two, the more important terms are called conditions, and the less important ones are called warranties. A condition is said to go to the root of the contract, whilst a warranty is said to be merely collateral and of lesser importance. Therefore in an ordinary contract, a breach of condition entitles the aggrieved person to rescind the whole contract, whereas the breach of warranty merely entitles him to claim damages.

In insurance law the situation is different, infact it is almost the exact opposite. A warranty, in insurance law, means the same as a condition in an ordinary contract. An insurer who discovers that the policy-holder or the insured has acted in breach of a warranty is entitled to avoid the policy. He is discharged from his promise to pay by virtue of the non-fulfilment of the warranty. If in a Burglary policy there is a warranty that a night-watchman shall be kept on the insured's premises, the insurer will be discharged and will not be called upon to make any payment under the policy if the insured fails to keep a night watchman.

Strict Compliance: A warranty must be strictly and literally fulfilled otherwise there is no contract (De Hahn v. HARTLEY (1786) 1 T.L.R. 343). A breach of the terms of a warranty discharges the insurer even if the loss is unconnected with the breach, and it is no excuse to a breach of warranty that the breach was innocent or that the warranty was not material. However, a breach may be excused on the ground that compliance would be unlawful, for instance owing to a subsequent change in the law, and an insurer may waive the breach.

Essential Characteristics of a warranty: The essential features of a warranty are as follows:-

(a) The warranty must be part of the written contract—it must be expressly written in the policy or incorporated into it by endorsement.

(b) The thing warranted need not be material to the risk insured against;

(c) The terms of the warranty must be literally fulfilled;

(d) A breach discharges the insurance company even though the loss has no connection with the breach.

Warranties in Proposal Forms: We have seen that the practice is for a proposer for insurance to fill in a proposal form which sets out certain questions he is to answer to enable the insurer assess the risk and to decide on whether to accept or reject the proposal. In most of these proposal forms, there is a declaration at the bottom of the form which reads something like this:-

" . . . . . I, the undersigned proposer warrant that the above questions are fully and truthfully answered and that I have not withheld or concealed any circumstance or any material information affecting the proposed insurance".

The effect of this declaration, where it exists, is to warrant all the information disclosed in the proposal form. If there is an untrue answer, even if it is made innocently, this amounts to a breach of warranty, which entitles the insurer to repudiate liability. Thus, in such a case, if the proposer has mistakenly given a wrong address, this would discharge the insurer from liability. We are lucky, however, that the majority of insurance companies in this country do not readily fall back on such minor breaches, except in exceptional circumstance, for instance, where the insurer suspects fraud, but is unable to prove it.

In the English case of DAWSON LIMITED v. BONNIN (1922) 2 A.C. 413, the proposal form completed by the insured contained a similar declaration to the one above, thus making every answer a warranty. In answer to a question in the proposal form, the insured had inadvertently given a wrong address as the place where the insured lorry would be kept, but this did not in any way increase the risk. The lorry was destroyed by fire. When the insured put in a claim, the insurance company repudiated liability on the ground of breach of warranty. The insured sued and the Court held that the warranty had been breached and the policy was thereby avoided.

In two recent Nigerian cases, both unreported, attempts had been made by learned counsel for the plaintiffs to defend a breach of warranty, using the following "novel" defences:-

(*a*) That the insured who had acted in breach of warranty owing to his quasi or semi-literacy, was unable to understand and appreciate the technical meaning of the term warranty, and

(*b*) That the status of the insured's business as a petty trader made it unreasonable to expect him to comply strictly with the warranty.

In one of these two cases the provisions of the Illiterates Protection Acts had been invoked in addition as a defence to the failure to comply with the warranty. All these new defences were rejected by the Courts. The two cases are important because they illustrate the importance of warranties in insurance law in Nigeria. The first case came up in the Lagos High Court in 1958, Suit No. LD. 33/1958. Between:

(1) B. N. AMAECHI)
(2) L. I. ANYANWU) PLAINTIFFS
(carrying on business in the name and style of MBAISE FANCY STORES).

v.

NORWICH UNION FIRE INSURANCE SOCIETY— DEFENDANTS.

The plaintiffs insured their shop with the defendant company against burglary. The policy was subject to a warranty to the effect that the insured would maintain certain specified books of account during the currency of the policy. A burglary occurred and it was in fact proved to the satisfaction of the court that there had been an actual forcible entry into the insured's premises on the night in question and that a considerable number of goods were removed by the thieves. However, some of the accounts books were not kept by the insured. The court held that the warranty had not been complied with and gave judgement for the defendant company. The learned trial judge had observed that the plaintiff's counsel had put forward what he described as "an interesting but untenable proposition, that as the defendant had contracted with a petty trader and as it is a notorious fact that petty traders in Nigeria do not keep proper books of accounts the defendants cannot reasonably require the plaintiffs to produce the sort of evidence which a competent businessman would be able to produce" (This was the judgement of Mr. Justice Bennet at the Lagos High Court.)

The second case: SUIT NO. JD. /42 /63
Between

ALEXANDER OKOLI (PLAINTIFF)

v.

WEST AFRICAN PROVINCIAL INSURANCE COMPANY LIMITED (DEFENDANT).

This case which came up at the Jos High Court before Mr. Justice J. P. Smith was almost on all fours with the previous one except that there was also a warranty to the effect that a nightwatchman shall be parading the insured's premises from 9 p.m: to 6 a.m. daily and the account books of the insured shall be kept in an iron and fire-proof safe at the close of business each day. The insured failed to comply with any of the warranties and the insurers repudiated liability on these grounds. The court decided in favour of the insurance company, and rejected the plaintiff's counsel's suggestion that the educational standing of the plaintiff and the unsophisticated nature of his business was such that he could not be expected to appreciate the far reaching effects of these warranties.

Warranty defined in the Marine Insurance Act, 1961:

Section 34 of this Act defines a warranty in the following words:-

Sec. 34 (1) "For the purposes of this section and of sections 35 to 42 (which relate to warranties) a warranty means a promisory warranty, that is to say, a warranty by which the assured undertakes that some particular thing shall or shall not be done, or that some condition shall be fulfilled, or whereby he affirms or negatives the existence of a particular state of facts."

Sec. 34 (2) "A warranty within the meaning of this section may be express or implied, and is a condition which shall be exactly complied with, whether it is material to the risk or not. If it is not so complied with, then, subject to any express provision in the policy the insurer shall be discharged from liability as from the date of the breach of warranty, but without prejudice to any liability incurred by him before that date".

Note: Implied warranties exist only in marine insurance policies because the Act provides that a warranty in a marine policy may be express or implied. In all other branches of insurance, a warranty must be express and must be part of the written policy or incorporated into the policy expressly by an endorsement.

Specimen Warranties:

Burglary Policy: "It is warranted that a nightwatchman shall patrol the insured premises between the hours of 9 p.m. and 6 a.m."

Life Policy: "It is warranted that the life assured is a person of temperate habits".

Motor Policy: "It is warranted that the insured vehicle shall be driven only by the insured".

Suggested Reforms:

It has been suggested by some Nigerian Lawyers that because the Illiterates Protection Act offers no protection to the semi-literate Nigerian petty trader and in the light of the far-reaching effects of warranties in insurance law, that insurers should be compelled by legislation to insert in all policies an Ibo, Yoruba, and Hausa translation of the Warranties attached to the policy. This school of thought also suggests that the declarations at the foot of proposal forms which are generally warranted and made the basis of the insurance contract should be translated into the three main languages of Nigeria. These suggestions, sound as they may appear, have, so far, not received the general support of the insurance industry, probably because of the extra administrative costs that their implementation might entail. In any event, to be really satisfactory, the translations should be extended beyond the three main languages to embrace the more important of the so-called "minority languages."

As a result of the provisions of the Insurance (Special Provisions) Decree No.40 of 1988 referred to earlier, the strict enforcement and the over-reaching effect of warranties in insurance transactions in Nigeria, has been greatly watered down by the provisions of Section (2) of that Decree, which states in effect that only material and relevant terms can give rise to the exercise of such rights in contracts of insurance, thus reducing the status of warranties to more or less the same level as conditions. That Section also stipulates that notwithstanding any provision in any written law or enactment to the contrary, where there is any breach of a term in an insurance contract, the insurer shall not be entitled to repudiate liability in respect of a claim on the grounds of a breach unless the breach amounts to a fraud or it is a breach of a fundamental term of the contract and in such a case it does not matter whether the relevant term is called a condition or a warranty in the insurance contract.

The Decree however makes it abundantly clear that nothing in the Section shall prevent the insurer from repudiating a contract of insurance on grounds of a breach of a material term before the occurrence of the loss or event insured against.

It has been suggested that the revolutionary changes introduced into the country's insurance laws under Decree No.40 of 1988 have become necessary as a result of the complaints made by insurance consumers concerning certain aspects of the insurance laws which were considered unduly favourable to insurers such as the strict and rigid application of the rule as regards warranties and the extension of the doctrine of non-disclosure in insuranc policies. Whatever the case, the official view is that these changes have been introduced primarily for the protection of the insuring public.

Although Decree No.40 of 1988 does not provide for a translation of the questions in proposal forms into the main languages of Nigeria for obvious administrative reasons, it stipulates, amongst others, that the proposal form or other application form for insurance shall be printed in easily readable letters.

CHAPTER VIII

AN ANALYSIS OF THE INSURANCE CONTRACT

(1) The proposal Form as the Basis of the Contract.
(2) The Policy as Evidence of the Contract—its layout terms and conditions.
(3) Endorsements and Cover notes.
(4) Construction or interpretation of the Policy.

Introductory: In Nigeria, as a general rule, the first step in the making of an insurance contract (other than marine insurance where broker's slips are used) is for the proposer to complete a proposal form giving details of the risk he proposes to insure. Thus the purpose of the proposal form is to elicit information concerning the nature of the risk proposed for insurance to enable the insurer assess the risk involved. Furthermore, as already pointed out, an essential feature of all contracts is that there must be an unrevoked offer, followed by an unqualified acceptance of that offer. The proposal form is the proposer's offer to the insurer which the insurer may accept or decline as he sees fit, usually depending on the information disclosed in the proposal form. Once the offer contained in the proposal form is accepted, it forms the basis of the contract to be embodied in the policy. In the light of the foregoing, it is evident that the proposal form occupies an important position in the practice of insurance. In addition to being the first documentary record of the nature of the transaction between the parties, it is also incorporated into the policy and thus forms the basis of the contract.

The policy on the other hand, is the printed document which contains the terms of the insurance contract. The policy is not the contract itself, but merely evidences the contract arising from the agreement reached by the parties. Its importance lies in the fact that in the event of any disputes arising as regards the terms of the contract, this can only be settled by referring to the policy, and in the absence of any ambiguities, the parties will be bound by the provisions of the policy.

In view of the importance of the proposal form and the policy form in the practice of insurance, we will now attempt to examine and analyse these documents with a view to ascertaining their legal and practical effects to the transaction.

The Proposal Form: We have seen that the purpose of the proposal form is to obtain particulars of the risk to be insured which is then presented to the insurer as an offer for the insurance contract. Dr. W. A. Dinadale (Director of Education, Chartered Insurance Institute, London) in his book, *Elements of Insurance* describes it as the means of communicating the offer to the insurers, and this is the primary purpose of the proposal form. Because they are widely distributed to Branches and Agents and an instrument of contact between insurer and insured, the forms are normally printed in an attractive style and displayed in the offices of the company and its Agents. On the back of each proposal form can usually be found a list of the types of insurance which are available from the Insurer and the forms are used as a vehicle for advertising the 'special' attributes of the Companies' policies.

Generally speaking, the body of the proposal form falls broadly into four or five sections. The first part asks questions about the proposer, his name, address, business or occupation, the second part seeks to obtain information concerning the risk proposed for insurance. For instance in a motor proposal, whether the vehicle to be insured is a private or commercial vehicle, its make, type of body, its registration number, where it will operate and the place where it will be garaged and who will drive etc. The third part of the form contains an assortment of questions concerning the proposer, his accident or claims history in respect of the particular type of insurance, whether other insurers have declined his proposal, cancelled his policy or refused to renew his policy. The fourth part contains certain questions to be answered by the agent introducing the business as regards his knowledge of the proposer and the risk proposed for insurance. The proposal form usually ends with a declaration which reads something like this:

"I, the undersigned, hereby warrant that the above statements and particulars are true and I hereby agree that this declaration shall be deemed to be of a promisory nature and shall form the basis of the contract between me and the XYZ Insurance Company Limited and I am willing to accept a policy subject to the terms and conditions prescribed by the Company therein and to pay the premium thereon." Proposal forms vary in their length depending on the nature of the risk, but the above represents a typical layout. A proposal form being merely an offer, its completion does not imply that cover is automatically effective. Unless, and until there is an unconditional acceptance of the proposal by the insurers, there is no contract. Thus, if the insurers accept subject to the insured paying the premium within a specified period, there is no insurance unless the premium is paid within the specified period. Similarly, if the proposer completes what he believes to be a proposal form for an endowment life policy, and the insurers issue him a whole life policy believing that the proposal was for a whole life policy, there is no contract, and the proposer is entitled to a refund of any premiums he might have paid over to the insurers. For there to be a valid insurance contract, the parties must be agreed on all the material terms (Allis CHALMERS v. FIDELITY & DEPOSIT COMPANY (1916) 32 T.L.R. 263). The material terms under an insurance policy are:

(1)   The definition of the risk.

(2)   The duration of the risk.

(3)   The premium to be paid by the insured, and

(4)   The sum insured or the amount to be paid by the insurer in the event of the thing insured against happening.

THE POLICY FORM

The policy, as we have explained, is a printed document in which is set down the terms and conditions governing the transaction. The modern tendency amongst all insurers is to have the policy in a printed form, and inside the printed form provision is made for the insertion of material information peculiar to the individual contract, such as, the insured's name, the sum insured the period of insurance, and a description of the thing insured. This portion of the policy is known as the schedule. Because of adverse criticisms by the public, insurers are now reducing the number of conditions in their policies, and the tendency now is to make the print less tiny and therefore less difficult to be read.

Although there is no special form prescribed by the law, and policies therefore take various forms, all policies in use in Nigeria have certain features in common. As a general rule, the body of the policy consists of five parts, (1) The preamble or recital Clause, (2) the Operative Clause, (3) the signature or Attestation Clause, (4) the Schedule, and (5) the Policy conditions.

1. The Preamble or Recital Clause: This is the opening section of the policy, it recites that there are two parties to the contract, the insured and the insurer, and the circumstances under which the insurance contract has been made.

A typical preamble or recital clause reads something like this: "WHEREAS the insured by a proposal and declaration dated as stated in the Schedule which shall be the basis of this contract and is deemed to be incorporated herein has applied to the Company for the insurance hereinafter contained and has paid or agreed to pay the premium as consideration for such insurance in respect of accident loss or damage occurring during the period of insurance."

2. The Operative Clause: This is the insuring clause. It states the scope or extent of cover granted by the policy, and enumerates the circumstances under which the insurers undertake to indemnify the insured.

The wording of the operative clause varies depending on the class of insurance concerned. For instance, the operative clause in the ordinary fire policy is comparatively shorter than that used in the private car comprehensive policy. The latter is grouped under three sub-headings: section one deals with loss or damage to the car itself, section two with liability to third parties, and secion three with medical expenses. Below is a typical clause in a fire policy:-

"THE COMPANY HEREBY AGREES with the insured (but subject to the conditions hereinafter printed, which are to be taken as part of this policy, and to such other conditions as are herein expressed) that if the property insured described in the Schedule, or any part thereof, shall be destroyed or damaged by fire and/or lightning, after payment of the premium, at anytime during the period of insurance stated in the Schedule, or before four o'clock in the afternoon of the last day of any subsequent period in respect of which the insured shall pay to the Company and it shall accept the sum required for the renewal of this policy, the Company will pay or make good all such loss or damage to an amount not exceeding in respect of the matters or matters specified in the Schedule the sums set opposite thereto, and not exceeding in the whole the total sum insured mentioned therein, nor exceeding in any case the amount of the insurable interest therein of the insured at the time of the happening of such fire."

3. **The Signature or Attestation Clause:** The attestation clause usually features at the end of the policy and contains the signature of the insurer or more accurately, that of the official responsible for the signing of policies. It reads something like this:-

"IN WITNESS WHEREOF this policy has been signed for and on behalf of the Company this........ day of .... 1966. Examined by............

Entered by ....

....

Signature"

4. **The Schedule:** The Schedule contains all the material information which is special to the individual policy and which could not be provided for in the general printed form. For instance, it contains the insured's name, his address, business or occupation, the policy number, the sum insured, the property insured or a description of the risk insured against, the period of insurance, the premium and the renewal date. Other information may feature in the schedule depending on the class of insurance concerned.

5. **The Policy Conditions:** All insurance policies are subject to certain conditions which declare the terms under which the insurance contract has been effected. There are two types of conditions, express conditions and implied conditions. The express conditions are those expressly set down by the parties whereas the implied conditions are those which the law would read into all insurance contracts even if they are not mentioned specifically by the parties. The implied conditions are:-

(a)   that the principle of utmost good faith shall be observed by the parties;

(b)   that the insured has an insurable interest in the subject-matter of the insurance;

(c)   that the subject-matter of the insurance is in existence at the time the insurance contract is made; and (*d*) that the subject-matter of the insurance has been sufficiently described so that it can be identified.

The express conditions contained in insurance policies vary according to the class of insurance, but certain conditions are common to all policies. For instance, all policies require the policy-holder to report to the insurer immediately or forthwith all accidents or losses. Broadly speaking, policy conditions deal with such matters as:

(*a*) Notification of accidents,

(*b*) Claims procedure,

(*c*) Right of Cancellation,

(*d*) Safety precuations to be taken by the insured,

(*e*) Contribution Condition (if the policy is one of indemnity).

(*f*) Arbitration Condition, which provides that all disputes arising under the policy have to be referred to an Arbitrator or arbitrators to be appointed by the parties.

The effect of breach of policy Condition: Breach of a condition in a policy entitles the aggrieved party to refuse to perform his own part of the contr ct, and in addition he may claim damages for the breach. Thus, if an aggrieved person (usually the insurer) discovers a breach of a policy condition, he may either elect to treat the contract as repudiated, in which case he is no longer bound to perform his part of the contract, or he may waive the breach and carry on with the contract as if there has been no breach. If an insurer elects to treat the contract as repudiated by the breach, he can successfully plead the breach as a defence in any subsequent action by the insured upon the contract.

A distinction is drawn between repudiating liability on the grounds of breach of policy conditions, and avoiding the policy on the ground of non-disclosure or the breach of 'the principle of utmost good faith. An aggrieved person repudiating liability on the ground of the breach of a policy condition accepts the existence of a binding contract a term of which he alleges has been breached, but an aggrieved person wishing to avoid the policy on the ground that there has been a breach of the principle of utmost good faith by the non-disclosure of a material fact, is in effect saying that there is no contract in existence between the parties. This distinction has serious legal consequences, for instance, the aggrieved person in the latter case cannot plead a condition or clause in the policy in his defence to an action arising from the policy.

ENDORSEMENTS

Most insurers prepare their policies in a standard printed form long before the risk is offered for insurance. The result is that quite often it does happen that the general provisions contained in the printed form are not appropriate for a particular case. In order to get the general policy form to fit the individual case, the practice amongst insurers is to modify the wording of the policy forms by means of endorsements which may be either handwritten, type-written, stamped or printed and affixed or pasted on to the body of the policy.

An endorsement is therefore a subsequent term or condition attached to a policy which has the effect of modifying the terms of the policy by either extending or restricting the cover granted by the general policy form. They are to insurance policies what codicils are to wills. Endorsements have the same effect as the policies to which they are attached, with the addition that, being subsequent in time to the basic policy form, the endorsement will prevail in the event of a conflict between the terms of the endorsement and the main policy form.

It is beyond the scope of this book to attempt a detailed discussion of the various forms of endorsements used by insurance companies, but it would suffice to note that they are used extensively for the purpose of modifying the general provisions of the policy. An endorsement may be added to a policy for the purpose of covering property or a risk not otherwise insured, for instance to extend the geographical limit in a motor policy. The Nigerian motor policy covers the insured only in respect of accidents within the Republic of Nigeria. If the insured is travelling to the Republic of Dahomey for a week end, he could approach his insurance company, which could then issue him an endorsement extending the policy to cover accidents in Dahomey. Similarly, a fire policy which insures a private dwelling house against loss by fire may be extended by endorsement to cover loss or damage by flood, tornado or earthquake.

Endorsements Limiting the Company's Liability: Endorsements are also issued to limit the liability of the insurer. For instance, if from the information contained in the proposal form in a motor proposal it is envisaged that the insured vehicle might be driven by a novice driver, the insurance company would almost invariably attach a NOVICE DRIVER'S CLAUSE to the policy. This endorsement stipulates that the policy-holder would bear a proportion of every loss (say, the first ₦25 of each loss) if at the time of the accident resulting in the loss the insured vehicle was being driven by a novice driver.

Endorsements noting Changes in the Subject Matter of the Insurance and Changes of Interest:

If the subject-matter is changed, for example where the insured sells his motor car and buys another one, short of taking out a new policy, an endorsement must be issued substituting the new car for the old. In the same way, if there has been a complete change of interest, for example where the policy-holder sells the insured property to a third party, an endorsement substituting the name of the new owner is necessary, as cover ceases from the moment the original insured ceases to have an insurable interest in the thing insured. This is most important, especially in motor insurance. There are several instances in this country where a policy holder has sold his motor vehicle and has purported, without the consent of the insurers, to have transferred the policy to the new owner. In one case the purchaser had claimed that "he bought the car together with the insurance". In the absence of an endorsement, such a purported transfer of the policy is of no legal effect and cover would cease as soon as the policy-holder parts with the insured motor car. (This point had been made in a previous Chapter, but because of its importance in the light of experience in this country, we make no apologies for the repetition).

COVER NOTES

Quite often, the proposer or the person seeking insurance protection, requires immediate cover pending the consideration and acceptance of his proposal by the insurers. If the insurers are agreeable and willing to go on cover temporarily whilst the proposal is being considered, they may do so and advise the insured informally, for instance, by word of mouth. Alternatively, they may issue a documentary evidence of the fact that they are on cover temporarily. This document which evidences such interim or temporary cover is known as a "cover note". It is usually granted for a limited number of days ranging from fifteen to thirty days, but the insurers always retain the right to cancel the cover during this period. The cover note is a temporary contract of insurance quite distinct from the one embodied in the Company's policy. Therefore, the conditions in the policy do not bind the insured to whom a cover note has been issued, unless, of course, the policy conditions are expressly incorporated into the cover note by reference.

For a cover note to be binding on insurers it must have been issued by an authorised official or agent of the company and it is in force only for the specified period, unless it is cancelled during that period. If an insured to whom a cover note has been issued changes his mind and obtains insurance from another company, he is bound to pay for the cover granted him on the cover note during the number of days that the first insurer remained on risk. The legal status of cover notes was discussed extensively in the case of MACKIE v. EUROPEAN ASSURANCE (1869) 21 L.T. 102, 104.

CONSTRUCTION OF POLICIES

The term construction of policies refers to the rules that the Courts would apply in the event of their being called upon to interprete the terms of insurance policies.

The object of all interpretation of a document is to ascertain and give effect to the intention of the parties to the transaction, and intention of the parties is to be ascertained from the document itself. An insurance policy is interpreted like any other contract or written instrument. The terms, words and phrases used in the policy are to be understood in their natural, ordinary and popular sense. The words will be given that meaning which an ordinary man of reasonable intelligence would give them, not the meaning that a philosopher or a scientist would attach to the words. Popular phrases must be given their popular meaning. Therefore if the words "mammy waggon", "bolekaja" or " Opi-Achara" feature in an insurance policy, these words would be given the popular meaning which the ordinary Nigerian attaches to them.

Technical Words: The general rule that words are to be given their popular ordinary meaning is subject to certain qualifications. Technical words or legal words are to be given their technical or legal meaning. Thus if the word "warranty" appears in an insurance document, it must be given its accepted insurance meaning. Similarly if the word "riot" appears in an insurance policy it must be given its meaning in criminal law (London & Lancashire Fire v. Bolands (1924) A C. 836, 847.

Ambiguity: If there is any ambiguity or doubt in the language used in the policy, that interpretation most favourable to the insured is to be accepted. It is a rule of construction that a document has to be constructed strictly against its maker where there is an ambiguity, and almost invariably, policies are prepared by the insurers. This rule is not really intended to give any special advantage to the insured as such, but it is devised so as to deprive the insurer of any undue advantages he might gain from his position as the maker of the policy.

Whole Policy is to be construed: In interpreting the terms of a policy, although individual words have to be given their ordinary meaning, the whole policy must be read so as to ascertain the intention of the parties, as indicated by the words and phrases they have used in the policy.

Proposal Form Incorporated into the Policy: If the proposal form is expressly incorporated into the policy, it must be read with the policy as part of the contract. Virtually all proposal forms used by insurers in this country contain a declaration to the effect that the information contained in the proposal form has been incorporated into the policy and will form the basis of the contract. The effect of this is that the information and declarations contained in the proposal form must be treated as part of the terms of the policy.

CHAPTER IX

UNDERWRITING AND RATING

UNDERWRITING

The word "Underwriter" as an insurance term originated from the practice of merchants in the 17th Century at Lloyd's Coffee house in London who accepted risks for insurance by merely signing their names and the proportions of the risks they were prepared to bear at the bottom of the "policy" slip. These merchants, who carried on the business of insurance as a sideline, came to be known as underwriters. They were the insurers of those days, and the term underwriter has passed on to their successors—the individual underwriters at Lloyd's of today in London and the insurance companies.

The term underwriter is also used in another sense. Most insurance companies have a responsible official whose main function is to scrutinize every proposal for insurance and to decide whether the risks proposed for insurance shall be accepted or rejected, and if accepted, on what terms. This official is called the company's underwriter and his department is called the underwriting department.

Functions of the Underwriting Department:

One eminent author once described insurance as a kind of manufacturing industry, and that the risk is the raw material, whilst certainty is the finished product. This writer goes on to point out that the quality of a manufactured product would depend on the quality of the raw material from which it is manufactured. Furthermore, that all manufacturing concerns maintain inspection departments and expensive laboratories to test the raw materials used in the industry in order to ensure that only the good quality raw materials are accepted. And where it is possible to use different quality grades, it is the duty of the inspection department to classify and allocate the raw materials into their different grades and uses. This writer then rightly concludes that the underwriting department of an insurance company has a similar function as the laboratory and inspection department of a manufacturing industry. For the underwriting department, its raw material is the risk proposed for insurance.

In the light of the remarks above, the functions of the under-writing department may be summarised as follows:-

(*a*)   To secure the most profitable risks; and

(*b*)   to ensure a wise and safe distribution of risks.

We will now discuss in some detail these duties of the underwriting department.

Duty in relation to the Selection of Risks: Experience has proved, and this is quite natural, that it is the bad risks, and not the good ones, which normally are offered for insurance, especially in those branches of insurance where it is not compulsory to insure. For instance, of a group of people in any community, the ones most anxious to obtain life assurance cover would be those in very poor health. People generally require insurance cover when they have cause to believe that there is an immediate possibility of the thing insured against happening. Thus, in a recent case in which the present author was involved as Solicitor for one of the parties, an insured person had stated that his only reason for taking out a burglary and money insurance was the fact that he had read in the local press that highway robbers were rampant on the Lagos-Benin-Asaba road over which he was to travel. He would not otherwise have thought of insuring his goods.

Insurers frown on the practice of offering only the bad risks for insurance. This is described in insurance terminology as "unfair selection" or "adverse selection" against the interest of the insurer, and the underwriting department is charged with the responsibility of ensuring that there is no unfair selection against the interest of the insurer.

Duty to ensure a Regular Increase in Volume of Business:

We have seen that insurance as a business, is based on what has been described as "the law of large numbers". This involves the contribution of money into a common fund by a large number of persons, and out of this common fund (which is held in trust for the "members" by the insurer) the unfortunate few who suffer losses are compensated. The larger the number of persons insured with a particular company, the more successful its scheme. In view of this fact, the underwriting department, along with its outside staff—

the agents and the inspectors, are charged with the responsibility of ensuring that the volume of business is always on the increase for each class of insurance underwritten by the particular insurer. The ideal is that each class of insurance should pay its way, for instance, it would not be a sound underwriting practice for the fire account to be used in supporting an unprofitable motor account over a long period.

Duty to Ensure an Equitable Distribution of Risks: To guard against the collapse of the insurer's business in the event of a catastrophe, the underwriting department must ensure that the insurer is not carrying an excessive amount of risk in any one location or on any one risk. For example, the Central Bank of Nigeria and its contents is worth several million pounds, similarly the "M.V. Aureol" together with its contents, passengers and equipment is worth several thousands of pounds. If either of these two big risks were insured by one company, in the event of a catastrophe, such as a big fire, the individual insurer would be financially crippled after paying for the loss. The underwriting department is charged with the responsibility of guarding against this eventuality by seeing to it that there is an equitable and wise distribution of risks.

Retention and Limits: Insurers have to decide well in advance their scale of limits in respect of any one class of risks and their retentions (that is the amount they retain for themselves) would depend on the insurers limit for the class of risk concerned. An insurer's limit is the maximum amount that he is prepared to lose on a given class of risks, whilst his retention is the maximum liability which the insurer finally assumes in respect of the particular risk.

The insurer's limits is primarily determined by his financial standing. A young insurance company with a share capital of only ₦50,000 might decide that its limits in respect of private dwelling houses in Lagos would be ₦2,000, whilst a bigger company with a capital of ₦200,000 might decide that its limits in respect of the same class of risks would be ₦10,000. Another factor that might influence an insurer's limit might be the extent of damage likely to be sustained in the event of a big loss.

In fixing his retention, the underwriter will be guided by the limit for that class of risk. Therefore, if this company's limit on private dwelling houses is ₦5,000, his retention would not normally exceed this amount. If the underwriter in our example is offered the insurance of a private dwelling house valued at, say, ₦10,000, he retains ₦5,000 and reinsures the remaining ₦5,000 with other insurers. The process of fixing retentions and distributing risks is the duty of the underwriting department of an insurance company.

RATING

The premium has been described as the monetary consideration payable by the insured to the insurer in return for the insurance cover granted by the policy. The question then is, how is this premium to be calculated? How much will a particular policy holder pay into the common pool in return for the cover he gets ? This is the province of rating.

There is very little literature on the subject of rating and for a young country like Nigeria, there is hardly any. Furthermore, the insurance underwriter's general approach to the problem of rating tends to vary from company to company and the procedure adopted in fixing the rates also varies depending on the nature of the risk and the class of insurance concerned. However, it is neither necessary nor possible to discuss the subject extensively in a work such as this one. It would suffice merely to state the general principles.

General Principles of Rating: In all classes of insurance the guiding principles in determining what rates to apply to a given risk are briefly as follows:

(1) The premium rate should be such as would provide enough funds to pay for losses and expenses leaving a small margin of profits for the Company's shareholders.

(2) The rates applied should be equitable, that is, it should be fair and reasonable.

(3) Each policyholder should contribute to the common fund in proportion to the value at risk and to the extent of the hazard introduced.

One and two above require no further comment. The third is the fundamental principle in insurance rating and demands some explanation. In order to ensure that each insured person contributes to the common fund in proportion to the value at risk and in accor-

dance with the hazards he introduces, the underwriter relies on
three guiding factors as follows: (a) Classification, (b) Discrimination and (c) Experience and Statistics of Previous losses.

(a) **Classification:** The first step is to classify the risks or
assign them to groups, depending on the nature of the risk.
Risks may be grouped according to the trade, business or
occupation of the proposer. For example, in a personal accident insurance, all the known professions and occupations
are grouped under three classes, with the least hazardous
ones under class one attracting a smaller premium, and the
most hazardous ones under class three attracting very high
premiums.

(b) **Discrimination:** After the risks have been classified there
is a further process of discrimination amongst each class,
and the risks are sorted into groups of (a) good risks, and
(b) bad risks of the particular class. Good risks, that is, the
non-hazardous ones attract a smaller premium rate, and
the more hazardous ones attract a higher premium rate.
For instance, in a fire policy, a Carpenter's Workshop, a
Petrol Station or a match factory, would attract a much
higher rate of premium than would a doctor's surgery or
a lawyer's chambers. Furthermore, a petrol station in an
area which is particularly susceptible to fires, would
attract a much higher rate of premium than one situated in a
locality that has never had a fire.

(c) **Experience or Statistics of Previous Losses:** As has
been pointed out earlier, insurers keep records and statistics
of previous losses both of the individual policy-holder and
of particular classes of risks. The individual proposer whose
claims experience or claims history is poor attracts a higher
rate of premium, and so does the proposer introducing a
risk which, from past experience, has been known to be
particularly hazardous.

How the Premium is Arrived at: By applying the principles
listed above, the underwriter decides what premium rate he would
charge, and having ascertained the rate, he applies it to the sum

insured of the value at risk and gets the premium. For example, the standard rate for a simple fire policy has been ascertained and fixed at 50k% per annum. Therefore for property valued at ₦400, the annual fire premium would be ₦1.

Competition: A most important factor which helps to keep insurance premium rates under control is competition. There are about sixty insurance companies in this country today. All these companies are engaged in a cut-throat competition, each striving to attract more and more clients at the expense of the others. In this atmosphere no company can afford to quote too high a rate as this will sooner or later drive it out of business, as people will, naturally be inclined to keep away from the expensive company.

CHAPTER X

REINSURANCE

A book on insurance would be incomplete without an appropriate reference to the subject of reinsurance. In ordinary language, the usual understanding is that whenever the prefix "re" is used in relation to any word, this suggests that something is repeated. For example, re-take or re-open. Therefore to re-insure would be taken to mean to insure again. This interpretation is quite reasonable in relation to reinsurance since the practice of reinsurance in effect involves the insuring again, by the original insurer of a risk already insured with the insurer concerned.

Re-insurance is the transfer of insurance business from one insurance company to another. The original insurer who obtained the business from the insured person is called the "direct insurer" or the "ceding company" and the company to which the business is transferred is called the reinsurer.

The system of reinsurance arose from the need of the original insurer to spread the risk he has undertaken. Under a reinsurance contract, the reinsurer takes over all or part of the liability contracted for by the ceding company and in return, the reinsurer gets a part or the whole of the premium as the case may be.

The reinsurance contract is only between the ceding company and the reinsurer. There is no contractual relationship between the reinsurer and the person insured under the ceding company's policy. Therefore in the event of a loss, the insured cannot bring an action against the reinsurers in order to enforce the reinsurance contract. Section II of the Marine Insurance Act, 1961, gives statutory force to this rule and provides that:-

Section (II) "The insurer under a contract of Marine insurance has an insurable interest in his risk, and may reinsure in respect of it; but unless the policy otherwise provides, the original assured shall have no right or interest in respect of such reinsurance."

Although section eleven of this Act specifically mentions marine insurance, it is submitted that this rule applies equally to all branches of insurance.

Advantages of Reinsurance

The system of reinsurance has many advantages, but the most important one is that it enables an insurance company to limit its liability on any one risk to an amount which represents the maximum that the company can conveniently pay in any one loss, and the insurer need not limit its acceptance to its own retention. Furthermore, reinsurance facilitates the spreading of risks and lessens the impact of a heavy loss. It helps in stabilizing the insurer's income and losses over a number of years, and makes statistics more reliable. For example, it is a known fact that an insurance company's premium income and its claim accounts fluctuate a great deal from year to year. One year might produce a premium income of, say, ₦100,000 and claims may take up about sixty percent of this amount. The following year might produce ₦150,000 in premiums with claims taking only one quarter of this amount, and so on. Despite these fluctuations in the gross premium income and the gross losses, the system of reinsurance makes it possible for the net results to remain fairly constant thus reducing the degree of annual fluctuation in a company's overall profit ratio over a period of years. The net result is the figure obtained after reinsurances have been deducted.

How reinsurance works in practice

The following hypothetical case would throw some light on the way reinsurance works in practice. Chief Babu, a local industrialist, has just completed a ₦100,000 dwelling house in Tinubu Square, Lagos, and he decides to insure it against damage by fire or tornado. He is on friendly terms with the manager of the XYZ insurance Company Limited and he therefore decides to insure this building with this company. Company XYZ on being approached by the Chief promptly issues out a policy covering the building to its full value of ₦100,000 against the perils of fire and tornado. Prior to this transaction, Company XYZ had decided that its limits on any private dwelling house in Lagos would be ₦10,000. But Chief Babu's property which the company has accepted to insure is valued at ₦100,000, well in excess of the company's limit on this class of risk. Therefore, the company having accepted the risk quickly proceeds to reinsure 9/10ths of it with other insurance companies whilst retaining 1/10th which represents its limit of ₦10,000. Company XYZ Limited in return for the cover it gets would have to pay over 9/10ths of the premium to the reinsurers.

In the event of the insured building being destroyed by either fire or tornado, the insured, Chief Babu, will be indemnified to the full extent of his loss by the ceding company, which would then approach the reinsurers to reimburse it for ninety percent of the loss. If for some reason, for example, insolvency, Company XYZ Limited is unable to pay the claim of their insured, Chief Babu, he, the insured, cannot claim from the reinsurers because he is not a party to the reinsurance contract between the ceding company and the reinsurers.

Methods of effecting reinsurance

Broadly speaking, there are two methods of arranging reinsurance cover. One is by facultative method, and the other is by the treaty method.

Facultative reinsurance

Facultative reinsurance was the earliest form of reinsurance, and is still widely practised at the present time in this country. Under the facultative reinsurance method each individual risk is offered by the ceding company to the reinsurer who may reject or accept as much of the risk as he sees fit. This form of reinsurance is so called because the reinsurer has the option of accepting or declining the risks according to the dictates of his faculty. Facultative reinsurance is more common in this country amongst local insurers than the alternative method of treaty reinsurance.

Treaty reinsurance

Treaty reinsurance is the exact opposite of facultative reinsurance. In the case of the treaty method, individual risks are not offered for reinsurance. The two parties, the ceding company and the reinsurer, enter into an agreement which provides that the reinsurer shall accept, without the option to decline, an agreed portion of all risks in excess of the ceding company's limits, subject to the terms of the treaty. The agreement between the parties is known as the treaty. There are three types of reinsurance treaties, namely, the QUOTA SHARE TREATY, THE SURPLUS TREATY, and the EXCESS OF LOSS TREATY.

Quota share treaty

The quota share treaty is also known as the fixed share treaty. As the name suggests the reinsurers under a quota share treaty agree to accept automatically, a fixed proportion of all insurances of a defined type written by the insurer. For example, the quota share treaty reinsurers may agree to accept fifty per cent of all fire insurances written by the direct insurer in which case the reinsurers would receive 50% of the premiums earned on that class of business and pay 50% of all claims.

The main advantage of the quota share treaty is that it is less expensive to administer than is the surplus treaty. It is also a very useful system of treaty reinsurance for a new insurance company with little underwriting experience.

Surplus treaty

Under the surplus treaty method of reinsurance, the direct insurer fixes a maximum retention, which is agreed with the reinsurers. Whenever the sum insured on a particular risk exceeds the agreed maximum retention, reinsurance becomes necessary, and the surplus over and above the retention, up to the sum insured is ceded to the treaty. Surplus treaties are usually arranged on the basis of slices known in insurance circles as "lines" and the treaty is limited to an agreed number of lines. The direct insurer retains its line, and the remaining lines are passed on to the respective reinsurers participating in the treaty programme. Each reinsurer may take one or more lines or even a fraction of a line in accordance with the terms of the treaty.

This example would illustrate how the surplus treaty method operates in practice: Assuming the direct insurer's retention is ₦1,000 and a ten line treaty has been arranged. Under a policy with a sum insured of ₦5,000, the risk would be shared out as follows between the parties:

The direct insurer retains: ₦1,000
The treaty reinsurer: ₦4,000

and the total sum insured would have been adequately distributed with the insurer retaining ⅕ of the risk and reinsurers, ⅘ Under this arrangement, reinsurers will also receive four-fifths of the premium and bear the same percentage of all claims.

The surplus treaty method of reinsurance has become fairly popular in recent years and is widely used in international reinsurance business. It has been suggested that this method of reinsurance is not suitable where there is a very large sum insured or where the limit of indemnity is high. It is definitely not recommended in liability insurances where the limit of indemnity is so high as to be almost unlimited in amount.

Excess of loss treaty

This type of treaty reinsurance provides that the direct insurer shall be liable up to a fixed amount in the event of a loss, and any claim in excess of that fixed amount would fall on reinsurers. For example, the treaty might provide that the ceding company will be liable for all claims up to ₦5,000 and any claim above this amount would fall on the reinsurers. In which case if there is a claim for say, ₦10,000, the direct insurer pays ₦5,000 and the treaty reinsurers will pay the balance of ₦5,000. If the claim had been for ₦5,000 or less, the direct insurer would bear the whole loss.

This type of treaty arrangement assists the ceding company in the sense that it ensures that the occasional large claim does not upset the profitability of the direct insurer's account for a particular class of insurance business in any one year. Because the treaty reinsurers under an excess of loss treaty only become liable when there are large claims, it is possible under such an arrangement for the direct insurer to make a profit in a given year when the reinsurers have made a loss. The reverse could also be the case.

Whereas under the quota share and surplus treaty methods the reinsurer receives a proportionate share of the premium paid by the policyholder, under the excess of loss treaty the reinsurer is paid a small percentage of the annual premium of the relevant class of insurance, and most times, the percentage of the annual premium which the insurer pays to the reinsurer is agreed rather arbitrarily.

The excess of loss treaty is generally used for liability insurances. It could also be used in cases where very large losses may be sustained, for example as a result of major disasters such as big fires, earthquakes and other major disasters. The important point to remember is that in the case of excess of loss treaty reinsurance, the reinsurance is not based on the sum insured, but on the amount of each individual claim. Usually, the practice is to ensure that the retention of the insurer is fairly high as the reinsurers are only called upon to make payment when the loss exceeds the insurers retention.

The treaty usually has an upper limit. For example, the re-insurers will bear any loss in excess of say ₦10,000 up to an upper limit of ₦250,000. An additional second layer treaty may then be arranged to take care of catastrophic losses in excess of the upper limit of ₦250,000.

Reinsurance Commissions

The cost of acquiring direct insurance business is heavier than the cost of obtaining reinsurance business. Because it costs the direct insurer more to obtain the business than it costs the reinsurer to get the same business, the practice is for the reinsurer to allow the direct insurer a reasonable percentage of the premium by way of commission to cover the insurer's acquisition costs. Some treaties also provide for profit commission to be paid to the insurer in appropriate cases depending on the terms of the treaty.

Reinsurance Pools

A recent development in insurance and reinsurance circles is the creation of reinsurance pools into which members cede part of their business on agreed terms. In most cases these pools are used for unusual or exceptionally heavy risks, such as aviation or atomic energy risks. Pools also exist for conventional insurance lines. In some cases, the whole premium income earned by each insurer involved in the pool in respect of the agreed class of risk is ceded to the pool. All losses arising, and any profits earned at the end of the insurance year would be shared in agreed proportions. The reinsurance pool idea seems to be catching on amongst insurers and reinsurers in the third world countries. One recent example of a successful reinsurance pool in the third-world countries is the F. A. I. R. Reinsurance pool which started operations in January 1974. It accepts from all members all classes of non-life insurance business excluding aviation, bond and credit insurance business.

The international character of reinsurance

Reinsurance has now developed into a highly specialised international business. There are, broadly, three kinds of reinsurers on the international reinsurance market, namely:

(a) The Purely Reinsurance Company;

(b) The Direct Insurer, who engages in reinsurance as a side-line; and

(c) Lloyd's Underwriters in London.

The purely reinsurance company

This class of reinsurer as the name suggests, is established mainly for the purpose of carrying on the business of reinsurance, and it does not as a rule, engage in direct business. Germany and Switzerland were the leaders in international reinsurance, and the earliest purely reinsurance companies had their homes in these two countries. With the great set-back suffered by the German reinsurance companies during the last war, Switzerland seems to be leading now. But since after the last war, London has become a very important international reinsurance market and most of the World's leading reinsurers are represented on the London market.

Until quite recently there were no African professional reinsurance companies. During the past five years however, a number of African countries have realised the importance of insurance and reinsurance, not only as a foreign exchange earner, but also as a factor in the development of their national economies and have set up their own national reinsurance companies. The Nigerian government responded to this trend recently and set up the Nigeria Reinsurance Corporation which has just commenced operations. In addition to its role as an international reinsurer, the Nigeria Reinsurance Corporation receives a 20% compulsory cession from every registered insurer in Nigeria in respect of each policy*[1]

Another new member of the international reinsurance community is the African Reinsurance Corporation. The African Reinsurance Corporation, as the name suggests is owned by the governments of African countries who are members of the Organisation of African Unity. It has its headquarters in Lagos, Nigeria. In accordance with the treaty establishing the African Reinsurance Corporation, all insurers in each member country must cede at least 5% of their treaties to the African Reinsurance Corporation. Section 2 (4) of the Nigeria Reinsurance Corporation Decree provides that the Nigeria Reinsurance Corporation "shall serve as the channel of ceding compulsory

---

*[1]   The Nigeria Reinsurance Corporation Decree is reproduced in full as Appendix III. Also for a detailed discussion on the functions of the Nigeria Reinsurance Corporation, see Chapter XIV.

cessions from the Federation of Nigeria to the African Reinsurance Corporation". Nigerian registered insurers are still allowed to place part of their reinsurance treaties with international reinsurers after the local· market capacity has been satisfied and subject to the Nigeria Reinsurance Corporation having been given the right of first refusal and a certificate to that effect obtained from the Nigeria Reinsurance Corporation.

In Nigeria, most of the country's Naira-related reinsurances are effected locally by the respective local companies on a facultative and reciprocal basis. However, subject to the conditions stated above as regards local capacity, and cessions to the Nigeria Re, the facilities of the world reinsurance market are utilised whenever necessary.

Advantages of international reinsurance

The main point in favour of international reinsurance is that it ensures that huge catastrophic losses in any one country do not fall entirely on the insurers of the particular country that has suffered the loss. By spreading the risk through international reinsurance, in the event of a catasprophe, the loss is spread throughout the insurance world, thus lessening the impact that it would have made on the resources of the country that suffered the catastrophe. For example, the Nigeria Airways, the National Electric Power Authority, and the Nigerian Ports Authority each owns property and assets worth several millions of Naira. Most of the property owned by these public corporations are insured with local insurance companies who, in turn, protect themselves by reinsurance, both locally and internationally. Should this country suffer a heavy disaster, such as an earthquake, the international reinsurers would be called upon to contribute their share of the loss and in this way, the impact on our local resources would be less.

Although they recognise the importance and the advantages of international reinsurance, most developing countries, including Nigeria, now pursue a policy aimed at increasing their domestic retention capacity so as to reduce the outflow of premiums abroad in foreign exchange for the purchase of reinsurance cover. In Nigeria, for example, the official policy is to ensure that the domestic market capacity has been fully utilized before any reinsurance business is placed abroad. To this end, most Naira-related risks such as Motor, General Accident and Life business are generally placed in the country while the foreign exchange-related risks such as general aviation, large target risks and major industrial risks including the country's oil risks are substantially reinsured abroad.

With the existence of the Nigeria Reinsurance Corporation, the African Reinsurance Corporation and the three privately owned professional reinsurance companies in the country -the Universe Reinsurance Company, the Continental Reinsurance Company and the G'obe Reinsurance Company, Nigeria is fast developing into a major African and third world reinsurance market. The three privately owned reinsurance companies joined the reinsurance scene between 1984 and 1987.

CHAPTER XI

CLAIMS SETTLEMENT

INTRODUCTORY
THE CLAIMS DEPARTMENT
GENERAL CLAIMS PROCEDURE

Introductory:

The settlement of claims is one of the principal functions of an insurance company. Without losses resulting in claims, there would have been no need for the insurance industry. The essence of the insurance contract is that the insurer agrees, in return for the premium paid by the insured, to indemnify or compensate the insured in the event of a loss. Therefore an insured person who has suffered a genuine loss within the meaning and intention of his policy need not feel reluctant or apologetic in approaching his insurance company for the settlement of his claim.

As was pointed out in an earlier chapter, insurance company are, in effect, trustees of the accumulated premium funds entrusted to their care. The beneficiaries of these funds are the policy-holders and the individual company's share-holders. Being trustees, insurers have a duty to ensure that the funds are not dissipated in the extravagant and indiscriminate settlement of claims. A company that indulges in the extravagant settlement of claims would sooner or later wind up, to the detriment of all those who have invested money in it either as share-holders or as policy-holders. Similarly, if all insurance companies indulged in this practice, there would have to be a general rise in premium rates, much against the overall interest of the insuring community.

On the other hand, there is a duty on the insurer to see to it that the policyholder who has suffered a genuine loss is adequately indemnified for his loss, as it would be inequitable to underpay where there is a valid claim. An insurance company which makes it a habit to underpay its claimants is not doing its business reputation any good.

Insurer's Duties in relation to Claims summarised:

In the light of the remarks above, the duties of an insurer in relation to the settlement of claims may be summarised as follows:

(a)   The Company has a duty not to overpay the insured or the claimant in the interest of the Company itself and the insuring Community as a whole;

(b)   The insurer or the Company has a duty not to underpay the insured or the Claimant in the interest of justice and equity.

The Claims Department:

Most insurance companies have a special department which deals with all matters relating to the settlement of claims or loss adjustment. This department is known as the Claims department, and at the head of the section is a Claims Manager or Claims Superintendent. Because of what has been described as the "psychological" attitude of claimants, it is important that the claims department should be manned by a staff of exceptional ability possessing a sound and extensive knowledge of insurance principles and policy conditions. Furthermore, the claims staff must have a thorough understanding of the human nature to the extent that they can recognise both the genuine and the fraudulent claimant, virtually at sight, and deal with such types appropriately.

The duty of the claims official is to settle claims equitably, and not to settle at the least amount that he can persuade the insured or the claimant to accept. Therefore a claims official dealing with an illiterate or ignorant policyholder or claimant who does not know his entitlements under the insurance contract, has a duty to enlighten the policyholder or the claimant as to his rights under the relevant policy. Similarly, the claims official must firmly resist an exaggerated or fraudulent claim. The ideal, which should be the aim of all insurance companies, is to settle all claims promptly and equitably.

General Claims Procedure:

Virtually all insurance policies contain a condition which lays down the procedure to be followed in the event of a loss, and the insured is well advised, in his own interest, to comply with these conditions. As a general rule, the claims condition in all policies stipulates that the procedure would be set in motion by the Insured when he gives some kind of notice to the Insurance Company that a loss has occurred. This notice should normally be in writing, but may be by telephone to the Company's office or through the Agent or Broker through whom the insurance was effected. (As an illustration, the relevant clause of the claims conditions in the Motor policy of one of the leading insurance companies in Nigeria is reproduced verbatim on page 118).

In this country at the present time, very few policyholders read through their policies before a loss occurs. Because of this, very few ever adhere to policy conditions as regards notification of a loss. A policy condition might stipulate that a loss must be reported forthwith, and in any event within three days. The Insured reports three weeks afterwards, quite ignorant of the condition in the policy concerning notification. This failure to report within the stipulated period is a breach of the terms of the insurance contract, and an insurer faced with such a situation would be acting entirely within his rights in repudiating liability. Luckily, most insurance companies in this country, probably out of fear of public reaction, do not insist on strict compliance with all the minor conditions contained in the policy, although experience tends to show that they do not hesitate to take advantage of such minor breaches where they suspect fraud on the part of the claimant.

Actions taken by an insurer upon receiving notification of a loss:

The details of claims procedure, naturally vary from company to company, but generally speaking, a well organised insurance office immediately it receives notice of a loss must take the following steps:-

(1) **Checking for cover:** The first step is to ensure that there is cover. This involves the examination of the Company's books and records to confirm, (*a*) that the relevant policy is in force, and (*b*) that the policy covers the event which is the subject of the claim or if a property claim, that the property in respect of which the claim is being made is insured by the policy; (*c*) that the claimant is the person entitled to claim under the policy; and finally, (*d*) that the peril or hazard which is said to have caused the loss is one contem-

plated by the policy. If the claim appears to be in order as a result of this preliminary enquiry, the claim is registered. that is, it is entered up in the Claims Register, and' a number is allocated to the Claim, and this number will feature in all correspondence relating to the claim. A claim form is then forwarded or handed over to the insured for completion. The claim form or accident report form will give the insured's own version of the circumstances of the loss or accident together with all the relevant information tha the insurer would require for the next step in the settlement of the claim.

(2) **Ascertain that a Loss has been suffered and the extent of the loss (Investigation of the Claim):** After (I) above, the next step is the investigation of the claim in order to confirm that a loss has in fact occurred within the terms of the policy, and if so, the extent of that loss. Having ascertained that a loss did occur, the claims official handling the claim must find out, (a) the cause of the loss, and (b) the extent of the loss in terms of money; and (c) the person primarily responsible for the damage. If these enquiry reveals that a third party was responsible for the loss or damage, the insurer might take steps to reimburse himself by exercising his subrogation rights against the third party. When the amount of the loss has been ascertained, a cheque for that amount is forwarded to the insured or claimant who will in return execute an appropriately worded discharge receipt in favour of the Company. The practice amongst insurers in this country is to send a discharge receipt to the claimant, and on the completion and return of the discharge receipt, the insurer then forwards his cheque in settlement.

In actual practice, the settlement of a claim is not always as easy as we have just enumerated above. In life assurance, for instance, the policy is valued and the amount payable in the event of a claim arising is known from the very beginning, so no difficulfy arises. All that is necessary in such a case is to confirm that the life assured is dead, and a doctor's certificate to this effect is enough then ensure that the policy, is in force and the claimant is the true beneficiary This is easy enough, and in normal circumstances, a life claim can be settle in a couple of days. But it is not so straightforward in the other brances of insurance. In the accident, marine, and fire departments, loss adjustments or claims settlement are a lot more complicated and negotiations tend to last longer.

SERIOUS CLAIMS

The procedure discussed above is the general claims procedure followed in respect of small and medium sized claims. In most of the big fire and accident claims involving thousands of pounds, there are usually several insurers involved in the one loss owing to the practice of reinsurance, and generally, the loss procedure takes the following form:-

As soon as the insurers are notified of a claim, they appoint an independent loss adjuster to act for them. (A loss adjuster is a person, or firm which specialises in the handling of insurance claims. They are comparatively rare in Nigeria today, but with the growth of insurance business, and with greater demand for their services, we are likely to see many more loss adjusters in the Country. There is at present at least one reputable expatriate firm of Loss Adjusters based in Lagos). Where there are many companies involved, as is usually the case with the big risks, such as the N.E.P.A. the Airways and the Nigerian Ports Authority, the loss adjuster is appointed by the leading company. (The leading company is the Company carrying the greatest percentage of liability). The loss adjuster once he is appointed is given the claim form and the relevent policy together with any other useful information available relating to the claim. Armed with these, he proceeds to the scene of the incident, ascertains the cause of the loss, checks on cover, and conducts a general investigation of the claim with a view to ascertaining that the policy conditions and warranties have been complied with. If he finds everything in order, he then agrees settlement with the insured, forwards his report to the insurers together with a recommendation as to the amount of the claim.

CHAPTER XII

CLAIMS SETTLEMENT UNDER INDIVIDUAL BRANCHES OF INSURANCE

In the preceding chapter, we discussed the subject of claims settlement procedure in a general sense. The detailed procedure in the settlement of a claim varies to some extent depending on the particular branch of insurance under which the claim is made. It is beyond the scope of this book to consider in minute details all aspects of claims settlement in relation to the various branches of insurance. Nevertheless, we will consider in some detail, the settlement of claims arising under the following branches of insurance, namely, FIRE, MOTOR and LIFE. The reason for taking our examples from these branches of insurance are twofold, firstly, because they represent the greatest areas of conflict between insurer and Insured in this country today, and secondly, because of the obvious differences that exist between the different classes.

Fire Insurance Claims:

Every fire policy lays down certain duties on both the insurer and the insured in the event of a claim arising under the policy. Provided the insured complies with the policy conditions generally, and in particular those relating to the notification and proof of the loss, the insurer is bound to indemnify him for his loss.

All fire policies issued in this country specifically provide that "on the happening of any loss or damage to the insured property, the insured shall forthwith give notice thereof to the Company and shall within fifteen days deliver to the Company proof of the loss or damage in writing". It follows from this condition that the insured must take the first step, that is, give immediate notice of the loss. The policy generally makes this and all the other stipulations conditions precedent to the liability of the insurer to indemnify the insured, and until the insured complies with this condition, no liability attaches to the insurer.

Immediate Notice of Loss: The purpose of this condition is to intimate the insurer that a loss in which it has an interest has occurred, and to enable the insurer take immediate steps to protect its own interests. For example, the insurer might wish to protect the salvage from further damage, or he might wish to collect evidence as to the cause of the fire before it is too late to do so. The policy condition provides that the notice must be forthwith or immediate, because any delay in advising the insurance company of the loss might prejudice the company's position. What constitutes immediate notice or notice forthwith depends on the circumstances of the particular case. In a normal case, notice should be given on the day the fire occurs, or at least, the following day. Except in very exceptional circumstances, notice given a month or even a week after the fire might not be held a compliance with the policy condition, and in such a case, the insurance Company would be entitled to repudiate liability, unless it waives the right to repudiate.

There are no reported Nigerian cases on the subject of notice in this context, but it is submitted that where the Nigerian Courts are called upon to decide on the question as to what constitutes "immediate notice" or "notice forthwith" within the terms of a fire insurance policy, the words "immediate" and "forthwith" would be given their ordinary popular dictionary meaning. (For an interesting discussion on this subject, see MacGillivary on Insurance Law, Fifth Edition, Vol. 2 at page 826). In an English case (R. v. Justices of Berkshire, 1878 4 Q.B.D., 469) the Court had this to say, per Cockburn, C. J., "It is impossible to lay down any hard-and-fast rule as to what is the meaning of the word "immediately" in all cases. The words "forthwith" and "immediately" have the same meaning. They are stronger than the expression "within reasonable time", and imply prompt vigorous action without any delay, and whether there has been such action is a question of fact having regard to the circumstances of the particular case". In this case, the relevant statute provided that something had to be done "immediately" and the Court held that a delay of four days was not a compliance with the statute. The decision might have been different had the appellant reasonably explained off the delay.

Proof of Loss: The policy condition in addition to providing that the insured shall give immediate notice of the loss, also requires the insured to produce proof of loss in writing within a specified number of days. This condition must also be complied with.

Having given immediate notice of the loss, and having proved his loss, the insured would have performed his own duties in relation to the claim, and the burden then shifts to the insurance company to play its own part.

Fire Loss Procedure from the Company's View Point:

As soon as it is notified of a fire claim, the first thing the insurance company should do is to ascertain that the policy on the property concerned is in force If the policy is in force, the next step would depend on whether the claim is a small one or a large one involving thousands of naira. If the claim is a small one, a claim form would be forwarded to the insured for completion. The claim form, amongst other things, requires information as to the time, date, and place of the fire, the cause and circumstances of the incident, the nature of the insured's interest, details of other insurances on the property, and details of previous claims by the insured.

Particulars of the Claims: On the reverse side of the claim form, the insured is required to state in detail the articles destroyed or damaged by the fire, the purchase price, the date of purchase, the value at the time of the fire, the value of the salvage, and the net amount being claimed for each article. At the end of the claim form is a declaration signed by the insured as to the truth of the information he has supplied in the claim form.

Buildings: If the claim is for fire damage to buildings, no information as to values is required, instead, the insured is required to forward repair estimates from builders or building contractors for the company's consideration and approval.

If after reading through the claim form the insurer considers the amount claimed reasonable, a discharge form is obtained and a cheque is forwarded to the insured in settlement of the claim. If, on the other hand the claim form discloses any unsatisfactory features or the amount claimed is considered unreasonable or exaggerated, the company may send either an inspector or a member of the claims department to interview the insured and negotiate settlement with him. When at the end of negotiations a figure is finally agreed, a discharge form incorporating a receipt is obtained from the insured to the effect that he accepts the agreed amount in full and final settlement of the claim.

Serious Fire Claims: Immediately an insurance Company is notified of a loss which is likely to be a serious one, the company will promptly appoint an independent loss adjuster to handle the claim on their behalf.

As soon as he is appointed, the loss adjuster would be given a copy of the policy under which the claim is made, and he would then proceed to the scene of the fire. On getting to the scene, he will immediately take steps to protect the salvage from further damage or loss, and would then proceed to ascertain the cause of the fire. From his findings, he sends out a preliminary report to the insurance company. This preliminary report will include an estimate as to what the loss is likely to cost. He obtains a completed claim form from the insured, and provided the property is covered and the policy conditions and warranties have been complied with, the loss adjuster will discuss the claim generally with the insured, and on the basis of the information available, an equitable amount would be agreed. When the adjuster and the insured have agreed an amount, say ₦50,000 as the total cost of the damage to the insured's property, the insured signs an "acceptance form" indicating his willingness to accept settlement at the agreed amount. The adjuster then forwards his final report together with the claim form and acceptance form to the insurance company for their consideration and approval. If the recommended figure is accepted by the insurer, a cheque is sent to the insured thus finalising the matter.

Loss Adjuster Must Act Independently: Although the loss adjuster is appointed and paid by the insurer, he is expected to function honestly, fairly, and independently in the execution of his duties.

Several Insurers Involved in One Big Loss: In most of the big fire claims, there are usually several insurance companies involved either as direct insurers or as co-insurers. For example, in March 1964, there was a big fire at the Industrial area in Apapa, Lagos, and property worth about ₦500,000 stored in a warehouse were destroyed. There were at least ten insurance companies interested in the loss. In such a case the practice is for the leading company, that is, the company with the largest interest, to appoint the adjuster. The adjuster sends his report to all the insurers, and in the end he apportions the loss, and each company issues a cheque settling its own share of the loss. The adjuster's fees are also similarly apportioned.

MOTOR CLAIMS

The claims condition in the motor policy, like that in the fire policy discussed in the preceding paragraphs, requires the insured to give immediate notice in writing to the Company of any accident. The following is the full wording of this condition as contained in the Motor policy issued by most of the leading insurers in Nigeria:

"Notice shall be given in writing to the Company immediately upon the occurrence of any accident or loss or damage and in the event of any claim. Every letter claim writ summons and or process shall be forwarded to the Company immediately on receipt by the insured. Notice shall also be given in writing to the Company immediately the insured shall have knowledge of any impending prosecution inquest or fatal inquiry in respect of any occurrence which may give rise to a claim under this policy. In case of theft or other criminal act which may be the subject of a claim under this policy the insured shall give immediate notice to the police and co-operate with the Company in securing the conviction of the offender".

The most essential requirements of this policy condition are:-

(a)   That the insured shall give to the Company immediate notice of the accident in writing;

(b)   That the insured shall forward every letter of claim and writ of summons to the company immediately he receives them; and

(c)   That the insured shall report all impending prosecutions of the driver or fatal inquiry (such as a Coroner's Inquest) to the Company.

As in all claims conditions, the purpose of this policy condition is to enable the company take steps to protect its interest. Technically, any breach of this or of any other term in the policy entitles the insurer to repudiate liability, but in practice, insurers almost invariably agree to waive all minor breaches especially when they have not been unduly prejudiced by such a breach.

General Loss Procedure:

As soon as a motor accident is reported to an insurer, the following three questions are raised:

(1)   Is there a valid insurance policy covering the policyholder's interest in the particular motor vehicle involved in the accident ? If the answer to this is yes, the next question then is;

(2)   Is the insured entitled to be indemnified under this policy ? If the answer is also in the affirmative, the insurer then has to direct his mind to the third point, and that is;

(3)   Is the insured liable to any third party in respect of either damage to that third party's property or for injury to his person.

The answer to both the first and second questions would be obtained by looking up the insurer's records. The answers would be in the affirmative if the records reveal (*a*) that the policy was in force at the material time, and (*b*) that the loss falls within the scope of cover granted by the policy, and (*c*) that the insured has complied with all the policy conditions.

Claim Form : To facilitate this initial inquiry a claim form, or to be more exact, an "accident report form" is completed by the insured.

CLAIMS UNDER INDIVIDUAL SECTIONS OF THE MOTOR POLICY

Introductory: Depending on the scope of cover granted by the policy, a motor claim may fall under any one or more of the under-mentioned sections, and the loss procedure would depend on the section under which the claim is made. A motor claim may be in respect of,

(*a*)   Accidental Damage to the Insured's Vehicle,

(*b*)   Theft of the Insured's Vehicle,

(*c*)   Fire Damage to the insured's vehicle,

(*d*)   Third Party Liability, arising either from damage to a third party's property, or death of or personal injury to a third party.

Scope of Cover:

Before we go on to consider the subject of claims, procedure under the individual sections of the motor policy, it must be noted that the owner or user of a motor vehicle has a choice of four types of motor policies. The higher the premium he is prepared to pay, the more extensive the cover he would obtain. The four kinds of motor policies are:

(1) The "Act" Policy;
(2) The Third Party Policy:
(3) The Third Party, Fire, and Theft Policy, and
(4) The Comprehensive Policy.

The "Act" Policy: This policy covers the insured to the extent of the minimum insurance cover he must have in order to comply with the compulsory insurance provisions of the Road Traffic Acts. (Under the Road Traffic Acts, no person is permitted to use a motor vehicle on the road unless there is a policy of insurance issued by an authorised insurer covering that person in respect of any liability that he may incur as a result of the death of or bodily injury to any person caused by, or arising from the use of the motor vehicle).

As the name suggests, the "Act" policy covers only this compulsory insurance requirement of the law. The policy does not insure against either liability for damage to property or liability to non-fare paying passengers travelling in the insured vehicle. Furthermore, the policy only covers accidents on public roads and highways, but not accidents on private property.

The Third Party Policy: In addition to granting cover similar to those granted by the "Act" policy, the third party policy also insures the policyholder against any liability he may incur in respect of damage to other people's property arising from the use of the motor vehicle.

The Third Party, Fire and Theft Policy: This policy in addition to granting the full third party cover described above, also insures the policyholder's motor vehicle against the risks of fire and theft.

The Comprehensive Policy:

As the term "comprehensive" suggests, the cover provided under the comprehensive motor policy is quite extensive, but this does not mean that all possible contingencies are covered under the policy. For instance, damage to the insured vehicle arising from normal wear and tear or ordinary mechanical breakdown is not covered, similarly, the policy expressly excludes, amongst others, liability in respect of (a) accidents outside the geographical area, and (b) accidents occasioned or caused by war or warlike operations, and civil war and riots.

Summary of the Scope of Cover: In addition to providing cover similar to those described above, the comprehensive motor policy insures against:-

(a) Loss of or damage to the insured vehicle;

(b) Medical expenses of the insured, his driver or any occupant of the insured vehicle at the time of an accident up to a specified amount; (This cover is limited to private cars).

(c) Solicitor's fees for the legal representation of the insured or his driver at any judicial proceeding arising from an accident which may give rise to a claim under the policy.

CLAIMS IN RESPECT OF DAMAGE TO THE INSURED'S VEHICLE.

Immediately an "own damage" claim is notified, the first step after obtaining a completed claim form would be to send the vehicle to a reputable garage for a repair estimate to be prepared. If the damage is serious and extensive, an Engineer may be appointed by the insurers to inspect and report on the vehicle. The Engineer's report which he would forward to the insurer would indicate the extent of damage, the probable cost of repairs, the pre-accident and the post-accident value of the vehicle. The Engineer would examine the repair estimate produced by the garage proprietors, and if he is satisfied that the repair estimate is reasonable, he would despatch it to the insurance company for approval, after which, repair work would proceed.

When the vehicle is finally repaired, the garage proprietor sends his repair invoice to the insurer for settlement. Where there is an excess under the policy, the insured pays the amount of the excess directly to the garage proprietor, together with any agreed contribution he is to make towards the cost of repairs for "betterment" (The term "betterment" has been explained on page 51).

Total Losses: An insured motor vehicle may become either an actual total loss after an accident, or a constructive total loss. There is an actual total loss when the motor vehicle is a complete wreck and is irreparable or when it ceases to exist, for instance, where the vehicle is burnt to ashes. On the other hand, there is a constructive total loss when the vehicle is damaged beyond economic repair, that is when the cost of repairing the damage to the vehicle would exceed its market value. For example, if the estimated cost of repairing a motor car valued at ₦400 is about ₦450, then it would be uneconomical to repair, and the claim would be dealt with as a constructive total loss.

Whether the claim is settled as an actual or constructive total loss, the effect to the insured is the same. In either case, the legal position is that the insured is entitled to have the vehicle replaced by the insurance company, with a vehicle of the same age, make, type and construction, and in much the same condition as the insured vehicle was immediately before the accident. Because of the obvious practical difficulty of making such a replacement, the general practice is to make a cash payment to the insured based on the market value of the vehicle immediately before the accident. As a rule, the motor dealers or the garage proprietors handling the claim are requested by the insurer to state the pre-accident market value of the vehicle, and this value forms the basis of settlement between the insurance company and the policyholder.

Ownership of the Salvage: When a claim is settled as a total loss, actual or constructive, and provided the insured has been indemnified, the ownership of the salvage passes to the insurers, who may sell it or deal with it as they see fit.

THEFT CLAIMS

Both the third party, fire and theft policy, and the comprehensive policy cover the risk of theft of the insured vehicle. The policy requires the insured to report the theft of the vehicle to the police forthwith, and this is a condition precedent which must be complied with by the insured before the insurer can entertain the claim.

The practice amongst insurers in this country is to allow some time to elapse, say, three to five weeks before the theft claim is settled. This is to allow the police sufficient time to conduct a search for the stolen vehicle with a view to effecting recovery. If after this search period the vehicle is not recovered, the claim is settled on the same lines as in the accidental damage claims discussed earlier.

Recovery of stolen Vehicle after insured is Indemnified:

In the event of the vehicle being recovered after the insured has been indemnified, it becomes the property of the insurer. But if it is recovered before the claim is settled, it is returned to the insured and no claim is made, except that if the vehicle is recovered in a damaged condition, the insurance company is liable for its repair, even if the particular policy did not cover accidental damage.

FIRE DAMAGE CLAIMS

The comprehensive policy and the third party, fire and theft policy insure against the risk of fire. Claims for loss of or damage to an insured vehicle by fire are treated on similar lines as accidental damage claims. If the vehicle is burnt to ashes and it therefore becomes a total loss, the insured is paid the market value of the vehicle immediately before the fire. If, on the other hand, the damage is only partial or minor and the vehicle can be economically repaired, the insurers would bear the cost of repairs.

Investigation of Fire Claims: Insurers tend to be extremely careful and scrupulous in the investigation of fire claims. They pay special attention to the question of the moral hazard of the insured in order to satisfy themselves as to the genuineness of the allegation that the fire was accidental.

THIRD PARTY PERSONAL INJURY CLAIMS

Introductory: Until quite recently, very few personal injury or death claims were made in Nigeria. In fact, in parts of the country, there used to be a strong moral and religious objection to the practice of "making money" out of an accident. And in those early days of motor insurance it might have been considered immoral and a disservice to the memory of the dead for a person to claim money from an insurance company in respect of his deceased relation. Those were the 'good old days' of the insurance industry in Nigeria. But today, the story is different. With greater sophistication, and the growth of an industrialised society, Nigerians are becoming more and more aware of their legal rights. The trend these days is that whenever personal injury results from a motor accident, claim is made, even when there is no legal liability!

No Legal Liability Unless there is Negligence or "Fault": Misunderstandings often arise because most claimants tend to lose sight of the fact that legal liability in respect of road accidents is not strict in Nigeria. To succeed in his claim, the claimant must show that the accident in respect of which he is claiming was caused as a result of some "fault" or negligence on the part of the driver of the insured vehicle involved in the accident. Quite often accidents do occur in circumstances where no negligence can be imputed to the driver. The accident may have resulted solely from the carelessness or negligence of the injured person. For instance, a pedestrian who suddenly rushes into the road in the face of approaching traffic, and is knocked down by an approaching car, has only himself to blame for his misfortune. Provided the driver had exercised reasonable care in the manner in which he drove and managed his vehicle at the material time, the pedestrian cannot make a successful claim in respect of the injuries he might have suffered as there was no negligence on the part of the driver.

Investigation: As soon as a third party personal injury claim is intimated, the insurer immediately proceeds to ascertain the circumstances of the alleged accident in an effort to determine whether or not there is liability, and if so, the extent of such liability. The extent of the insurer's liability would of course depend on the nature and extent of the injury suffered by the claimant. Statements would be obtained from the driver, his passengers and any independent eye witnesses of the accident. The investigation of the claim might include a visit to the scene of the accident. If the accident was witnessed or investigated by the police, a copy of the abstract of the police report may be obtained and this is usually quite useful. In more complicated cases, the insurer would seek legal opinion from their lawyers. To ascertain the extent of injury, a medical report would have to be obtained as well.

At the end of the investigation, the insurer is in a position to assess the claim. The information obtained as a result of this investigation may show,

(a)   that the insured or his driver was at fault, or that the insured was only partially at fault and that the claimant substantially or equally contributed to the accident by his own negligence. or finally,

(b)   that there was no negligence on the part of the insured or his driver.

If the facts reveal that the insured was either entirely or partly negligent, the parties, usually, but not invariably, through their lawyers would endeavour to agree a reasonable 'out-of-Court' settlement. If they are unable to agree, the matter may proceed to Court.

If, on the other hand, the facts clearly show that there was no negligence on the part of the insured, the insurance Company would normally turn down the claim, unless it voluntarily elects to make an ex-gratia payment.

EX-GRATIA PAYMENTS

An Ex-Gratia Payment is a payment made out of grace and favour not based on any legal obligation. Quite often, insurance companies find it necessary to settle a claim either in part or in full despite the fact that there is no legal liability to make any payment under the terms of the relevant insurance policy. Such payments are quite common in Nigeria, especially where the insurance company considers the claimant or policyholder an important connection, or probably where the insurer believes that such payments would promote its corporate image and enhance the insurer's reputation thereby encouraging others to insure with the particular insurance company.

There is a school of thought which maintains that insurance companies should not make ex-gratia payments but should only settle claims where there is legal liability. In spite of this school of thought, ex-gratia payments remain quite popular and every year insurance companies in Nigeria pay out several millions of naira in claims where on a strict interpretation of the policy there would be no legal liability.

Third Party Death Claims: These are treated on much the same lines as third party personal injury claims. Proof of death is required and the insurer would insist on some evidence to show that the deceased was killed in the accident which is the subject of the claim. To determine quantum, the insurer would ascertain the age, occupation and earning capacity of the deceased at the time of his death. The practice in Nigeria today is to ask the claimants to produce the deceased's tax receipts for the last three years of his life. Finally, the claimants must be capable of giving a good discharge to the insurer, that is, they must be the authorised representatives of the deceased's estate.

THIRD PARTY PROPERTY DAMAGE CLAIMS

The procedure in the handling of claims in respect of damage to third party property is similar to those discussed above in relation to third party personal injury claims. The detailed method of investigation and settlement would depend on the nature of the third-party property damaged, which may be goods, buildings or land.

Investigation: The third party's claim must be thoroughly investigated in order to determine the question of liability, and the extent of damage. Where there is liability, an early attempt must be made to settle, so as to avoid a high consequential loss claim. Provided there is liability on the part of the insured, the third party claimant is entitled to the full market value of his damaged property (if totally destroyed) or the full cost of repairs, in the case of a minor damage. In addition, the third party is entitled to a reasonable amount in respect of his consequential losses Thus, where Mr Atta's stationary 'motor car is damaged as a result of the careless driving of Mr. Bassey, Mr. Atta is entitled to,

(*a*)   the cost of repairing his vehicle to its pre-accident condtion, and,

(*b*)   reasonable consequential losses, for instance, the cost of hiring another vechile whilst his damaged motor car was undergoing repairs. Consequential losses, to be recoverable, must be reasonable, especially as the claimant plaintiff has a common law duty to mitigate damages.

Motor Vehicles: If the subject of the third party's claim is a motor vehicle, the claim would be settled on the same lines as the own damage claim discussed earlier. If the damage is repairable, this method of settlement would be applied, and if not repairable, the claim is settled as a total loss.

Inter-Office Sharing Agreements: In most of the collision cases involving two or more vehicles, an inter office sharing agreement applies. The most popular of these agreements is the "Knock-for-Knock" agreement. Briefly, the Knock-for-Knock Agreement, in its simplest form, provides that if there is a collision and damage is sustained by vehicles insured by any of the parties to the agreement, each insurer pays his own damage, irrespective of legal liability. For example, car 'A' is properly parked on its own side of the road, and car 'B', carelessly driven, collides with car 'A' in its stationary position damaging it quite extensively. It is quite clear from the circumstances of the accident that the driver of car B was at fault. If the two vehicles in our example, are comprehensively insured with two different insurers who are subscribers to the Overseas Knock-for-Knock Agreement, each insurer would bear the cost of repairing its own car and no claim is made on the insurer or owner of the car whose driver caused the accident.

The Knock-for-Knock Agreement is an agreement between insurers, and does not in any way affect the legal rights of the respective policy-holders. Therefore an insured person, inspite of the operation of the agreement, is free to bring an action against the tortfeasor in order to recover his uninsured losses.

LIFE ASSURANCE CLAIMS

The settlement of life assurance claims is a little less complicated than the settlement of losses under the other branches of insurance. This is because the amount to be paid by the insurer is agreed at the time the policy is effected, and there is no question of negotiation when the claim arises.

Broadly, there are two main types of life policies issued in Nigeria today. These are, (a) the Whole life policy and (b) the Endowment policy. In the whole life policy the claim becomes payable only when the life assured dies. All that the claimant needs to do in order to get the policy money is to prove to the insurance Company that the life assured has died, and that he is the person entitled to receive the money. In the case of the endowment policy, the policy "matures" for payment, either at the end of the policy period, or at the death of the life assured, whichever is the earlier in time. It follows from the foregoing, that a claim under a life policy (except where the policy is terminated for some reason and a surrender value is paid) may be either a death claim, or an Endowment claim under a "mature" policy. The procedure in the handling of each type of claim is discussed below:

Death Claims: All life policies specifically stiplulate that death claims will be settled only when the claimant produces satisfactory proof to the insurance company of the age and death of the life assured, and of the title of the claimant.

On being notified of the death of the life assured, the first step taken by the insurer is to look up the index of lives assured kept by the company to ascertain the number of policies on the life of the deceased. A folder is then opened in respect of each policy, and in this folder will be placed the original proposal papers together with all correspondence concerning the claim. The claimants are then requested to produce evidence of death, which will consist of (*a*) a Death Certificate, and (*b*) a Declaration of Identity. Unless the age of life assured had already been admitted, the claimant must produce proof of age. As a general rule, birth certificates and passports are accepted as evidence of age.

Importance of the Age of the life assured:

In all classes of life assurance, the age of the life assured is of considerable importance because premium rates are based on the age of the life assured at the time the insurance was effected. The older the life assured, the higher the premium. To avoid misunderstandings when a claim arises, it is best to produce evidence of age at the outset, when the life assured is still available. In the event of the age stated in the policy being incorrect, the amount due under the policy would be subject to adjustment.

Evidence of Title: When satisfactory evidence of death has been submitted to the insurer, and age is confirmed, the next step is to ascertain the identity of the person or persons entitled to receive the policy money. The person claiming title to the proceeds of the policy is usually required to substantiate his claims by producing proof that he is entitled to the money. This is because life policies are a kind of proprietary right of the class known as choses-in-action, and are freely assignable from one person to another. Assignments of life policies should be notified to the insurer because priority depends on the date on which notice was given to the insurer and not necessarily on the date of assignment.

Proof of Title: Where the grantee, (that is, the person who took out the life policy, otherwise known as the assured) and the deceased life assured are different persons, and no notice has been received affecting the title to the policy, it is prima facie proof of title if the policy document is produced. But if other persons have acquired interests in the policy the claimant would be required to produce all documents of title for inspection by the insurance company's Solicitors. If the documents are in order, settlement would be recommended by the solicitors. The test in determining title should be, can the claimant give the insurer a good discharge ? If he can give a good discharge, which cannot be successfully challenged, then he is entitled to the proceeds of the policy.

Where the assured and the life assured are one and the same person (that is, where the assured effected the policy on his own life), and there has been no dealing in the policy, the policy moneys are payable to the personal representatives of the deceased for his estate. In Nigeria, the practice is to insist on a Grant of Representation, (in the form of Probate or Letters of Administration) before payment is made. When a grant of Representation has been obtained, the money is paid to the person or persons entitled under the Grant to administer the estate of the deceased or to the Federal Administrator General if he is administering the estate.

Amount Paid: The amount finally paid to the person entitled is the sum assured which is stated in the policy, plus any bonus that may have accrued if the policy is a with-profit policy, less any loans or outstanding premiums.

CLAIMS UNDER MATURING ENDOWMENT POLICIES

Arrangements for the payment of claims under "maturing" endowment policies are started long before the due date. All policies which would mature in a particular year are sorted out and entered up in a "maturities book". Two or three months to the due date, a folder is made up in which will be placed the original proposal papers together with all the correspondence relating to the claim.

Letter of Admission: As the due date approaches, a Letter of Admission of the claim is sent to the policyholder drawing his attention to the approaching maturity of the policy. This letter would contain a statement showing the amount payable and the date on which it falls due for payment. If the age of the life assured has not been admitted, this letter would ask for evidence of age to be submitted as no payment would be made until proof of age has been produced. The policyholder is further requested in this letter to produce the policy for cancellation when payment has been made.

Notices Affecting Title: If the notices affecting the title to the policy have been received, the letter of admission will list these notices, and the claimant will be required to produce all the relevant documents for inspection by the insurance Company's lawyers.

Discharge Form: As soon as the question of title has been resolved, a form of discharge is prepared by the insurer and forwarded to the person entitled to receive the money, for completion and signature. This form when properly executed, discharges the insurer from all liability under the policy. On the due date a cheque covering the amount of the claim is forwarded to the person entitled, thus finalising the matter.

CHAPTER XIII

DISCHARGE OF LIABILITIES UNDER LIFE ASSURANCE POLICIES

Discharge by Performance

Discharge by Breach
  (i) Payment of Surrender Values
  (ii) Breach by Life Office

Discharge by Novation

Discharge by Agreement of the Parties.

As in every other form of contractual obligation, there are four possible ways in which the contractual obligation under a life assurance policy can be terminated, namely;
- (a) By performance
- (b) By Breach
- (c) By novation i.e. by the making of a new contract; and
- (d) By the agreement of the parties.

(*a*) **Discharge by Performance:** The term performance in this context refers to the fulfilment of the conditions and stipulations of the contract in every respect. If each party to the contract has performed his part of the obligations under the contract, the contract is said to have been discharged by performance. Thus in a whole life policy if the assured or the life assured has paid his premiums fully and complied with all the terms of the contract and then dies, there is a complete discharge of the contract by performance when the insurers pay to his legal owners the sum assured under the whole life policy. Similarly, regarding endowment assurances, by survival to the maturity date when the Company pays over the sum assured (and bonuses in the case of a with-profit policy) in discharge of the contract.

(*b*) **Breach:** A contract may be discharged by a breach of the terms of the contract, but the injured then either acquires the right to sue the defaulter for damages or in appropriate cases to apply for an order for specific performance or an injunction. In life assurance in this Country the most common form of breach is the failure on the part of the insured or assured to pay the premium. Insurance Companies do not compel the insured to pay his life premiums, but the policy usually provides that in the event of the assured failing to pay the premium within a stipulated period the policy would lapse, or in the alternative the benefits under the policy would be reduced if the policy has earned a surrender value. The practice in Nigeria is that where the policy has been in force for less than two or three years before the assured fails to pay the premium, the policy lapses and the company forfeits the premium paid to date as compensation for the breach. But where the non-payment of premium arises after the policy has earned a surrender value (i.e. it has been in force for a considerable number of years) the insured is given the option of either taking a paid-up policy with lesser benefits or of accepting the surrender value of the policy. This then takes us to the controversial subject of surrender values.

Surrender Value Defined: The surrender value of a life policy is the cash value of the policy at any given date. It represents the cash amount that the insurer pays to the assured if he surrenders the policy in place of the prevailing cash value of the policy thereby terminating the original contract. The surrender value of a life policy is usually determined by an insurance actuary by applying a well defined scientific process. In calculating the surrender value of each policy, the actuary must take the following factors into account:

(*i*) the commission paid to the agent who introduced the business;
(*ii*) The medical expenses incurred by the Company;
(*iii*) the Stamp duty paid to the Inland Revenue Authorities;
(*iv*) administrative expenses which include the cost of documentation, rents, staff salaries and similar items of expenditure;
(*v*) the cost of life assurance cover.

The first three factors can easily be ascertained and fixed amounts easily allocated to them, but the last two factors cannot easily be determined by a Court of law or an arbitrator. The universal practice is to accept the surrender value of the particular policy as vouched by the insurance Company's actuary. Perhaps the existence of competition and the fear of losing business to other companies should compel insurers to pay reasonable surrender values to their policy-holders.

Recently, the Insurance Department which was formerly a Division of the Ministry of Trade, insisted that all insurance Companies operating in Nigeria, must show very clearly in their life policies, the minimum guaranteed surrender values payable to their policy holders in the event of a surrender. This is a most interesting development and certainly goes a long way to protect the interests of the insuring public. Although the Insurance Division of the Ministry of Trade did not specify the minimum surrender value which the Companies must guarantee, it would appear that the figure that has gained general acceptance is one-third of the total premiums paid subject to the policy having been in force for at least two years and subject to two or three years' premiums having been paid. We reproduce below the full text of the surrender value clause contained in a Life policy issued by a leading Nigerian insurer:

"This Policy acquires a surrender value after two years' permiums have been fully paid. If at least three years' premiums shall have been paid, the surrender value shall not be less than one-third of the premiums paid".

Where the policy is silent on the subject of surrender value, the attitude of insurers is that the payment of a surrender value is a privilege and not a right. Thus the insurers view the payment of a surrender value to a policyholder as a concession and not a right which he can insist on enforcing. The basis of this reasoning is that in effecting the insurance, the parties agreed that the policy would run its whole term of years if an endowment policy or until the death of the life assured if a whole life policy. By surrendering the policy the insured is acting in breach of contract and he therefore has no right to dictate terms. This reasoning may be valid, but it is hoped that the current trend referred to above will solve most of the controversy over the subject of surrender values.

Breach by Life Office: It is unusual for a life insurance Company to act in breach of the terms of a life policy. But what is the legal position, where an insurance Company suddenly decides not to continue to do life business ? What is the effect of all the life policies issued by that Company where these policies are still in force and the policyholders are still willing and able to keep their policies alive by paying their premiums regularly but the insurer is unwilling to accept. In this case the surrender value cannot be said to be adequate compensation to the insured. It is submitted that the insured is entitled to some compensation for "breach of contract" on the part of the insurer. Surely when the policy was effected the parties intended that the policy would run its full term. By its decision to wind-up its operation, the insurance company is acting in breach of the contract and it is not an adequate compensation merely to offer the insured the surrender value of the policy fixed by the company's own actuaries. Furthermore, the insured may have in the meantime become a substandard risk and therefore uninsurable or the cost of obtaining insurance cover may have increased substantially for him in comparison with the period when he effected his original insurance with the insurer who now wishes to wind-up. Even in a case of winding-up by order of the Court, the receiver or liquidator should ensure that the policyholders have rights in preference to the shareholders.

(c) **Novation:** In the case of a discharge arising by novation the obligations under the original contract are released in place of obligations assumed by another person. In this case the parties agree to have a new contract in place of the original contract.

(d) **Agreement:** As pointed out earlier, the Nigerian Law allows freedom of contract. Therefore just as the parties, i.e. the insured and the insurer, have entered into a contract of insurance as evidenced in the life policy, they may, by agreement bring the transaction to an end. For example, the insurer and assured or policyholder may agree that if the assured surrenders the life policy for a cash payment the policy shall become terminated. Similarly, they may also agree to alter the terms of the policy, for example by converting a whole life policy to an endowment or by converting a "with profit" twenty year endowment policy to a "without profit" endowment for ten years. Quite often it is difficult to determine whether there has been a mere alteration of the original contract or whether it has been cancelled entirely and a new one effected. This can create serious and different legal consequences as far as title to the policy proceeds are concerned. On the authority of the English case of ROYAL EXCHANGE ASSURANCE v. HOPE (1928) Ch. 179; (1927) All E.R. Rep. 67) it is safe to assume that the Courts would hold that it is a mere variation and not a new policy where no fresh policy has been issued and no fresh stamp duty has been paid and no new number has been assigned to the contract.

In this case the life assured effected a temporary term assurance and then assigned the policy to Hope. He (the life assured) subsequently arranged with the company to extend the term for three months and died during the extended term. His legal personal representatives claimed the proceeds of the policy on the ground that there was a new contract. The court held that since there was no new policy issued and no new policy number was allocated and no fresh stamp duty was paid, there was no new contract.

CHAPTER XIV

GOVERNMENTAL CONTROL AND STATE INTERVENTION IN INSURANCE

(1) Introductory
(2) Reasons for governmental control
(3) Governmental control in Nigeria
(4) Conditions for carrying on insurance business in Nigeria
(5) Insurance Decree 1976

Introductory

In the early days of insurance in Nigeria, there was no form of state or governmental control of the insurance industry. The policy of the successive governments had been to allow the insurance companies almost complete freedom of action within the provisions of the ordinary commercial laws of the land.

As time went on, it became clear to the governments that this policy of no supervision was subject to abuse as it meant in theory, if not in practice, that any one, irrespective of his background was free to set up an insurance company provided he was able to comply with the very limited requirements of those early days. There were in fact, some isolated cases in which some dubious promoters incorporated insurance companies, or purported to incorporate insurance companies, undercut premium rates, collected substantial amounts of premiums and went underground as soon as the claims started rolling in. Fortunately, for us in Nigeria, it did not require any major failure of an insurance company before the principles of governmental control of insurance business was accepted as a matter of policy by the Nigerian governments. The position today is that there is now a reasonable degree of governmental control and supervision of the activities of insurance companies in the country. The various legislations and governmental regulations governing the activities of insurance operations in Nigeria will be discussed later in this chapter together with a brief examination of the various methods by which governmental control is exercised.

Reasons for Governmental Control

In practically all civilised countries, there is some degree of governmental control or regulation of the insurance business. Many writers on the subject have suggested various reasons,in support of the principle of governmental control. For instance, it has been suggested that control is exercised because of the special or peculiar nature of the insurance transaction. Whereas in an ordinary commercial transaction in which A pays for an article, for example, a motor car, he examines the car and if satisfied; he pays for it and takes delivery, in the case of an insurance transaction he pays a premium in return for a promise. So that all that A takes away from the insurer in return for the amount he has paid (the premium) is a promise from the insurer that he (the insurer) will pay a certain sum of money on the happening of a specified event, which may or may not happen. It is therefore necessary for the government to intervene to ensure that the kind of person or group of persons who sell these promises are men who can be relied upon to honour their obligations when the time to do so comes. Furthermore, in the absence of a comprehensive social insurance scheme, most people take out life assurance policies to protect themselves and their families against death and old age. For some of these people it is their only life savings. The government therefore has a duty to protect the savings of such individuals by ensuring that the insurance companies are properly run and that the owners or promoters of these companies do not run away with these savings or premiums collected from the unsuspecting public. Other reasons have been suggested, for example, the insured's inability to understand the technical nature of insurance in support of governmental control, but all these reasons early indicate that the primary purpose of governmental control is the necessity to protect the interests of policyholders against possible exploitation by unscrupulous insurers.

Governmental Control in Nigeria

Governmental control was first introduced into an independent Nigeria by the Insurance Companies Act, 1961, which was passed by the Federal parliament a year after the country attained full independence. The Insurance Companies Act, 1961, introduced for the first time in Nigeria the necessity for registration, i.e. licensing as distinct from incorporation. Before the coming into effect of the 1961 Act, all that was necessary was for the insurance company to be incorporated as an insurer. As soon as it received the certificate of incorporation, it was free to commence business but by Section 7 of the 1961 Act, the insurer after its incorporation, must apply for registration in the prescribed form to the insurance control authority in the Federal Ministry of Trade which under the 1961 Act, was the Registrar of Insurance. If the registrar (as he then was), is satisfied that the prescribed conditions for registration have been complied with by the insurer, he would register the applicant as an insurer and notify the insurer in writing accordingly and notice of the registration shall be published in the Federal Government gazette.

The 1961 Act has since been repealed and the present legislation which governs the control and operations of insurance organisations is the Insurance Decree 1976. This comprehensive decree re-enacted certain provisions of the Insurance Companies Act of 1961 and other legislations and regulations governing the business of insurance prior to its coming into effect and has generally modified and up-dated the rules and regulations governing the business of insurance in Nigeria. Some of the more important provisions of this decree are summarised later in this chapter.

CONDITIONS FOR CARRYING ON INSURANCE BUSINESS IN NIGERIA AND THE CONDITIONS TO BE FULFILLED BY AN APPLICANT FOR REGISTRATION AS AN INSURER

No person is allowed to carry on any class of insurance business. in Nigeria except:

(i)   a company duly incorporated as a limited liability company under or pursuant to the companies decree 1968;

(ii) a co-operative insurance society registered under any enactment or law relating to co-operative societies; or

(iii) a mutual insurance company.

Furthermore, in accordance with the provisions of the Insurance Decree 1976, no insurer shall commence or carry on insurance business in Nigeria unless the insurer is registered under or pursuant to this decree.

Application for Registration

Every application for registration as an insurer shall be made to the Director of Insurance in the prescribed form and be accompanied by such other documents or information as the Director may direct or require. Life insurance business and non-life insurance business shall each be subject to separate application and registration.

The Director shall register an applicant as an insurer if he is satisfied as to all of the following matters:-

(a) that the class of insurance business will be conducted in accordance with sound insurance principles;

(b) that the applicant being one of the bodies referred to in section 3 (1) of this Decree is duly established under the applicable law and has a paid-up share capital as specified in section 8 of this Decree for the relevant class of insurance business;

(c) that the relevant statutory deposit specified in section 9 of this Decree has been paid to the Central Bank and the applicant has submitted a certificate from the Central Bank to that effect;

(d) that the arrangements relating to re-insurance treaties in respect of the classes of insurance business to be transacted are adequate and valid;

(e) that the proposal forms, terms and conditions of policies are in order and acceptable;

(f) that there is at least one competent and professionally qualified person to man each department of insurance business;

(g) that the directors and shareholders are persons, who have not been involved in or been found guilty of fraud;

(h) that the name of the applicant is not likely to be mistaken for the name of any other insurer who is or has been an insurer, or so nearly resembling that name, as to be calculated to deceive;

(i) that the applicant has paid the fee prescribed for registration;

(j) that it is in the interest of public policy that the applicant be registered,

the Director shall register the applicant as an insurer by issuing a certificate of registration and notifying the insurer in writing accordingly; and notice of the registration (including registration pursuant to section 6 (4) of this Decree) shall be published in the Gazette.

Cancellation of Registration

The Insurance Decree 1976 also empowers the Director of Insurance in certain circumstances to cancel the registration of an insurer when he is satisfied:-

(a)   that the class of insurance business of the insurer is not being conducted in accordance with sound insurance principles; or

(b)   that the technical reserves in respect of unexpired risks and outstanding claims are inadequate, as required by the provisions of section 17 of this Decree; or

(c)   that the insurer has ceased to carry on insurance business of the class assigned to it for at least one year in Nigeria; or

(d)   that the insurer has applied in writing for the cancellation of its registration as an insurer; or

(e)   that a judgment obtained in any court of competent juris-diction in Nigeria against the insurer remains unsatisfied for 30 days; or

(f)   that the insurer is carrying on simultaneously with insurance business any other business which is detrimental to the insurance business of the insurer; or

(g)   that the business of the insurer has been transferred to or amalgamated with the business of any other insurer; or

(h)   that the insurer has refused to submit to an examination of its books, as provided for in this Decree; or

(i)   that the insurer has failed to comply with the provisions of section 19 (4) of this Decree; or

(j)   that the insurer has failed to maintain adequate and valid re-insurance treaties; or

(k)   that the insurer lacks expertise; or

(l)   that the insurer has persistently contravened the provisions of section 8 of the National Insurance Corporation of Nigeria Decree 1969 relating to compulsory re-insurance or has failed to comply with any other enactment relating to re-insurance in Nigeria; or

(m)   that the net assets of the insurer are below the minimum paid-up capital and the capital has not been made good within the time stipulated by the Director; or

(n)   that the insurer persistently fails to pay claims promptly; or

(o)   that the insurer has failed to set up the special reserves as prescribed under section 17 (1) of this Decree; or

(p)   that the insurer has established a branch office or branch offices without the approval of the Director; or

(q)   that the insurer acts in any manner without the approval of

the Director in cases where this Decree requires such approval;
(r) that the insurer has been wound up or otherwise dissolved,
or has gone into liquidation,
the Director shall give notice in writing to the insurer of his intention
to cancel the registration of the insurer in respect of a particular class
or both classes of insurance business and the provisions of section
6 of this Decree shall apply to any such notice as if it were a notice to
reject an application for registration.

Insurance Decree 1976

This Decree, otherwise known as Decree No. 59 of 1976 came
into force on the 1st December 1976. It is a most comprehensive
enactment aimed at cleaning up the insurance business in Nigeria
thereby producing a healthy, sophisticated and efficient insurance
industry.

The main objections which the Federal Government of Nigeria
intends to achieve as a result of this important enactment has been
beautifully summarised in non-technical language in a DAILY TIMES
editorial of Monday, December 13, 1976, as follows:-

"The implementation of the provisions of Decree No. 59 of
1976 (otherwise known as Insurance Decree 1976) is bound
to have a general cleansing and therefore healthy effect on the
business as it is practised in Nigeria. Reading through the provisions of the decree, there is clear evidence that in formulating
them, the Federal Government has sought to achieve two broad
objectives, among others. The first is to ensure that insurance
companies are lawfully established and are run at all times along
sound insurance principles. The second broad objective of the
decree is to give better protection to members of the general
public who deal with insurance companies, while at the same
time being fair to insurance companies operating in this country.
Before the relevant legislation was tightened up, some Nigerians
established insurance businesses under the erroneous impression
that it was another way of getting rich quickly, without really
working hard. That was why they were rather clever and enthu-
siastic in persuading clients to take up various insurance policies;
but they went to great lengths to avoid settling claims (many
of them legitimate) if and when they arose. Of course, there
were a few honourable exceptions to these malpractices which

did not endear many clients to insurance companies. If the provisions of Decree No. 59 of 1976 are rigorously applied, these abuses would be totally eliminated."[1]

The Decree has introduced some fundamental changes in the laws and regulations affecting the business of insurance in Nigeria. In addition to laying down new conditions for carrying on insurance business in Nigeria, it raised the minimum paid-up share capital from the original ₦100,000 to ₦800,000 for a composite company, that is, a company doing both life and non-life business. The relevant section provides that "no insurer shall carry on insurance business in Nigeria unless the insurer has and maintains at all times, while carrying on that business a paid-up share capital of the following amounts as the case may require, that is—

(*a*) in the case of life insurance business, not less than ₦500,000;

(*b*) in the case of non-life insurance business, not less than ₦300,000 and

(*c*) in the case of re-insurance business, not less than ten times the amount specified in paragraph (a) above or, as the case may require, in paragraph (b) above.

It also introduced the idea of statutory deposits as a further safeguard. Other important innovations introduced by the Decree relate to the appointment and removal of chief executives of insurance companies. Under Section 12 of the Decree, the appointment of chief executives of insurance companies are subject to the approval of the Director of Insurance, and any change of chief executive must be notified to the Director of Insurance. The Decree further provides that all insurance policies or certificates of insurance and changes therein require the approval of the Director of Insurance. It also stipulates that where an insurer carries on both classes of insurance business, there shall be a separation of accounts and reserve funds between life and non-life business. In Section 15, the Decree lists out the books and records that must be kept and maintained at the principal office of the insurer as follows:

(*a*) the memorandum and articles of association or other evidence of the constitution of the body concerned;

(*b*) a record containing the names and addresses of the owners of the insurer (whether known and called shareholders or otherwise howsoever);

---

1 See DAILY TIMES of Nigeria, Monday, December, 1976.

(c)   the minutes of any meeting of such owners, and of the policy-making executive (whether known and called the board of directors or otherwise howsoever);

(d)   a register of all policies, in which shall be entered in respect of every policy issued, the name and address of the policy-holder, the date when the policy was effected, and a record of any transfer, assignment or nomination, of which the insurer has notice;

(e)   a register of claims in which shall be entered every claim made together with the date of claim, the name and address of the claimant and the date on which the claim was settled, or in the case of a claim which is rejected the date of rejection and the grounds thereof, or in the case of litigation, the particulars thereof and the decision of the court in the matter;

(f)   a register of investments showing those which are attributable to the reserves and those which are not and also any alteration in their values from time to time;

(g)   a register of assets;

(h)   a register of re-insurance ceded, showing separately those ceded in Nigeria and those ceded abroad;

(i)   a cash book;

(j)   current accounts books; and

(k)   a register of open policies in respect of marine insurance transactions.

In respect of life insurance business the following additional records shall be kept and maintained, that is —

(a)   a register of assured under group policies;

(b)   a register of loans on policies;

(c)   a register of cash surrender values; and

(d)   a register of lapsed and expired policies.

On the subject of reserves, the Decree makes it mandatory for every insurer to set up the following technical reserves in respect of each class of insurance business, that is —

(a)   reserves for unexpired risks;

(b)   reserves for outstanding claims; and

(c)   contingency reserves to cover fluctuations in securities and variations in statistical estimates.

Insurance Agents and Brokers

For the first time in the history of insurance in Nigeria, the Decree introduced the idea of licensing in respect of insurance agents and brokers. Under the Decree, no person is allowed to transact insurance business as an agent unless he is licensed as such. The procedure for obtaining such a licence is laid down by the Decree. Similarly, no person is allowed to transact business in Nigeria as an insurance broker unless he is licensed as such under the provisions of the Decree and to obtain such a licence, the applicant must in addition to other requirements, deposit a sum of ₦25,000 on a fixed deposit basis with the Central Bank of Nigeria. Furthermore, the Director of Insurance, in addition to having been given powers to investigate the activities of insurance companies, is also empowered to investigate agents and brokers.

Premium rates and commissions

The Decree also introduced restrictions on general increases in premium rates and commissions. Commission rates applicable in respect of each class of business is also stipulated.

Rating committee to review rates

An ad hoc committee to be known as the rating committee made up of representatives of the Federal Ministries of Trade, Finance and Economic Development, the Accident Insurance Association of Nigeria and the Nigerian Insurance Association and one other independent Nigerian citizen has also been created by the Decree to review premium rates and commissions from time to time.

Settlement of motor accident claims

A time limit of ninety days is set during which all motor accident claims must be settled where the insurer admits or is not disputing liability. Where the insurer does not accept liability "it must deliver a statement in writing disclaiming such liability" not later than ninety days from the date on which the claim was intimated to the insurer.

Dispensation with Police report in certain motor accident cases

One of the most controversial subjects in the handling of motor claims in Nigeria in recent years has been the subject of the police report. Some insurers are said to hold the view that on no account must a motor claim be settled unless the claimant produces a police report as part of the proof of his loss. Because of the difficulty and delay in producing these reports, many genuine claimants have suffered untold hardship and delay in having their claims settled. Also, it has been consistently alleged that a few insurers often took advantage of the absence of a police report as an excuse for repudiating liability even in cases where adequate proof had been obtained or are easily obtainable from other independent sources, such as the evidence of eye witnesses. In the light of this situation and as a result of the importance which insurers attach to the police report, motorists involved in accidents likely to lead to a claim on their insurers would go to any length to ensure that the police report when finally obtained is in their favour. Even minor accidents involving two vehicles and without any personal injuries had to·be witnessed and reported upon by the police. This, in some cases, especially in the big cities, contributed to the regular traffic chaos witnessed in these cities and the resultant economic loss to the nation.

Section 45 of the decree is aimed at solving this problem. The section provides that where a motor claim arises out of an accident involving one or more motor vehicles, it shall not be necessary, if there is sufficient evidence of proof of loss.or damage, for any claimant to deliver a police report thereon to the insurer:

> "provided that where death of, or serious bodily injury to a person is involved in any such accident, the provisions of this section shall not apply. Without prejudice to any other mode of proof, it shall be sufficient evidence of proof of loss or damage for the purposes of this section if -
>
> (a)   where only one person is involved in the accident, the person delivers a statement of the facts to the insurer concerned together with a statement of any eye witness to the accident, if any; or
>
> (b)   where more than one party is involved in the accident, each party delivers a statement of the facts to the insurer or insurers concerned and the alleged facts do not differ in any material particular".

Settlement of claims generally

One ˒f the complaints generally made against insurers by some members of the public is that insurance claims are quite often not settled promptly. The decree has, to a great extent provided an answer to this. Section 7 of the decree lists the conditions under which the Director of Insurance may cancel the certificate of registration of a registered insurer and one of these conditions is where the insurer persistently fails to pay claims promptly. Therefore an insurer who makes it a matter of regular practice to delay the settlement of claims stands the risk of having its licence cancelled. This provision should operate to the advantage of the insuring public as no responsible insurer would wish to risk losing its licence.

Insurance of imports

One other major change introduced by the decree with rather vital economic consequencies is the provision under section 46 which stipulates that every insurance in respect of goods to be imported into Nigeria must be effected with an insurer registered in Nigeria in accordance with the provisions of the Decree. This important piece of legislation has automatically altered the character of the marine insurance industry in Nigeria and has substantially increased the marine market capacity of the country.

The Director of Insurance

Under the 1961 Act, governmental supervision of insurance operations had been carried out on behalf of the government by the registrar of insurance who is an official under the Federal Ministry of Trade. This official had very limited powers of control but the Insurance Decree 1976 has abolished the post of registrar of insurance and created a new one known as the Director of Insurance. The responsibility for the administration and enforcement of the provisions of the Insurance Decree 1976 and all the regulations made thereon are vested on the Director of Insurance and his deputies. In view of the very wide powers conferred on the Director of Insurance by the Decree and in view of the extensive provisions of the Decree, the office of the Director of Insurance is a very responsible one[*1]

[*1.] The full text of the Insurance Decree 1976 together with the Insurance Regulations 1977 are attached to this volume as appendix I & II respectively.

THE NIGERIA REINSURANCE CORPORATION DECREE 1977

Another important piece of legislation affecting the insurance industry in Nigeria passed in recent times by the Federal Government is the Nigeria Reinsurance Decree 1977 which was promulgated on the 14th day of June, 1977. This Decree which is otherwise known as Decree No. 49 of 1977, is presumed to have come into force on the 1st July 1976 which is stated as its commencement date. The Decree in Section 1 established the Nigeria Reinsurance Corporation and gave it the "power, within or outside Nigeria, to effect or carry on reinsurance of any class of insurance business, including life insurance business, and to reinsure against loss of any kind arising from any risk or contingency in respect of any matter whatsoever"*²

COMPULSORY LEGAL CESSION OF 20% OF ALL POLICIES

The decree also made it compulsory for every registered insurer to reinsure with the Corporation "in respect of every insurance policy issued or renewed by it an amount equal to 20% of the sum insured in the policy........., and the registered insurer shall forthwith pay over to the Corporation an amount equal to 20 per cent of the premium received by the registered insurer on the policy whether such business relates to new business or renewal. The Nigeria Reinsurance Corporation is also empowered to operate as an international reinsurer in the world reinsurance market and also to serve as the channel of ceding compulsory cessions from the Federation of Nigeria to the African Reinsurance Corporation.

In addition to the legal cessions of 20% of all policies to be ceded from all registered insurers to the Corporation, the Corporation shall have the right of first refusal of any reinsurance business from Nigeria before such business is placed in the international reinsurance market. Furthermore, where the Corporation has exercised its right of first refusal as conferred upon it by the Decree, the Corporation shall issue a certificate to this effect to the insurer before such reinsurance business is placed abroad. The Decree also repealed those sections of the National Insurance Corporation of Nigeria Decree 1969 relating to reinsurance. *¹

---

2. See Section 1 & 2 of Decree No. 49, 1977.

1   The National Insurance Corporation of Nigeria Decree 1969 is reproduced in full as Appendix VI to this volume.

The Decree also directs that the Insurance Decree 1976 shall apply to the Corporation to the same extent as it applies to insurers under that decree and insofar as the provisions of the Insurance Decree 1976 are not inconsistent with those of the Nigeria Reinsurance Decree.

BOARD OF DIRECTORS

The Board of Directors of the Corporation is its policy making body and subject to the direction of the Commissioner, it is respon-sible for the overall policy and general management of the Corporation. The Board is made up of about eleven members, including the chair-man of the board, the Permanenrt Secretaries of the Federal Ministries of Finance, Economic Development and Trade, a maximum of 6 persons "who by their character and experience in matters relating to accountancy, law, finance, insurance or economics, who in the opinion of the commissioner, are suitable for appointment as members of the board" and the Managing Director of the Corporation who is also the chief executive of the Corporation.

SHARE CAPITAL OF THE CORPORATION

The authorised share capital of the Nigeria Reinsurance Corpora-tion is ₦10,000,000 divided into 10,000 shares of ₦1,000 each and this may be increased from time to time by the commissioner with the approval of the Federal Executive Council.

RECOVERY OF UNPAID PREMIUM FROM REGISTERED INSURERS

The procedure to facilitate the efficient and prompt recovery of premiums from registered insurers has been set up by the Decree under Section 9. This section provides that in any action brought against an insurer by the Corporation for non-payment of premiums due to the Corporation, the production by the Corporation of a certificate signed by the Director of Insurance, setting out the name of the defendant and the amount of premium due shall be sufficient evidence of the amount so due, and sufficient authority for the court to give judgement for the said amount.

DUTY OF ALL REGISTERED INSURERS TO FURNISH INFORMATION TO THE NIGERIA REINSURANCE CORPORATION

The Decree makes it mandatory upon all registered insurers to

produce to any person authorised by the Managing Director of the
Corporation, upon the production by that person of a duly authenticated document showing his authority, such books of accounts,
records, documents and to supply copies and extracts from such
books, records, documents, and to furnish such other information
as may reasonably be required for the purposes of enforcement of
the provisions of the Decree.

The Decree makes it a criminal offence punishable with a fine of
₦500 or a term of twelve months imprisonment or both if any person
gives false information for purposes of the Decree.

In addition to its role as a national as well as an international reinsurer, the Nigeria Reinsurance Corporation is also expected
like other leading reinsurers and by virtue of its leadership position
in the Nigerian insurance industry to give positive leadership in
improving the quality of insurance and reinsurance service in the
country. It is expected, for example, as indicated in the decree, to run
courses and training programmes, not only for its own staff, but also
for the staff of all its ceding companies. Since it is directly affected
by the claims and other business experience of all other insurance
companies in the market, it must take steps to ensure a high standard
of insurance underwriting and service generally in the market. The
full text of the Nigeria Reinsurance Decree 1977 has been reproduced
in this volume as appendix III.

By conceiving and promulgating the Insurance Decree 1976 and the
Nigeria Reinsurance Decree 1977, the Federal Government of Nigeria
has laid a solid foundation for a strong and healthy insurance market
not only in Nigeria but for the whole of Africa especially in view of
the active involvement of the Nigerian insurance market in both
the activities of the African Reinsurance Corporation with its headquarters in Nigeria, and the African Insurance Organisation. It is
now for all the practitioners of insurance, the control authorities
and the insuring community to ensure the successful implementation
of the provisions of these decrees to the benefit of all concerned.

CHAPTER XV

MISCELLANEOUS MATTERS

UNIINSURABLE RISKS
WAR RISKS AND DAMAGES
ARBITRATION
AGENCY (in relation to insurance transactions)
NATIONAL INSURANCE
DEVELOPMENT IN AGRICULTURAL AND HEALTH INSURANCE
AGRICULTURAL INSURANCE HEALTH INSURANCE
PRINCIPLES OF LIABILITY IN TORTS–Negligence and Nuisance
THE NEED FOR INSURANCE-PROTECTION

UNINSURABLE RISKS:

In chapter 1 of this book, we stated that the insurance industry has grown so much in recent years that practically every known risk or contingency can be insured against, and we mentioned in particular the risks of twin-birth and even the possibility of a breach of promise. Although insurance is growing daily and insurers are prepared to cover most known contingencies, there are however certain classes of risks or contingencies which are regarded by the insurance industry as uninsurable. It is not possible to draw a comprehensive list of such risks or contingencies. But the deciding factor is usually the financial capacity of either the individual insurer or of the insurance industry. A newly incorporated insurance company is usually very selective in the classes of risks it accepts for insurance but as its financial position gets stronger it extends the scope of its activities and tries on new risks. Similarly as the industry grows and gets more sophisticated so does the list of insurable risks or perils grow.

WAR RISKS AND DAMAGES:

Policies covering property on land (as opposed to property on the high seas) do not generally grant cover in respect of war damage. Various types of endorsements are used by the insurance industry to exclude the risk of war damage. Insurers regard war damage as entirely beyond their financial capacity. The risks of destruction of property in modern warfare are so great and far beyond the collective financial resources of the whole industry. Therefore it would be financially suicidal for insurers to insure against such risks. Imagine for one moment what would have been the fate of the insurance Companies in Nigeria if they had insured most of the property damaged during the last civil war against the risks of war damage. They would have been crippled financially as the property damaged far exceeded the total resources of all the insurance Companies in Nigeria. War risks insurances are better handled by Governments whose resources are usually much stronger. Marine insurers are prepared to grant cover in respect of war risks or war damage to both hull and cargo on payment of a small extra premium as such risks are considered to be within their resources.

In life assurance, death arising from war or war-like operations is covered unless the policy specifically states that it is not covered. Thus where the policy is silent on this, death from any cause is covered and the insurers must pay. In recent years however, most life policies issued by the leading insurers in Nigeria embody an endorsement which reads as follows:

"In the event of death of the life assured resulting, directly or indirectly, from war, whether declared or undeclared, from warlike action, civil war, insurrection, riot, civil commotion or other acts of violence originating from any political or civil unrest, the company's liability under this policy shall be limited to the amount of the surrender value of this policy at the time of death, less any indebtedness under it."

Where a policy is subject to this endorsement, the maximum liability of the insurer in the event of death arising from war or warlike operations etc. is the surrender value of the policy at the material time.

ARBITRATION

Arbitration is the settlement of a dispute by the decision of one or more persons called arbitrators. The decision of an arbitrator is called an award, and it can be enforced by legal process in the same way as the judgment of a law court.

Parties to a contract, especially commercial contracts, may agree that all disputes arising under the contract would be settled by arbitration rather than by the normal method of litigation in the law Courts. A contract subject to an arbitration clause is known as an arbitration agreement. The law on the subject of Arbitration is governed by the Arbitration Act (formerly Ordinance) Cap 13, Laws of Nigeria 1958 Volume 1 at p. 98. Section 3 of this Act provides that a submission shall be irrevocable and would have effect as an order of Court. Therefore, once a party has contracted to settle all disputes by this means, it remains binding on him for the duration of the contract and he cannot revoke it by a unilateral act.

Almost all insurance policies effected in Nigeria are subject to an arbitration clause. Reproduced below is a typical arbitration clause as contained in a Nigerian-Motor policy:

"All differences arising out of this policy shall be referred to the decision of an Arbitrator to be appointed in writing by the parties in difference or if they cannot agree upon a single Arbitrator to the decision of two Arbitrators one to be appointed in writing by each of the parties within one calendar month after having been required in writing so to do by either of the parties or in case the Arbitrators do not agree of an Umpire appointed by the Arbitrators before entering upon the reference. The Umpire shall sit with the Arbitrators and preside at their meetings and the making of an Award shall be a condition precedent to any right of action against the Company. If the Company shall disclaim liability to the insured for any claim hereunder and such claim shall not within twelve calendar months from the date of such disclaimer have been referred to arbitration under the provisions herein contained then the claim shall for all purposes be deemed to have been abandoned and shall not thereafter be recoverable hereunder".

Application for Stay of Proceedings: If one of the parties to an arbitration agreement institutes legal proceedings in contravention of the submission, the other party to the agreement may apply to the Court by motion under Section 5 of the Arbitration Act for a stay of proceedings. Thus, if a dispute arises under an insurance policy subject to an arbitration clause similar to the one above, and the insured refuses to comply with the clause and proceeds straight to Court, the insurer may apply to the court for a stay of proceedings whilst the matter is referred to arbitration in accordance with the terms of the policy. Section 5 of the Arbitration Act reads as follows:-

"If any part to a submission, or any person claiming through or under him, commences any legal proceedings in any court against

any other party to the submission or any other person claiming
through or under him, in respect of any matter agreed to be referred,
any party to such legal proceedings may at any time after appea-
rance, and before delivering any pleadings or taking any other
steps in the proceedings, apply to that court to stay the proceedings,
and that court if satisfied that there is no sufficient reason why
the matter should not be referred in accordance with the submission,
and that the applicant was, at the time when the proceedings were
commenced, and still remains, ready and willing to do all things
necessary to the proper conduct of the arbitration, may make an
order staying the proceedings".

Discretion of Court to stay proceedings: The power to stay
proceedings under Section 5 of the Act is at the discretion of the
Court, but the application will be granted in all proper cases, especially where arbitration is made a condition precedent as in the clause
recited above. The applicant for a stay must satisfy the Court that
he is ready and willing to refer the matter to arbitration and that
he would do everything possible to facilitate the arbitration. Having
done so, the burden then shifts to the plaintiff in the action (the
respondent in the application) to show cause why he should not
comply with his agreement to refer disputes to arbitration.

Powers of Arbitrators and Method of Appointment: The
rules relating to the powers and method of appointment of Arbitrators and Umpires, and the procedure and control of proceedings
are contained in the Arbitration Act and its schedule. These rules
operate in the absence of a contrary intention expressed in the submission. Parties may therefore expressly vary the provisions of the
Act, for example, by naming the person or persons who may be
appointed arbitrators, their method of appointment, and their
powers. Where the parties lay down their own arbitration condition,
this must be complied with by each party to the contract.

Advantages of Arbitration: Advocates of arbitration as a
means of settling disputes claim that it has the following advantages,
firstly, the proceedings are faster than a hearing in Court; secondly,
it is conducted in private and therefore avoids the adverse publicity
that might result from a public hearing; and, thirdly, it is inexpen-
sive.

AGENCY

In insurance terminology, an agent is someone who introduces business to the insurer on commission, whereas in ordinary language, an agent is understood to mean anyone employed to do some act for another. The person on whose behalf the agent is acting is known as his principal.

In the strict legal sense, an agent is a person employed to bring his principal into contractual or legal relations with third parties. Once the agent has brought his principal and the third party into contractual relations, he drops out. In the leading English case of TOWLE & COMPANY v. WHITE (1873) 29 L.T. 78, an agent was defined as "a person invested with a legal power to alter his principal's legal relations with third parties"

Formation and Termination of Agency:

An agency may arise either by express appointment, or by implication. Express appointment is where the agent is specifically appointed as such by some deliberate act on the part of the principal. An agent expressly appointed may be appointed orally, that is by word of mouth, or in writing. The appointment may be by deed, in which case it is written, signed, sealed and delivered. This is the method adopted when the agent is invested with a power of attorney. As a general rule, insurance agents in Nigeria are appointed in writing, but not usually under seal. The letter of appointment states, in clear language, the terms of appointment, the different classes of insurance transacted, and the rates of commission applicable. (Any prospective policyholder in doubt as regards the scope of the insurance agent's authority, should inspect the agent's letter of appointment. This should indicate the extent to which the agent's acts are binding on his principal, the insurer). Any person who has contractual capacity may appoint an agent to act for him, and provided the agent acts within the scope of his authority (that is, acts within the specific powers given to him), his acts bind his principal. If the agent acts beyond the terms of his appointment, the principal is not bound by his acts. Thus in J. A. O. ODUFANADE v. A. ROSSEK (1960) F.S.C. 358, the Nigerian Federal Supreme Court held that the agent was not entitled to be paid commission by the principal as *the act in respect* of *which commission* was being claimed was outside the terms of appointment.

Agency Arising by Implication: In this case, there is no express appointment, but the law holds that agency has arisen by virtue of either the conduct of the parties or because of the peculiar circumstances. Agency by implication arises in two ways—(a) By necessity, or (b) by the operation of the principle of estoppel. Agency by necessity originated in marine insurance when the master of a ship is compelled as of necessity to discard or throw away goods entrusted to him so as to save the voyage or other more valuable goods. In such circumstances, the law regards the master of the ship as an agent of necessity. Similarly, a wife deserted and unprovided for by her husband, may become an agent of necessity and the husband becomes liable, as principal for her necessaries.

By Estoppel: A principal who has represented or behaved to a third party in such a way as to suggest to that party that the purported agent is clothed with the principal's authority, is estoppel from denying such previous representation, if the third party had altered his legal position relying on such representation. For example, if Mr. X had been in the habit of sending his clerk A to buy goods on credit from Kingsway Stores and on each occasion, he, Mr. X settled the bills, a state of agency is implied, and Mr. X in subsequent proceedings will be estopped from denying that the clerk A is his agent. This was the principle on which the English case of MURFITT v. ROYAL INSURANCE COMPANY LIMITED, (1922) 38 T.L.R. was decided. In this case, the plaintiff had approached an insurance agent for fire cover in respect of his orchard. The agent agreed to cover the risk pending the insurer's decision after reading through the proposal papers. A fire occurred during this period of "temporary cover", and the insurers declined the risk after seeing the proposal form, but before they had any knowledge of the fire. The plaintiff sued and the insurers pleaded that the agent had no authority to give cover. The plaintiff called evidence to show that the agent had in the past given him such "temporary cover" and that on each such occasion the insurers subsequently ratified the insurance cover given by the agent. The Court held that the insurers were liable as the agent had implied authority. By ratifying such previous acts, they had, in effect, represented to third parties that they would ratify the agent's acts in excess of his authority, and they were thus estopped from declining the cover.

Scope of the Agent's Authority: From the foregoing it is clear that the principal is bound by the acts of the agent if the agent acts within the scope of his authority. Where the appointment is in writing and *the terms and the scope of the agent's authority* are expressly noted in the written document, there is no difficulty, and all that is necessary is to ascertain the scope of the agent's authority by looking at the written document. If the agent acts in excess of his authority, the principal is not liable—J. A. O. Odufanade v. A. Rossek (1960) F.S.C. 358, supra. Therefore where an insurance agent employed merely to introduce business on commission, proceeds to issue cover and admit claims, the principal (the insurer) is not bound by the acts of the agent as he has acted beyond the scope of his authority. The agent is personally liable to the aggrieved third party for breach of warranty of authority. (The decision would be different if the insurers, in our example, had been in the habit of ratifying such acts of the agent—MURFITT v. ROYAL INSURANCE COMPANY LIMITED) supra). In such a situation, an implied authority will be presumed.

Ratification: This is the act of adopting, (by the principal) or giving approval to the unauthorised act of an agent.

Insurance Agent Completing Proposal Form: For purposes of obtaining insurance business, the insurance agent, as opposed to the broker, is an agent of the insurer on whose behalf he is acting. The insurer relies on the information supplied in the proposal form in order to assess the risk proposed for insurance. It is the duty of the proposer to complete the proposal form. If the proposer employs the insurance agent to complete the form for him, which the proposer adopts by signing it, it is submitted that the agent in completing the proposal form, is the agent of the proposer, and the proposer will be responsible for any untrue statements contained in the proposal form even if he did not read through the form to check the answers supplied by the agent. There is no Nigerian authority for this proposition, but this was the principle on which the English case of BIGGAR v. ROCK LIFE INSURANCE COMPANY (1902) 1 K.B. 516, was decided.

Termination of an Agency: An agency may end either by revocation or by termination. Subject to a few exceptions, (for example, where there is agency coupled with an interest, or where a power of attorney is stated to be irrevocable) a principal may, at any time, revoke the authority he has conferred on the agent, and when he revokes, the agency comes to an end. Thus, when an insurance company feels that it is no longer in its best interest to retain an agent, it may revoke the agent's appointment by notifying the agent together with all persons who have dealings with the agent. This question of notice to persons who have dealings with the agent is of great importance, because in the absence of such notice, the insurer may be held liable for the acts of the agent even after he has ceased to be his agent. Revocation is the commonest method of terminating insurance agencies; but an agency may terminate as a result of death, insanity, or bankruptcy (or dissolution) of one of the parties. It may also come to an end by agreement between the agent and the principal. Just as the principal may terminate the agency by revocation, the agent may terminate the agency by renunciation if he finds it no longer in his interest to continue to act as agent to the particular principal.

NATIONAL INSURANCE

Insurance as an economic institution, is divided into two parts: (1) Commercial or private insurance, which is a contract voluntarily entered into by the parties, and (2) National or social insurance, which is a devise by the State in fulfilment of its obligations to cater for the welfare of those of its citizens who may suffer serious economic distress arising from social misfortunes beyond their control, such as sickness, unemployment, or old age.

In terms of development, commercial insurance was first in time. It was only at the beginning of this century that the insurance idea was borrowed by the modern welfare states in order to devise a system to insure or protect the state against the effects of those more common misfortunes that may fall upon the citizens of the State concerned. Germany under Bismack was the first country to introduce a system of social insurance, followed by Great Britain, the Scandinavian countries, the American States, and other countries.

Distinction between National Insurance and Private Insurance:

Whereas commercial or private insurance is effected by a person in order to cover himself, or in the case of life assurance, his dependants, against accidental misfortunes, such as a motor accident, fire or death, National or Social Insurance is organised, sponsored and administered by the State in order to insure or protect itself against certain economic hazards such as sickness, unemployment and such other misfortunes which could befall its citizens. Commercial Insurance is administered by private insurers, but National insurance is administered by the State through a government department. For example, the British Social insurance scheme is administered by the Ministry of Pensions and National Insurance, and in Nigeria, our comparatively limited social insurance scheme under the National Provident Fund Act, 1961, is administered by the Federal Ministry of Labour.

Contributions and Benefits: Contribution rates and benefits payable in the event of a claim are all standardised and are stated in the relevant statute setting up the scheme, and no actuarial principles are applied in fixing the 'premium' rates. No policies of insurance are issued, and the scheme is compulsory for all those who fall within the provisions of the Act establishing the Social insurance scheme.

Scope of the Scheme: A comprehensive Social insurance Scheme, subject to the contribution terms in the relevant statute being complied with, covers the Insured person and provides benefits in respect of unemployment, sickness, industrial injuries, death, old-age or retirement pensions, and maternity allowance for working women. In each case, when the disability arises payments are made to the insured person in accordance with the provisions of the Act.

The Fund: The fund from which the Scheme is maintained is raised from the contributions of the insured persons and their employers, and this may occasionally be subsidised by the State as the need arises.

National Provident Fund Act, 1961: Social insurance was first introduced into Nigeria in 1961 under the provisions of the National

Provident Fund Act of that year. This was a fairly modest effort, but certainly a good beginning, although the scheme has been rather severely criticised in recent years. It is hoped that with time, Nigeria will device a fairly comprehensive and efficiently run social insurance scheme. The National Provident fund scheme as it stands now is rather restricted in its scope. It is, at best, a compulsory saving scheme by the class of worker covered, against unemployment and old age, the only difference being that the worker's savings are augmented by the contributions of his employer.

DEVELOPMENT OF AGRICULTURAL AND HEALTH INSURANCE IN NIGERIA

As far as the handling of risks is concerned, insurance is easily the most useful creation of the human mind. Its principles have been extended and adapted to protect victims of different kinds of hazards associated with modern living conditions, including agricultural and health risks.

Although agricultural and health insurance risks have been fully covered for many years on a fairly large scale in the insurance markets of most developed countries, these classes of insurance, because of their peculiar and sophisticated nature have been slow in developing in the Nigerian insurance market. In view of their social and economic importance, we will discuss the basic scope of these classes of insurance indicating the extent of their availability in the Nigerian market today.

Agricultural Insurance: Agriculture is easily the most important sector of any economy and until the arrival of the oil boom days, Nigeria was essentially an agricultural nation and we depended mainly on our agricultural products for survival. Because of the agricultural sector it follows that agricultural insurance should be a vital class of insurance necessary to support this important economic sector. Unfortunately, despite its importance, agricultural insurance has been slow in developing in Nigeria.

Agricultural insurance is concerned with the insurance protection of farmers and investors in agriculture against risks of economic loss as a result of the operation of some of the risks associated with modern agriculture. Under a typical agricultural insurance programme, loss or damage to crops arising from such natural causes as floods, frost, hail and other severe or adverse weather conditions may be covered; while livestock mortality from certain animal diseases may also be insured against. Although agricultural insurance is practised in Europe and in a few African insurance markets such as Mauritius and Zimbabwe for example, insurers in Nigeria have been reluctant to embark on this type of insurance because of its hazardous and unpredictable nature. They have always maintained that this is a class of business that can best be handled as a special government scheme as is the case in some countries, with or without the involvement of traditional insurers.

Because of the importance which the Federal Government attaches to the development of agriculture, and in order to promote investments in agriculture, the Federal Government responded a few years ago by establishing the Nigerian Agricultural Insurance Company. The agricultural insurance scheme operated by this largely state-owned insurance company operates almost like a social service with the primary objective of promoting agricultural development in the country by indemnifying the insured farmers against specified agricultural losses. The company is wholly owned by the Federal Government which funds the company's insurance programme up to about 70%, with the remaining 30% contributions from some major financial institutions such as the Central Bank, the Nigeria Reinsurance Corporation and the National Insurance Corporation. We understand that the company would maintain a special reserve fund in the region of N200 million to meet the cost of indemnifying farmers for their insured losses.

At present, the number of farmers benefiting from the scheme is limited as insurance coverage is limited to maize, rice, poultry and livestock. It is expected that before long other widely cultivated crops such as cotton, cowpea, yam and cassava as well as certain species of livestock not yet covered would be added to the scheme.

Health Insurance: Undoubtedly, one of the most useful developments from the insurance concept in recent times has been its general application to the many and assorted needs of mankind especially during periods of personal difficulties and hardships.

In practically all African societies, it is generally accepted that a good health is the best that anyone can ask for and that is why we say that health is wealth, and every sensible person will spare no effort in ensuring that he or she remains in good health all the time. Unfortunately however, despite all the precautions that we may take, people still become victims of different types of accidents and diseases.

As in other types of insurance, health insurance does not guarantee that accidents or diseases will not occur. ˙ On the contrary, what the health insurance programme undertakes to do is to compensate the insured victim for any monetary or economic loss which may occur as a result of the accident or disease in accordance with the terms of the relevant health insurance contract or programme.

There are broadly two types of health insurance programmes, namely, the national health insurance programme run by the state, like a social insurance scheme under which citizens or certain categories of citizens contribute to a state-sponsored National Health Insurance Scheme and in return for these contributions the insured persons receive certain benefits specified under the scheme such as free medical advice and treatment, maternity cash benefits as well as weekly or monthly payments during periods of incapacity for work as a result of disability arising from sickness or accident. Some national health insurance programmes may include a number of other benefits including old age payments and unemployment benefits.

*See Daily Times of 24/3/89 Page 20, and Nigerian Tribune of 24/3/89 Page 4 for report on scope of Nigerian Agricultural Insurance Company (NAIC) Scheme.

At present, there is no state or national health insurance scheme in Nigeria but the subject has become very topical in recent years. The Federal Government has established a number of expert committees to examine the subject and to recommend an appropriate scheme for consideration by the government. From all indications, Nigeria may soon join those countries that have adapted the insurance concept and used it to fashion out a National Health Insurance Scheme. Since government cannot easily afford to maintain a free medical service programme for all Nigerians with its many other social and economic problems crying out for attention, we believe that a contributory national health insurance programme will be a useful device for achieving a better health-care delivery system for the country.

The other form of health insurance is the private contract or commercial type sold by insurance companies on a commercial basis to individuals and corporate bodies for their employees. Insurers in different markets generally offer different types of policies with a wide variety of benefits under different names. Some are called Permanent Health policies or Permanent Sickness policies while others are just extensions of the ordinary individual or group personal accident policies to cover losses and injuries arising from accidents or some specified diseases.

A typical health insurance contract of this nature would ay benefits to the insured on accidental death or injury as well as weekly benefits for temporary disablement due to sickness.

Subject to the insured being able to pay the appropriate premiums, schemes are available to cover the cost of hospital treatment and other medical expenses at home and sometimes abroad, but an overall cost limit may be placed on the number of claims that will be paid in one year.

As indicated above, Group Permanent Health Insurance policies are available to employers and a number of employers anxious to reduce their medical bills tend to take advantage of such group policies by arranging group schemes for their employees and the families of such employees.

Although a few insurance companies in Nigeria have been marketing individual and group health insurance schemes in the country for many years, this type of insurance is not yet sold on a large scale in the country for a number of reasons, the main one being that insurers are quite cautious and selective in their underwriting of such risks at present and in any event the demand is still quite limited.

PRINCIPLES OF LIABILITY IN TORTS

A tort is an actionable civil wrong which is not a breach of contract. An eminent English jurist defines it as: "An act which causes harm to a determinate person, whether intentionally or not, not being the breach of a duty arising out of a personal relation or contract, and which is either contrary to law, or an omission of a specific legal duty, or a violation of an absolute right". (Sir Frederick Pollock). Professor Salmond describes it as "A civil wrong for which the remedy is a common law action for unliquidated damages, and which is not exclusively the breach of a contract, or the breach of a trust or other merely equitable obligation".

It follows from these definitions that to constitute a tort, three factors must exist:

(a)   There must be some act or omission on the part of the tort-feasor (*i.e.* the person committing the wrongful act) which is not a breach of the terms of a contract or a trust.

(b)   The act or omission must not be authorised by law.

(c)   The act or omission must result in some damage to the plaintiff or the person injured.

The difference between a tort and a contract is that in a contract, the obligation is assumed by the defendant voluntarily whereas in a tort, the duty or obligation is fixed by law. In spite of this difference, there are occasions when a wrongful act could be both a breach of contract and a tort. In such a case, the aggrieved party (the plaintiff) has a choice of suing in either contract or in tort. For example, if Mr. Eke goes to his surgeon for a surgical operation to remove his appendix, and the doctor after the operation carelessly forgets to remove his scissors from poor Mr. Eke's stomach, and Mr. Eke suffers as a result of the doctor's carelessness. In this example, the doctor has committed both a breach of contract and the tort of negligence, and Mr. Eke may sue in either contract or in tort.

There are a number of torts, and it is believed that the number of torts will continue to increase as new torts are created. The following number amongst the more common torts in this country: negligence, nuisance, trespass, assault and battery, defamation—libel and slander, malicious prosecution, and false imprisonment. From an insurance point of view, the most important is the tort of negligence, followed by the tort of nuisance. We will restrict this brief survey to these two torts (the reader interested in a more detailed study is referred to any of the standard works on the Law of Torts).

Negligence: Negligence is the tort which arises as a result of the defendant's failure to take reasonable care. It was defined in the leading case of BLYTH v. BIRMINGHAM WATERWORKS COMPANY (1856) II Ex., at p. 784), as follows: "Negligence is the omission to do something which a reasonable man, guided upon those considerations which ordinarily regulate the conduct of human affairs, would do, or doing something which a prudent and reasonable man would not do". The law expects every one to take reasonable care to avoid those acts or omissions which one can reasonably foresee are likely to injure ones neighbour. For instance, the law expects a lorry driver driving through a busy street to concentrate on his driving as his failure to do so might lead to his losing control of the vehicle. If this happens, the driver's "neighbours" might get injured. The driver owes a duty of care to his neighbours, and neighbours in this context are all those "persons who are so closely and directly affected by my act that I ought reasonably to have them in contemplation as being so affected when I am directing my mind to the acts or omissions which are called in question" per Lord Atkin, in Donoghue v. Stevenson (1932) A.C., at p. 580.

To succeed in an action of negligence, the plaintiff must prove three things, first, he must prove that the defendant owes him a duty of care, secondly, he must prove that the defendant acted in breach of that duty to take care, and thirdly, that he suffered some damage as a result of that breach. What constitutes a duty of care is a question of law for the judge to decide and to prove that the defendant acted in breach of this duty of care, the plaintiff must produce evidence of the negligent act of the defendant's which constitutes the breach. This is purely a question of fact. Having proved (a) and (b) above, the plaintiff then has to prove this damage.

Res ipsa loquitur: (The thing speaks for itself). Where the doctrine of res ipsa loquitur applies, all that the plaintiff has to prove is the accident, and the burden of proof then shifts to the defendant who then has to explain (if he can) how the accident could have happened without some negligence on his part. The case usually cited in support of this doctrine is the case of BYRNE v. BOADLE (1863) 2 H.&C. 722. In this case a barrel of flour rolled out of an open doorway on the upper floor of the defendant's warehouse and fell upon the plaintiff, who was passing by along the street below. It was held by the Court that this was sufficient evidence of negligence as the plaintiff had, by merely proving the accident, produced enough facts which could lead to a reasonable inference that the defendant had been negligent. (The judgement of Mr. Justice Quashie-Idun (Ibadan High Court) in the case of D. S. OLAIYA v. J. F. OSOSAMI (1959) W.R.N.L.R. throws some light on this doctrine.

NUISANCE

There are two types of nuisance—private and public, and both have the same common element of unlawful annoyance except that public nuisance is essentially a crime, whilst private nuisance is a tort actionable at the instance of the aggrieved person. We will restrict our discussion to private nuisance which is a tort.

A private nuisance consists of any wrongful interference or annoyance which causes damage to an occupier or an owner of land in relation to his right to the enjoyment of the land. There are different kinds of wrongful interference that would constitute a nuisance. For instance, it is a nuisance to allow branches of trees to project over into adjoining land, or to allow annoying animals to enter into neighbouring land, or to allow water, smell, disease germs, noise, heat or smoke to escape into some other person's land. The person who plays his records until very late at night to the annoyance of his neighbours is committing the tort of nuisance.

Nuisance is actionable only at the instance of the party in possession of land (either as occupier or as owner) who must have suffered actual damage as a result of the nuisance. To constitute a nuisance, there must be the element of continuity, that is, the nuisance must have continued for some time. For example, if Mr. Umo decided to have a swinging and rather noisy party, which lasts until very late into the night, to the annoyance of his neighbour Mr. Edet. Mr. Edet can only succeed in an action for nuisance if this noisy party is continuous and not if it is only an isolated or an occasional event.

The Need for Insurance Protection: In modern times, claims based on the torts of negligence and nuisance have tended to attract very heavy court awards. It is therefore of the utmost importance for the average citizen to have himself adequately protected with insurance cover. In a recent English case, the defendant had left a railway carriage door open, and a Railway porter lost both legs when he stumbled and fell in trying to close the door. He sued the defendant for negligence and obtained judgment against the defendant for a total sum of £6,727. The defendant was not insured, and the Court ordered that he should pay £2 every week to the porter for the rest of his life until the judgement debt is cleared. There are very many circumstances in which the ordinary Nigerian citizen could incur a huge financial liability running into thousands of pounds, as a result of a negligent act. For instance, if Mr. "A" carelessly strikes a match to light his cigarette at the petrol station, this single act could result in a fire damage to other peoples property to the extent of several hundreds of pounds. Similarly, if Mr. B allows some poisonous gas to escape from his premises to adjoining land and the neighbours suffer damage as a result of the escaping gas, Mr. B would be liable in an action of nuisance. In either case, if the injured party sues, he might get judgement for any amount. (There is no limit to the amount a Court can award in such a case). If the defendant or the tortfeasor is uninsured, he might be crippled financially for the rest of his life. Almost all insurers in this country issue a variety of policies to cover the insured against his legal liability to members of the public arising from any of these torts. The commonest of these are, the public liability, professional indemnity, and the workmen's Compensation and Employer's liability policies.

The recent case at the Lagos High Court (Suit No. LD/459/69 Ope-Olu Banjo v. L.C.C.) in which the Lagos High Court awarded damages of ₦50,000 to a Lagos Lawyer for loss of one arm confirms that the Nigerians Courts will award quite substantial damages in appropriate cases, and the citizen should always obtain insurance cover to protect himself against having to bear the full effect of such heavy awards.

CHAPTER XVI

THE FUTURE OF INSURANCE AND THE INSURANCE INDUSTRY IN NIGERIA

A realistic forecast of the future, in any situation must be based to some extent on the experience of the past and existing trends. Therefore in forecasting the future of insurance in Nigeria, one must be guided by the experience of the industry in the recent past and by the present day trends. Guided by these considerations, one must then answer the question - what does the future hold in store for insurance and the insurance industry in Nigeria?

The principal function of insurance is to give protection against economic losses and to indemnify or compensate the policyholder in the event of a loss. In the case of a businessman or an industrialist the existence of the facilities offered by a modern insurance industry makes it possible for the businessman or industrialist to take business risks and to make investments in commerce and industry which he would not normally have made in the absence of an organised insurance service. This is why insurance is said to be the "handmaiden of commerce and industry" and this is also why one eminent Nigerian once described insurance as the business that exists to ensure the existence and survival of other businesses. The insurance industry of any country is closely tied up to the economy of that country. As the economy of that country grows, so does its insurance industry. A primitive society has no need for a modern insurance service - the extended family system takes care of all such needs, but as the society marches into the technological age, so does its insurance industry grow.

During the years between 1960-1975, Nigeria has made tremendous progress socially and economically. The growth in our national economy, has resulted in the expansion of the insurance industry in Nigeria both in terms of volume of business handled and in the quality and scope of insurance service available in the market. In 1960 for example, we had only about 20 Insurance companies operating in the country. These were mostly foreign and the gross national premium income was less than three million pounds sterling and only a few classes of insurance were transacted in the local market. By

1970, the number of companies had increased to well over 40 and the premium income had increased by well over 500%. Furthermore the classes of insurance available in the market had increased considerably. There was also a marked improvement in the quality of insurance service available in the Nigerian market. The period between 1971 and 1976 witnessed an even greater improvement in the overall performance of the Nigerian insurance industry. The gross national premium income of the whole market in 1974 had risen to about ₦50 million but by 1976 it had gone up to about ₦200 million. Almost every class of insurance business is available in the Nigerian market of today. This remarkable growth in the gross national premium income of the insurance companies in Nigeria also reflect the trends in our national economy. A booming economy produces a boom in the growth of the industry,

It would naturally be expected that an economic depression would have the opposite effect. But despite the economic slide of the years between 1979 and 1987, the insurance industry still managed to thrive, and in 1987, the annual premium of the Nigerian market was approximately ₦650 million. In the light of the present growth rate of 20% per annum, the insurance industry in Nigeria would still appear to have a great future, and it is estimated that by 1995 the annual gross premium of the market will have risen to more than ₦1 billion.

These general remarks about the development of insurance over the years and the anticipated growth in the years to come, also apply to individual branches of insurance. Life insurance for example, is still virtually untapped in the country. Only a very small population of the country have life policies. In a country with a population of well over 100 million, only 250 life policies were in force in 1971. By 1976, it is estimated that the number of life policies in force in Nigeria had doubled to about 500,000

For a population of over 100 million, the volume of Life business in Nigeria is about the lowest in Africa when related to the population. At present, it accounts for over 25% of the market premium, with about one million life policies in force. Although this growth rate is remarkable, the volume of Life business transacted in the country is still relatively low.

The Structural Adjustment Programme introduced in the country in 1986 as a means of restructuring the economy and making it more self-reliant, resulted in a substantial devaluation of the national currency in relation to other currencies. This, in turn, led to a considerable fall in the disposable income available to the Nigerian insurance consumer. The overall effect of all these is that Life insurance companies in the country are finding it increasingly difficult to sell more Life policies, whilst some existing policy holders are surrendering their policies.

Another development that is causing some alarm in the insurance industry is the serious in-roads which the banks appear to be making in the pension business. A pension scheme may be insured or not insured at the discretion of the parties concerned. The traditional view of the insurance industry worldwide is that it is wiser and more efficient to have pension schemes insured. Unfortunately, the position in Nigeria today is that if they are insured, the benefits, when paid, are taxed. As a result, insurers in Nigeria are complaining that the banks have exploited this position to their advantage by campaigning vigorously for the management of pension funds set up by other organisations, and so far, the banks have succeeded in winning over a number of pension schemes set up by their clients.

This development is seen by Life insurers in the country as a major threat to the development of group life insurance and pensions business. To this end, it has been suggested that insurers should make appropriate representations to the tax authorities to remove any form of discriminatory tax on the insured pension benefits so as to place them on equal footing with the banks as far as this development is concerned.

Whatever the outcome, the ultimate responsibility for popularising their products, in this case the insurance policies, rests on the insurers. Therefore, if they want to check the in-roads being made in their territory by the banks they must devise more attractive benefits and incentives to the ultimate consumer who has to make the decision as to what cover to buy.

Despite the adverse effects of inflation on the development of life assurance, the indications are that the growth of life assurance protection in Nigeria has very good prospects. There are still millions of Nigerians without life assurance cover. With better designed life policies, tailored to Nigerian conditions and with better marketing techniques, life assurance will continue to develop in Nigeria. Furthermore, with continued improvements in living conditions and an increased supply of money, more people will take advantage of life assurance as a means of providing for their dependants in the event of their premature death and also as a means of saving for old age and unforeseen contigencies.

Marine Insurance: Traditionally, Marine insurance is regarded as the oldest branch of insurance, but it is comparatively new to Nigeria, having been introduced into the country by the early European traders at the beginning of this century to support their international trade. In each country, the volume of marine insurance business depends on the volume of that country's international trade.

The volume of marine insurance business in the country has increased substantially as a result of the compulsory insurance of imports into the country as stipulated by the 1976 decree.

From 1978 many companies established marine departments. Nigeria has become one of the fastest growing marine markets in the world. Gross premium for Marine and Aviation business rose from ₦53 million in 1977 to ₦82 million in 1978. It dropped to ₦65 million in 1979 because of government economic policies aimed at regulating certain imports. However, it pushed up again, and in 1980, the figure stood at ₦85 million, and rose again to ₦117 million in 1982. With the introduction of the Structural Adjustment Programme (SAP) in July 1986, the premium income increased significantly in 1987 to ₦273.6 million.

However, with the increase in the volume of marine insurance, came a high incidence of claims; some of them for extremely vast sums of money. Nigeria became a high-risk area for marine cargo insurance. A loss ratio of 33.6% was recorded for Marine and Aviation business in the in 1979, 21% in 1982, 18.8% in 1983 and 20.7% in 1985. The government attempted to correct this trend by opening more ports. The insurers deployed survey teams to counter pilferage as well as adopting the Nigerian classified clause to monitor the age of ships coming into ports.

By the beginning of 1980, the government started adopting austerity measures to deal with the growing economic crisis in the market. One of these measures was a sharp cut-back on imports. Gross premium for marine insurance fell as the total imports into the country fell by 11% in 1984 (₦8.6 million) and by 30% in 1985. Both the Structural Adjustment Programme (SAP) and its corollary, the Second-Tier Foreign Exchange Market (SFEM) in 1986 was a further attempt to re-structure the seriously ailing economy plagued by the effects of global economic recession. It led to a drastic cut in imports with the resultant decline in insurance.

Fire Insurance: Another class of insurance business which has witnessed very substantial growth in recent years in Nigeria is Fire insurance. The indications are that this growth will continue although it has been suggested in some circles that the future tendency might be for large industrial concerns with modern fire fighting equipments and other fire loss prevention facilities to do away with fire insurance and adopt self insurance measures. This is most unlikely especially in view of our recent fire experience. The fear of major fire disasters such as the one that occurred at Mobil Oil Tank at Apapa in 1981 which cost more than ₦10 million and a number of other major losses will deter large companies from contemplating doing away with fire insurance. Another major disaster that occurred was at Aswani Textile Industry in 1982 which was followed in 1983 by the major fire loss involving the Nigerian External Telecommunications' (NET) building which cost insurers about ₦30 million.

In the face of these occasional major fire disasters, no company would take the risk of not being insured. The best course of action open to any reasonable manager of a large company with good fire hazard features should be to negotiate for better premium rates.

From all accounts it will be reasonable to conclude that Fire insurance has a great future in Nigeria and that the demand for Fire insurance would continue to increase in the foreseeable future. Despite the prevailing economic situation and the fact that industrial activity has been slowed down as a result of the prevailing poor economic situation, Fire insurance premiums have been increasing over the years. For example, in 1975 this class of business attracted a gross annual premium of ₦21 million, increasing to ₦55 in 1979 and ₦70.7 million and ₦88.7 million in 1981 and 1982 respectively.

Although Fire insurance premiums are increasing yearly, the loss experience is also increasing in the sense that there are more fire claims today than was the case in the past. In the past, Nigerian Fire insurance business used to be amongst the most profitable in the world for insurers but with increased industrialisation the picture is changing. For example, in 1983 the industry recorded a gross Fire premium of ₦98.3 million but suffered a loss ratio of 38% as against 20.9% recorded in the previous year. The indications are that whereas Fire insurance premiums would continue to increase, the loss ratio would also unfortunately increase. The insurance industry seem to be aware of this development and are therefore pioneering efforts aimed at promoting fire prevention and general loss prevention measures. The Nigerian Fire Protection Association as well as the Faculty of Risk Management are all committed to the prevention of fire and other losses and the promotion of risk management principles with a view to reducing national waste, and both organisations as well as other loss prevention measures are supported by the insurance industry.

Fire insurance should be made compulsory

It has been suggested in some circles that in view of the disastrous consequences of fire losses to the Nigerian community, the government should intervene and make it compulsory for every property especially in the big cities to be insured against fire. It is argued that the philosophy which led to the introduction of compulsory motor insurance is relevant to some extent in respect of fire insurance, especiall where a fire started negligently in one property spreads to cause damage to adjoining property of innocent victims and in some cases, inflicting death or bodily injuries to such parties. If this idea is accepted and government makes fire insurance compulsory, this should lead to further increase in the volume of fire business handled by insurance companies in the country.

Other related problems that should engage the attention of fire insurance managers in the years ahead include the problem of accumulation of risks arising from the increasing growth of factories, large warehouses and office blocks located in the same area and the problem of explosions arising from the large electrical installations, gas works and chemical and petroleum industries now being established all over the country. Whilst it is certain that fire insurance will grow substantially in the years ahead, fire insurance managers have serious problems to cope with as indicated above and more large fire losses will be experienced. To be able to bear and absorb these losses, rates must be reasonable, but above all, fire insurers must encourage fire prevention programmes. In appropriate cases, premium discounts should be allowed where the insured has taken reasonable steps to reduce the fire hazard to his projects or premises.

Motor vehicle insurance has been steadily showing a decline since 1979 when it accounted for 29% of the gross premium income of the Nigerian insurance market (as opposed to 40.2% in 1976). In 1985 the premium fell to an all time low of 21%. Many factors account for this, but the primary cause is the cutback in the importation of vehicles into the country and the reduction in domestic production of vehicles. Further, there was a withdrawal of car loans and allowances to workers in 1978-79. Even though this was restored in 1983, the decline continued. The introduction of the Structural Adjustment Programme (SAP) in 1986 led to the devaluation of the Naira, and placed motor vehicles completely out of the budget of most Nigerians.

The effect of this increase in the price of motor vehicles has led to a corresponding increase in the cost of premiums, consequently, there has been a sharp reduction in the number of vehicle insurance policies, with many insured being unable to pay the high premiums needed for comprehensive insurance and resorting to lesser covers, like Third Party and Theft covers.

Two incidental effects of this rise in the value of motor vehicles are firstly, the drastic increase in the rate of motor thefts, and secondly the prohibitive repair costs of most vehicles. Both of these trends will naturally adversely affect the motor vehicle insurance business. It is therefore understandable that the loss ratio of the motor business has risen from 62.8% in 1979 to 79.3% in 1985. It is hoped that when the economy picks up, matters will improve.

Another class of accident insurance business which has a good future in Nigeria is public and emplyers' liability insurance. As the citizens of Nigeria become more and more sophisticated and therefore more conscious of their legal rights, so will the demand for liability insurances increase. The substantial damages awarded by the courts in the few liability cases that have been litigated to judgement have already compelled many potential defendants to take out various types of liability insurance policies to protect themselves against these risks. In the light of recent experience, the indications are that the demand for liability insurances, such as those offered by the products liability policy, the public liability and the personal liability policies and the employers' liability and workmen's compensation policies will increase substantially.

Employer's Liability: Since the government passed the Workmen's Compensation Decree in 1987, there has been a substantial increase in the volume of this class of business. This decree makes it compulsory for every employer to insure against his legal liabilities for industrial or other injury to his employees.

Professional indemnity insurance is another section of accident insurance business which has a great future. As more claims are made on professionals for their professional negligence or breaches of duty, so will the need for professional indemnity increase. In some professions, it is in fact a pre-requisite for the issue of a professional licence or registration that the applicant effects a professional indemnity insurance. For example, section 28 of the Nigerian Insurance decree 1976 makes it compulsory for a broker to take out a professional indemnity policy before he can obtain a licence to practise as such. Other professions make similar demands. This professional requirement has helped to popularise professional indemnity insurance.

Until quite recently, it was most unusual for Nigerians to take out personal liability insurance cover in spite of the fact that this type of cover which is most valuable to the ordinary citizen, can save him a lot of misery in the event of his incurring some tortious liability in his personal capacity. For example, a private citizen may incur personal liability as a result of the negligent handling of his bicycle or by some careless act of his resulting in the injury or death of a third party. These risks can be covered under a personal liability policy at a relatively small premium. For example, an annual premium of less than ₦20 will obtain cover up to a limit of indemnity of about ₦10,000 for anyone event. Personal accident insurance will also expand in the future. In the recent past, only very few leading professionals or persons employed by large commercial organisations effected this kind of cover. The situation is changing and different types of personal accident insurance for individuals and groups are now being sold in the Nigerian market. With increased air travel and industralisation, more of this type of policy will be sold.

With the various construction works taking place in the country, contractors-all-risks insurance and the various types of liability, bonds and surety business associated with projects of this nature have become quite popular. Demands for these classes of insurance will continue in the foreseeable future. In view of the adverse experience of insurers in other parts of the world in respect of bonds and surety business, Nigerian insurers should approach this class of business cautiously. The Nigeria Reinsurance Corporation should give the lead in ensuring that only companies with properly trained bond underwriters are allowed to underwrite these classes of risks and there should be uniformity in underwriting terms and conditions.

In addition to bonds and contract guarantees, other types of miscellaneous accident business that will grow include engineering, fidelity guarantees, householders and houseowners insurances.

Credit insurance, that is insurance against bad debts, also has a good future. In fact, the need for credit insurance already exists and it now remains for insurers in Nigeria to devise ways of making the business of credit insurance worthwhile from both the insured and the insurers points of view. At present Nigerian insurers are reluctant to develop this class of business but with more efficient business management, more reliable records and statistics by the average Nigerian private businessman, insurers may be persuaded to consider introducing credit insurance on a substantial scale.

Another important class of insurance business which definitely will grow in the near future is aviation, that is, the insurance of aircrafts and the liability of aircrafts operators. This is a very highly specialised line of business and in view of the high value of aircrafts, most of the aviation insurance business of many African countries, including Nigeria, are transacted in the London and other major world insurance markets. In the case of Nigeria, only a small proportion of the country's aviation insurances had hitherto been retained in the Nigerian market. This practice will continue for some time.

In 1984 an Aviation Pool was formed to cater for the medium-sized and small aircrafts, excluding Nigerian Airways. The pool was formed mainly to reduce the out flow of aviation premiums from Nigeria. The pool has 17 foundation members and is managed by the National Insurance Corporation of Nigeria (NICON). So far the pool has been doing profitable business, starting with a gross premium income of ₦.64 million in 1984 and rising to ₦1.1 million in 1987 the loss ratio for each of the years of its existence has been under 4%.

The facts stated above clearly indicate that the insurance business has a great future in Nigeria. As stated earlier in this book, experience has shown that the more the economy of a country grows, so does its need for insurance protection increase. Indeed, it could be said that the very growth of the economy is encouraged to a considerable extent by the availability of insurance protection. Nigeria's economy has been growing steadily in the past few years and the insurance needs of the country is also growing daily. Existing forms of insurance are being developed and expanded and new types of cover to suit local conditions are being marketed as the demand for them arises. With improvements in the quality of the insurance service offered by the industry, and with improvements in the public image of the insurance industry, it is evident that the business of insurance in Nigeria will enjoy further exceptional growth.

The future of the insurance industry itself

Up to this point we have been discussing the future of the business of insurance, and the anticipated growth in the volume of business and the different forms of insurance cover. We will now direct our attention to a brief examination of the future of the industry itself and the future pattern of its development. The insurance industry in the world is predominantly divided into three types: (i) Those cases where the industry is a state monopoly, in which case, there is only one and in some cases, two or more state owned insurance companies, (ii) those cases where there is a mixture of private and state owned insurance companies with or without foreign partici- pation, and finally (iii) those where the insurance industry is wholly privately owned with limited control by the state.

At the early stage of insurance business in Nigeria, the market was entirely dominated by foreign owned insurance companies, and there was very little state intervention. The companies were free to transact the business as they saw fit and to invest their profits in accordance with their own interests. Shortly after independence, the first Insurance Act of 1961 was passed, regulating to some extent, the conduct of insurance business in the country. But the ownership and the control of the 20 or more insurance companies operating in the country then remained predominantly in foreign hands. By 1970 there were about 50 insurance companies operating in the market, partly foreign and partly indigenous with a few government owned insurance companies. The position today, as stated earlier, is that there are now 95 insurance companies in the market, some state owned, others privately owned, either foreign or indigenous. The Federal Government has also acquired substantial equity interests of about 49% of the shares in all the viable foreign owned insurance companies. There is now a national reinsurance company known as the Nigeria Reinsurance Corporation which has compulsory legal cessions in the form of 20% of each policy issued by every insurer in the market. The leading direct insurance company in the market is the National Insurance Corporation of Nigeria owned by the Federal Government. There are also other insurance companies owned by various state governments. The situation in the market is that these insurance companies participate freely and in open competition with one another. There is no nationalisation of the market as such. However, there is limited governmental intervention aimed at protecting the national economy, ensuring that the business is run on sound insurance principles, and above all, that the interests of the public generally are not exploited in any way by the insurance companies. The indications are that in keeping with the national policy, this trend will continue in the foreseeable future. The industry must however be prepared and equipped to face up to the challenges of the future and live up to its responsibilities.

In their own interest, insurers in Nigeria must take more positive steps to improve their collective public image. Steps must be taken not only to educate the public about the various types of insurance cover available in the market but the public must be educated on the value of insurance to both the individual and the nation.

With increased advancement in the fields of science and modern technology, the business of insurance will become more complex and sophisticated. The Nigerian insurance industry must be equipped to meet these challenges of the future. Insurance managers and other insurance practitioners must be better educated than their predecessors. The industry must intensify and modernise its training and educational programmes. It should sponsor the setting up of insurance chairs, fellowships and grants in Nigerian Universities to further promote researches in different branches of insurance. It should sponsor and promote the writing of books and articles on various branches of insurance and allied subjects. More graduates and highly educated persons should be recruited into the industry.

The insurance manager and the future

In the past, the insurance industry in Nigeria had been managed either on the basis of management by intuition or on a trial and error basis depending on the disposition of the particular manager. Scientific management principles were never considered let alone applied. The days of management by trial and error are gone. The insurance manager of the future must be prepared to apply modern management techniques in the running of his business. He must plan, organise, ,control and direct the affairs of his company in a scientific manner. He must ensure that his staff are adequately motivated and in keeping with the present policy of the Nigerian government, the welfare of his staff of all categories should be of special concern to him and his company.

The idea of management by objectives — the setting of objectives and targets, have been found to be most relevant in the management of a modern insurance company. The Nigerian insurance manager should examine these and other management principles and where appropriate, apply them in the running of his company. The Nigerian insurance manager of the future must have a broad outlook. He must not be sectional, tribalistic or be guilty of ethnicity in his approach to matters. In view of the fact that insurance is an international business, he must, whilst taking steps to protect his own national interests, adopt an international outlook. He must not be found wanting in his knowledge of world affairs. The manager must ensure that his company keeps abreast of international developments in all aspects of insurance and allied subjects.

Finally, the insurance manager of the future must always remember that the days are gone when his primary concern was to ensure that his company was run profitably. The manager now has much wider responsibilities to his company, his staff, his policyholders and the entire community or the nation. He must ensure that his company is run successfully in accordance with his company's policies and set objectives. In doing so, he must take into account and protect the interests of the shareholders, policyholders and employees of the company, and above all, the general interests of the community and the nation as a whole. The manager should encourage his company to apply its profits, not only for the benefit of the company's shareholders and policy holders, but also for the welfare of the staff and that of the community generally. For example, by way of donations to charities, the sponsoring of developments and other welfare programmes.

Records and statistics

It is also the responsibility of the industry to maintain records and statistics. Reliable records and statistics are most vital for the success of any insurance organisation. Unfortunately, however, the insurance industry in Nigeria in the past was not noted for its efficiency in keeping records and statistics of its operations. Whilst individual companies may have kept proper and accurate records of their operations, the industry as such has not been as successful in record keeping as it has been in other areas. No institutions can plan adequately without accurate records and statistics. The insurance industry in Nigeria in the years ahead will require more reliable figures and statistics. Every company should keep proper and reliable records of all its operations and a centralised system should be devised to keep records of the activities of the entire market. This is one more area in which the Nigeria Reinsurance Corporation, the Insurance Control department of the Federal Ministry of Trade, the department of statistics and the Universities could play an active part. With the increasing use of the computer and other modern accounting gadgets in the running of insurance companies in Nigeria, record keeping should be a lot easier.

One other subject which could influence the future development of the insurance industry in Nigeria, is the attitude of insurance companies to the settlement of claims. The commonest charges levelled against insurers in Nigeria is that they are quick enough in the collecting of premiums, but that when it comes to the settlement of claims, they often hesitate. Although this is generally exaggerated, there is usually some degree of truth in a few of these complaints. To justify their existence and to achieve further growth, insurers must adopt a proper and progressive attitude to the settlement of claims. The policyholder who has taken out an insurance policy has done so because he fears that the event insured against could happen and that this would result in his making a claim on his insurance company. Therefore the only time when an insured person really needs his insurance company is when he has a claim to make. The way he is received and the manner in which his claim is handled by his insurance company would determine his future attitude to both the company and the insurance industry as a whole. Insurers must therefore aim at giving maximum co-operation and satisfaction to all their clients in the handling of their claims. All genuine claims must be settled promptly and equitably in accordance with settled insurance principles. This point had been made earlier in this book, but because of its importance, we make no apologies for committing this repetition.

The code of conduct of the Insurance Institute of Nigeria

The Insurance Institute of Nigeria, which is the professional and educational body for Nigerian insurance professionals, has a Code of Conduct which came into force recently. This Code of Conduct enjoins members to be honest, efficient and fair in their dealings with policyholders and the public in general. Members are also required to obey the laws of the land in their business dealings and to observe at all times, the insurance principles of utmost good faith in its widest context. Insurers in Nigeria should ensure that all their employees adhere to the Institute's Code of Conduct. In fact, it is submitted that it is not only in the interest of the insurance industry but also in the national interest that all insurance practitioners should be made to subscribe to this Code of Conduct which should be rigidly enforced. Government and the industry's support should be sought to make it compulsory for all qualified persons and others fully employed in the business of insurance, holding positions of assistant superintendents and above to join the Insurance Institute of Nigeria and subscribe to this Code of Conduct. A disciplinary committee with recognised status and authority should be appointed to enforce the provisions of the Code. The full text of the Institute's Code of Conduct is attached to this volume as Appendix VIII.

In summary, it is reasonable to state that the indications are that the insurance industry in Nigeria has a great future. The business will grow and new forms of insurance will be introduced and existing ones will be tailored to meet Nigerian needs. The business of insurance will become more complex and require sophisticated management techniques and equipments. Because of this growth, the industry will require better trained technicians and skilled and disciplined managers to cope with the increased responsibilities and complexity of the business. The insurance managers of the future will have to apply modern management techniques in the running of their organisations. Social responsibility and accountability will become significant features in the industry. State intervention and governmental control will increase in order to ensure that the insurance industry operates in accordance with the national interests and on sound insurance principles.

Although the state might increase its interests and participation in the business of insurance, the pattern of the Nigerian insurance market should remain basically healthy, free and competitive. The future trend, however, will, to a great extent, depend on the performance of the industry as a whole and the manner in which it copes with its responsibilities to the nation in general.

In his then famous Jaji address*1, the former Nigerian Head of State, General Olusegun Obasanjo pointed out some of the ills and shortcomings of the Nigerian society. As the New Nigeria editorial of Friday, 16th September 1977 put it, the former Head of State "lamented that inspite of all efforts, Nigeria has failed to become a disciplined, fair, just and humane African society". Also in his Anniversary Day Broadcast on the 1st October 1977, the former Head of State stated *inter alia*, that the objectives of his government is to establish for Nigeria a society and an economy virile enough to ensure for its members an ever-increasing standard of living. He appealed to all Nigerians to conduct all their affairs honestly and in accordance with the national interest. Other leading Nigerians have made similar appeals urging all Nigerians to be honest and fair in all their business and private activities.

Insurance proprietors and managers, as controllers of an important section of the national economy, must respond positively to these appeals. Their investment, financial, and other policies must always be in line with national objectives. The practitioners of insurance and all those who execute insurance company policies must subscribe to, and conduct their affairs in accordance with the code of conduct of the Insurance Institute of Nigeria referred to above. Provided the insurance industry in Nigeria acts in accordance with the objectives and ideals enunciated above, and runs its business in accordance with sound insurance principles, complying at all times with the provisions of the laws of the land, it has nothing to fear and should be able to cope with the challenges of the future.

Keynote address by General Obasanjo at the Command and Military Staff College, Jaji on Monday, September 12, 1977.

APPENDICES

INSURANCE DECREE 1976

ARRANGEMENT OF SECTIONS

PTF Low
Price Edition

ARRANGEMENT OF SECTIONS—*continued*

Decree No. 59

[*1st December* 1976]   Application of this Decree

THE FEDERAL MILITARY GOVERNMENT
hereby decrees follows:—

PART I—PRELIMINARY

1.—(1) This Decree shall apply to all insurance business and insurers other than insurance business carried on by or insurers of the following descriptions, that is—   Commencement.

(a) a friendly society, that is an association of persons established with no share capital for the purpose of aiding its members or their dependents where such association does not employ any person whose main occupation is the canvassing of other persons to become members of the association or the collecting of contributions or subscriptions towards the funds of the association from its members;

(b) a pensions fund;

(c) a company or any other body (whether corporate or unincorporate) or person whose business is established outside Nigeria, engaged solely in re-insurance transactions with an insurer authorised by or pursuant to the provisions of this Decree to carry on any class of insurance business but not otherwise howsoever.

2.—(1) For the purposes of this Decree, insurance business shall be divided into two main classes, that is—

(a) life insurance business; and

(b) non-life insurance business.

(2) Non-life insurance business shall be sub-divided into the following categories—

(a) fire insurance business;

(b) aaccident insurance business;

(c) motor vehicle insurance business;

(d) workmen's compensation insurance business;

(e) marine, aviation and transport insurance business; and

(f) miscellaneous insurance business, being insurance business not falling under any of the foregoing paragraphs of this subsection.

(3) For the purposes of this Decree—

(a) any part of an insurance business may be treated as belonging to a particular class of insurance business; and

(b) re-insurance of liabilities under an insurance policy shall be treated as insurance business of the class to which such policy would have belonged if it had been issued by the re-insurer.

PART II—REGISTRATION

Conditions
for carrying
on insurance
business in
Nigeria, etc.
1968 No. 51.

3.—(1) No person shall carry on any class of insurance business in Nigeria except—

(a) a company duly incorporated as a limited liability company under or pursuant to the Companies Decree 1968;

(b) a co-operative insurance society registered under any enactment or law relating to co-operative societies; or

(c) a mutual insurance company.

(2) Subject to the provisions of this Decree, no insurer shall commence or carry on insurance

business in Nigeria unless the insurer is registered under or pursuant to this Decree.

(3) Where on the coming into operation of this Decree any insurer is carrying on insurance business in Nigeria, the insurer may apply within three months thereafter to be registered but shall cease to carry on insurance business of any description in Nigeria after the expiration of six months from the coming into operation of this Decree unless, prior to the expiration of the said period, such insurer is registered to continue the particular class or classes of insurance business in respect of which application had been made by the insurer.

(4) For the purposes of subsection (1) (c) of this section, any seven or more persons may, by subscribing their names to a memorandum of association and otherwise complying with the requirements of this Decree as to registration, form a mutual insurance company the aim of which shall be to use any profit derived from their operations to reduce the cost of insurance undertaken by its members.

Application for registration.

4.—(1) For the purposes of this Decree life insurance business and non-life insurance business shall be subject of separate application and registration.

(2) Every application for registration as an insurer shall be made to the Director of Insurance in the prescribed form and be accompanied bu such other documents or information as the Director may direct or require.

5.—(1) The Director shall register an applicant as an insurer if he is satisfied as to all of the following matters, that is—

Registration as insurer.

(a) that the class of insurance business will be conducted in accordance with sound insurance principles;

(*b*) that the applicant being one of the bodies referred to in section 3 (1) of this Decree is duly established under the applicable law and has a paid-up share capital as specified in section 8 of this Decree for the relevant class of insurance business;

(*c*) that the relevant statutory deposit specified in section 9 of this Decree has been paid to the Central Bank and the applicant has submitted a certificate from the Central Bank to that effect;

(*d*) that the arrangements relating to re-insurance treaties in respect of the classes of insurance business to be transacted are adequate and valid;

(*e*) that the proposal forms, terms and conditions of policies are in order and acceptable;

(*f*) that there is at least one competent and professionally qualified person to man each department of insurance business;

(*g*) that the directors and shareholders are persons, who have not been involved in or been found guilty of fraud;

(*h*) that the name of the applicant is not likely to be mistaken for the name of any other insurer who is or has been an insurer, or so nearly resembling that name, as to be calculated to deceive;

(*i*) that the applicant has paid the fee prescribed for registration;

(*j*) that it is the interest of public policy that the applicant be registered,

the Director shall register the applicant as an insurer by issuing a certificate of registration and notifying the insurer in writing accordingly; and notice of the registration (including registration pursuant to section 6 (4) of this Decree) shall be published in the *Gazette*.

(2) If the Director is not satisfied as to any of the matters referred to in subsection (1) on which he is required to be satisfied, he shall give notice in writing to the applicant of his intention to reject the application.

6.—(1) Any person aggrieved by the proposal of the Director to reject an application for registration as an insurer may, within sixty days after the date of the notice of intention to reject the application, lodge with the Permanent Secretary a notice of appeal to the Commissioner.

(2) The notice of appeal under subsection (1) above shall be in writing setting out the grounds on which it is made, and the Permanent Secretary shall transmit the notice with any other relevant documents to the Commissioner within fourteen days after the date of its receipt by the Permanent Secretary.

(3) The Commissioner shall give a decision on any appeal lodged in accordance with this section not later than thirty days after the date of its receipt by him.

(4) The Permanent Secretary shall, unless the appeal is withdrawn, give notice in writing to the applicant of the decision of the Commissioner (which shall be subject to no appeal); and if the appeal is allowed the Permanent Secretary shall cause the Director to register the person as an insurer and notify him in writing accordingly.

(5) Where an appeal is allowed by the Commissioner, the Permanent Secretary shall cause notice thereof to be published in the *Gazette* and in such other manner to ensure wide publicity thereof as he may determine.

Review of application in certain cases.

7.—(1) If, in the case of any registered insurer, the Director is satisfied—

(a) that the class of insurance business of the insurer is not being conducted in accordance with sound insurance principles; or

(b) that the technical reserves in respect of unexpired risks and outstanding claims are inadequate, as required by the provisions of section 17 of this Decree; or

(c) that the insurer has ceased to carry on insurance business of the class assigned to it for at least one year in Nigeria; or

Cancellation of registration

(*d*) that the insurer has applied in writing for the cancellation of its registration as an insurer; or

(*e*) that a judgement obtained in any court of competent jurisdiction in Nigeria against the insurer remains unsatisfied for 30 days; or

(*f*) that the insurer is carrying on simultaneously with insurance business any other business which is detrimental to the insurance business of the insurer; or

(*g*) that the business of the insurer has been transferred to or amalgamated with the business of any other insurer; or

(*h*) that the insurer has refused to submit to an examination of its books, as provided for in this Decree; or

(*i*) that the insurer has failed to comply with the provisions of section 19 (4) of this Decree; or

(*j*) that the insurer has failed to maintain adequate and valid re-insurance treaties; or

(*k*) that the insurer lacks expertise; or

(*l*) that the insurer has persistently contravened the provisions of section 8 of the National

Insurance Corporation of Nigeria Decree 1969 relating to compulsory re-insurance or has failed to comply with any other enactment relating to re-insurance in Nigeria; or

(*m*) that the net assets of the insurer are below the minimum paid-up capital and the capital has not been made good within the time stipulated by the Director; or

(*n*) that the insurer persistently fails to pay claims promptly; or

(*o*) that the insurer has failed to set up the special reserves as prescribed under section 17 (1) of this Decree; or

(*p*) that the insurer has established a branch office or branch offices without the approval of the Director; or

(*q*) that the insurer acts in any manner without the approval of the Director in cases where this Decree requires such approval;

(r) that the insurer has been wound up or otherwise dissolved, or has gone into liquidation,

the Director shall give notice in writing to the insurer of his intention to cancel the registration of the insurer in respect of a particualr class or both classes of insurance business and the provisions of section 6 of this Decree shall apply to any such notice as if it were a notice to reject an application for registration.

(2) Where no appeal is lodged as provided for under section 6, the Director shall with the approval of the Commissioner cancel the registration of the insurer and notice of such cancellation shall be published in the *Gazette*.

8.—(1) No insurer shall carry on insurance business in Nigeria unless the insurer has and maintains at all times, while carrying on that business, a paid-up share capital of the following amounts as the case may require, that is— Requirements as to minimum paid-up share capital.

(a) in the case of life insurance business, not less than ₦500,000;

(b) in the case of non-life insurance business, not less than ₦300,000; and

(c) in the case of re-insurance business, not less than ten times the amount specified in paragraph (a) above or, as the case may require, in paragraph (b) above.

(2) The Commissioner may by an Order published in the *Gazettee* increase the amounts specified in subsection (1) of this section, so however that no amendment of the said subsection (1) shall come into force before the expiration of the period of twelve months beginning with the date on which the Order is made.

9.—(1) Every person intending to carry out insurance business in Nigeria after the commencement of this Decree shall deposit the share capital referred to in section 8 of this Decree (hereinafter referred to as the "statutory deposit") with the Central Bank Additional requirements as to share capital.

and keep deposited with Central Bank such statutory deposit at all times during which such person is lawfully carrying on insurance business in Nigeria under or pursuant to the provisions of this Decree:

Provided that the Director may permit any insurer referred to in section 3 (3) of this Decree to pay the statutory deposit at any time before the expiration of the period of six months after the coming into operation of this Decree.

(2) The Director shall, after the registration of an insurer pursuant to section 5 of this Decree, cause to be released to any such insurer a sum not exceeding 50 *per centum* of the statutory deposit paid by the insurer in respect of each class of insurance business but where registration is refused or is subsequently cancelled the whole of the statutory deposit shall, subject to the other provisions of this Decree, be released to the person concerned:

Provided that in the case of any insurer referred to in section 3 (3) of this Decree, the requirements of this subsection as to statutory deposits shall be satisfied if not less than 50 *per centum* of the relevant statutory deposit is so deposited with the Central Bank.

Treatment of statutory deposit.

10.—(1) Where an insurer suffers a substantial loss, that is such loss as it can not reasonably meet from its own resources, the Director may, upon application therefor by the insurer, approve the withdrawal from the statutory deposit of an amount of not more than 25 *per centum* of the deposit and any amount so withdrawn shall be replaced by the insurer not later than thirty days after the date of such withdrawal.

(12) The statutory deposit shall not be regarded as assets held by the insurer, so however that it shall be available, in the event of the cancellation of its certificate of registration or of the winding up of the insurer, for the discharge of the liabilities arising out of policies of the insurance business transacted by the insurer and remaining undischarged at the time of the winding up.

PART III—MODE OF OPERATION OF INSURERS

Certain Changes to be notified to Director

11.—(1) Every insurer shall on the day it is registered to commence or continue business in Nigeria have a principal office to which all communications and notices may be addressed, so however that a postal box address or a private mail bag address shall not by itself only be sufficient for the purposes of the foregoing requirement.

(2) Notice of the situation of the principal office or any subsequent change thereof shall be given within twenty-one days thereof to the Director who shall record the same.

(3) If an insurer carries on business without complying with the requirements of this section, it and every officer thereof shall be liable to conviction to a fine of ₦10 for every day during which the insurer so carries on business.

(4) The fact that the address of an insurer is included in its application or in its annual return or any other return to the Director shall not be taken to satisfy the obligation imposed by this section.

(5) Where the insurer is a company incorporated under or pursuant to the Companies Decree 1968, it shall ensure that its principal office under this Decree shall be the same as its registered office within the meaning of that Decree.

12.—(1) No insurer shall appoint a chief executive thereof (whether designated as the managing director, executive chairman or otherwise howsoever) unless—

   (a) the insurer has served on the Director a written notice that it proposes to appoint that person to that position and containing such particulars as may be prescribed; and

   (b) the Director has, before the expiration of a

Notification of location of principal offic e to

1968 No. 51.

Appointment of chief executives subject to approval of Director.

period of 30 days beginning with the date of service of that notice, notified the insurer that there is no objection to that person being so appointed.

(2) Any notice served the insurer under subsection (1) (*a*) above shall contain a statement signed by the person proposed to be appointed that it is served with his knowledge and consent.

(3) The Director may, before the the expiration of the period mentioned in subsection (1) (*b*) above, serve a notice of objection to the appointment of proposed chief executive and give the insurer and that person a period of 21 days within which to make written representations to the Commissioner through the Permanent Secretary.

(4) The Permanent Secretary shall, as soon as may be thereafter, give notice in writing to the insurer and the proposed chief executive of the decision of the Commissioner which decision shall be subject to no appeal.

(5) If an insurer carries on business without complying with the requirements of this section, it and the proposed chief executive shall be liable on conviction to a fine of ₦10 for everyday during which the insurer so carries on business.

Change of chief executive to be notified to Director.

13.—(1) A person who becomes or ceases to be the chief executive of any insurer shall, before the expiration of a period of 7 days beginning with the day on which he does so, notify the insurer in writing of such matters as may be prescribed.

(2) An insurer shall give written notice to the Director of the fact that any person has become or ceased to be a chief executive thereof and of any matter which any such person is required to notify the insurer under subsection (1) above and that notice shall be given before the expiration of the period of 21 days beginning with the day on which that fact or matter comes to the insurer's knowledge.

(3) Any person who makes default in complying with subsection (1) of this section shall be guilty of an offence and liable on conviction to a fine of ₦500

Insurance Policies

14.—(1) Subject to subsection (4) below, no insurance policy or certificate of insurance shall be issued and no contract of insurance shall be entered into by any insurer without the prior approval of the Director and no rider, clause, warranty or any endorsement whatsoever shall be attached to, printed or stamped upon any document containing any such policy, certificate or contract or deleted therefrom unless the form of such rider, clause, warranty or endorsement or the matter to be deleted has the prior approval of the Director.

All insurance policies, etc. and changes therein to be approved.

(2) Any policy or certificate issued or any contract entered into in contravention of subsection (1) of this section shall not be void but may .be avoided by the other party or parties concerned; not being the insurer.

(3) Any insurer that issues any policy or certificate or enters into any contract otherwise than in compliance with subsection (1) of this section shall be guilty of an offence and liable on conviction to a fine of ₦2,000.

(4) Where the form of any policy, certificate, contract, rider, clause, warranty or endorsement or deletion therefrom referred to in this section is one of a standard class, that is where any one such form does not deviate from the others in that particular class in any material particular, then only six copies of any such form need be referred to the Director for the purposes of this section.

Accounts and Audit

15.—(1) Every insurer shall keep and maintain

Records to be kept.

at its principal office the following, that is—

(a) the memorandum and articles of association or other evidence of the constitution of the body concerned;

(b) a record containing the names and addresses of the owners of the insurer (whether known and called shareholders or otherwise howsoever);

(c) the minutes of any meeting of such owners, and of the policy-making executive (whether known and called the board of directors or otherwise howsoever);

(d) a register of all policies, in which shall be entered in respect of every policy issued, the name and address of the policy-holder, the date when the policy was effected, and a record of any transfer, assignment or nomination, of which the insurer has notice;

(e) a register of claims in which shall be entered every claim made together with the date of claim, the name and address of the claimant and the date on which the claim was settled, or in the case of a claim which is rejected the date of rejection and the grounds thereof, or in the case of litigation, the particulars thereof and the decision of the court in the matter;

(f) a register of investment showing those which are attributable to the reserves and those which are not and also any alteration in their values from time to time;

(g) a register of assets;

(h) a register of re-insurance ceded, showing separately those ceded in Nigeria and those ceded abroad;

(i) a cash book;

(j) current accounts books; and

(k) a register of open policies in respect of marine insurance transactions.

(2) In respect of life insurance business the following additional records shall be kept and maintained, that is—

(*a*) a register of assured under group policies;

(*b*) a register of loans on policies;

(*c*) a register of cash surrender values; and

(*d*) a register of lapsed and expired policies.

(3) Where an insurer makes default in complying with any provision of subsection (1) or (2) of this section, the insurer and every officer thereof who is in default shall be liable on conviction to a fine of ₦500.

16.—(1) Where an insurer carries on both classes of insurance business, all the receipts of each of those classes of insurance business shall be entered in a separate and distinct account and shall be carried to and form a separate insurance fund with the appropriate name, that is either the life insurance fund or the non-life insurance fund.

Separation of accounts and reserve funds.

(2) Each insurance fund shall represent the liabilities in respect of all contracts of insurance of that particular class and shall consist—

(*a*) in the case of life insurance business, of a sum not less than the mathematical reserves; and

(*b*) in the case of non-life insurance business, of the reserves for unexpired risks and reserves for outstanding claims including, in the case of the latter, reserves estimated to provide for the expenses of adjustment or settlement of such claims.

(3) The insurance fund of each particular class—

(*a*) shall be as absolutely the security of the policy-holders of that class as though it belonged to an insurer carrying on no other business than insurance business of that class;

(*b*) shall not be liable for any contracts of the insurer for which it would not have been liable had the business of the insurer been only that of insurance of that class; and

(*c*) shall not be applied, directly or indirectly, for any purposes other than those of the class of business to which the fund is applicable.

Reserves.

17.—(1) Every insurer shall set up and maintain the following technical reserves, applicable thereto in respect of each class of insurance business, that is—

(a) reserves for unexpired risks;

(b) reserves for outstanding claims; and

(c) contingency reserves to cover fluctuations in securities and variations in statistical estimates.

(2) With respect to non-life insurance business, the insurer shall maintain the following reserves, that is—

(a) with respect to non-life insurance business (other than marine insurance business) reserves for unexpired risks, the amount of which shall not be less than 45 *per centum* of the total net premiums and, in the case of marine insurance business, the amount of which shall bot be less than 75 *per centum* of the net premium;

(b) reserves for outstanding claims, the amount of which shall be equal to the total estimated amount of all outstanding claims together with a further amount representing 20 *per centum* of the estimated figure for outstanding claims in respect of claims incurred but not reported at the end of the last preceding year; and

(c) contingency reserves, the amount of which shall not be less than 3 *per centum* of total premiums or 20 *per centum* of net profits (whichever is greater) and the amount shall accumulate until it reaches the minimum paid-up capital or 50 *per centum* of the net premiums (whichever is greater).

(3) With respect to life insurance business, the insurer shall maintain the following reserves—

(a) a general reserve fund which shall be credited with an amount equal to the net liabilities on policies in force at the time of the actuarial valuation; and

(b) a contingency reserve which shall be credited with an amount equal to 1 *per centum* of premiums or 10 *per centum* of profits (whichever is greater) and the reserve shall accumulate until it reaches the amount of minimum paid-up capital.

18.—(1) Every insurer shall at all times in respect of the insurance business transacted by it in Nigeria invest and hold invested in Nigeria assets equivalent to not less than the amount of the funds in such insurance business as shown in the balance sheet and the revenue accounts of the insurer.

Investments.

(2) Subject to the other provisions of this section, the assets of the insurer shall not be invested in property and securities except—

(a) securities specified under the Government and Other Securities (Local Trustees' Powers) Act and the Trustee Investments Act 1962; *Cap. 78. 1962 No. 13.*

(b) shares in or other securities of a society registered under any law relating to co-operative societies;

(c) loans to building societies approved by the Commissioner;

(d) loans on real property, machinery and plant in Nigeria;

(e) loans on life policies within their surrender values;

(f) cash on deposit in, or bills of exchange accepted by, licensed banks;

(g) such other investments as may be prescribed.

(3) An insurer shall not be treated as satisfying the requirements of this section unless not less than 25 *per centum* of the total assets of the insurer is invested in the securities mentioned in paragraph (a) of sub-section (2) of this section.

(4) No insurer shall—

(a) in respect of non-life insurance business invest more than 10 *per centum* of the assets in real property, or

(b) in respect of life insurance business invest more than 25 *per centum* in real property.

(5) Any investment made by an insurer otherwise

than in compliance with the provisions of this section shall be treated as non-admitted assets.

(6) In this section references to real property include references to an estate in land in fee simple, a lease or a right of occupancy.

Statements of accounts, etc.

19.—(1) Every insurer shall not later than 31st May in each financial year submit in writing to the Director the following documents—

(*a*) a balance sheet duly audited showing the financial position of the insurance business of the insurer, at the close of that year together with a copy of the relevant profit and loss account which the insurer is to present to its share holders at its annual general meeting; and

(*b*) a revenue account applicable to each class of insurance business for which the insurer is required to keep a separate account of receipts and payments.

(2) Every insurer transacting life insurance business shall submit annually to the Director in the prescribed form, the following—

(*a*) an abstract of the report of an actuary and valuation report of insurance business;

(*b*) a summary and valuation of the life policies; and

(*c*) a table showing premiums, policy reserve values and guaranteed surrender values, together with the relationship between premiums paid and such guaranteed, surrender values.

(3) The Director may require an insurer transacting life insurance business—

(*a*) to cause the person who, for the time being, is its actuary to make an investigation into its financial condition (including evaluation of its liabilities) in respect of that business, as at a specified date;

(*b*) to cause an abstract of that person's report of the investigation to be made and submitted to him;

(c) to prepare and submit to him a statement of its life insurance business or part thereof as at that date; and

(d) to show him sufficient evidence that at least 75 *per centum* of the actuarial surplus declared has been applied as reversionary bonus additions.

(4) Every insurer transacting life insurance business shall at the expiration of each financial year prepare with reference to that year in the prescribed form a statement and exhibit of the life policies and submit it together with such other documents and information relating to the relevant accounts and balance sheet (including copies of reports on the affairs of the insurer for the financial year as submitted to the policy holders or share holders of the insurer) as the Director may from time to time require.

(5) Upon the receipt of the documents mentioned in the foregoing subsections of this section, the Director shall, if it appears to him that any statement furnished by an insurer under any of the said provisions is inaccurate, or not prepared in the prescribed form, or defective in any material particular—

(a) require from the insurer such further information as he may consider necessary;

(b) call upon the insurer to submit for his examination any book of accounts, register or any other documents;

(c) require from any insurer that the authenticity of any statement submitted shall be confirmed on oath, or by a sworn declaration;

(d) refuse to accept the insurer's annual statement unless or until the inaccuracies have been corrected or the deficiencies have been supplied; and any insurer who fails, neglects or refuses to produce any book, or give any information as may be required by the Director under this section shall be guilty of an offence and liable on conviction to a fine of ₦2,000.

(6) No insurer shall distribute any dividends until it has received a statement in writing from the Director to the effect that it has complied with all the provisions relating to statutory annual returns.

(7) Every insurer shall in each financial year, after receipt of the statement mentioned is subsection (6) above, publish its general annual balance sheet together with its profit and loss account in at least one newspaper having wide circulation in Nigeria.

Audit.

20.—(1) The balance sheet, profit and loss account and revenue account of every insurer, in respect of insurance business transacted by such insurer shall be audited annually by an auditor approved in that behalf by the Director and no auditor shall be so approved if he is an emplyee, manager or director of the insurer.

(2) At the conclusion of the audit the auditor shall issue a certificate signed by him stating whether in his opinion—

(a) he has obtained adequate information from the books and records;

(b) the books of the insurer have been properly kept and the affairs and transactions of the insurer have been correctly recorded;

(c) the accounts and balance sheet are in accordance with the information given to him for the purposes of his audit;

(d) the accounts and balance sheet are in accordance with the applicable provisions of this Part of this Decree; and

(e) the balance sheet and the profit and loss account, respectively, give a true and fair view of the financial position of the insurer.

PART IV—AMALGAMATIONS AND TRANSFERS

Procedure on amalgamation or transfer.

21.—(1) Subject to the provisions of this section, no insurer shall—

(a) amalgamate with any other insurer carrying

on life insurance business or workmen's compensation insurance business; or

(*b*) transfer to or acquire from any other insurer,
any such insurance business or part thereof,
unless the transaction is sanctioned by the
Federal Revenue Court (hereinafter referred
to as "the court").

(2) If any of the class of insurance business
mentioned in subsection (1) of this section is intended
to be amalgamated with any other insurance business
or where any insurer or any such class of insurance
business is intended to be transferred, in whole or
in part, the insurers concerned shall apply to the
court to sanction the proposed amalgamation or
transfer, as the case may be.

(3) Before an application is made to the court
to sanction any transaction under this section, notice
of intention to make the application together with a
statement of the nature of the amalgamation or transfer
shall, at least three months before the application
is made, be published in the *Gazette* and be served
on the Director; and certified copies of each of the
following documents shall, during the three months
aforesaid, be kept open for inspection by the members
and policy-holders at the principal and branch offices
of the insurers concerned, that is—

(*a*) a draft of the agreement or deed under which
it is proposed to effect the amalgamation
or transfer;

(*b*) balance sheets in respect of the insurance
business of each of the insurers concerned
in such amalgamation or transfer, prepared
in the prescribed form;

(*c*) actuarial reports in respect of the life insurance
business of each of the insurers concerned
prepared in the prescribed form; and
prepared in the prescribed form; and

(*d*) a report on the proposed amalgamation or
transfer, prepared by an independent actuary.

(4)   The deed or agreement under which an amalgamation or transfer, as the case may be, is proposed to be effected shall be available for inspection without payment of any fee by policy-holders and share holders at all reasonable times in all the offices of the insurers in the Federation, for a period of twenty-one days after the publication of the notice in the *Gazette*.

(5)   The court in its discretion may sanction the arrangement, if it is satisfied that no sufficient objection has been established by those entitled to be heard and, for the purposes of this subsection, it shall be sufficient objection if it appears to the court that policy-holders representing not less than one-fifth of the total number insured by any of the insurers carrying on the business concerned, dissent from the amalgamation or transfer, as the case may be.

(6)   If an amalgamation or transfer under this section is sanctioned by the court, no policy-holder shall be regarded as having abandoned any claim which he would have had against the original insurer or to have accepted in place thereof the liability of another insurer, unless he or his agent has signed a written document abandoning that claim and accepting in place thereof, the liability of that insurer and any such objecting policy-holder shall have the right to cancel his contract, in which case he will be entitled to reclaim the portion of premium corresponding to the unexpired term of the risk insured by him or the mathematical reserve in the case of life assurance.

(7)   The transferring concern shall not be licensed anew to undertake the same class or, as the case may be, classes of insurance until after the expiration of five years from the issue of the sanction of the court.

Documents to be deposited with Director after amalgamation or transfer.

22.   Within three months after the date of completion of the amalgamation or transfer of insurance business under section 21 of this Decree, the insurer carrying on the amalgamated business or to whom the business is transferred, as the case may be, shall furnish in duplicate to the Director—

(*a*) certified copies of statement of assets and liabilities of the insurers concerned in the amalgamation or transfer together with a statement of the nature and the terms of the amalgamation or transfer;

(*b*) a certified copy of the agreement or deed under which the amalgamation or transfer had been effected;

(*c*) certified copy of the actuarial or other reports upon which the agreement or deed was founded; and

(*d*) a declaration signed by each of the insurers concerned that to the best of their knowledge and belief every payment made or to be made to any person whatsoever on account of the amalgamation or transfer is therein fully set forth and that no other payments beyond those set forth have been made or are to be made either in money, policies, securities or other valuable consideration by or with the knowledge of any of the parties to the amalgamation or transfer

PART V—WINDING UP

23. A petition for the winding up of an insurer may be presented to the court either—

Winding up petition.

(*a*) by not less than fifty policy-holders, each such policy-holder having a policy that has been in force for not less than three years, on the grounds specified in sections 209 and 210 & the Companies Decree 1968; or

(*b*) by the Director on any of the following grounds—
(*i*) that the insurer has failed to comply with the requirements of section 7 (1) of this Decree; or
(*ii*) that the insurer, having failed to comply with any of the aforementioned requirements has continued such failure or having contravened any of the provisions of the said section 7 (1) has continued such contravention for

a continuous period of six months, after notice
of such failure or contravention had been
conveyed to the insurer by the Director; or
(*iii*) that the registration of the insurer has
been cancelled in accordance with section
7 (2) of this Decree; or

(*iv*) that it appears from the annual statements
furnished by the insurer under section 19
or from the results of any investigation made
under section 37 of this Decree that the insurer
is insolvent,

and the Companies Decree 1968 shall have
effect, subject to this Decree, as if the petition
were one presented under that Decree.

Prohibition on voluntary winding up.   24. Notwithstanding the provisions of the Companies
Decree 1968 or any other enactment, no insurer who
transacts life insurance business shall voluntarily
wind up his business except for the purpose of effecting an amalgamation or transfer under this Decree.

PART VI—INSURANCE AGENTS AND BROKERS

Licensing of insurance agents.   25.—(1) No person shall transact business as
an insurance agent unless he is licensed in that behalf
under this Part of this Decree.

(2) Application for a licence as an insurance agent
shall be made to the Director in the prescribed form
and be accompanied by the prescribed fee and such
other documents as may be prescribed.

(3) If the Director is satisfied that the applicant
has satisfied the requirements of this section or such
other requirements as may be prescribed, he shall
license the applicant as an insurance agent and notice
thereof shall be published in the *Gazette*.

(4) A licence issued under this section shall entitle
the holder thereof to act as an insurance agent for
the insurer or insurers named therein and shall, subject
to this section, be renewable every year upon payment

of the prescribed fee.

(5) Any person—

(*a*) who is a minor;

(*b*) who is of unsound mind; or

(*c*) who had, prior to the date of his application, been convicted by a court of any offence in the nature of criminal misappropriation of funds or breach of trust or cheating,

shall not be entitled to be licensed as an insurance agent under this Decree; and any insurance agent who, after having been licensed, is found to be a minor or subsequently suffers any of the disabilities mentioned in paragraph (*b*) or (*c*) above, shall have his licence cancelled.

26.—(1) Every insurer who employs the services of insurance agents and every person who acts for an insurer in that behalf shall maintain a register showing the name and address of every such insurance agent and the date on which his services were employed and, where applicable, terminated.

Duties of insurers and agents inter se.

(2) Every premium collected by an insurance agent shall be paid to the insurer not later than 15 days after receipt thereof; and where payment is not feasible, either because of the remoteness of the agent from the insurer or otherwise howsoever, the agent shall effect a transfer of the funds within the said period.

(3) Any insurance agent who contravenes subsection (2) of this section shall be guilty of an offence and shall on conviction—

(*a*) for a first offence, be liable to a fine of ₦100;

(*b*) for the second offence, be liable to a fine of ₦200; and

(*c*) for the third offence, be liable to a fine of ₦500, and in addition his licence shall be cancelled and he shall be disqualified from being again licensed as an insurance agent.

(4) Any person who transacts business as an insurance agent without having been licensed in

that behalf under this Decree shall be guilty of an offence and liable on conviction to a fine of ₦500 or imprisonment for two years or to both such fine and imprisonment; and in addition the court shall make an order requiring such a person to refund any sums collected by him while so transacting business to the rightful owners thereof or other persons entitled thereto.

(5) Any insurer who knowingly or recklessly transacts any insurance business with any person mentioned in subsection (4) of this section shall be guilty of an offence and shall be liable on conviction to a fine of ₦1,000 and the court may make such additional order as to the refund of the sums involved as in the said subsection (4).

Registration of insurance brokers, etc.

27.—(1) No person shall transact business in Nigeria as an insurance broker unless he is licensed in that behalf under of this Part of this Decree.

(2) Application for registration as an insurance broker shall be made to the Director in the prescribed form and be accompanied by the prescribed fee and such other documents as may be prescribed.

(3) If the Director is satisfied—

(a) that the applicant has the prescribed qualifications; and

(b) that the applicant has unlimited liability; and

(c) that the applicant has deposited a sum of ₦25,000 on a fixed de_sit basis with the Central Bank,

the Director shall register the applicant as an insurance broker by issuing him with a certificate of registration and notice thereof shall be published in the *Gazette*.

(4) If the Director is not satified as to any of the matters referred to in subsection (3) on which he is required to be satisfied, he shall give notice in writing to the applicant of his intention to reject the application.

(5) Any person aggrieved by the proposal of the

Director to reject an application for registration as an insurance broker may give notice of appeal and the provisions of section 6 of this Decree shall apply as if references therein to the applicant were references to an applicant under this section.

(6) A certificate issued to an insurance broker shall be valid for one year and shall, subject to this section, be renewable every year upon payment of the prescribed fee.

(7) If, in the case of any licensed broker, the Director is satisfied that such broker—

(a) has knowingly or recklessly contravened the provisions of this Part;

(b) has made any statement for the purpose of obtaining a licence which is false in a material particular;

(c) has been found guilty by a court of competent jurisdiction of fraudulent or dishonest practices (including misappropriation of clients' money); or

(d) has materially misrepresented the terms and conditions of any policy or contract of insurance which he has sold to clients or seeks to sell to prospective clients,

the Director shall give notice in writing of his intention to cancel the licence or to refuse its renewal and the provisions of section 6 of this Decree shall apply as if references therein to applicant were references to a licensed broker under this subsection.

28.—(1) Every insurance broker shall have and maintain at all times a professional indemnity insurance cover for an amount of not less than ₦50,000 or 25 *per centum* of its annual brokerage income during the last preceding year, whichever is greater.

Requirements as to conduct of business of broker.

(2) Every premium collected by the broker shall be paid to the insurer not later than 30 days after receipt thereof; and where payment is not feasible, either

because of the remoteness of the broker from the insurer concerned or otherwise howsoever, the broker shall effect a transfer of the funds within the said period.

(3) Any broker who contravenes subsection (2) of this section shall be guilty of an offence and shall on conviction—

(a) for a first offence, be liable to a fine of ₦500;

(b) for the second offence, be liable to a fine of ₦1,000; and

(c) for the third offence, be liable to a fine of ₦2,000; and in addition the certificate of such broker shall be cancelled and the person or, where this is a firm, the persons constituting the firm, shall be disqualified from being again involved in the setting up of the business of an insurance broker under this Decree either by himself or themselves or in conjunction with any other person or body.

(4) Any person who transacts business as an insurer broker without having been registered in that behalf under this Decree shall be guilty of an offence and liable on conviction—

(a) in the case of a body corporate to a fine of ₦5,000; or

(b) in the case of an individual, each such individual and, in the case of a firm or other combination of persons (not being a body corporate), each officer of the firm or other such body, to a fine of ₦2,000 or imprisonment for two years or to both such fine and imprisonment; and in addition, the court may order any such person mentioned in this section to refund the sums involved to the rigthful owners thereof or other persons entitled thereto.

(5) Any insurer who knowingly or ·recklessly transacts any insurance business with any person mentioned in subsection (4) of this section shall be

guilty of an offence and liable on conviction to a fine of ₦5,000 and the court may make such additional order as to the refund of the sums involved as referred to in the said subsection (4).

29.—(1) Every registered insurance broker shall keep records of all insurance business handled by such broker and for the purposes of this section, separate records shall be kept by such broker with respect to—

(a) insurance business entered into with insurers registered under or pursuant to this Decree; and

(b) subject to subsection (2) below, insurance business entered into with persons outside Nigeria

(2) No registered insurance broker shall enter into any contract of insurance with any person outside Nigeria except with the prior approval of the Director and any contract entered into otherwise than in compliance with the provisions of this subsection shall be void.

Records of transactions, etc.

30. For the purposes of satisfying himself as to whether or not the provisions of this Part are being complied with, the Director may at any time—

(a) authorise an investigator to conduct an examination of any agent or registered insurance broker as may be reasonable in the circumstances; and

(b) by notice in writing require any agent or broker to produce any document or information on any matter relating to the insurance business negotiated or to be negotiated or solicited by any such agent or broker.

Power of Director to investigate agents and brokers.

31.—(1) In this Part and in the other provisions of this Decree, all references to brokers shall be construed as including references to adjusters; and for the purposes of this Decree an "adjuster" means any person or body (whether corporate or unincorporate) who for money or other valuable consideration acts

Application of certain provisions of this Decree to adjusters, agents and brokers.

for or on behalf of any insurer in adjusting claims arising from insurance contracts or policies issued by any such insurer or in negotiating for or effecting settlement of claims in connection with any such transaction.

(2) The provisions of section 8, (2) 9 and 10 of this Decree shall apply to a deposit under paragraph (c) of section 27 (3) of this Decree as they apply in relation · to the amounts and deposits respectively mentioned in those sections.

(3) The provisions of section 3 (3) of this Decree shall apply in relation to agents and brokers carrying on business at the commencement of this Decree as they apply in relation to insurers under that section.

(4) For the avoidance of doubt, where under this section it is provided that certain provisions are to apply, such provisions shall have effect subject to such modifications ; amendments or omissions as would bring them into line with the general intendment of this section including, where applicable, textual amendments to forms.

PART VII—PREMIUM RATES AND COMMISSIONS

Restrictions on general increases in premium rates.

32.—(1) No insurer either by itself or as a member of an association of insurers sl all make a general increase in the rates of premiuₗ ıs charged oₗ to be charged with respect to any class cf insurance business or any division thereof except with the prior approval of the Director; and any insurer thℷt makes a general ncrease otherwise than in compliance with this sub-ection shall be guilty of an offence and liable on conviction to a fine of ten times the amount of the premiums charged and received by such insurer.

(2) Any insurer who increases rates of premiums otherwise than in compliance with subsection (1) of this section shall be liable to either of the following additional penalties, that is—

(a) suspension of its cperations in respect of new

insurance business for a period of not less than six months or more than three years; or

(*b*) cancellation of its certificate of registration; and in addition to either of the foregoing, every · such insurer shall refund the excess payment to every person making such excess payment or to other persons entitled thereto.

(3) The penalties referred to in subsection (2) of this section shall be imposed by the Director and any insurer that feels aggrieved may appeal to the Commissioner in accordance with the provisions of section 6 of this Decree; and the decision of the Commissioner in any such appeal shall be final.

33.—(1) There may be appointed from time to time by the Commissioner, an ad hoc committee to be known as the Rating Committee which shall consist of— *Rating Committee to review rates.*

(*a*) a representative of the Federal Ministry of Trade (not being the Director) as chairman;

(*b*) a representative each of the Federal Ministries of Finance and Economic Deveopment;

(*c*) two representatives of the Accident Insurance Association of Nigeria;

(*d*) one representative of the Nigerian Insurance Association; and

(*e*) such other members (not being more than three) as the Commissioner may think fit.

(2) The functions of the Rating Committee shall be—

(*a*) to examine and determine reasonable and adequate premium rates chargeable for similar risks in any class of insurance business or part thereof, having regard to past, current and prospective claims experience of insurers and also the nature of the risks;

(*b*) to group risks by class for the purpose of ascer-taining minimum and maximum rates chargeable thereof;

(*c*) to ensure that rates are non-discriminatory

except in accordance with well-established customs and rules of the trade;

(*d*) to consider factors that should be taken into consideration in fixing rates and premiums;

(*e*) to examine and consider applications for general increase in rates and premiums with a view to making recommmendations thereon having regard to general anti-inflationary measures prescribed or to be prescribed by the Government and;

(*f*) to review insurance commissions from time to time.

Insurance commissions.

34.—(1) No insurer shall pay by way of commission to any insurance agent or broker or any other intermediary, an amount—

(*a*) exceeding 10 *per centum* of the premium in respect of motor vehicle, workmen's compensation or contractor's all risks and engineering insurance; or

(*b*) exceeding 15 *per centum* of the premium in respect of any other subdivision (not being one mentioned in paragraph (*a*) above) of non-life insurance business.

(2) No alteration in the rates of commission mentioned in subsection (1) of this section shall be made except with the prior approval of the Director.

(3) Any person who pays, or any person who receives, any commission otherwise than in compliance with the provisions of this section shall be guilty of an offence and liable on conviction to a fine of ₦1,000 plus an additional fine being an amount equal to such excess commission.

PART VIII—ADMINISTRATION AND ENFORCEMENT

Director of Insurance, etc.

Director of Insurance, etc.

35.—(1)There shall be appointed by the Federal Public Service Commission a Director of Insurance for the purposes of this Decree whose office shall be in the Department of Government for which responsibility is assigned to the Commissioner.

(2) There shall be appointed a Deputy Director of Insurance, such officers in the grades of Superintendent and Inspector of Insurance and such other public officers as may be necessary for the administration and enforcement of this Decree.

(3) It shall be the duty of any person mentioned subsections (1) and (2) of this section, while in exercising his powers under this Decree, not to interfere unreasonably with the affairs of persons affected by his activities.

(4) Any power conferred on the Director by virtue of this Decree may be exercised by the Deputy Director or any other public officer who produces an instrument signed by the Director or Deputy Director authorising him, either generally or on any special occasion, to exercise the power on his behalf and references to the Director in this Decree shall be construed accordingly.

36.—(1) Without prejudice to the generality of section 35 (2) of this Decree, there shall be appointed a public officer to be known as the Chief Actuary and other actuaries in subordinate grades as may be necessary to assist the Chief Actuary in the discharge of his functions. *Appointment of Chief Actuary, etc.*

(2) The Chief Actuary shall advise and assist the Director, particularly with respect to the technical administration and enforcement of this Decree concerning actuarial matters and such other matters as the Director may delegate to him.

Powers as to Inspection

37.—(1) Without prejudice to the other powers conferred upon him under or pursuant to this Decree, the Director shall, once every two years, authorise any person (in this Decree referred to as "investigator") *Powers of investigation.*

to conduct an examination of each insurer registered pursuant to this Decree for the purpose of satisfying himself as to whether or not the provisions of this Decree or of any regulations made thereunder are being complied with.

(2) Without prejudice to the mode of the conduct of the examination by the investigator, any such investigator shall have power to—

(a) intervene in the checking of the cash in hand, cash accounts and otherwise verify the liquid and other assets of the insurer;

(b) check all the main and auxiliary books of accounts, registers and other papers and correspondence connected with the insurer's business;

(c) verify the investment of the capital and statutory reserves; and

(d) verify the legality or otherwise of any insurance business transacted by the insurer.

(3) Upon the completion of an examination under this section, the investigator shall make a report thereon to the Director who shall take such action (if any) as may be necessary in the circumstances to ensure compliance with the relevant provisions of this Decree by the insurer concerned ôr such action as is provided for in the other provisions of this Decree.

(4) The Director may (whether or not any other penalty is provided for breach thereof in this Decree) cancel the certificate of registration of any insurer who refuses an examination under this section or who, in purported compliance therewith, refuses to furnish any information which such insurer may be required to furnish for the purposes of an examination under this section.

Power to suspend insurer from underwriting new business. 38.—(1) If, after the submission of the report referred to in section 37 of this Decree, it appears to the Director—

(a) that the insurer is in an unsound condition

or that its method of transacting its business is such as to render its continued operation hazardous to its policy-holders or potential policy-holders; or

(b) that it has failed to maintain the statutory reserves; or

(c) that it has failed to maintain adequate management control; or

(d) that it has failed generally to comply with the provisions of this Decree or of regulations made thereunder and that such failure cannot be corrected within a reasonable period of time,

the Director may suspend such insurer from undertaking any new insurance business for such period as, in his opinion, would enable the insurer to remove such deficiencies.

(2) Any such insurer may, after removing such deficiencies, be permitted by the Director to resume its full operations but before doing so, the Director shall require the insurer to submit a business plan showing the estimated receipts and disbursements, as well as the bases for the foregoing, projected for the next succeeding three years and shall, in addition, satisfy himself that such plan is based on sound insurance principles.

39.—(1) If after the expiration of the period mentioned in section 38 (1) of this Decree, it appears to the Director that the insurer has refused to, or continues to be unable to, remove any of the deficiencies mentioned in the said section, the Director may appoint an interim manager to take charge of the assets and liabilities, and management control of such insurer.

Appointment of interim manager for suspended insurer.

(2) Notwithstanding the memorandum and articles of association or other constitutional instrument of any insurer, the interim manager shall have and exercise all powers necessary to restore the viability of the insurer concerned; and without prejudice to the generality of the foregoing, any such manager shall have power—

(a)   to collect all moneys and debts due to the insurer;

(b)   to enter into or continue any pending legal proceedings by or against the insurer but in the insurer's name;

(c)   to take all such steps as to preserve the assets of the insurer;

(d)   to do any thing relating to the employment and disciplinary control (including dismissal) of all employees of the insurer;

(e)   to confirm or revoke or otherwise vary any decision of the previous management and board of directors or other controlling body of the insurer.

(3) The remuneration and incidental expenses of the interim manager appointed under this section shall be borne by the insurer.

(4) The interim manager shall be under the supervision of the Director and shall make such periodic and other reports to the Director as the Director may from time to time direct.

(5) If it appears at any time to the Director—

(a)   that the affairs of the insurer have been restored on sound insurance business basis; or

(b)   that the continuation in business of the insurer would be hazardous to the policyholders, the Director shall terminate the appointment of the interim manager on such terms as may be appropriate in the circumstances.

(6) Where the Director terminates the appointment of the interim manager for the reason mentioned in subsection (5) (b) of this section, the Director shall cancel the certificate of registration of the insurer concerned.

(7) In this section references to "interim manager" include references to an insurance company or other body (whether corporate or unincorporate) appointed in that behalf.

40.—(1) In every case where the certificate of registration of an insurer is cancelled pursuant to any provision of this Decree, the Director may, unless the insurer is a company being wound up by the court, appoint a receiver to immediately take charge of its assets and to collect and gather in all other assets due to the insurer and administer same as expeditiously as possible for the benefit of the policy holders and creditors thereof.

(2) The receiver shall so soon as may be thereafter apply to the court for the winding up of the insurer and for this purpose, the provisions of the Companies Decree 1968 relating to the winding up of companies by the court shall, subject to section 41 of this Decree, apply.

41.—(1) This section has effect in relation to the winding up of an insurer, being a company carrying on life insurance business.

(2) The liquidator shall, unless the court otherwise orders, carry on the life insurance business of the company with a view to its being transferred as a going concern to another insurance company, whether an existing company or a company formed for that purpose; and in carrying on that business as aforesaid, the liquidator may agree to the variation of any contracts of insurance in existence when the winding up order is made but shall not effect any new contracts of insurance.

(3) The court may, if it thinks it fit and subject to such conditions (if any) as it may determine, reduce the amount of the contracts made by the company in the course of carrying on life insurance business.

(4) The Director may at any time appoint, and the court on the application of the liquidator may appoint, an independent actuary to investigate the life insurance business of the company and the actuary shall report to the appointing authority, as the case may require, on the desirability or otherwise of that business being continued and on any reduction in

the contracts made in the course of carrying on that business that may be necessary for its successful continuation.

(5) The Director or the liquidator may make an application in the name or on behalf of the company under section 23 of this Decree.

Power as to production of books, etc.

42.—(1) Any power conferred upon the Director by virtue of this Decree to require an insurer, broker, agent or other person to produce books or other documents shall include power—

(a) if the books or documents are produced—
   (i) to take copies of them or extracts from them, and
   (ii) to require that insurer, broker, agent or other person or any person who is a present or past officer or auditor thereof, or is or was at any time employed by any of them to provide an explanation of any such book or document;

(b) if the books or documents are not produced, to require the person who was required to produce them to state, to the best of his knowledge and belief, where they are.

(2) In this section "books or documents" include accounts, deeds, writings, registers, ledgers and documents of all descriptions.

PART IX—MISCELLANOUS AND SUPPLEMENTARY

Settlements of claims

Settlement of claims generally.

43.—(1) Where civil proceedings are taken in court in respect of any claim under a policy of insurance and judgment is obtained against any person insured by a policy of insurance then, notwithstanding that the insurer may be entitled to avoid or cancel or may have avoided or cancelled the policy, the insurer shall, subject to this section, pay to the persons entitled to the benefit of any such judgment the sum payable (including costs and interest on such sum) not later than 30 days from the date of delivery of such judgment.

(2) No sum shall be payable by an insurer under the provisions of subsection (1) above—

(a) in respect of any judgment unless before or within seven days after the commencement of the proceedings in which the judgment was given the insurer had notice of the bringing of the proceedings; or

(b) in respect of any judgment so long as execution thereon is stayed pending an appeal; or

(c) in connection with any liability if before the happening of the event, which gave rise to the liability, the policy was cancelled by mutual consent or by virtue of any provision contained therein and either—

(i) before the happening of such event the certificate of insurance was surrendered to the insurer or the person to whom the certificate of insurance was delivered made a statutory declaration stating that the certificate of insurance had been lost or destroyed and so could not be surrendered, or

(ii) after the happening of such event but before the expiration of fourteen days from the taking effect of the cancellation of the policy the certificate of insurance was surrendered to the insurer or the person to whom the certificate of insurance was delivered made a statutory declaration that the certificate of insurance had been lost or destroyed and so could not be surrendered, or

(iii) before or after the happening of the event or within a period of fourteen days from the taking effect of the cancellation of the policy the insurer had commenced proceedings under this Decree in respect of the failure to surrender the certificate of insurance.

(3) No sum shall be payable by an insurer under the provisions of this section if in an action commenced before or within three months after the commencement

of the proceedings in which the judgment was given he has obtained a declaration that apart from any provision contained in the policy, he is entitled to avoid it on the ground that it was obtained by the non-disclosure of a material fact or by a representation of fact which was false in a material particular or if he has avoided the policy on the ground that he was entitled to do so apart from any provision contained in it:

Provided that an insurer who has obtained such a declaration in an action shall not thereby be entitled to the benefit of the provisions of this subsection in respect of any judgment obtained in any proceedings commenced before the commencement of that action unless before or within seven days after the commencement of that action he has given notice thereof to the person who is plaintiff in the action under the policy specifying the non-disclosure or false representation on which he proposes to rely and that he intends to seek a declaration and any person to whom notice of such action is given may, if he desires, be made a party thereto.

Time within which motor accident cases must be settled.

44. Subject to section 43 of this Decree, in every case where a claim made in writing by the insured or any other party entitled thereto under an insurance policy in relation to a motor vehicle accident, the insurer shall—

  (a) where it accepts liability, settle the claim not later than ninety days from the date on which the claim was delivered to it; or

  (b) where it does not accept liability, deliver a statement in writing disclaiming such liability to the person making the claim or his authorised representative not later than ninety days from the date on which such person delivered his claim to such insurer.

Dispensation with police repor* in certain motor accident cases.

45.—(1) Where any claim referred to in section 43 or 44 of this Decree arises out of an accident involving one or more motor vehicles, it shall not be necessary, if there is sufficient evidence of proof of loss or damage, for any claimant to deliver a police report thereon to the insurer:

Provided that where death of, or serious bodily injury to, a person is involved in any such accident, the provisions of this section shall not ap

(2) Without prejudice to any other mode of proof, it shall be sufficient evidence of proof of loss or damage for the purposes of this section if—

(a) where only one person is involved in the accident, the person delivers a statement of the facts to the insurer concerned together with a statement of any eye witness to the accident, if any; or

(b) where more than one party is involved in the accident, each party delivers a statement of the facts to the insurer or insurers concerned and the alleged facts do not differ in any material particular.

Insurance of Imports

46.—(1) Subject to subsection (2) of this section, every insurance in respect of goods to be imported into Nigeria shall, as from the commencement of this Decree, be made with an insurer registered under this Decree and, accordingly, the provisions of any law, contract or instrument shall be construed with such modifications, amendments and omissions as would bring them into line with the general intendment of this section of this Decree; and without prejudice to the generality of the foregoing, every letter of credit or such similar document issued by any bank or other financial institution in Nigeria in respect of such goods shall be on a carriage and freight basis only.

Insurance of imports to be effected with insurers in Nigeria, etc.

(2) Notwithstanding subsection (1) of this section, where in any particular case an insurance broker satisfies the Director that by reason of the exceptional nature of the risk in, or emanating from, Nigeria or other exceptional circumstances, it is not reasonably practicable to effect the insurance with an insurer

registered under this Decree, the Director may in writing permit such broker to effect such insurance with insurers outside Nigeria.

(3) Any person who effects any insurance otherwise than in compliance with the provisions of subsections (1) and (2) of this section shall be guilty of an offence and liable on conviction to a fine of ₦2,000 plus an additional fine equal in amount to the total commission received by any such person in any such transaction.

Rebates and Loans

Certain rebates prohibited.

47.—(1) No person shall offer, either directly or indirectly, as an inducement to any person to take out or renew or continue an insurance contract in respect of any kind of risk relating to lives and property in Nigeria—

(a) any rebate of the whole or part of the commission payable under this Decree; or

(b) any rebate of the premium shown on the policy, except such rebate as may be allowed in accordance with the published prospectus or table of the insurer.

(2) Any person who offers or receives any rebate otherwise than as provided for in subsection (1) of this section shall be guilty of an offence and shall be liable on conviction to a fine of ₦1,000.

Restriction on loans to directors, etc.

48.—(1) No insurer shall grant loans to any officer of the insurer, except—

(a) loans on life policies issued to such person by the insurer; and

(b) loans normally forming part of the terms and conditions of service of such officer.

(2) Every insurer who grants and every officer thereof who receives any loan otherwise than as provided for in subsection (1) of this section shall be guilty of an offence and every such insurer or officer shall on conviction be liable to a fine of double the amount of such loan.

General Penalties

49.—(1) Every offence under this Decree shall, subject to the rules of court, be tried in the Federal Revenue Court and references in this Decree to "court" or "the court" shall be construed accordingly.

(2) Without prejudice to the powers of the Attorney-General of the Federation under the Constitution of the Federation, the Director may initiate criminal proceedings and prosecute same under his own name.

50.—(1) If any person required to furnish returns or information to the Director pursuant to this Decree fails to furnish such returns or information, he shall be guilty of an offence and liable on conviction to a fine of ₦1,000 or imprisonment for six months or to both such fine and imprisonment.

(2) If a person in purported compliance with a requirement to furnish returns or information as aforesaid knowingly or recklessly makes a statement in the return or gives information which is false in any material particular, he shall be guilty of an offence and liable on conviction to a fine of ₦500 or imprisonment for three months or to both such fine and imprisonment.

51. Any person who wilfully obstructs, interferes with, assaults or resists any public officer in the performance of his duties under this Decree or aids, invites, induces or abets any other person to obstruct, interfere with, assault or resist any such officer shall be guilty of an offence liable on conviction to a fine of ₦500 or imprisonment for three months or to both such fine and imprisonment.

52.—(1) Any insurer who distributes dividends otherwise than in compliance with section 19 (6) of this Decree shall be guilty of an offence and liable on conviction to a fine of ₦2,000.

(2) Any insurer who encumbers, or disposes of •

Margin notes:

Jurisdiction and prosecutions.

1963. No. 20.

Offences as to returns.

Obstruction of public officers.

Offences by insurers in relations to dividends. and investments.

investments or who does any other thing whatsoever which results in diminishing the security offered by any investments made pursuant to this Decree shall be guilty of an offence and liable on conviction to a fine of ₦3,000.

Misrepresentation by public officers

53.—(1) Any public officer who, in the discharge of his duties under this Decree, presents to another public officer, who is to take a decision thereon or do any other act in relation thereto, information which is false or false in any material particular, shall be guilty of an offence unless he proves that such information was supplied to him by another person and that he exercised all such diligence to prevent the commission of the offence as he ought to have exercised having regard to the nature of his functions in that capacity and to all the circumstances.

(2) Any public officer found guilty of an offence under subsection (1) of this section shall be liable on conviction to a fine of ₦1,500 or imprisonment for six months or to both such fine and imprisonment.

Additional penalties to be imposed on insurers.

54.—(1) Notwithstanding any other provision of this Decree, in any case where an insurer fails to pay any fine imposed for any offence under this Decree within 30 days from the imposition thereof, or, in case of an appeal to a higher court and where no further appeal is made, 30 days from t e confirmation of the judgment of the lower court, he Director may in writing suspend such insurer from writing any new insurance business for such period not being less than 12 months as he may think fit.

(2) If the insurer fails to pay the fine referred to in subsection (1) of this section within the period of suspension mentioned in that subsection, the Director shall cancel the certificate of registration of the insurer.

Additional penalties: officers of insurers, brokers and agents, etc.

55.—(1) Where an offence under this Decree has been committed by a body corporate, or firm or other association of individuals, any person who at the time of the commission of the offence was an officer thereof or was purporting to act in such capacity shall severally be guilty of that offence and liable to be proceeded against and punished for the offence in like manner as if he had himself committed the offence, unless he proves that the act or omission constituting the offence took place without his knowledge, consent or connivance.

(2) In this section and the other provisions of this Decree, "officer"—

(a) in relation to a body corporate, includes every director, chief executive, manager or secretary;

(b) in relation to a firm, includes every partner or other officer thereof;

(c) in relation to any other association of individuals, every person concerned in the management of the affairs of such association.

56.—(1) No person other than an insurer or broker registered pursuant to this Decree or an agent so licensed shall, after the expiry of six months from the coming into operation of this Decree, use the word "insurance" or any derivative thereof as part of his business name or for describing the nature or object of such business.

Restriction on use of the word "insurer" or "underwriter".

(2) No person other than an insurer registered pursuant to this Decree shall, after the expiry of six months from the coming into operation of this Decree, use the word "underwriter" or any derivative thereof as part of his or its business name or for describing the nature or object of such business.

(3) Any person who uses the word "insurer" or "underwriter" otherwise that in compliance with the provisions of subsection (1) or (2) of this section shall be guilty of an offence and liable on conviction to a fine of ₦5 for every day or part thereof upon which the name or description is so used.

Supplementary

57.—(1) Any person may, on payment to the Director of the prescribed fee, inspect or make copies of any

Inspection of documents, etc.

document or obtain certified copies of any documents in the custody of the Director under this Decree.

(2) No fee shall be paid to the Director for information supplied by him as to the chief executive in Nigeria of an insurer and the address of the principal office in Nigeria of an insurer.

Copies where documents produced to the Director.

58.—(1) Where an original document is produced to the Director it shall be accompanied by two copies duly certified as true copies for retention by the Director unless the Director dispenses with production of the copies, or any copy.

(2) Where a copy only of a document is produced, the Director may require production of further evidence to account for the absence of the original; and if he is satisfied, two copies shall be prepared, and when duly certified on behalf of the insurer, shall be retained by the Director unless the Director dispenses with their production.

(3) For the purposes of this section a document shall be deemed to be duly signed or certified if it appears to be signed on behalf of the insurer by the chief executive in Nigeria of the insurer or is issued under seal or, as the case may be, is signed by some person approved by the Director.

Service of process.

59.—(1) Service of process in any legal proceedings against an insurer registered pursuant to this Decree may be effected at the principal office of the insurer in Nigeria.

(2) In any case where the principal office of the insurer in Nigeria has ceased to exist, process in any legal proceedings against such insurer may be served at the office of the Director and service on the Director, in any such case, shall be deemed to be service on the insurer.

Fees.

60.—(1) The fees payable for registration as an insurer shall be such as may be prescribed.

(2) Where fees are to be prescribed under this Decree-

or are specified therein such fees shall be prescribed
or, as the case may be, may be varied from time to
time by regulations made by the Commissioner.

61. The Commissioner may make regulations generally   Regulations
for the purposes of this Decree and, without prejudice
to the generality of the foregoing, such regulations
may make different provisions for different classes
of insurers or of insurance business.

62. In this Decree, unless the context otherwise   Interpreta-
requires— "actuary" means—   tion.

(*a*) a person having prescribed actuarial qualifications; or

(*b*) a member of a professional actuarial society
or institute approved by the Director;

"auditor" means a person enrolled or regis-
tered as an accountant pursuant to the Institute   1965 No. 15.
of Chartered Accountants Act 1965;

"Central Bank" means the Central Bank   Cap. 30.
of Nigeria established pursuant to the Central
Bank of Nigeria Act;

"Commissioner" means the Federal Commissioner
charged with responsibility for insurance;

"co-operative insurance society" means a society
registered under any enactment or law relating to
co-operative societies and which carries on the business
of insurance and of which, by its constitution, all
policy holders are members thereof;

"court" means the Federal Revenue Court;

"Director" means the Director of Insurance appointed
pursuant to section 35 of this Decree;

"financial year" means one calendar year;

"industrial life policy" means a policy whereby
the insurer assumes a contingent obligation dependent
on human life, in an amount not exceeding the sum
of ₦2,000 in return for a premium or the promise
of a premium payable at intervals not exceeding two
months, if the insurer has expressly or tacitly undertaken to send a person from time to time to the policy

holder or to his residence or place of work to collect the premiums;

"insurance" includes assurance;

"insurance agent" means a person licensed as such pursuant to · this Decree authorised by an insurer to solicit risks and collect premiums on its ·behalf for which he receives or agrees to receive payment by way of commission or other remuneration· from the insurer;

"insurance broker" means a person registered pursuant to section 27 of this Decree ·and includes an adjuster;

"insurance business" includes re-insurance business and references to contracts and business of insurance shall be construed accordingly;

"insurance policy"·includes a cover note;

"insurer" means a person who is carrying insurance risks and is registered under this Decree for that purpose;

"life insurance business" includes annuity business that is to say, the business of effecting contracts of insurance for the granting of annuities on human life, and if so provided in the contract of insurance, disability and double indemnity accident benefits; and "non-life insurance business" means any insurance business other than life insurance business;

"life policy" means any instrument by which the payment of money is assured on death (except death by accident only) or the happening of any contingency being the termination or the continuance of human life or any instrument evidencing a contract which is subject to payment of premiums, for a term dependent on human life;

"mutual insurance company" has the meaning assigned thereto by section 3 (4) of this Decree;

"officer" has the meaning assigned thereto by section 55 of this Decree;

"pensions fund" means a programme for providing regular payments out of an accumulated fund to retired employees for life;

"policy-holder" means the person who for the

time being is the legal holder of the policy for securing
the contract with the insurer;

"prescribed" means prescribed by regulations
under this Decree;

"registered" means registered for the purposes
of this Decree.

63.—(1) On the appointed day, the Insurance Compa- Repeals and
nies Act 1961 and the Insurance (Miscellaneous Provi- savings.
sions) Act 1964 shall, subject to the provisions of 1961 No. 53.
this section, stand repealed.

(2) Nothing in this Decree shall be construed so 1964 No. 19.
as to prohibit the continuation of an inspection by
inspectors appointed under any enactment hereby
repealed, begun before the appointed day and section
38 of this Decree shall apply to a report of inspectors
appointed under any such repealed enactment as it
applies to a report of investigators appointed under
section 37 of this Decree.

(3) Any register kept under the enactments hereby
repealed shall be deemed part of the register to be
kept under the corresponding provisions of this Decree.

(4) Funds and accounts constituted under this
Decree shall be deemed to be in continuation of the
corresponding funds and accounts constituted under
the enactments hereby repealed.

(5) Where any offence, being an offence for the continuance of which a penalty was provided, has been
committed under any enactment hereby repealed,
proceedings may be taken under this Decree in respect
of the continuance of the offence after the commencement of this Decree, in the same manner as if the
offence had been committed under the corresponding
provisions of this Decree.

(6) In this section, "the appointed day" means
the day of coming into operation of this Decree.

Companies
Decree 1968 to
supplement
this Decree.

64. The provisions of this Decree are without prejudice to the application of the Companies Decree 1968 to insurers under this Decree which are companies registered under that Decree:

1968 No. 51.

Provided that where any of the provisions of the Companies Decree 1968 is inconsistent with any provision of this Decree, this Decree shall prevail.

Citation and
commencement.

65.—(1) This Decree may be cited as the Insurance Decree 1976.

(2) This Decree shall be deemed to have come into operation on the 1st day of December 1976.

MADE at Lagos this 7th day of December 1976.

LT.-GENERAL O. OBASANJO.
Head of the Federal Military Government,
Commander-in-Chief of the Armed Forces,
Federal Republic of Nigeria

EXPLANATORY NOTE

*(This note does not form part of the above
Decree but is intended to explain its support)*

The Decree repeals the Insurance Companies Act 1961 and the Insurance (Miscellaneous Provisions) Act 1964 and, while re-enacting some of the provisions of those repealed enactments, prescribes additional measures for the registration of insurers and makes fresh provisions for the licensing of insurance agents and registration of insurance brokers.

Provisions are contained in the Decree specifying time-limits within which motor accident claims are to be settled, prohibiting general increases in premium rates (except with the prior approval of the Government), while other provisions relate generally to the better management and regulation of insurance business in Nigeria.

INSURANCE DECREE 1976
(1976 No. 59)

Insurance Regulations 1977

ARRANGEMENT OF REGULATIONS

Regulation

PART I—FORMS

1. Application for registration as an insurer.
2. Certificate of registration.
3. Cancellation of registration, etc.
4. Certificate of solvency.
5. Balance sheet, etc.
6. Statement of life insurance business.
7. Report of actuary.
8. Valuation balance sheet, etc.
9. Auditor's certificate.
10. Application form for brokers and adjusters.
11. Registration form for brokers and adjusters.
12. Notice to cancel registration of broker or adjuster.
13. Application form for agents.
14. Licence form for agents.
15. Notice of cancellation of agent's licence.

PART II—PARTICULARS

16. Particulars of chief executives of insurers.
17. Particulars required on resignation of chief executive.
18. Agents.
19. Brokers and adjusters.

INSURANCE DECREE 1976

(1976 No. 59)

Insurance Regulations 1977

Commencement : 17th January 1977

In exercise of the powers conferred by section 61 of the Insurance Decree 1976, and of all other powers enabling me in that behalf, I, Major-General Mohammed Shuwa, the Federal commissioner for Trade, hereby make the following regulations:—

PART I—FORMS

Application for registration as an insurer.

1.—(1) For the purposes of section 4 of the Decree, an application for registration as an insurer shall be in Form 1 in Schedule 1 to these regulations and be accompanied, where applicable, by the following documents, that is—

(*a*) a copy of table of premium rates and their basis including occupational extra rating and standard policy forms of each class of insurance business carried on or proposed to be carried on by the applicant: Provided that in the case of marine, aviation and transit insurance business, the requirements of this section shall be complied with only in so far as such rates and forms are available;

(*b*) if the applicant is a person carrying on or proposing to carrying on life insurance business, statements, signed by an actuary, as to the calculation of premium rates and non-forfeiture values as to advantages, terms and conditions offered or proposed to be offered;

(*c*) the memorandum and articles of association or other evidence of the constitution of the body concerned;

(*d*) a list containing the name and address of each director or other similar officer of the body concerned;

(*e*) a list containing the name, qualifications and experience and address of the head or proposed . head of each department of the body concerned;

(*f*) a certified copy of the certificate of incorporation;

(*g*) a list showing the names, addresses, occupation for the past ten years of each director;

(*h*) a statement of the class or classes of business to be carried out;

(*i*) in case of life insurance business, also a statement as to the method of distributing profits, as between policy holders and shareholders.

(2) Where an application for registration is made by an insurer which, on the coming into operation of the Decree, was carrying on insurance business in Nigeria, the application shall be accompanied by the following additional documents, that is—

(*a*) a certificate as to the solvency of the applicant· signed, in the case of life insurance business, by an actuary and in the case of non-life insurance business, by any other person authorised in that behalf by the applicant;

(*b*) a certified copy of the balance sheet duly audited showing the financial position of the insurance business of the applicant at the close of the last preceding financial year, together with a copy of the relevant profit and loss account;

(*c*) a certified copy of the revenue account in respect of the insurance business carried on by the applicant in the last preceding financial year; and

(*d*) in the case of life insurance business, a statement in respect thereof covering the last preceding financial year.

Certificate of registration

2.—(1) Form 2 (*a*) is hereby prescribed as the form of certificate of registration of an insurer.

(2) Form 2 (*b*) is hereby prescribed as the form of registration to continue as an insurer for the purposes of section 3 (3) of the Decree.

Cancellation of registration, etc.

3.—(1) Forms 3, 4, 5 and 6 are hereby prescribed as the forms in respect of the following matters, respectively, that is—

(*a*) notice of the Director's intention to reject an application pursuant to section 5 (2) of the Decree;

(*b*) notice of the decision of the Commissioner allowing an appeal against the Director's intention to reject such application;

(*c*) notice of the Director's intention to cancel the registration of an insurer pursuant to section 7 (1) of the Decree; and

(*d*) notice of the decision of the Commissioner allowing an appeal against the Director's intention to cancel such registration.

(2) Forms 3, 4 and 6 shall apply with all necessary textual alterations, amendments, omissions and any other modification whatsoever, to brokers and adjusters.

Certificate of solvency.

4. Forms 7 and 8 are hereby prescribed as the forms of—

(*a*) certificate of solvency of an insurer in respect of insurance business carried out by such insurer other than life insurance business; and

(*b*) certificate of solvency of an insurer in respect of life insurance business carried out by such insurer.

Balance sheet, etc.

5. Forms 9, 10, 11, 11*a*, 12, 12*a*, 13 and 14 are hereby prescribed where applicable, as the forms of—

(*a*) balance sheet;

(*b*) profit and loss account;

(*c*) profit and loss appropriation account;

(*d*) revenue account in respect of life insurance

business; and

(*e*) revenue account in respect of insurance business other than life-insurance business.

6. Form 15 is hereby prescribed as the form of statement of life insurance business.

Statement of life insurance business.

7. Form 16 is hereby prescribed as the form of abstract of report of an actuary and statement of long term business.

Report of actuary.

8. Forms 17, 18 and 19 are hereby prescribed respectively as the forms of—

Valuation balance sheet, etc.

(*a*) summary and valuation of policies;

(*b*) valuation balance sheet; and

(*c*) specimen policy reserve values and minimum surrender values.

9. Form 20 is hereby prescribed as the form of certificate to be furnished by an auditor in respect of the audit of the accounts of an insurer's business in Nigeria

Auditor's certificate.

10. Form 21 is hereby prescribed as the form of application for registration as a broker or, as the case may be, an adjuster.

Application form for brokers and adjusters.

11. Form 22 is hereby prescribed as the form of registration or renewal of registration of a broker or, as the case may be, of an adjuster.

Registration form for brokers and adjusters.

12. Form 23 is hereby prescribed as the form of notice of the Director's intention to cancel a certificate of registration of a broker or, as the case may be, of an adjuster pursuant to section 27 (7) of the Decree.

Notice to cancel registration of broker or adjuster.

13. Form 24 is hereby prescribed as the form of application for registration as an agent.

Application form for agents.

14. Form 25 is hereby prescribed as the form of the licence to be issued to a broker whose application is approved.

Licence form for agents.

15. Form 26 is hereby prescribed as the form of notice of cancellation of the licence of a broker pursuant to section 25 or, as the case may require, section 26 of the Decree.

Notice of cancellation of agent's licence.

PART II.— PARTICULARS

Particulars of chief executives of insurers.

16. The particulars required pursuant to section (12) (a) of the Decree are—

    (a) the curriculum vitae of the prospective appointee indicating in detail his academic, professional, administrative and other qualifications; and

    (b) the detailed career history of the said prospective appointee.

Particulars required on resignation of chief executive.

17. The matters required pursuant to section 13 (1) of the Decree are—

    (a) that the letter of termination of appointment of the chief executive or, as the case may be, of his resignation shall contain reasons for such termination or resignation;

    (b) that in either case mentioned in paragraph (a) above, the chief executive concerned shall prepare a report containing his general observations of the business of the insurer; and

    (c) any other matter that the said chief executive thinks should be brought to the attention of the insurer concerned.

Agents.

18. The documents required pursuant to section 25 of the Decree are—

    (a) a letter of appointment from each insurer concerned; and

    (b) in the case of an application for renewal of a licence, a statement from each insurer concerned that the accounts of the preceding financial year have been settled.

Brokers and adjusters.

19. The documents required pursuant to section 27 of the Decree are—

    (a) the curriculum vitae indicating in detail the academic, professional, administrative and other qualifications of the prospective chief executive of the applicant including—

        (i) evidence that the said chief executive is a holder of either an A.C.I.I. or A.C.I.B. diploma, or (*ii*) evidence that the said chief executive has been principally engaged in insurance business for a continuous period of not less than five years on the date of, or at any time prior to the date of, application for registration; and

(*b*) in the case of an application for renewal of registration, a declaration by the applicant to the effect that all premiums collected during the preceding financial year have been paid over to the insurers concerned.

PART III.—FEES

20.—(1) Pursuant to the Decree, the fees specified in column 2 of Schedule 2 to these regulations shall apply with respect to the corresponding matters set out in column 1 therein. Fees:

(2) Notwithstanding paragraph (1) above, the Director may in cases where he considers it in the public interest so to do, dispense with the fee for any inspection of documents.

PART IV.—SUPPLEMENTARY

21. Every form or other document required to be furnished pursuant to the Decree or these regulations shall be printed or typed. Forms to be printed.

22. Any document purporting to be a document executed under the seal of office of the Director or Deputy Director or any other duly authorised public officer appointed pursuant to sections 35 and 36 of the Decree or, as the case may require, any document not sealed but merely authenticated by the signature of any of the aforementioned officers, shall be received in evidence and shall, unless the contrary is proved, be presumed to be so executed or, as the case may require, so authenticated without proof of signature. Evidence.

23.—(1) In these regulations, unless the context otherwise requires— Interpretation.

"accident insurance business" means the business of assuming the obligation of an insurer under any policy of insurance upon the happening of personal accident, whether fatal or not, disease or sickness, or any class of personal accidents, disease or sickness;

"fire insurance business" means the business of assuming the obligation of an insurer under any policy against loss by or incidental to fire;

"marine, aviation and transit insurance business" includes the business of assuming the liabilities of an insurer under policies insuring, otherwise than as incidental to some other class of insurance business—

(a) vessels or aircraft or machinery, tackle, furniture or equipment of vessels or aircraft; or

(b) goods, merchandise or property of any description whatsoever on board vessels or aircraft; or

(c) the freight of, any other interest in or relating to vessels or aircraft; or

(d) against damage arising out of or in connection with the use of vessels or aircraft, including third party risks; or

(e) risks incidental to the repair or docking of vessels, including third party risks; or

(f) transit risks (whether the transit is by sea, inland water, land or air, or partly one and partly another) including risks incidental to the transit insured from the commencement of the transit to the ultimate destination covered by the insurance, but not including risks the insurance of which is motor vehicle insurance business; or

(g) any other risks the insurance of which is customarily undertaken in conjunction with or as incidental to any business referred to in paragraphs (a) to (f) of this definition;

"motor vehicle insurance business" means the business of effecting contracts of insurance against loss of, or damage to or arising out of or in connection with the use of, motor vehicles, including third party risks.

24.—(1) These regulations may be cited as the Insurance Regulations 1977.

Citation and repeal.

(2) The Insurance Companies Regulations 1968 are hereby revoked and the Insurance Companies (Amendment) Regulations 1973 are consequentially repealed.

L. N. 92 of 1968
L. N. 31 of 1973.

SCHEDULES

SCHEDULE 1 *Part I of Regulations*

FORMS

FORM 1

(*Under the Insurance Decree* 1976)

APPLICATION FOR REGISTRATION AS AN INSURER

(*a*) ....

To the Director of Insurance,
Lagos.

1. This application for the registration of the above-mentioned applicant as an insurer under the Insurance Decree 1976 is made on its behalf by (*b*) ....directors of the applicant by whom this application is signed.

2 (*a*) The applicant is a company incorporated and registered under the Companies Decree 1968 and its registration number is (*c*) ....

3. The name of the applicant is as stated above and its registered office within the meaning of section 105 (2) of the Companies Decree 1968 or (in the case of a company established outside Nigeria) its place of business in Nigeria within the meaning of section 369 of that Decree is (*e*)..

The particulars of the Share Capital of the applicant are as follows:—

(*i*) Authorised Share Capital (*f*) ₦ ....

(*ii*) Issued Share Capital (*g*) ₦ ....

(*iii*) Paid Up Share Capital   (*h*) ₦ ....

5. The class or classes of insurance business (if any) carried on in Nigeria by the applicant on the date of the coming into operation of the Insurance Decree 1976 are as follows :—

(*i*) ....

6. The class or classes of insurance business in respect of which this application is made are as follows:—

(*j*) ....

7. For the purposes of section 11 of the Decree, it is proposed that the principal office of the applicant shall be at (*k*) ....

and that its chief executive shall be (*l*) ....

8. In accordance with regulation 1 of these Regulations, this application is accompanied by a certified copy of each of the following documents that is to say:—

(*a*)
(*b*)
(*c*)
(*d*)
(*e*)
(*f*)
(*g*)
(*h*)
(*i*)
(*j*)
(*k*)
(*l*)

9. The fee of ₦ (*m*)..................payable in respect of this application has been paid to the Government of the Federation and credited to the appropriate Head of Revenue vide Treasury Receipt No.

(*n*).....................of......................................(*o*).

10. We have been duly authorised by the applicant to make this application on its behalf.

DATED...19......

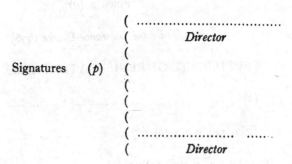

Signatures (*p*)

NOTES

I. Where not applicable, insert a dash or "n.a."

II.(*a*) Insert the name under which the applicant is incorporated and/or registered as a corporate body under the laws of any country.

(*b*) Insert the number of directors (not being less than two) by whom the application is signed.

(*c*) Insert the registration number under the companies Decree 1968.

(*d*) Insert the name of the country under which the applicant is incorporated and/or registered as a corporate body.

(*e*) Insert the address.

(*f*) Insert the amount of the authorised share capital.

(*g*) Insert the amount of the issued share capital.

(*h*) Insert the amount of the paid up share capital.

(*i*) Insert the class or classes of that insurance business.

(*j*) Insert the class or classes of the insurance business in respect of which the application is made.

(*k*) Insert the address of the place which it is proposed shall be the principal office.

(*l*) Insert the name, qualifications and experience of the person who it is proposed shall be the chief executive.

(*m*) Insert the amount of the fee paid.

(*n*) Insert the number of the Treasury receipt.

(*o*) Insert the date of the Treasury receipt.

(*p*) To be signed by at least two directors.

FORM 2 (*a*)

(*Under the Insurance Decree* 1976)

CERTIFICATE OF REGISTRATION AS AN INSURER

(*a*) ....

Registration No. (*b*) ....

It is hereby certified that (*a*)...has this

(*c*)...day of...19........... been
registered as an insurer under the Insurance ~~Decree 1976~~ to carry
on the following class or classes of insurance business:—

(*d*) ....

Signature (*e*) ....
Director of Insurance

NOTES

(*a*)   Insert the name of the insurer which is being certified as
        registered.
(*b*)   Insert the registration number of the insurer under the Insu-
        rance Decree 1976.
(*c*)   Insert the date of the registration.
(*d*)   Insert the class or classes of insurance business which the
        insurer is authorised to carry on.
(*e*)   To be signed by the Director or a Deputy Director.

FORM 2 (*b*)

(*Under the Insurance Decree* 1976)
CERTIFICATE OF REGISTRATION TO CONTINUE AS AN INSURER

(*a*) ....

Registration No. (b) ....

It is hereby certified that (a)..has this

(c)...day of ....19.......... been
registered to continue as an insurer under the Insurance Decree
1976 to carry on the following class or classes of insurance business:—

(d) ....

....

....

Signature (e) ....

Director of Insurance

NOTES

(a) Insert the name of the insurer which is being certified as
registered.
(b) Insert the registration number of the insurer under the
Insurance Decree 1976.
(c) Insert the date of the registration.
(d) Insert the class or classes of insurance business which the
insurer is authorised to carry on.
(e) To be signed by the Director of Insurance or a Deputy Director.

FORM 3*

(*Under the Insurance Decree* 1976)

NOTICE OF INTENTION TO REJECT AN APPLICATION FOR REGISTRATION AS AN INSURER

(a) ....

Notice is hereby given to (a)...that the

Director of Insurance intends to reject your application for registration as an insurer, on the following grounds, that is to say—

(b) ....

2. Unless before (c)...........................you lodge with the Permanent Secretary, Federal Ministry of Trade, a notice of appeal in writing under section 5 of the Insurance Decree 1976, setting out the grounds on which it is made, your application shall be deemed to have been rejected.

DATED...19..........

Signature (d)   ....

Director of Insurance

NOTES

This form shall apply with all necessary modifications to brokers and adjusters.
(a)   Insert the name and address of the applicant.
(b)   Insert the grounds on which the Director intends to reject the application.
(c)   Insert a date which is sixty days after the date of the notice.
(d)   To be signed by or on behalf of the Director of Insurance

FORM 4*

(*Under the Insurance Decree* 1976)

NOTICE OF DECISION ALLOWING AN APPEAL AGAINST THE DIRECTOR'S INTENTION TO REJECT AN APPLICATION FOR REGISTRATION AS AN INSURER

(a) ....

Notice is hereby given that in exercise of the powers conferred under section 6 of the Insurance Decree 1976, the Federal Commissioner for Trade has on (b)...............................allowed your appeal against the intention of the Director of Insurance to reject your application for registration as an insurer.

DATED...19.........

Signature (c) ....
Permanent Secretary

NOTES

This form shall apply with all necessary modifications to brokers and adjusters.

(a) Insert name and address of applicant.

(b) Insert the date of the decision.

(c) To be signed by or on behalf of the Permanent Secretary, Federal Ministry of Trade.

FORM 5

(*Under the Insurance Decree* 1976)

NOTICE OF DIRECTOR'S INTENTION TO CANCEL THE REGISTRATION OF AN INSURER

(a) ....

Registration No. (b) ....

Notice is hereby given to (a)...............................that the Director, of Insurance, in exercise of the powers conferred on him under section 7 of the Insurance Decree 1976, intents to cancel your registration as an insurer, on the following grounds, that is to say:—

(c) ....

2. Unless before (d)....................................you lodge with the Permanent Secretary, Federal Ministry of Trade, a notice of appeal against this notice, in accordance with section 6 of the Decree, the Director shall proceed to cancel your registration as an insurer.

DATED...19...........

Signature (e) ....
Director of Insurance

NOTES

(a)   Insert the name and address of the insurer, the registration of which the Director intends to cancel.

(b)   Insert the registration number of the insurer under the Insurance Decree 1976

(c)   Insert the grounds on which the Director intends to cancel the registration of the insurer.

(d)   Insert a date being not less than sixty days after the date of the notice.

(e)   To be signed by or on behalf of the Director of Insurance.

FORM 6

(Under the Insurance Decree 1976)

NOTICE OF DECISION ALLOWING
AN APPEAL AGAINST THE DIRECTOR'S INTENTION
TO CANCEL THE REGISTRATION OF AN INSURER

(a)..

Notice is hereby given that in exercise of the powers conferred under section 6 of the Insurance Decree 1976, The Federal Commissioner for Trade has on (b)..allowed your appeal against the intention of the Director of Insurance to cancel your registration as an insurer.

DATED...19...........

Signature (e) ....
Permanent Secretary

NOTES

This form shall apply with all necessary modifications to brokers and adjusters.

  (a) Insert the name and address of the appellant.
  (b) Insert the date of the decision.
  (c) To be signed by or on behalf of the Permanent Secretary, Federal Ministry of Trade.

FORM 7

(*Under the Insurance Decree* 1976)

CERTIFICATE OF SOLVENCY OF AN INSURER IN RESPECT OF INSURANCE BUSINESS OTHER THAN LIFE INSURANCE BUSINESS

(a)...

To the Director of Insurance,
Lagos.

    This certificate witnesseth that the above-mentioned insurer, having its head office at (b)..carries on the following classes of insurance business, that is to say (c) ....
    And that during the preceeding financial year that is to say, from ....19......... to...19........., to the best of our knowledge, information and belief the value of the assets of the insurer aforesaid in respect of the insurance business, other than life insurance business, carried on by it exceeded the value of its liabilities by...(e)

DATED..19.........

....
Actuary or Director

....
Chief Executive

....
Auditor

NOTES

(a) Insert the name of the insurer or applicant.
(b) Insert the address where the head office is situated.
(c) Insert the class or classes of insurance business.
(d) To be signed by an actuary or a director, the chief executive and an auditor.
(e) Insert amount.

FORM 8

(Under the Insurance Decree 1976)

CERTIFICATE OF SOLVENCY OF AN INSURER IN RESPECT OF LIFE INSURANCE BUSINESS

(a) ....

To the Director of Insurance,

Lagos.

This certificate witnesseth that as respects the above-mentioned insurer, having its head office at (b).. and carrying on life insurance business, the liabilities under its life policies, in respect of business carried on in Nigeria did not exceed the amount of the life insurance fund relating to that business at the end of the preceding financial year, that is to say as at the................................

day of..19..........

DATED...19...........

Signature (c) ....

Actuary

NOTES

(a) Insert the name of the insurer or applicant.
(b) Insert the address where the head office is situated.
(c) To be signed by an actuary.

FORM 9

(Under the Insurance Decree 1976)

BALANCE SHEET

As at 31st December, 19......... in respect of life insurance Business

transacted in Nigeria by the ....

(Name of Insurer)

PART A—LIABILITIES

19.........   19.........

1. Amount of Capital
   Authorised
   Issued
   Paid-Up
2. Contingency Reserve *(a)*
3. Life Funds
   Ordinary branch
   Industrial branch
   Pensions
4. Outstanding Claims, admitted or Intimated
5. Amounts due to insurers
6. Amounts due to insurance agents
7. Amounts due to policyholders
8. Other Liabilities *(b)*
9. Other sums owing by insurer *(b)*
10. Balance of Profit and Loss Appropriation
    Account

TOTAL

FORM 9

PART B: ASSETS

19............   19............

1. Federal Governmnet Securities (*c*) ....
2. State Government Securities (*c*)   ....
3. Securities of Semi-governmental bodies (*c*)
4. Other bonds and stocks   ....
5. Real Estate   ....
6. Mortgage Loans on real estate (*c*)   ......
7. Loans made to policy-holders   ....
8. Other Loans (*c*)   ....
9. Outstanding Premiums (*d*) ....
10. Amounts due from Insurers   ....
11. Amounts due from Insurance Agents and
    Brokers   ....
12. Cash (*a*) on deposit account   ....
    (*b*) in hand and on current account   ......
13. Bills of exchange   ....
14. Interest, Dividends and Rents   ....
    (*a*) Outstanding   ....
    (*b*) Accrued but not due   ....
15. Equipment, Furniture and Supplies   ......
16. Other Assets (*c*)   ....
17. Balance of profit and loss   ....
    Appropriation Account.   ....

                              TQTAL

                    (....
                    (*Director*
                    (
                    (....
Signature (*e*)   (*Chief Executive*
                    (
                    (....
                    (*Auditor*

NOTES

(*a*) This denotes amounts voluntarily set aside out of profits and other surpluses which are not designed to meet any liability, contingency, commitment, or diminution in value of assets known to exist as at the date of the balance sheet.

(*b*) These must be specified on a separate sheet.

(*c*) Items 1 to 6, 8 and 16 must be specified on a separate sheet showing yields on each security.

(*d*) Either this item must be shown net as to reinsurance and commission or the ceded reinsurance payable and the commission must be provided for amongst the liabilities of this balance-sheet (items 11 and 12).

(*e*) To be signed by a director, the chief executive and the auditor who makes the audit.

FORM 9

PART C

ANALYSIS OF THE INVESTMENTS SHOWN IN THE BALANCE SHEET AND OF THE DEPOSITS

	Investment			Deposits made by undertaking		Deposits in the undertaking belonging to third parties	
a	*b*	*c*	*d*		*e*	*f*	*g*
Investments	In national securities	In foreign securities	In the country	Abroad		From the country	From abroad
1. In State securities and bonds, etc.							
2. In real estate							
3. In mortgages							
4. In private securities with fixed interest							
5. In stock and similar securities							
6. In cash and currency							
7. In other investments and loans (specify)							
8. TOTAL							
9. % of Total							

FORM 10

(Under the Insurance Decree 1976)

BALANCE SHEET

As at 31st December 19............ in respect of the Non-Life Insurance

Business transacted in Nigeria by the ....

(name of insurer)

PART A.—LIABILITIES

	Insurance Business	
	Non-Life	Total
	₦	₦
1. Amount of capital:		
Authorised		
Issued		
Paid up		
2. Contingency Reserve (a)		
3. Accident Insurance Fund		
4. Fire Insurance Fund		
5. Employers' Liability Insurance Fund		
6. Motor Vehicle Insurance Fund		
7. Transport Insurance Fund		
8. Miscellaneous Insurance Fund		
9. Outstanding claims, admitted or intimated		
10. Amounts due to insurers		
11. Amounts due to insurance agents		
12. Amounts due to policyholders		
13. Other sums owing by insurer		
14. Other liabilities (b)		
15. Balance of Profit and Loss		
Appropriate Account		
TOTAL		

PART B.—ASSETS

	Insurance Business	
		Total
	N	N
1. Federal Government securities (c)		
2. State Government securities (c)		
3. Securities of semi-governmental bodies (c)		
4. Other bonds and stocks (c)		
5. Real estate (c)		
6. Mortgage loans on real estate (c)		
7. Loans made to policyholders		
8. Other loans (c)		
9. Outstanding premiums (d)		
10. Amounts due from insurers		

PART B.—ASSETS

	Insurance Business	
		Total
	N	N
11. Amounts due from insurance agents		
12. Cash (a) on deposit account		
(b) in hand and on current account		
13. Bills of exchange		
14. Interest, dividends and rents		
(a) outstanding		
(b) accrued but not due		
15. Equipment, furniture and supplies		
16. Other assets (c)		
17. Balance of Profit and Loss Appropriation Account		
TOTAL		

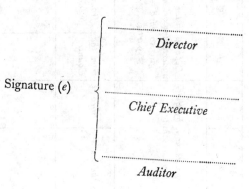

Signature (*e*)
Director

Chief Executive

Auditor

NOTES

(*a*) This denotes amounts voluntarily set aside out of profits and other surpluses which are not designed to meet any liability, contingency, commitment, or diminuation in value of assets known to exist as at the date of the balance sheet.

(*b*) These must be specified on a separate sheet.

(*c*) Items 1 to 6, 8 and 16 must be specified on a separate sheet

(*d*) Either this item must be shown net as to reinsurance and commission or the ceded reinsurance payable and the commission must be provided for amongst the liabilities of this balance sheet (items 11 and 12).

(*e*) To be signed by a director, the chief executive and the auditor who makes the audit.

FORM 10

PART C

ANALYSIS OF THE INVESTMENTS SHOWN IN THE BALANCE SHEET AND OF THE DEPOSITS

a	b	c	d	e	f	g
	Investments		*Deposits made by the undertaking*		*Deposits in the undertaking belonging to third parties*	
	In national securities	*In foreign securities*	*In the country*	*Abroad*	*from the Country*	*from abroad*
1. In State securities and bonds, etc.						
2. In real estate						
3. In mortgages						
4. In private Securities with fixed interest						
5. In stock and similar securities						
6. In cash and currency						
7. In other investments and loans (specify)						
8. TOTAL						
9. % of Total						

FORM 11

(*Under the Insurance Decree* 1976)

PROFIT AND LOSS ACCOUNT

For the year ended..19..........

in respect of Life Insurance Business transacted in Nigeria by the..........

....

(*name of insurer*)

	₦		₦
Interest, dividends and rents (*a*)		Taxes on insurer's profits (*b*)	
Deduct: income tax thereon		Loss on realisation of investments (*d*)	
Profit on realisation of investments			
Appreciation of investments (*c*)		Depreciation of investments (*d*)	
Profits transferred from Revenue Account (details to be given)		Loss transferred from Revenue Accounts (details to be given)	
Other income (to be specified)		Other expenditure (to be specified)	
Balance being loss for the year carried to Appropriation Account		Balance for the year carried to Appropriation Account	

Signatures (*e*)

> ....
> *Director*
>
> ....
> *Chief Executive*
>
> ....
> *Auditor*

NOTES

In this Account must be reported all gains and losses on capital transactions and on revaluation of assets, non-recurring expenses and losses and income and expenditure not directly connected with the underwriting of risks.

(*a*)   Interest dividends and rents relating to the investments of insurance funds have to be carried to the Revenue Accounts.

(*b*)   All property, profit and similar taxes, licence fees and other public burden have to be carried to the Revenue Accounts.

(*c*)   Amounts which have not been credited to any particular fund or account and irrespective of whether they have actually been received or not.

(*d*)   Amounts which have not been charged to any particular fund or account and irrespective of whether they have actually been paid or not.

(*e*)   To be signed by a director, the chief executive and the auditor who makes the audit.

FORM 11 (*a*)

(*Under the Insurance Decree* 1976)

PROFIT AND LOSS APPROPRIATION ACCOUNT

For the year ended...19...........

In respect of Life Insurance Business transacted in Nigeria by the...........

....

(*Name of Insurer*)

	₦		₦
Balance brought forward from last year		Balance being loss brought forward from last year	
Balance for the year brought		Balance being Loss for the	

from Profit and loss Account
(as in Form 10) ....

year brought from
Profit and Loss Account
(as in form 10)......   ....

Dividends to share-
holders   ....,

Bonuses to Policy-
holders   ....

Balance being loss at end of
the year as shown in the
Balance Sheet   ....

Transfer to any particular
Funds or Accounts
(details to be given)   ....

Signatures·(a)

{

....
Director

....
Chief Executive

....
Auditor

NOTE

(a)   To be signed by a director, the chief executive and the auditor
who makes the audit.

FORM 12

(*Under the Insurance Decree* 1976)
PROFIT AND LOSS ACCOUNT

For the year ended...19..........

in respect of Non-Life Insurance Business transacted in Nigeria by the

....

| PTF Low
Price Edition |

(*Name of Insurer*)

	N		N
Interest, dividends and rents	....	Taxes on insurers' profits (*b*)	....
Deduct: Income tax thereon	....		
Profit on realisation of investments	....	Loss on realisation of investments (*d*)	....
Appreciation of investments (*c*)	....	Description of investments (*d*)	....
Profits transferred from Revenue Accounts (details to be given)	....	Loss transferred from Revenue Accounts (details to be given)	....
Other income to be specified	....	Other expenditure (to be specified)	....
Balance being loss for the year carried to Appropriation Accounts	....	Balance for the year carried to Appropriation Account	....

Signatures (*e*)

Director

Chief Executive

Auditor

Notes

In this Account must be reported all gains and losses on capital transactions and on revaluation of assets, non-recurring expenses and losses, and income and expenditures not directly connected with the underwriting of risks.

(*a*) Interest, dividends and rents relating to the investment of insurance funds have to be carried to the Revenue Accounts.

(*b*) All property, profit and similar taxes, licence fees and other public burden have to be carried to the Revenue Accounts

(c) Amounts which have not been credited to any particular ·fund or account and irrespective of whether they have actually been received or not.

(d) Amounts which have not been charged to any particular fund or account and irrespective of whether they have actually been paid or not.

(e) To be signed by a director, the chief executive and the auditor who makes the audit.

FORM 12 (*a*)

(*Under the Insurance Decree* 1976)

PROFIT AND LOSS APPROPRIATION ACCOUNT

For the year ended..19............

In respect of Non-Life Insurance Business transacted in Nigeria by the

....

(*Name of Insurer*)

₦	₦
Balance brought forward from last year	Balance being loss brought forward from last year ....
Balance for the year brought from Profit and Loss Accounts (as in Form 12)	Balance being loss for the year brought from Profit and Loss Account (as in form 12) ....
	Dividends to shareholders Bonuses to Policy-holders ....
Balance being loss at end of the year as shown in the Balance Sheet	Transfer to any particular Funds or Accounts (details to be given) ....

Signatures (a) {

....
Director

....
Chief Executive

....
Auditor

NOTE

(a)   To be signed by a director, the chief executive and the auditor who makes the audit.

FORM 13*

(Under the Insurance Decree 1976)

REVENUE ACCOUNT IN RESPECT OF LIFE INSURANCE BUSINESS REVENUE ACCOUNT

For the year ended..19..........

In respect of the Life Insurance Business transacted in Nigeria by the

....

(Name of Insurer)

PART A: INCOME

		N	N	N
Amount of Life Insurance Fund at the beginning of the Reserve for outstanding claims Premium:-(a)				....
single	....	....	......	......	....	....
first year	......	....	......	......	....	....
renewal	......	....	......	......	......	....

Add · Reinsurance accepted: Locally ....
Abroad ....
Deduct: Reinsurance ceded: Locally ....
Abroad ....
Premiums for own account ....
Consideration for annuities ....
Deduct: Reinsurance ceded ....

Investment Income:—
interest ....
dividends ....
real estate income ....

Deduct: Income tax thereon ....
Increase in book value of assets ....
Profit on sale of assets .... ——
Other income (to be specified) ....
Transferred from Appropriation Account ....
Loss transferred to Profit and Loss Account ....

Part B: Expenditure

Claims paid under policies:—			**N**	**N**	**N**
By death	......	......	......	......	....
By additional accidental death		......	......	......	....
By maturity	......	......	......	......	....
By disability	......	......	......	......	....

Deduct: Reinsurance recoveries ....
Net claims paid ....
Reserve for outstanding claims ....

Deduct: Reinsurance recoveries ——
Annuities ....
Deduct: Reinsurance recoveries ....

Surrenders (*b*) .... ——
Bonuses in cash (*c*) ....
Bonuses in reduction of premiums (*c*) ......

Commission to insurance agents ....
Deduct: Reinsurance ....
Compensation of agents not paid by commission ————
Expenses of management:—

1. Salaries (other than to agents) ....
2. Travelling expenses ....
3. Contribution to staff pension fund ....
4. Director's fees ....
5. Auditor's fees ....
6. Medical examiners' fees ....
7. Legal expenses ....
8. Advertisement ....
9. Printing and stationery ....
10. Postage, telegrams and telephone ....
11. Rent for offices (*d*) ....
12. General office maintenance .... ————

13. Other expenses of management (to be
    specified) ....
Decrease in book value of assets . ...
Loss on sale of assets ....
Other expenditure (to be specified) ....
Profit transferred to Profit and Loss Account
Amount of Life Insurance Fund at the end of the
year as shown in the Balance-sheet ....

Signature (*e*)

> ....
> *Director*
>
> ....
> *Chief Executive*
>
> ....
> *Auditor*

Notes

(a)   Including Premiums:—
     (*i*) for reinsurance accepted;
     (*ii* for disability and accidental death benefits;
     (*iii*) for group insurance;
     (*iv*) payable by application of dividends (bonuses).
(b)   Including surrenders of bonus, less reinsurance recoveries (if any).
(c)   Less reinsurance recoveries (if any).
(d)   Including rent for offices belonging to and occupied by insurer.
(e)   To be signed by a director, the chief executive, and the auditor who makes the audit.

A Revenue Account in Form 13 must be rendered in respect of each branch (ordinary and industrial) of life insurance business for which a separate fund is maintained.

Form 14*

(*Under the Insurance Decree* 1976)

REVENUE ACCOUNT IN RESPECT OF INSURANCE BUSINESS OTHER THAN LIFE INSURANCE BUSINESS REVENUE ACCOUNT

For the year ended...19.........

in respect of the............ ....Insurance Business transacted

in Nigeria by the   ....

(*Name of Insurer*)

Part A: Income

Amount of ....Insurance Fund at the   ₦
beginning or the year:
Reserve for unexpired risks   ....

Liability in respect of outstanding claims   ....

Additional reserve (if any)   ....
Premiums:—

         Direct Business

Add: Reinsurance accepted locally   ....

         Reinsurance accepted abroad   ....

Deduct: **Reinsurance ceded locally**   ....

         Reinsurance ceded abroad   ....
Premiums for own account   ....

Interest, dividends and rents (*a*)   ....
Deduct: Income-tax thereon   ....

Other income (to be specified)   ....

Transferred from Appropriation Account   ....

Loss transferred to Profit and Loss Account   ....

PART B: EXPENDITURE

Claims paid under policies: (*b*)   **N**
  relating to:

         Previous years   ....

         Current year   ....
Deduct: Reinsurance recoveries relating to: ....

         Previous years   ....

         Current year   ....
Net Claims paid:
Commission: Direct Business   ....

Add: Reinsurance accepted   ....

Deduct: Reinsurance ceded......   ....

Net Commission   ....
Expenses of management (c)   ....
Other expenditure (to be specified)   ....
Profit transferred to   ....

Profit and Loss Account   ....
Amount of......................Insurance Fund at the end of
  year as shown in the Balance-Sheet:
  Reserve for unexpired risks being..........per cent of the
    premium income of the year   ....

Liability in respect of outstanding claims   ....

Additional reserve (if any)   ....

NOTES

(a) All interest, dividends and real estate income relating to the investment of the respective insurance fund must be reported hereunder.

(b) Expenses incurred in settling claims must not be included in this item.

(c) Expenses of management in respect of the total non-life insurance business must be specified in Part C of this Form.

A Revenue Account in Form 14 must be rendered in respect of each class of insurance business.

PART C: EXHIBIT

EXPENSES OF MANAGEMENT IN RESPECT OF THE TOTAL INSURANCE BUSINESS OTHER THAN LIFE INSURANCE BUSINESS

		Loss Adjustment Expenses (1)	*Other underwriting Expenses* (2)	*Investment Expenses* (3)	*Total Expenses* (4)
1.	Salaries				
2.	Contribution to employees' pension fund				
3.	Directors' fees				
4.	Travelling expenses				
5.	Legal expenses and auditing				
6.	Advertising				
7.	Printing and stationery				
8.	Equipment				
9.	Office rent and maintenance				
10.	Postage, telegrams and telephone				
11.	Associations' fees, etc.				
12.	Other expenses of management (to be specified)				
	Expenses of Management (as shown in) Revenue Accounts				

Signatures (*a*)

$\left\{\rule{0pt}{4em}\right.$ ....
Director

....
Chief Execute

....
Auditor

Notes

(*a*) To be signed by a director, the chief executive and the auditor who makes the audit.

Form 15*

(*Under the Insurance Decree* 1976)

STATEMENT OF LIFE INSURANCE BUSINESS

Part A—Statement of New Life Policies

For the Year Ending ....19............

in respect of the Life Insurance Business transacted in Nigeria by the

....

(*Name of insurer*)

	New life insurance business in respect of which a premium has been paid in the year			
	Number of Policies	Sums Insured (a)	Single Premiums (b)	Yearly renewable premiums (c)
ORDINARY INSURANCE POLICIES (c)		₦	₦	₦
A With participation in profits:				
Whole life insurance				
Endownment insurances				
Temporary insurances				
Others				
B Without participation in profits:				
Whole life insurance				
Endowment insurances				
Temporary insurances				
Others				
TOTAL				
Thereof: ceded for re-insurance				

GROUP INSURANCE POLICIES				
Permanent insurance plan	(d)			
One-year renewable term plan	(d)			

ANNUITY CONTRACTS	Number of Contracts	Annuities per annum	Consideration	
			Single (b)	Renewable (b)
Immediate				
Deferred				
Total				

Signatures (e)

....
Director

....
Chief Executive

NOTES

(*a*)   Only the main benefit is to be reported; benefits from contracts supplemental to life policies are to be excluded.

(*b*)   The amounts are to be stated to the nearest naira.

(*c*)   Including policies accepted for reinsurance, if any.

(*d*)   Indicate in parenthesis the number of persons insured thereunder.

(*e*)   This Statement must be signed by a director and the chief executive.

* *A separate statement must be submitted in respect of insustrial insurance policies.*

PART B—POLICY EXHIBIT

For the Year Ending...19..........
in respect of the Life Insurance Business transacted in Nigeria by the

....

(*Name of insurer*)

	Ordinary Life Insurance Policies (a)			Annuities	
	Number of Policies	Sums insured	Reversionary bonus additions	Number of contracts	Annuity per annum
1. Policies at beginning of year (b) ...... 2 (thereof; policies ceded for reinsurance)	₦	₦	₦		₦
Additions during year 2. New policies issued					
3. Old policies revived					
4. Policies increased (i) by bonuses allotted .... (ii) otherwise					
5. Old policies changed					
6. TOTAL					
Deductions during year 7. By death					
8. By survival					
9. By happening of contingencies insured against other than death					
10. By expiry of term under temporary insurance					
11. By surrender of policy					
12. By forfeiture or lapse					
13. By decrease: (i) By surrender of					

bonus				
(*ii*) by change into paid up policy				
(*c*) otherwise				
14. By change of policy.....				
15. By being not taken up				
16. TOTAL				
17. Policies existing (*c*) at end of year ...... (thereof: policies ceded for reinsurance				
18. Applications declined during year				
19. Supplemental accident insurance policies existing at end of year				

Signature (*d*)   { ....
                       Director

                     ....
                       Chief Executive

NOTES

(*a*)   Including temporary insurance policies.

(*b*)   Only the main benefit is to be reported; benefits from contracts supplemental to life policies are to be excluded from lines 1 to 18.

(*c*)   Including policies accepted for reinsurance, if any; a separate statement must be submitted in respect of:

(*i*) industrial life insurance policies; and

(*ii*) group insurance policies (with indication of number of persons insured thereunder).

(*d*)   This statement must be signed by a director and the chief executive.

FORM 16

(*Under the Insurance Decree* 1976)

FORM OF ABSTRACT OF THE REPORT OF AN ACTUARY AND STATEMENT OF LIFE INSURANCE BUSINESS VALUATION REPORT

Report of an Actuary on an investigation into the financial position of a life insurer

NOTES

(*a*)   Report and statements must be so arranged that the numbers and letters of the paragraphs correspond with those of the requirements of this Form. The amounts stated therein shall be to the nearest naira.

(*b*)   Separate reports and statements must be furnished throughout in respect of ordinary and industrial life insurance business.

(*c*)   Every report and annexed statement prepared in accordance with this Form shall be signed by an actuary and shall contain a certificate by him to the effect that he has satisfied himself as to the accuracy of the valuations made for the purposes thereof and of the valuation data.

PART A.—REQUIREMENTS

Every such report shall show:—

1. The valuation date.

2. The general principles and full details of the methods adopted in the valuation of the particular groups of insurance as shown in Form 17 including statements on the following points:—

(*a*)   the method by which the net premiums taken credit for in the valuation (thereinafter called "net premiums") have been arrived at;

(*b*)   the method by which the valuation age, period from the valuation date to the maturity date, and the future premium terms, have been treated for the purpose of the valuation;

(*c*)   the method of allowing for—

(*i*) the incidence of the premium income; and

PTF Low
Price Edition

(*ii*) premiums payable otherwise than annually;

(*d*)   the methods by which provision has been made for the following matters, namely:—

(*i*) the immediate payment of claims;

(*ii*) future expenses and profits in the case of limited payment;

(*iii*) the reserve in respect of lapsed policies, not included in the valuation, but under which a liability exists or may arise;

(*e*)   whether under the valuation method adopted any policy would be treated as an asset;

(*f*)   the manner in which policies on substandard lives have been dealt with.

3. The table of mortality used in the valuation. If rated, state degree of rating up or down as the case may be.

4. The rate of interest assumed in the valuation.

5. The proportion which that part of the annual premiums reserved as a provision for future expenses and profits bears to the total of the annual premiums, separately specified in respect of insurances with and without participation in profits.

6. The basis adopted in the distribution of profits as between the insurer and policy-holders and how such basis was determined.

7. The general principles adopted in the distribution of profits among policy-holders, including statements on the following points, namely:—

(*a*)   how these principles were determined;

(*b*)   the number of years' premiums to be paid, period to elapse and other conditions to be fulfilled before a bonus is allotted;

(*c*)   the conditions of vesting of the bonus.

8.—(1) The total amount of profits arising during the intervaluation period, including profits paid away and sums transferred to reserve funds or other accounts during that period, and the amount brought forward from the preceding valuation and the allocation of such profits—

(*a*)   to interim bonus paid,

(*b*)   among the participating policy-holders,

(*c*)   among the shareholders of the insurer (if any),

(*d*)   to reserve funds,

(*e*)   as carried forward unappropriated.

(2) Specimens of bonuses allotted as a result of the valuation to policies for ₦1,000—

(a) for the whole term of life affected at the respective ages of 20, 30 and 40, and having been in force respectively for five years, ten years and upwards at intervals of ten years;

(b) for endowment insurances effected at the respective ages of 20, 30 and 40 for endowment terms of fifteen, twenty, and thirty years and having been in force respectively for five years, ten years and upwards at intervals of ten years; together with the amounts apportioned under the various manners in which the bonus is receivable.

PART B.—STATEMENTS

The following statements shall be annexed to every Report namely:—

(a) A Consolidated Revenue Account for the inter-valuation period, i.e. the period to the valuation date of the present valuation from the valuation date of the last preceding valuation or, in case where no such valuation has been made, from the date on which the insurer began to carry on business. The Consolidated Revenue Account shall be made in a form corresponding to Form 13 of these regulations.

(b) A Summary and Valuation of the Policies included at the valuation date in Form 17.

(c) A Valuation Balance Sheet in Form 18.

(d) A Policy Exhibit for the inter-valuation period in a form corresponding to Part B of Form 15 of these regulations.

(e) A statement of Specimen Policy Reserve Values held or required to be held according to the methods adopted in the valuation, and specimen Minimum Surrender Values in Form 19 together with a statement of the method pursued in calculating such minimum surrender values. These shall be shown in respect of whole life insurance policies for ₦1,000 with premiums payable throughout life and in respect of endowment insurance policies maturing at age 55, effected at the respective ages 20, 30, 40 and 50.

(f) A statement, separately prepared in reespect of policies with and without participation in profits, showing:—

(i) as respect whole life insurance policies the total amounts insured (specifying sums insured and reversionary bonuses separately), grouped according to the ages attained at the valuation date;

(*ii*) as respects endowment insurance policies the total amounts insured (specifying sums insured and reversionary bonuses separately), grouped according to the years in which the policies will mature for payment.

(*g*)   A statement as respects any policies in force under which premiums cease to be payable, whether permanently or temporarily, during disability arising from sickness or accident, showing the total amount of the office premiums payable.

(*h*)   A statement as respects any group insurance policies, showing the total premiums received and claims paid since the date as at which the last statement was prepared under this Form, or where no such statement has been prepared since the date on which the insurer, began to transact group insurance business, and the premium reserve or the reserve for unexpired risks and the outstanding claims at the valuation date.

(*i*)   A statement as respects immediate annuities on single lives for the whole term of life, showing for each attained age the total amount of such annuities.

(*j*)   A statement as respects deferred annuities showing the specimen reserve values for annuities of one thousand naira which will be produced on maturity on the basis of valuation adopted at age 60.

(*k*)   A statement respecting the average rate of interest yielded by the assets, whether invested or uninvested, constituting the life insurance fund of the insurer for each of the years covered by the valuation date.

This average rate shall be calculated by dividing the interest of the year by the mean fund of the year; and for the purposes of any such calculation the interest of the year shall be taken to be the whole of the income credited to the life insurance fund during the year after deduction of income tax charged thereon, and the mean fund of the year shall be ascertained by adding a sum equal to one-half of the amount of the life insurance fund at the beginning of the year to a sum equal to one-half of that fund at the end of the year, and deduction from the aggregate of those two sums an amount equal to one-half of the interest of the year.

(*l*)   A certificate signed by the chief executive of the insurer that full and accurate particulars of every policy under which there is a liability either actual or contingent has been forwarded to the actuary for the purpose of the investigation.

FORM 17

(Under the Insurance Decree 1976)

SUMMARY AND VALUATION OF THE POLICIES

OF THE..............................

(Name of Insurer)

AS AT..................19........

Group	Description of Transactions	Particulars of the Policies for Valuation (a)						Valuation		
		Number of Policies	Sums Insured	Bonuses 1	Bonuses 2	Office Yearly Premiums	Net Yearly Premiums	Sums Insured and Premiums	Net Yearly Premiums	Net Liabilities
A	Insurance with participation in profits:									
	Whole Life									
	Endowment . . .									
	Educational Endowment .									
	Other classes (to be specified) (b)	*	*							
	Extra Premiums (c) . .									
	TOTAL	*								

(1) Guaranteed.
(2) Non-guaranteed.

Form 17 Continued

B	Insurance without participation in profits:								
	Whole Life								•
	Endowment . . .								•
	Educational Endowment								•
	Other classes (to be specified) (*d*) . . .								•
	Extra Premiums (*c*)								•
	TOTAL . . .	• •		•					•
	Total Insurance:								•
	(A) and (B) thereof: ceded for reinsurance		•						•
C	TOTAL, INSURANCE FOR OWN ACCOUNT .								•
D	Group Insurances less reinsurance:		•						•
E	Annuities on Lives—								
	Immediate . . .								
	Deferred . . .								
	TOTAL, ANNUITIES LESS REINSURANCE								
	TOTAL: (C) AND (D) AND (E)								•

....
Director

....
Chief Executive

....
Actuary

Signatures (*e*)

Notes

(*a*) Including policies accepted for reinsurance, if any.
(*b*) Policies with a waiver of premiums during disability are to be shown separately.
(*c*) Including the charge for any risk not provided for in the minimum contract premium.
(*d*) Policies without participation in profits but with a guaranteed rate of bonus are to be specified separately.
(*e*) To be signed by a director, the chief executive and the actuary by whom the investigation was made.

• A separate form must be submitted in respect of industrial life insurance policies.

FORM 18

(*Under the Insurance Decree* 1976)

VALUATION BALANCE SHEET

As at ....19.........in respect of. the
Life Insurance Business transacted in Nigeria by the ....

....

(*name of insurer*)

	N
Net liability under life insurance transactions as shown in the Summary and Valuation of Policies ...... Surplus, if any	Life Insurance Fund as shown in Balance Sheet .... Deficiency, if any ....

(
(
(
(*Signatures* (*a*)
(
(
(
(

....
Director

....
Chief Executive

....
Actuary

NOTE

(*a*) To be signed by a director and the chief executive of the insurer and by the actuary by whom the investigation was made.

(*Under the Insurance Decree* 1976)

FORM OF SPECIMEN POLICY RESERVE VALUES AND MINIMUM SURRENDER VALUES

SPECIMEN POLICY RESERVE VALUES AND MINIMUM VALUES

Under...(*a*) policies for ₦1,000 according to the method adopted in the valuation or in force at the date of valuation of the................

(*name of insurer*)

Number of annual premiums paid up to the valuation date	Age at entry : 20		Age at entry : 30		Age at entry : 40		Age at entry : 50	
	Policy Reserve Value	Minimum Surrender Value	Policy Reserve Value	Minimum Surrender Value	Policy Reserve Value	Minimum Surrender Value	Policy Reserve Value	Minimum Surrender Value
2.								
3.								
4.								
5.								
6.								
7.								
8.								
9.								
10.								
15.								
20.								
25.								

NOTE—(*a*) Insert the words "Whole Life Insurance" and/or "Endowment Insurance Policies maturing at age 55" as appropriate.

FORM 20

(Under the Insurance Decree 1976)

CERTIFICATE TO BE FURNISHED BY AN AUDITOR IN RESPECT OF THE ACCOUNT OF A REGISTERED INSURER IN NIGERIA

CERTIFICATE

To the Director of Insurance,
Lagos.

I have examined the books relating to insurance business carried on by..(a) being an insurer during the financial year ended 31st December, 19.........In my opinion, the books of (a)............................have been properly kept and the affairs and transactions of the insurer have been correctly recorded. The accounts and balance sheet are in accordance with the information given to me and with the provisions of the Insurance Decree 1976 and reflect a true and fair view of the financial position of the insurer.

I have verified by actual inspection the investments and cash as at 31 st December, 19.........and adequate provision has been made for doubtful debts.

All the information I require has been supplied to me and the books appear to me to have been properly kept.

DATED at........................this....................day of.......................19.........

Signed (b)...
Auditor

(a)   Insert the name of the insurer.
(b)   To be signed by the Auditor.

FORM 21*

(Under the Insurance Decree 1976)

APPLICATION FOR REGISTRATION/RENEWAL OF REGISTRATION AS AN INSURANCE BROKER UNDER THE INSURANCE DECREE 1976

(a) ....

To the Director of Insurance,
Lagos.

This application for registration as an insurance broker under the Insurance Decree 1976 is made by the applicant, whose name is given above or on its behalf by the undersigned.

The applicant's principal place of business is...

....

Qualifications and experience of the applicant or of its Chief Executive are as follows ....

....

....

....

The Registration/Renewal fee of ₦.. payable in respect of this application has been paid to the Government of the Federation vide Treasury Receipt No. ....
of.., 19..........

The applicant has deposited with the Central Bank of Nigeria on a fixed deposit basis, the sum of ₦.. vide Central Bank receipt No...........................of..............................
....19..........

Details of insurance transactions handled by the applicant are as follows:

....

....

DATED this..day of................ ....19............

Signature..•..............

*Applicant or authorised
representative*

NOTE

(*a*)   Insert name of applicant.

**This form shall apply to adjusters and, accordingly, all reference
to "broker" therein should be altered to read "adjuster"*

FORM 22*

(*Under the Insurance Decree* 1976)

CERTIFICATE OF REGISTRATION/RENEWAL AS AN INSURANCE BROKER

(Registration No. RB...)

It is hereby certified that..has this..........................day

of..19............ been registered/had its registration
renewed under the Insurance Decree 1976..for the
period of.......... ....19......... to..............................19............
to transact the business of an insurance broker.

Signature:..

Director of Insurance

*This form shall apply to adjusters (see note to form 21).

FORM 23

(Under the Insurance Decree 1976)

NOTICE OF DIRECTOR'S INTENTION TO CANCEL THE CERTIFICATE OF REGISTRATION OF AN INSURANCE *BROKER

Notice is hereby given that in exercise of the powers conferred under section 27 of the Insurance Decree 1976, the Director of Insurance intends to cancel your certificate of registration as an insurance broker on the following grounds..

....

Unless within 60 days from the date of this notice you lodge with the Permanent Secretary, Federal Ministry of Trade, a notice of appeal against this notice, your registration shall be deemed to have been cancelled.

DATED this.............................day of..19...........

Signature:..
Director of Insurance

This form shall apply to adjusters (see note to form 21).

FORM 24

(Under the Insurance Decree 1976)

APPLICATION FOR LICENSING/RENEWAL OF LICENCE AS AN INSURANCE AGENT UNDER THE INSURANCE DECREE 1976

To the Director of Insurance,
Lagos.

I,...
hereby apply for a licence/renewal of a licence as an insurance agent under the Insurance Decree 1976 to canvass for the classes of insurance business listed below on behalf of the Principal named below:—

Name and Address of Principal	Classes of business to be canvassed for	Registration No. of the Principal

2. The relevant returns of business in respect of the preceding year of agency are attached hereto.

3. Authority from my Principal, to act on its/their behalf is also attached.

4. The Licensing/Renewal fee of ₦...................................payable in respect of this application has been paid to the Government of the Federation vide Treasury Receipt No...................of.............19 ....

DATED this...................................day of..............................19.........

Signature...
Applicant

FORM 25

(*Under the Insurance Decree* 1976)

LICENCE AS AN INSURANCE AGENT UNDER THE INSURANCE DECREE 1976

Licence No. LA...

It is hereby certified that...has this...................day of..................19......... been licensed/had its licence renewed under the Insurance Decree 1976 for the period of ....19........to.................................19..........

to canvass for the following classes of insurance business, on behalf of the Principal named below:—

Name and Address of Principal	Registration No. of Principal	Classes of Business for which licence is issued

DATED this...day of.....................................19.........

Signature...

Director of Insurance

FORM 26

(*Under the Insurance Decree* 1976)

NOTICE OF CANCELLATION OF LICENCE AS AN INSURANCE AGENT

(a) ....

Notice is hereby given that pursuant to section 25/26 (b) of the Insurance Decree 1976, the Director of Insurance has with effect from..19.........cancelled your licence as an insurance agent. Henceforth it shall be unlawful for you to canvass for any insurance business on behalf of any Principal in the Federation of Nigeria.

DATED this...day of.....................................19.........

Signature...

Director of Insurance

NOTES

(a)   Insert name of agent.
(b)   Delete whichever is inapplicable.

SCHEDULE 2

Regulation 20

FEES

Column 1	*Column* 2
	Rates
	₦
(1) The fee for registration as an insurer shall be—	
(a) in respect of life insurance business	500
(b) in respect of insurance business other than life insurance business	500
(2) For the certificate of registration as an insurer or a certified copy thereof	6
(3) For the registration of a notice of the winding up or dissolution of an insurer	4
(4) For the registration of an amalgamation of two or more insurers	6
(5) For the inspection by each person of documents in the custody of the Director relating to a particular insurer	1
(6) For a copy or extract of any document, whether certified or not, in the custody of the Director—	
(a) not exceeding 216 words	2
(c) exceeding 216 words, for the 1st 216 words, ₦2 and for each folio of 72 words or part thereof in excess of 216 words	1
(7) Fee for registration as a broker/adjuster	200
(8) Renewal fee of certificate of registration of a broker/adjuster	100
(9) Fee for licence as agent	100
(10) Renewal fee of licence of an agent	25

MADE at Lagos this 17th day of January 1977.

MAJOR-GENERAL M. SHUWA,
Federal Commissioner for Trade

Explanatory Note

(This note does not form part of the above Regulations but is intended to explain the purpose thereof)

The regulations, among other things, prescribe the forms of registration of insurers, brokers or adjusters and agents, fees payable and other matters required to be prescribed pursuant to the Insurance Decree 1976.

NIGERIA REINSURANCE CORPORATION
DECREE 1977

Deree No. 49

Commence-
ment.   [1st *July* 1976]

THE FEDERAL MILITARY GOVERNMENT
hereby decree as follows:—

Constitution and Functions of the Corporation, etc.

**Establish-
ment of the
Nigeria Re-
insurance
Corporation.**

1.—(1) There shall be established a corporation
to be known as the Nigeria Reinsurance Corporation
(hereinafter in this Decree referred to as "the Corporation") which shall be constituted in accordance
with and shall have such powers and duties as are
conferred on it by the following provisions of this
Decree.

(2) The corporation shall be a body corporate with
perpetual succession and a common seal.

(3) The corporation may sue or be sued in its corporate name and may hold, acquire, and dispose of any
property movable or immovable.

**Functions of
the Corpora-
tion.**

2.—(1) Subject to the provisions of this Decree,
the Corporation shall have power, within or outside
Nigeria, to carry on reinsurance of any class of insurance
business, including life insurance business, and to
reinsure against loss of any kind arising from any risk
or contingency in respect of any matter whatsoever.

(2) Without prejudice to the generality of section (1)
of this section the Corporation shall have power to
do any of the following things, that is—

(a) to reinsure with any insurer carrying on insurance
or reinsurance business, any risk undertaken
by the Corporation and for that purpose to

enter into reinsurance contracts; and '

(b) to accept the reinsurance of any part of risks undertaken by any other person (being risks such that the corporation has power to reinsure against) and to retrocede any part of such risk.

(3) Save as may be expressly provided for by an order made under Subsection (5) below, the Corporation shall have power to do anything or to enter into any transaction which in the opinion of the Board is calcu-lated to facilitate the due performance of the functions of the Corporation under this Decree, and in particular the Corporation may—

(a) acquire any undertaking of any registered insurer or acquire, hold or have any shares or stock in, or any financial interest in any such undertaking;

(b) acquire and invest in any other profitable business;

(c) assist in organising training schemes for employees of any registered insurer.

(4) The Corporation shall serve as the channel of ceding compulsory cessions from the Federation of Nigeria to the African Reinsurance Corporation.

(5) Where the Commissioner is of the opinion that it is in the public interest so to do, he may, with the prior approval of the Federal Executive Council, by Order published in the *Gazette* abridge or restrict the powers of the Corporation to any extent necessary; and when so abridged or restricted the powers of the Corporation shall be exercisable subject to and in accordance with the provisions of the order, and not otherwise.

(6) For the avoidance of doubt, it is hereby declared that the foregoing provisions of this Decree relate only to the capacity of the Corporation as a statutory corporation, and nothing in the said provisions shall be construed as authorising the disregard by the Corporation of any rule of law.

3.—(1) There shall be a Board of Directors of the Corporation (hereinafter referred to as "the Board") — Board of Directors.

which shall, subject to the general direction of the Commissioner, be responsible for the overall policy and general management of the Corporation.

(2) The Board shall comprise the following, that is to say—

(a) a Chairman, who shall be a person of integrity and of good standing with wide experience in industry, commerce, finance or administration as well as specialised knowledge of the working of insurance;

(b) the Permanent Secretary, Federal Ministry of Finance or his representative;

(c) the Permanent Secretary, Federal Ministry of Economic Development or his representative;

(d) the Permanent Secretary, Federal Ministry of Trade or his representative;

(e) the Managing Director of the Corporation;

(f) a number of directors, not being more than six, being persons who by their character and experience in matters relating to accountancy, law, finance, insurance or economics are, in the opinion of the Commissioner, suitable for appointment as members of the Board.

(3) The Chairman and the members of the Board under paragraph (f) of subsection (2) above shall be appointed by the Federal Executive Council on the recommendation of the Commissioner and shall, subject to this section, hold office on such terms and conditions as the Federal Executive Council may, from time to time, determine.

(4) The Chairman and members of the Board under paragraph (f) of subsection (2) above shall hold office for three years and shall be eligible for reappointment.

(5) The Chairman or any member of the Board under paragraph (f) of subsection (2) above may resign his appointment by a letter addressed to the Commissioner and the resignation shall take effect from the date on which the letter is received by the Commissioner.

(6) The supplementary provisions of Schedule 1

to this Decree shall have effect in relation to the procedure at meetings of the Board and such other matters as are specified therein.

(7) The reference in subsection (2) of this section to the representative of a Permanent Secretary is a reference to such officer of the Ministry of which that Permanent Secretary has responsibility as may be appointed by the Permanent Secretary to represent him.

4.—(1) Subject to subsection (2) below, the Corporation shall be liable to taxation under any applicable law (including liability for any duty, rate, levy or other charge whatsoever whether general or local properly levied and payable).

Corporation not to be exempted from taxation, etc.

(2) Nothing in this section shall be construed as imposing liability for company income tax upon the Corporation until such time as the amount in the general reserve fund of the Corporation is for the first time equal to twice the amount of the paid-up capital of the Corporation.

5.—(1) The Commissioner may give to the Board directions of a general or of a special nature with regard to the exercise of the functions of the Corporation; and, as the case may require, it shall be the duty of the Chairman, the Board and the Managing Director to comply with the directions unless matters of policy are in dispute.

Directions by the Commissioner.

(2) In the application of subsection (1) above, where the Commissioner intends to initiate a policy affecting the exercise of the functions of the Corporation, he shall consult with the the Board and in the event of disagreement between the Commissioner and the Board over the implementation of that policy, the policy and any directive issued in that respect, shall stand suspended, so however that if any part of the policy so in dispute is severable from any other aspects of the policy not in dispute, the policy or the directive issued shall be suspended only in respect of the part

in dispute; and thereafter the policy, or the part in dispute, so suspended shall, upon its being referred by the Commissioner to the Federal Executive Council, be affirmed, modified, or rejected by that Council, and the Council may give such directions thereon as it thinks fit.

Extended application of Insurance Decree 1976 No. 59.

6.—(1) The Insurance Decree 1976 shall apply to the Corporation to the same extent as it applies to insurers under that Decree; and accordingly, and in so far as the provisions of the Insurance Decree 1976 are not inconsistent with those of this Decree, the Corporation shall, where applicable, comply with the requirements of that Decree as if the Corporation were an insurer registered pursuant to that Decree and the Insurance Decree 1976 shall in relation to the Corporation have effect and be construed accordingly.

(2) The provisions of subsection (1) of this section shall apply *mutatis mutandis* to the National Insurance Corporation of Nigeria established pursuant to the National Insurance Corporation of Nigeria Decree 1969.

1969 No. 22.

Compulsory reinsurance with the Corporation by registered insurers; Schedule 2, etc.

7.—(1) Subject to subsection (2) below, a registered insurer shall, in respect of every insurance policy issued or renewed by it on or after 1st January 1978 reinsure with the Corporation an amount equal to 20 *per cent* of the sum insured in the policy, upon and subject to the provisions of Schedule 2 to this Decree; and the registered insurer shall forthwith pay over to the Corporation an amount equal to 20 per cent of the premium received by the registered insurer on the issue or, as the case may be, renewal of the policy.

(2) The Corporation shall, in respect of any reinsurance ceded to it pursuant to section (1) above by a registered insurer, pay to such registered insurer commission at such rate as the Corporation may determine after taking into account any applicable commercial consideration; but no profit commission shall be payable on such cessions.

(3) In respect of reinsurance business above the legal cession, that is the percentage of cession specified in subsection (1) of this section, the Corporation shall have the right of first refusal of any reinsurance business from Nigeria before such business is placed in the international reinsurance market.

(4) Where the Corporation exercises the right of first refusal conferred upon the Corporation under subsection (3) of this section, the Corporation shall issue a certificate to this effect to the insurer before such reinsurance is placed abroad.

(5) Sections 4 (2) (a), 8 and 9 Schedule 2 of the National Insurance Corporation of Nigeria Decree 1969 (which deal with reinsurance) are, hereby, accordingly repealed.

1959 No. 22.

8.—(1) Without prejudice to the provisions of section 7 (2) of this Decree, where any registered insurer contravenes or fails to comply with any requirement of that section and thereby evades or fails to pay any amount of premium which is due from and payable by it under section 7 (1) of this Decree, the amount of the premium so unpaid shall—

Recovery of unpaid premiums from registered insurer.

(a) notwithstanding any other enactment, be a first charge on the property of the registered insurer: and

(b) be a debt due to the Corporation, and the Corporation may sue for and recover that amount in any court of competent jurisdiction from the registered insurer.

(2) In any action brought under subsection (1) above, the production by the Corporation of a certificate signed by the Director of Insurance setting out the name of the defendant and the amount of premium due shall be sufficient evidence of the amount so due, and

sufficient authority for the court to give judgment for the said amount.

Duty of registered insurer to furnish information.

9.— It shall be the duty of every registered insurer to produce to any person authorised by the Managing Director of the Corporation, upon the production by that person of a duly authenticated document showing his authority, such books of accounts, records, documents and to supply copies and extracts from such books, records, documents and to furnish such other information as may reasonably be required for the purposes of sections 7 and 8 or any other provision of this Decree.

General Financial Provisions

Share capital of the Corporation etc.

10.—(1) The authorised capital of the Corporation shall be ten million naira divided into 10,000 shares of ₦1,000 each out of which there shall be issued such proportion as may be resolved by the Board and approved by the Commissioner and all the issued share capital shall be subscribed by and paid up at par by the Federal Government upon the establishment of the Corporation.

(2) Any further portion of the authorised capital of the Corporation may be called up as the Board may, with the approval of the Commissioner, from time to time resolve and the Federal Government shall subscribe and pay up at par the amount so called up.

(3) The Commissioner may, from time to time, with the approval of the Federal Executive Council, increase the share capital of the Corporation, by order published in the *Gazette* and, as soon as may be after any such increase, the Board may make calls for the additional shares on such terms and conditions as the Board may determine.

General reserve fund.

11.—(1) The Corporation shall establish a general reserve fund to which shall be allocated from the net profits of the Corporation at the end of each financial year of the Corporation—

(*a*) 50 per cent of the net profits of the Corporation for the year, when at the end of the year the fund is less than the authorised capital of the Corporation;

(*b*) 25 per cent of the net profits of the Corporation for the year, when the fund is equal to or exceeds the authorised capital of the Corporation.

(2) After any allocation has been made in terms of subsection (1) above the balance of the net profits shall be paid to the Federal Government.

12. The liability of any holder of shares in the Corporation shall be limited to the amount, if any, unpaid on the shares held by the holder.

Liability of Share-holder limited.

Managing Director Secretary, etc.

13.—(1) There shall be an employee of the Corporation who shall be called the Managing Director and who shall be the chief executive officer of the Corporation and shall be responsible for the day to day management of the affairs of the Corporation.

Managing Director of the Corporation.

(2) The Managing Director shall be appointed by the Federal Executive Council on the recommendation of the Commissioner.

(3) Any person appointed as the Managing Director shall not, while he is the holder of that office, be the holder of the office of a director in any bank, corporation, company or any other concern except with the approval of the Commissioner.

14.—(1) There shall be appointed by the Corporation a Secretary to the Corporation who shall not be a member of the Board.

Secretary to the Corporation.

(2) The Secretary shall be responsible to the Chairman and the Managing Director and be under their direction and control.

(3) The Secretary shall keep the records and conduct the correspondence of the Corporation and perform such other duties as the Chairman or Managing Director

may from time to time direct and without prejudice to the generality of the foregoing the Secretary shall be responsible for the following matters, that is to say—

(a) making arrangements for meetings of the Board;

(b) preparing the agenda and the minutes of such meetings;

(c) conveying decisions of the Board to members of the Board; and

(d) arranging for payments of fees and allowances and all other matters affecting members of the Board.

Retirement benefit fund for employees of the Corporation.

15.—(1) The Board shall make rules for the establishment and maintenance of a fund to be known as the Nigeria Reinsurance Corporation Pension and Welfare Fund for providing pensions to employees of the Corporation, and in the case of injuries to such employees or of their death while engaged on the Corporation's business, for providing benefits to them or their dependants.

(2) Provision shall be made by the rules for the payment of contributions to the said fund by the Corporation or the employees of the Corporation or by both, as the Commissioner may direct or require.

(3) Rules made for the purposes of this section shall not have effect until approved by the Commissioner.

Accounts, Returns and Information

Accounts and audit.

16.—(1) The Corporation shall keep proper accounts and proper records in relation thereto and shall, in respect of each financial year, prepare a balance sheet, a profit and loss account, revenue accounts and other statements and abstracts, in accordance with the requirements of the Insurance Decree 1976.

1976 No. 59.

(2) The accounts of the Corporation shall be audited by auditors in Nigeria appointed annually and on such remuneration as may be fixed by the Board with the approval of the Federal Executive Council.

(3) The auditors shall, on completion of the audits of the accounts of the Corporation for each financial year, prepare and submit to the Board the following two reports, that is to say—

(a) a general report setting out the observations and recommendations of the auditors on the financial affairs of the Corporation for that year and on any other important matters which the auditors may consider necessary to bring to the knowledge of the general public; and

(b) a detailed report containing the observations and recommendations of the auditors on all aspects of the operations of the Corporation for that year.

Miscellaneous and Supplementary

17. If any person in giving information for the purposes of this Decree or any regulation thereunder, makes any statement which he knows to be false in any material particular, or recklessly makes any statement which is false in a material particular, he shall be guilty of an offence and liable on conviction to imprisonment for a term of twelve months or to a a fine of ₦500 or to both such imprisonment and fine.

False information.

18. The Corporation shall not be wound up except by or under the authority of an enactment.

Winding up the Corporation.

19. Without prejudice to any other power of the Commissioner under this Decree to make regulations for any special purposes, regulations may be made by the Commissioner generally for the purposes of this Decree.

Regulations.

20. In this Decree, unless the context otherwise requires—

Interpretation.

"the Board" has the meaning assigned to it in section . 3 of this Decree;

"the Chairman" means the Chairman of the **Board**;

"the Commissioner" means the Federal Commissioner charged with responsibility for insurance;

"the Corporation" means the Nigeria Reinsurance Corporation established under section 1 of this **Decree**;

1976 No. 59.   "Director of Insurance" means the Director appointed pursuant to the Insurance Decree 1976;

"the Managing Director" means the Managing Director of the Corporation appointed pursuant to section 13 of this Decree;

"policy" in relation to insurance includes every writing whereby any contract of insurance is made or agreed to be made;

"registered insurer" means, without prejudice to section 6 of this Decree, any person (other than the Corporation) registered as an insurer under the Insurance Decree 1976.

Citation and commencement.   **21.**—(1) This Decree may be cited as the Nigeria Reinsurance Corporation Decree 1977.

(2) This Decree shall be deemed to have come into operation on 1st July 1976.

SCHEDULES

SCHEDULE 1   *Section* 3 (6)

SUPPLEMENTARY PROVISIONS WITH RESPECT TO PROCE-
DURE AT MEETINGS, ETC. OF THE BOARD

1964. No. 1.   1. Subject to this Decree and section 26 of the Interpretation Act 1964 (which provides for decisions of a statutory body to be taken by a majority of its members and for the person presiding to have a second or casting vote), the Board may make standing orders regulating the proceedings of the Board or any committee thereof, in particular, as respects—

(a) the holding of meetings;

(b) notices to be given of such meetings and proceedings thereat;

(c) the keeping of minutes, and the custody, production and inspection of such minutes; and

(d) the opening, keeping, closing and auditing of accounts.

2. Every meeting of the Board shall be presided over by the Chairman or, if the Chairman is unable to attend any particular meeting, by another member appointed by the members present at the meeting to act as chairman for that particular meeting.

3. The quorum for meetings of the Board shall be six and the quorum for meetings of any committee of the Board shall be determined by the Board.

4. Where standing orders made under paragraph 1 above provide for the Board to co-opt persons who are not members of the Board such persons may advise the Board on any matter referred to them by the Board but shall not be entitled to vote at a meeting of the Board.

5. The affixing of the seal of the Corporation shall be authenticated by the signatures of the Chairman and another member of the Board authorised either generally or specifically by the Board to act for the purpose, and of the Managing Director or some other employee of the Corporation authorised either generally or specifically to act for the purpose.

6. Any document purporting to be a document executed under the seal of the Corporation authenticated as provided for in paragraph 5 above shall be received in evidence and shall, unless the contrary is proved, be presumed to be executed.

7. Any contract or instrument which if made or executed by any person not being a body corporate would not be required to be under seal, may be made or executed on behalf of the Corporation by any person generally or specifically authorised to act for the purpose by the Corporation.

8. Any member of the Board who has a personal interest in any contract or arrangement entered into or proposed to be considered by the Board shall forthwith disclose his interest to the Board and shall not

vote on any question relating to the contract or arrangement.

9. The validity of any proceedings of the Board shall not be affected—

(a) by any vacancy in the membership of the Board; or

(b) by any defect in the appointment of a member of the Board; or

(c) by reason that a person not entitled to do so took part in the proceedings of the Board.

SCHEDULE 2 *Section* 7 (1)

1. The liability of the Corporation shall commence simultaneously with that of the registered insurer.

2. All loss settlements properly made by the registered insurer shall be binding on the Corporation.

3. The registered insurer shall furnish the Corporation on such forms and at such times as the Board may specify, particulars of the cessions to be made and shall advise the Corporation of any material alteration affecting such cessions.

4. Accounts shall be rendered by the registered insurer to the Corporation at times to be prescribed by the Board and shall also contain matters likewise to be so prescribed.

MADE at Lagos this 14th day of June 1977.

LT.-GENERAL O. OBASANJO
Head of the Federal Military Government,
Commander-in-Chief of the Armed Forces,
Federal Republic of Nigeria

EXPLANATORY NOTE

(This note does not form part of the above Decree but is intended to explain its purport)

The Decree sets up the Nigeria Reinsurance Corporation to undertake reinsurance business within and outside Nigeria. The minimum legal cession is 20 per cent of all sums assured under life and non-life insurance business.

Accordingly, certain of the functions of the National Insurance Corporation of Nigeria relating to reinsurance have been transferred to this new body.

APPENDIX IV

REGISTERED INSURANCE COMPANIES AS AT 31ST JULY, 1989

NAME AND REGISTERED OFFICE	*CLASSES WRITTEN*
1. ACEN Insurance Company Ltd. 7th Floor Great Nigeria House. 47/57 Martins Street, Lagos.	Fire, Accident, Motor, Workmen's Compensation Aviation & Transport and Miscellaneous Insurance Business.
2. ACIL International Ins. Co. Limited 17 Zik Avenue. P.O. Box 9129, Enugu.	Motor and Fire InsuranceBusiness.
3. African Alliance Insurance Company Limited, 112 Broad Street, P.O. ,Box 2276, Lagos.	Life Assurance only.
4. African Development Insurance Company Limited 149/153 Broad Street, P.O. Box 5061, Lagos.	Life, Motor Vehicle, Marine, Aviation, Accident Workmen's Compensation and Miscellaneous Insurance Business.
5. African Insurance Company Limited, 134 Nnamdi Azikiwe Street, P.O. Box 274, Lagos.	Fire, Accident Motor Vehicle, Workmen's Compensation, Marine, Aviation & Transit & Miscellaneous Insurance Business.
6. African Ivory Insurance Company Limited, 10 Sanni Adewale Street, P.O. Box 10009, Lagos.	Fire, Motor Vehicle Marine Aviation & Transit & Miscellaneous Insurance Business.

7. African Prudential Insurance
Company Limited
Church House.
29 Marina.
P.O. Box 2358, Lagos.

Life, Fire, Marine
Accident & Miscellaneous Ins.
Business.

8. African Trust Ass. Co. Ltd.
Plot 90, Block 'C' Latif
Salami Street, Along Express
Way, Ajao Estate, Mafoluku
Oshodi — Lagos State.

Motor Vehicle, Marine
Fire, Accident and
Miscellaneous Insurance
Business.

9. American International
Insurance Company (Nigeria)
Limited,
200 Broad Street,
P.O. Box 2577,
Lagos.

Life, Fire, Accident,
Motor Vehicle, Workmen's
Compensation, Marine,
Aviation & Transit and
Miscellaneous Insurance
Business.

10. Amicable Assurance Co. Ltd.
126/130 Nnamdi Azikwe Street
P.O. Box 4715,
Lagos.

Life, Accident, Motor
Vehicle, Workmen's
Compensation, Marine
Miscellaneous Ins. Business.

11. Arrowhead Insurance Co. Ltd.
131 Broad Street,
P.O. Box 6071,
Lagos.

Motor Vehicle, Fire
Marine & Miscellaneous
Insurance Business.

12. Atlantic Insurance Co. Ltd.
31 Otukpo Road,
(High Level),
Makurdi, Benue State.

Fire, Motor Vehicle,
Workmen Compensation &
Miscellaneous Insurance
Business.

13. Achor Insurance Company Ltd,
5 Barracks Road,
P.M.B. 1151,
Uyo Akwa Ibom State.

All Classes of Insurance
Business expect life.

PTF Low
Price Edition

14.   Bendel Insurance Company   Life, Fire, Accident
      Limited,   Motor Vehicle, Workmen's
      119 Sapele Road,   Compensation, Marine,
      P.O. Box 607,   Aviation & Transit &
      Benin City.   Miscellaneous Insurance
                                        Business.

15.   Blue Star Insurance Company   Fire, Accident Motor
      Limited,   Vehicle, Workmen's
      P.O. Box 8231,   Compensation, Marine
      18 Moloney Street,   Aviation & Transit &
      Lagos.   Miscellaneous Insurance
                                        Business.

16.   British American Insurance   Life, Accident, Motor
      (Nigeria) Limited   Vehicle, Workmen's
      35 Simpson Street,   Compensation, Marine,
      P.O. Box 2654,   Aviation and Transport
      Lagos.   and Miscellaneous
                                        Insurance Business.

17.   City Union Insurance Co. Ltd.   Motor Vehicle, Fire
      66 Campbell Street,   Accident, Aviation &
      P.O. Box 51982,   Transit, Workmen's
      Ikoyi.   Compensation, Marine &
      Lagos.   Miscellaneous Ins. Business.

18.   Commerce Assurance Co. Ltd.   Fire, Accident, Motor
      47/48 Breadfruit Street,   Vehicle, Workmen's
      P.O. Box 6406,   Compensation
      Lagos.   Miscellaneous Insurance
                                        Business.

19.   Confidence Insurance Co. Ltd.   Fire, Accident, Motor
      Toyin Building,   Vehicle, Workmen's
      46 Oba Adesina Road,   Compensation, Marine,
      P.O. Box 685,   Aviation, Transport &
      Akure.   Miscellaneous Ins. Business.

20.   Corporate Alliance & General   Fire, Motor, Personal
      Insurance Company Limited   Accident, Marine,
      182/184 Broad Street.   Transport and Aviation,

P.O. Box 72942,
Victoria Island,
Lagos.

Workmen's Compensation
Miscellaneous Insurance
Business.

21. Crusader Insurance Company
(Nigeria) Limited,
23/25 Martins Street,
P.O. Box 2101,
Lagos.

Life, Accident, Motor
Vehicle, Workmen's
Compensation, Marine and
Transit & Miscellaneous
Insurance Business.

22. Credit bonds Insurance Co.
Limited,
172A Aba Road, P.M.B. 5355,
Port Harcourt.

All Classes of Insurance
Business Except Life.

23. Destiny Insurance Company
Limited,
Destiny House,
Ikot EkpeneRoad,
P.M.B. 1150, Uyo,
Cross River State.

Accident, Fire, Motor
Vehicle, Workmen's
Compensation, Marine and
Miscellaneous Insurance.

24. Executive Insurance Company
6 Sanni Adewale Street,
2nd Floor, P.O. Box 4511,
Lagos, Island.

Fire, marine, Aviation and
Transport, Motor Vehicle,
and Miscellaneous
Insurance Business.

25. Express Insurance Company
Limited,
136 Nnamdi Azikiwe Street,
P.O. Box 3853,
Lagos.

Fire, Accident, Motor
Vehicle Workmen's
Compensation, Marine
Aviation & Transit and
Miscellaneous Insurance
Business.

26. Finance Assurance Corporation
of West Africa Limited,
N.I.D.B., House, 5th Floor,
18 Waff Road,
P.O. Box 7978, Kaduna.

Fire, Accident, Motor
Vehicle, Marine Aviation
and Transport and
Miscellaneous Ins. Business.

27. Financial Assurance Company   Life, Assurance Business,
     Limited,   Fire, Motor Vehicle,
     7th and 8th Floor,   Worksmen's Compensation,
     1–4 Balogun/Breadfruit Street, Marine, Aviation & Transit
     P.O. Box 9265,   and Miscellaneous Ins. Business.
     Lagos.

28. Fire Equity & General   Fire, Motor Vehicle,
     Insurance Company Limited   Accident, Workmen's
     13/15 Lake Street,   Compensation, Marine
     Lagos.   Insurance.

29. First Nigeria Insurance
     Company Limited,
     181 Sultan Road,
     P.O. Box 3134,
     Kaduna.

30. Foundation Insurance Co.   Fire, Accident, Motor
     6 Mazu Lane,   Vehicle, Marine, Aviation
     P.O. Box 255,   Transport, Workmen's
     Owerri.   Compensation & Miscellaneous
     Imo State.   Insurance Business.

31. Golden Insurance Company   Fire, Motor, Vehicle,
     Investment House,   Accident Workmen's
     25/25 Broad Street,   Compensation Marine
     P.O. Box 2852,   Aviation Transport and
     (1st Floor Room 111) Lagos.   Insurance Miscellaneous

32. Grand Union Assurance Ltd.   Fire, Motor Vehicle,
     2 Creek Road, Apapa,   Marine, Aviation,
     P.O. Box 1494   Transit and
     Lagos.   Miscellaneous Insurance
                                     Business.

33. Great Nigeria Insurance   Life, Fire, Accident,
     Company Limited,   Motor Vehicle, Workmen's
     39/41 Martins Street,   Compensation, Marine,
     P.O. Box 2314,   Aviation & Transit and
     Lagos.   Miscellaneous Insurance Business.

34. Great Providence Assurance
Company Limited
Trade house 8th Floor,
11 – 13 Hiwo Ona,
Atire Street,
P.O. Box 10396,
Lagos.

Fire, Accident, Motor
Vehicle, Workmen's
Compensation, Miscellaneous
Insurance Business.

35. Greenland Insurance Co.
Limited,
7 Association Avenue,
Ilupeju,
P.M.B. 1108,
Yaba, Lagos.

Motor Vehicle Insurance
Business only.

36. Guinea Insurance Company
Limited,
1st Floor Investment
21/25 Broad Street,
P.O. Box 1135, Lagos.

Fire, Accident, Motor Vehicle,
Workmen's Compensation,
Marine, Aviation & Transit and
Miscellaneous Insurance Business.

37. Hallmark Assurance Co.
Plot 5B Okigwe Road,
P.M.B. 1339,
Owerri, Imo State.

Fire, Motor Vehicle, Marine,
Aviation, Transport &
Miscellaneous Insurance
Business, Life.

38. Herwa Insurance Company
226 Apapa Road,
P.O. Box 9472,
Lagos.

Fire, Accident, Motor Vehicle
Workmen's Compensation, Marine,
Aviation, Transit & Miscellaneous
Insurance Business.

39. Heritage Assurance Co.
Limited,
Investment House,
21 – 25 Broad Street,
P.O. Box 9386, Lagos.

Fire, Accident, Motor Vehicle
Workmen's Compensation, Marine
Aviation and Transport and
Miscellaneous Insurance
Business.

40. Inter-Continental Ass.   Fire, Accident, Motor Vehicle
    Company Limited,   Workmen's Compensation, Marine,
    31/33 Martins Street,   Aviation and Transport and
    P.O. Box 244,   Miscellaenous
    Lagos.

41. International Insurance   Fire, Accident, Motor Vehicle
    Group,   Marine and Miscellaneous
    14 Apongbon Street,   Insurance Business.
    P.O. Box 50725, Lagos.

42. Jubilee Insurance Co.   Fire, Motor Vehicle, Marine
    Limited,   Aviation, Transport
    28 Aba Road, Afrinsuru   Miscellaneous Insurance Business.
    House, Port Harcourt
    P.O. Box 4204,
    Port Harcourt.

43. Kapital Insurance Co. Ltd.   Fire, Accident, Motor Vehicle
    Gidan Dan Bakore,   Workmen's Compensation, Marine
    1st Floor,   Aviation and transit and
    15C Murtala Moh. Way,   Miscellaneous Insurance Business.
    P.O. Box 2044,
    Kano.

44. King David Insurance Co.   Fire, Motor, Marine and
    Block A Plot 8 Dual   Miscellaneous Insurance
    Carriage Way,   Business.
    Gbagada Industrial
    Estate.
    P.O. Box 262,
    Ebute Metta, Lagos.

45. Lasaco Assurance Co. Ltd.,   Motor Vehicle, Fire, Marine
    L.S.D.P.S. House,   Aviation & Transit Workmen's
    Nnamdi Azikiwe/Ali Balogun   Compensation, Accident and
    Street, Lagos.   Miscellaneous Insurance
                                  Business, Life.

46. Law Union and Rock
   Insurance Co., (Nig.)
   Limited,
   88/92 Broad Street,
   P.O. Box 944,
   Lagos.

   Fire, Accident, Motor Vehicle
   Workmen's Compensation, Marine
   Aviation and Transit &
   Miscellaneous Insurance
   Business.

47. Leadway Assurance
   Company Limited,
   Leadway House,
   NN 28/29 Constitution
   P.O. Box 458,
   Kaduna.

   Fire, Accident, Motor Vehicle,
   Workmen's Compensation, Marine
   Aviation & Transit and
   Miscellaneous Insurance
   Business.

48. Liberty Assurance Company
   (Nigeria) Limited
   Liberty House,
   P.O. Box 1505,
   Iwo Road,
   Ibadan.

   Fire, Accident, Motor Vehicle
   Marine, Aviation & Transport &
   Miscellaneous Insurance Business.

49. Lister Insurance Co.
   (Nigeria) Limited,
   Plot G & H Ring Road,
   P.M.B. 5546,
   Ibadan.

   Fire, Motor Vehicle, Marine
   Miscellaneous Insurance Business.

50. Lombard Insurance
   Company Limited,
   Ashaku House Building,
   13 – 15 Lake Street,
   P.O. Box 169,
   Lagos.

   Fire, Accident, Motor Vehicle,
   Marine, Aviation & Transit,
   Workmen's Compensation and
   Miscellaneous Insurance
   Business.

51. Manilla Insurance Co.
   Limited,
   1 Barracks Road,
   P.M.B. 1085,
   Calabar,
   Cross River State.

   Life Fire, Accident, Motor
   Vehicle, Workmen's Compensation
   Marine, Aviation & Transit and
   Miscellaneous Insurance
   Business.

52.   Marine and General   Life, Accident, Fire Motor
      Assurance Co. (Nig)   Vehicle, Workmen's Compensation
      Limited,   and Transit & Miscellaneous
      194 Broad Street,   Insurance Business.
      P.O. Box 3657,
      Lagos.

53.   Maximum Insurance Co.   Fire Accident, Motor Vehicle
      Limited,   and Workmen's Compensation
      Rational Building   Insurance Business.
      (4th Floor),
      6 Lagos Bye-Pass
      Oke Bola,
      P.M.B. 5307, Ibadan.

54.   Mercury Assurance Co.   Fire, Accident, Motor Vehicle
      Limited,   Workmen's Compensation, Marine
      17 Martins Street,   Aviation and Transit and
      P.O. Box 2003   Miscellaneous Insurance
      Lagos.   Business.

55.   Metropolitan General   Fire, Motor Vehicle, Marine,
      Insurance Co. Limited,   Aviation and Transport and
      30 Ogui Road,   Insurance Business.
      P.O. Box 1276
      Enugu, Anambra State.

56.   Milverton Insurance   Motor Vehicle, Miscellaneous
      Company Limited,   Insurance Business only.
      Milverton House,
      11 Akinbayo Street,
      Papa – Ajao Near Isolo
      Mushin,
      P.M.B. 1145,
      Lagos.

57.	Mulumba Assurance Co. Limited 2B Western Avenue, Alaka Bus–Stop Surulere, P.O. Box 578, Lagos.	Fire, Motor Insurance Business only.
58.	National Insurance Corporation of Nigeria 5 Customs Street, P.O. Box 1100, Lagos.	Life, Fire, Accident, Motor Vehicles, Workmen's Compensation, Marine, Aviation and Transit and Miscellaneous Insurance Business.
59.	N.E.M. Insurance Co. (Nigeria) Limited, N.E.M. House, 22A Borno Way, Ebute Metta P.O. Box 654, Lagos.	Life, Fire, Accident, Motor Vehicle, Workmen's Compensation, Marine, Aviation & Transit and Miscellaneous Insurance Business.
60.	National Co-operative Insurance Society of Nigeria, 35 Ado Bayero Road, P.O. Box 4733, Kano.	Fire, Motor Vehicle, Marine Miscellaneous, Insurance Business.
61.	New – Line Insurance Company Limited, 46 Burma Road, P.M.B. 1230, Apapa, Lagos.	Fire, Accident, Motor Vehicle Workmen's Compensation, Marine, Aviation and Transport and Miscellaneous Insurance Business.
62.	New-Gate Insurance Co. Limited, 10 Sanni Adewale Street, 2nd Floor, P.O. Box 9186 Lagos.	Motor Vehicle, Marine, Aviation and Transport, Fire and Miscellaneous Insurance Business

63. Nigeria Reliance Insurance
    156 Herbert Macaulay
    Street, Ebute Metta,
    Lagos.

    Motor Vehicle, Marine,
    Miscellaneous Insurance
    Business.

64. Nigeria Alliance
    Assurance Corporation
    Limited,
    SW8/491C Lagos Bye-Pass,
    Oke – Ado,
    P.O. Box 10706
    Ibadan.

    Fire, Marine, Aviation and
    Transit, Motor Vehicle
    Workmen's
    Compensation Miscellaneous
    Insurance Business.

65. Nigerian Agricultural
    Insurance Company
    Limited NICON
    House No. 5 Custom Street,
    P.O. Box 1100, Lagos.

    Miscellaneous Insurance
    Business Crop and Live-Stock
    (Agricultural Insurance).

66. Nigerian French Insurance
    Company Limited,
    Plot 8 block K.
    Isolo Express way,
    P.O. Box 5570
    Lagos.

    All Classes of Insurance
    Business.

67. Noble Assurance Company
    80 School Road, Aba
    Imo State,
    P.O. Box 5505.

    Fire, Accident, Motor Vehicle
    Workmen's Compensation, Marine
    Aviation and Transport and
    Miscellaneous Insurance Business.

68. Nigeria Exchange Insurance
    Company Limited
    Victory Lodge SW7/3
    Lagos Bye-Pass Oke–Bola,
    P.O. Box 1602,
    Ibadan.

    Motor Vehicle, Marine, Aviation
    and Transport Accident and Fire.

69. Palm Beach Insurance
    Company Limited
    1 Temple Avenue,
    G.R.A. Enugu,
    P.O. Box 630,
    Enugu,
    Anambra State.

    Life, fire, Accident, Motor
    Vehicle, Workmen's
    Compensation, Marine,
    Aviation, Transit.

70. Pacific Insurance Co.
    (Nig.) Limited
    69 Obafemi Awolowo Way,
    P.O. Box 6608,
    Lagos.

    Fire, Accident, Motor
    Vehicle, Marine, Aviation
    Transit and Miscellaneous
    Insurance Business.

71. People's Insurance Co.
    Limited,
    N61/770A Oluseun House,
    Oyo Road Near Coca-Cola
    P.O. Box 9810, U.I.
    Post Office,
    Ibadan.

    Marine, Aviation, Transport
    Motor Vehicle, Accident and
    Fire, Insurance Business.

72. Philanthropy Insurance
    Company Limited,
    45/47 Balogun Street,
    P.O. Box 2712,
    Lagos.

    Fire, Accident, Motor Vehicle,
    Workmen's Compensation
    Insurance Business.

73. Phoenix of Nigeria
    Assurance Company Ltd.
    Mandilas House,
    96/102 Broad Street,
    P.O. Box 2893, Lagos.

    Fire, Accident, Marine
    Aviation and Transit, Motor
    Vehicle, Workmen's
    Compensation and Miscellaneous
    Insurance Business.

74. Piccadilly Insurance Co.
    SW8/340 Lagos By-Pass
    Oke – Ado,
    P.O. Box 637,
    Ibadan, Oyo State.

    Fire, Marine, Motor Vehicle,
    Workmen's Compensation and
    Miscellaneous Insurance
    Business.

75.	Prestige Assurance Co. Ltd. P.O. Box 650, Chellarams House, 54 Marina (12th Floor), Lagos.	Fire, Motor Vehicle Marine, Aviation, Transit, Accident, Workmen's Compensation and Miscellaneous Insurance Business.
76.	Progressive Insurance Co. Akure/Owo Road, P.O. Box 17, Akure, Ondo State.	Fire, Accident, Motor Vehicle, Workmen's Compensation and Miscellaneous Insurance Business.
77.	Prudential Union Assurance Company Limited, 27/29 Martins Street, P.O. Box 3552, Marina, Lagos.	Motor Vehicle, Fire Accident, and Miscellaneous Insurance business.
78.	Profound Assurance Co. Limited, 37 Zik Avenue, Anambra State.	Fire, Motor Vehicle, Accident, Marine, Aviation Transport and Insurance Business.
79.	Royal Exchange Assurance (Nigeria) Limited, New African House, 31 Marina. P.O. Box 112, Lagos.	Life, Fire, Accident, Motor Vehicle, Workmen's Compensation, Marine, Aviation.
80.	Safeway Insurance Co. Ltd., L.S.D.P.C. House, 7th Floor, Nnamdi Azikiwe Street, P.O. Box 10287, Lagos.	Motor Vehicle, Accident Marine Aviation, Transport and Miscellaneous Insurance Business.
81.	Sazo Insurance Co. (Nigeria) Limited, SW8/106 Lagos Bye-Pass, P.O. Box 2556, Oke–Ado U.I. Post Office, Ibadan.	Fire, Accident, Motor Vehicle, Workmen's Compensation, Marine, Aviation, Transport and Miscellaneous Insurance Business.

82. Sentinel Assurance Co. Ltd.,   Fire Accident, Motor Vehicle,
126 Broad Street,   Workmen's Compensation, Marine
P.O. Box 3003,   Aviation and Transit and
Lagos.   Miscellaneous Insurance
Business.

83. Star Insurance Company   Motor Vehicle & Miscellaneous
115 Ikorodu Road,   Insurance Business.
Igbobi,
Yaba, Lagos.

84. Sun Insurance (Nigeria)   Fire, Accident, Workmen's
(16th Floor) Unity House   Compensation, Motor Vehicle,
37 Marina,   Marine, Aviation Transit and
P.O. Box 2694   Miscellaneous Insurance
Lagos.   Business.

85. Tabs Assurance Limited   Fire, Accident, Motor Vehicle,
175 Zik Avenue Uwani   Workmen's Compensation, Marine
P.O. Box 106,   Aviation, Transit and
Enugu.   Miscellaneous Insurance Business.

86. The Gate–Way Insurance   Life, Fire, .Accident, Motor
19 Commercial Lay-out   Vehicle, Workmen's
Murtala Mohammed Road,   Compensation and Miscellaneous
P.M.B. 1399,   Insurance Business.
Ilorin,
Kwara State.

87. The Lion of Africa   Life, Accident, Motor Vehicle
Insurance Company Ltd.,   Workmen's Compensaiton, Marine
St. Peter's House,   Fire,Aviation, and Transit
3 Ajele Street,   Miscellaneous Insurance
P.O. Box 2055, Lagos.   Business.

88. The Niger Insurance Co.   Life, Fire, Motor Vehicle
Limited,   Workmen's Compensation, Marine
47 Marina,   Aviation and Transport
P.O. Box 2718,   Miscellaneous Insurance
Lagos.   Business.

89.	The Nigeria General Insurance Company 1 Nnamdi Azikiwe Street, Tinubu Square, P.O. Box 2210, Lagos.	Life, Fire, Accident Motor Vehicle Workmen's Compensation, Marine, Aviation and transit and Miscellaneous Insurance Business
90.	The United Nigeria Insurance Co. Limited, 55 Marina, P.O. Box 2780, Lagos.	Fire, Accident, Motor Vehicle, Workmen's Compensation, Marine, Aviation and Transit and Miscellaneous Insurance Business.
91.	The Universal Insurance Company Limited, Unisure House Plot E. Independence Layout Enugu, P.O. Box 360, Enugu.	Life, Fire, Accident, Motor Vehicle, Workmen's Compensation Transit Aviation Marine and Miscellaneous Insurance Business.
92.	The United Nigeria Life Insurance Company Ltd. 55 Marina, P.O. Box 588, Lagos.	Life, Accident, Motor Vehicle, Workmen's Compensation, Marine and Miscellaneous Insurance Business.
93.	Towergate Insurance Co. Limited P.M.B. 2177, Oke – Ilewo Round-about Ibara – Abeokuta.	Fire, Accident, Motor Vehicle, Workmen's Compensation Marine, Aviation, Transport and Miscellaneous Insurance Business.
94.	Total Insurance Company Limited, 44 Norman Williams Street Ikoyi, Lagos.	Fire Motor, Accident, Marine Workmen's Compensation and Miscellaneous.

95. Trans Nigeria Assurance Company Limited Aje House Annex, Lebanon Street, P.O. Box 2205, Ibadan, Oyo State.

Life, Fire, Accident, Motor Vehicle, Workmen's Compensation, Marine, Aviation and Transport and Miscellaneous Insurance Business.

96. Triumph Assurance Co. Limited, N6/329 Vision House, Mokola Oyo Road, P.O. Box 12142, Ibadan.

Fire, Accident, Motor Vehicle, Workmen's Compensation, Marine, Aviation and Transit and Miscellaneous Insurance Business.

97. Unity Life & Fire Insurance Company 9 Nnamdi Azikiwe Street, P.O. Box 3681, Lagos.

Life, Fire, Accident, Motor Vehicle Workmen's Compensation, Marine, Aviation and Transit and Miscellaneous Insurance Business.

98. Unitrust Insurance Co. Limited, 4/6 Oil Mill Street, P.O.Box 3650, Lagos.

Fire, Accident, Motor Vehicle, Marine, Aviation, Transport, Workmen's Compensation Miscellaneous Insurance Business.

99 Valid Assurance Co. Limited, 12/14 Broad Street, P.O. .Box 5715, Lagos.

Fire, Accident, Motor Vehicle, Workmen's Compensation, Marine and Transport and Miscellaneous Insurance Business.

100. Veritas Insurance Company Limited, 19 Martins Street, 3rd Floor, Lagos.

Fire, Accident, Motor Vehicle, Marine, Aviaiton and Transit Workmen's Compensation and Miscellaneous Insurance Business.

101. Vigilant Insurance Co.   Motor Vehicle, Marine Fire, and
     Limited,   Miscellaneous Insurance Business.
     150 Nnamdi Azikiwe Street,
     Idumota,
     P.O. Box 8218,
     Lagos.

102. West African Provincial   Fire, Accident, Motor Vehicle,
     Insurance Company Ltd.   Workmen's Compensation,
     27/29 King George V. Road,   Miscellaneous Insurance Business.
     Onikan, Lagos.

103. World-Wide Insurance   Fire, Motor Vehicle Marine,
     Company Limited,   Aviation, Transport and
     Magazine Jericho Road,   Miscellaneous Insurance
     P.M.B. 5272,   ·Business.
     Ibadan.

104. Yankari Insurance Co.   Fire, Motor Vehicle, Marine
     Limited,   Aviation, Transport, Accident
     Ahmadu Bello – Way   and Miscellaneous Insurance
     P.O. Box 2122,   Business.
     Bauchi.

LIST OF REGISTERED INSURANCE BROKERS AS AT AUGUST 1987 TOGETHER WITH THEIR ADDRESSES AND CLASSES OF BUSINESS WRITTEN

Name and Registered Officer	Classes Written
1. Accord Nigeria Insurance Brokers 2B Western Avenue, Alaka, Box 3781, Surulere, Lagos.	All classes of insurance business.
2. Adehmos Brokers (Insurance Consultants), 47 Murtala Mohammed Road, P.O. ,Box 802, Ilorin.	All classes of insurance business.
3. African Insurance Brokers and Company 27/29 Martin Street, Lagos.	All classes of insurance.
4. Akin—George Life and Pensions Consultants Pensions Managers and Consultants 10 Bode Thomas Street, Surulere, P.O. Box 2279, Lagos.	Life and pensions only.
5. Alfam Insurance Brokers 29 Berkley Street, Lagos.	Fire and General business including Life assurance.
6. All States Insurance Brokers 77 Ibrahim Taiwo Road, P.O. Box 12315, Kano.	All classes of insurance business.
7 Alli—Balogun and Company (Insurance Brokers) Plot Al, Ahmadu Bello Way, P.O. Box 1007, Kaduna	All classes including Pension.
8. Alm—Adam Insurance Brokers 11 Adebambo Street, Obanikoro, Ikorodu Road, Lagos.	All classes
9. Alpha Brokers 59 Chime Avenue, New Haven, P.O. Box 1179, Enugu.	All classes of insurance including Reinsurance, Pension Consultancy and Risks Management.
10. Alrisk Insurance Brokers 43 Yesufu Sanusi Street, P.O. Box 2401, Surulere, Lagos.	All classes of insurance business.
11. Amfa Insurance Consultants Sw8/794 Challenge Road, P.O. Box 4349, Ibadan.	All classes including Life and Pensions and Loss Adjusting of all classes.

12.	Anopit Insurance Brokers Plot 445 Airport Road, Kano	All classes of insurance business.
13.	A.O. Ogunkeye and Company (Insurance Brokers) Nw5/197 Adamasingba/Adekunle Fajuyi Road, Ibadan.	All classes of insurance.
14.	Aremott Banwill and Company 9 Toyin Street, P.O. Box 5395, Ikeja, Lagos.	All classes of insurance business.
15.	Ark Stewart Wrightson Nigeria 11 Karimu Kotun Street, Victoria Island, P.O. Box 3771, Lagos.	General Broking i.e. Fire, Accident, Marine and Pension, C.A.R./E.A.R. Bonds etc.
16.	Askar Insurance Brokers, 32 Lewis Street, Onward House, Lagos.	All classes of insurance business.
17.	Austine and Associates, 64/66 Ojuelegba Road, Surulere, P.O. Box 4632, Lagos.	All classes.
18.	Bafot Insurance Brokers 14 Market Street, Marina, Behind Leventis Stores, P.O. Box 60482, Ikoyi	
19.	Baklay Insurance Brokers 27 Beirut Road, Kano	All classes of insurance.
20.	Ban—Doy (Brokers) Company 97 Obafemi Awolowo Way, P.M.B. 21541, Ikeja, Lagos	All classes of insurance business.
21.	Banki Brithwaite and Company 20 Little Road, Sabo, Yaba, Lagos.	Insurance broking.
22.	Barrow Lloyds Insurance Brokers 5 Little Road, Yaba, Lagos	All classes of insurance.
23.	B.C. Madiebo and Company 31/33 Martins Street, P.O. Box 244, Lagos.	All classes of business.
24.	Bellcrest Insurance Brokers and Consultants, 30 Ikwerre Road, P.O. Box 1856, Port Harcourt.	All classes of insurance.
25.	Benevolent International Loss Adjusters 39 Herbert Macaulay Street, Yaba, P.O. Box 897, Lagos.	All classes of insurance business including recoveries.

No.	Name and Address	Classes
26.	Bidac, Insurance Brokers 66 Falolu Road, Surulere,	All classes of insurance business.
27.	BOS Insurance Consultants and Company, Plot 2 Liberty Stadium Road, P.O. Box 175, Ibadan.	All classes of insurance.
28.	City Insurance Brokers 95 Ojuelegba Road, Surulere, P.O. Box 2683, Lagos.	All classes of insurance business.
29.	City Loss Adjusters (Nigeria) 50 Western Avenue, P.O. Box 2056, Surulere, Lagos.	All loss adjusting, Cargo Supt. Surveys and Engineering services.
30.	Clement Ado Insurance Brokers 6th Floor, 17 Martins Street, Lagos.	All classes of insurance.
31.	Colenson Brokers Nigeria 47 Fashoro Street, Surulere, Lagos.	All classes of insurance business.
32.	Consolidated Brokers 77 Alhaji Masha Road, P.O. Box 516, Surulere, Lagos.	All classes including Reinsurance.
33.	Constant Insurance Brokers of Nigeria 101 Ibrahim Taiwo Road, P.O. Box 2326 Kano.	All classes.
34.	Continental Brokers 46 Queen's Street, Alagomeji, Yaba, P.O. Box 60369, Ikoyi, Lagos.	All classes of insurance business.
35.	Continental Loss Adjusters (Nig) Company 23 Association Avenue, Ilupeju, Lagos.	All Classes of Adjustment.
36.	Crown Insurance Brokers 29 Burma Road, Apapa, Lagos.	All Classes of Insurance
37.	Darasco Brokerage Company N3/809A, Queen Elizabeth Road Mokola, Ibadan.	All Classes of Insurance.
38.	Datum Insurance Brokers 213/215, Ikorodu Road, P.O. Box 9922, Ikeja, Lagos.	All Classes of Insurance business.
39.	Diligence Insurance Brokers 14, Rwang Pam Street, P.O. Box 6844 Jos, Plateau State.	All Classes of Insurance business.

40.	Eagle Insurance Brokers 149/153, Broad Street P.O. Box 2294, Lagos.	All Classes of Insurance
41.	Everyman & Company 8 Sulu Gambari Road P.O. Box 289, Ilorin Kwara State.	All Classes of Insurance business.
42.	Eliwad Consultants (Insurance Brokers) 44 Stadium Road, Ilorin, Kwara State	All Classes of Insurance
43.	Famak and Company Sw9/152A, Aba Alamu Road Apata, P.O. Box 2862, Ibadan.	All Classes of Insurance business.
44.	Femi Johnson and Company 1 Alhaji Jimoh Odutola Road P.M.B. 5035, Ibadan.	All Classes.
45.	Fidelity Bond Incorporated Insurance Brokers, 108 Obafemi Awolowo Way P.O. Box 859, Ikeja, Lagos.	All Classes.
46.	Financo Brokers, 75 Douglas Road, P.O. Box 2832, Owerri.	All Classes of Insurance.
47.	First Nationwide Insurance Brokers Consultants, E9/902, Iwo Road, P.O. Box 7291 Secretariat Post Office, Ibadan.	
48.	Frank O. Harris Company Nigeria 2, Oyekan Road, Yaba P.O. Box 4835, Lagos.	All Classes of Insurance Life and Pensions inclusive.
49.	Fortune Insurance Brokers and Consultants Desam House, Marian Road, Ext. P.O. Box 1578, Calabar.	All Classes of Insurance.
50.	Gaskiya Insurance Brokers Company 3 Kanta Road, P.O. Box 327, Kaduna.	All Classes.
51.	Glanvill Enthoven and Company Nigeria 14th Floor, Western house Nigeria 14th Floor, Western House 8/10 Broad Street, P.M.B. 2273, Lagos.	Incorporated Insurance brokers for all classes of business.
52.	Glanvill Enthoven Reinsurance Brokers 14th Floor, Western House 8/10 Broad Street, P.M.B. 2273, Lagos.	All Classes — Reinsurance.

53. Glanvill Enthoven Life and pensions
    Consultants   All forms of Life and
    14th Floor, Western House   Pensions Insurances.
    8/10 Broad Street, Lagos.

54. Global Risk Associates
    3rd Floor, 208/212 Broad Street
    P.O. Box 2150, Lagos.   All Classes of Insurance

55. G.N. Bishop Insurance Brokers
    8/10 Broad Street   All Classes of Insurance
    Lagos.   except Life.

56. Graham Miller and Company Nigeria
    Investment House
    21/25 Broad Street   All Loss Adjusters and
    P.O. Box 26/75   Surveys.
    Lagos.

57. Grand Metropolitan Associates
    243/245, Apapa Road, Ijora   Survey of Marine and Non–
    P.O. Box 9732, Lagos.   Marine Claims.

58. Hakash and Company
    9 Alagbede Street, Lagos.
    P.O. Box 50628, Falomo, Lagos.   All Classes.

59. H. Clarkson, Edu and Partners
    172 Broad Street, P.O. Box 2853, Lagos.   All Classes.

60. Heritage Insurance Brokers
    13 Okesuna Street, Lagos.   All Classes.

61. Hogg Robinson Nigeria
    221 Ikorodu Road
    P.O. Box 1156, Lagos.   All Classes.

62. Home and Overseas Insurance Brokers
    (Inc)
    60 Old Market Road, P.O. Box 1047,
    Onitsha.   All Classes.

63. HPS Adjusters   International Loss Adjusters,
    6 Sanni Adewale Street   Marine Cargo, Surveyors
    P.O. Box 7933   Claims, Investigators and
    Lagos.   consultants, Recovery Agents

64. Ifebogun and Company   Life, Fire, Accident, Motor
    Sw8/1358, Lodge Street   Vehicle, Workmen's Com-
    Oke—Ado, P.O. Box 285, Ibadan.   pensation Contractors all
                                                 Risks, Marine Aviation and
                                                 Transport and all other
                                                 classes of insurance.

65.	Insurance Brokers of Nigeria 90 Ladipo Street, Matori Industrial Estate, Mushin P.O. Box 2010, Lagos.	All Classes of Insurance.
66.	Interbroker and Company 80 Adebola Street, P.O. Box 2409, Surulere	All Classes
67.	Intercotra Limited (Lloyd's Agency Division) 13/15 Wharf Road, P.O. Box 155, Apapa.	All Classes.
68.	Interlink Associates and Company Nigeria 77/79, Apapa Road, Ebute-Metta (West) P.O. Box 390, Surulere, Lagos.	All Classes including Life
69.	International Chartered Insurance Brokers Co. 8 Sanni Adewale Street (2nd Floor), Lagos.	All Classes of Insurance Business.
70.	International Loss Adjusters 19 Eric Moore Close, Iganmu Surulere, P.O. Box 8704, Lagos.	Adjustment of Fire, Bur– glary, Marine & Aviation Claims, including survey of some risks.
71.	JAGSNO (Insurance) Surveyors and Consultants 5 Ashanti Road, P.O. Box 954, Apapa, Lagos.	All Classes.
72.	J. Akin—George and Company 10 Bode Thomas Street Surulere, P.O. Box 2279, Lagos.	All Classes
73.	KAL and KAY Insurance Brokers Company	All Classes of Insurance
	Plot 21, Ikorodu Road, Ilupeju Estate P.O. Box 2292, Surulere, Lagos.	All Classes of Insurance
74.	KESS Insurance Brokers Block 2, Edewor Shopping Centre P.O. Box 1079, Warri, Bendel State.	All Class of Insurance.
75.	KIND Insurance Brokers and Consultants 13A Egunjenmi Street Dugbe, Alawo, P.O. Box 247, Ibadan.	All Classes of Insurance
76.	KOLFAC and Company 12 Nnamdi Azikiwe Street P.O. Box 5305, Lagos.	All Classes

77. KOGUNA BABURA and Company
    13 Bello Road, Kano, P.O. Box 2589,
    Kano.   All Classes.
78. Lambert Willis and Associates
    Ashakun House, 13/15, Lake Street,
    Lagos.   All Classes.
79. Landway Insurance Brokers Company
    149 Herbert Macaulay Street, Yaba.   All Classes.
80. Martin—Dele and Company (Insurance
    Brokers)
    22 Itolo Street, Off Eric Moore, Road   All Classes of Insurance
    P.O. Box 1220, Surulere, Lagos.   except life.
81. Median and Shepherds Nigeria
    (Insurance Brokers)
    21/25 Broad Street, Investment House
    (7th Floor) P.O. Box 9334, Lagos.   All Classes
32. Melpon Insurance Consultants (Insurance
    Brokers)
    12 Rafiu Shitta, Alaka Estate, Surulere
    P.O. Box 51767, Ikoyi, Lagos.   All Classes.
83. Minet Nigeria (Insurance Brokers
    Represented at Lloyds)
    Rear Ground Floor, NUJ Building,
    Plot PC3, Alakija Adeyemo Street,
    Victoria Island, Lagos. P.M.B. 1155,
    Apapa.   All Classes.
84. Monitor Insurance Brokers
    82 Azikiwe Road
    P.M.B. 7475, Aba, Imo State.   All Classes.
85. Navianco Insurance Brokers
    1 Allen Avenue, Ikeja
    P.O. Box 60092, Ikoyi, Lagos.   All Classes.
86. Nigerian Life and Pensions Consultants
    312 Ikorodu Road, P.O. Box 1156, Lagos   Life and Pensions brokerage.
87. Noble Lonndes Nigeria and Company
    7 Taofeek Lawal Street, Off
    Raymond Njoku Street   All Classes of Insurance.
88. O.B.A. Insurance Brokers
    23/25 Martins Streets   All Classes of Insurance
    Lagos.   Business.
89. Ola Esan and Company
    3—7 Nnamdi Azikiwe Street   All Classes including Life
    P.O. Box 3118, Lagos.   and Pensions.

PTF Low
Price Edition

90.   Oriwu Insurance Brokers
      21 Shipeolu Street
      P.O. Box 1400, Shomolu, Lagos.   All Classes of Insurance
                                              Business.
91.   Overseas and Nigeria Insurance Brokers
      5A, Aerodrome Road, Apapa, Lagos.   All Classes of Insurance.
92.   Perils Technical Company Inc.
      78 Marina Road, P.O. Box 931, Calabar   All Classes of Insurance
93.   Perfect Insurance Brokers
      LL16, Ahmadu Bello Way
      P.O. Box 1182, Kaduna, Kaduna State.   All Classes of
94.   Premier Brokers
      4, Market Road, Level Crossing
      P.O. box 447, Enugu.   All Classes of Business.
95.   Rahama Insurance Brokers
      Plot 6, Hadejia Road, P.O. Box 4245,
      Kano.   All Classes of Insurance.
96.   Prudence Insurance Brokers and
      Consultants
      Plot 21, Ikorodu Road
      Ilupeju, Lagos.   All classes
97.   Risk consultants (Insurance Brokers)
      Oladipo Street, Matori Industrial Estate
      Mushin, P.M.B. 1142, Apapa.   All Classes
98.   Romans Eneli Flynn and Company
      49 Awolowo Road, P.O. Box 1168,
      Ikoyi, Lagos.   All Classes.
99.   Ronsik International Insurance Brokers
      Ltd.
      6th Floor, 3 Breadfruit Street, Lagos. All Classes of Insurance
                                              Business.
100. Russel (Brokers) Nigeria Company
      48 Sakpoba Road, Benin City.   All Classes.
101. Sakina Insurance Brokers and Company
      4, Maiduguri Road
      P.O. Box 442, Bauchi, Bauchi State.   All Classes.
102. Samash Broker and Company
      55, Balogun Street, (2nd Floor)   All Classes.
103. SCIB Nigeria and Company
      St. Peter's House,
      3 Ajele Street, Lagos.   All Classes.
104. Secure Insurance Brokers
      40/41 Commercial Avenue
      Sabo, Yaba.   All Classes.
105. S.I. Osas and Company
      P.O. Box 1186, Agodi, Ibadan.   All Classes.

106.	Slof Union Insurance Brokers 178 Palm Avenue, Mushin Lagos.	All Classes.
107.	SOA Adjusters and Partners 21/25 Broad Street P.O. Box 10019, Lagos.	Loss Adjusters in Marine, Aviation, Fire, Burglary, Theft, Valuation in Plant and Machinery.
108.	SONIC Insurance Brokers and Pensions Consultants 6 Oturkpo Road, Makurdi.	All Classes.
109.	Standard Insurance Consultants Sw9/637c I.C.C. Layout, State Hospital Road, P.O. Box 4245, Ibadan.	All Classes.
110.	STAR Brokers 106 Nnamdi Azikiwe Street, P.O. Box 9241, Lagos.	All Classes.
111.	Starbright Insurance Brokers 70A Alhaji Masha Road, Surulere P.O. Box 3622, Lagos.	All Classes.
112.	T.A. Brithwaite (Insurance Brokers) and Company 47 Marina, P.O. Box 785, Lagos.	All Classes of Insurance and Reinsurance Business.
113.	TIME Insurance Brokers 42 Association Avenue, Ilupeju P.O. Box 1086, Yaba, Lagos.	All Classes of Insurance including Pensions and Life.
114.	TOMOH Insurance Brokers 540 Ikorodu Road, Maryland P.M.B. 8886, Ikeja, Lagos.	All Classes of Insurance
115.	Triumph Brokers Services 6 Allen Avenue, Ikeja Lagos.	All Classes of Insurance, Life and Pensions Consultancy.
116.	UNI—Chartered Brokers 9 Nnamdi Azikiwe Street P.O. Box 10592, Lagos.	All Classes.
117.	United Modern Insurance Brokers 1 Ilodibe Road, Awada Layout P.O. Box 1443, Onitsha.	All Classes of Insurance including Reinsurance.
118.	WAN's Brokerage 13 Sabiu Ajose Crescent Surulere, Lagos.	All Classes.
119.	Yinka Omilani and Associates 46 Burma Road, P.M.B. 1230 Apapa.	Cargo Superintending, Survey and Loss Adjusting, Marine.

APPENDIX VI

NATIONAL INSURANCE CORPORATION OF NIGERIA DECREE 1969

ARRANGEMENT OF SECTIONS

Commencement.

Decree No. 22

[1st *July* 1969]

THE FEDERAL MILITARY GOVERNMENT
hereby decrees as follows:—

Constitution and Functions of the Corporation etc.

Establishment and constitution of the Corporation.

1.—(1) There shalll be for the purposes of this Decree a corporation to be known as the National Insurance Corporation of Nigeria (hereinafter in this Decree referred to as "the Corporation") which shall be constituted in accordance with and shall have such powers and duties as are conferred on it by, or by virtue of, the following provisions of this Decree.

(2) The Corporation shall be a body corporate with perpetual succession and a common seal.

(3) The Corporation may sue or be sued in its corporate name and may hold, acquire, and dispose of any property movable or immovable.

Board of Directors.

2.—(1) The governing body of the Corporation shall be a Board of Directors (hereinafter in this Decree referred to as "the Board") which, subject to this Decree, shall consist of not less than seven or more than nine directors of whom one director shall be appointed Chairman and one other director shall be the Managing Director appointed under section 21 of this Decree, but in no circumstances shall the position of Chairman be held by the Managing Director.

(2) The Chairman shall be appointed by the Federal Commissioner charged with responsibility for trade (in this Decree hereafter referred to as "the Commissioner"), and the provisions of section 3 (2) of this Decree shall apply in respect of any such appointment.

(3) All members of the Board, except the Managing Director, but including the Chairman, shall be appointed to serve as part-time members.

(4) The Board shall be responsible for the determination of the overall policy of the Corporation, and in particular with regard to the financial, economic and operational programmes of the Corporation, and for ensuring the implementation of such policy; but the Board shall not in implementing such policy have or exercise any of the executive functions of the Corporation vested in the Managing Director pursuant to section 21 of this Decree.

3.—(1) The membership of the Board shall be composed of:—

Composition of the Board of Directors etc.

   (a) the Managing Director;

   (b) the Permanent Secretary, Federal Ministry of Finance or in his absence such member of his Ministry, not below the rank of senior assistant secretary, as he may designate to represent him;

   (c) the Permanent Secretary, Federal Ministry of Economic Development or in his absence such member of his Ministry, not below the rank of senior assistant secretary, as he may designate to represent him;

   (d) the Permanent Secretary, Federal Ministry of Trade or in his absence such member of his Ministry, not below the rank of senior assistant secretary, as he may designate to represent him;

   (e) such number of other directors not being

less than three or more thah five as the Commissioner may, with the approval of the Federal Executive Council, appoint as independent persons from amongst persons not holding offices in the public service of the Federation or of a State therein.

(2) Appointments of members of the Board under paragraph (*e*) of subsection (1) above, and of the Chairman, shall be made by the Commissioner only after first satisfying the Federal Executive Council in respect thereof that the persons concerned are persons of integrity, and of good standing in the community from which they are to be drawn. In addition, the Federal Executive Council must be satisfied that such persons are persons of eminence in, or have wide experience of, and have shown capacity in the field of industry, commerce, finance or administration and also have specialised knowledge of the working of an insurance business, so as to be capable of discharging the functions of their office in a manner satisfactory to the Commisssioner.

Schedule 1.

(3) The supplementary provisions contained in Schedule 1 to this Decree shall have effect in relation to the Corporation, the Board and the other matters there mentioned.

Functions of the Corporation.

4.—(1) Subject to the provisions of this Decree, the Corporation shall have power, within or outside Nigeria, to carry on any class of insurance business, including life insurance business, and to insure and reinsure against loss of any kind arising from any risk or contingency and in respect of any matter whatsoever.

(2) Without prejudice to the generality of subsection (1) of this section the Corporation shall have power to do any of the following things, that is,—

(a) to insure any property of the Government of the Federation or of tne Government of any State in the Federation or of any statutory corporation;

(b) to insure any property in which any government mentioned in paragraph (a) of this subsection or any statutory corporation has any interest (including any property held on trust for such government or corporation);

(c) to reinsure with any insurance company, reinsurance company, or association of underwriters, any risk undertaken by the Corporation and for that purpose to enter into reinsurance contracts;

(d) to accept on reinsurance any part of risks undertaken by any other person (being risks such that the Corporation has power to insure against) and to retrocede any part of such risks;

(e) to act as insurance agent or insurance broker in relation to any insurance, and in particular in relation to the insurance of any property mentioned in paragraphs (a) and (b) of this subsection.

(3) Save as may be expressly provided by an order made under subsection (4) below, the Corporation shall have power to do anything or to enter into any transaction which in the opinion of the Board is calculated to facilitate the due performance of the functions of the Corporation under this Decree, and in particular the Corporation may—

(a) acquire any undertaking of any registered insurer or acquire, hold or have any shares or stock in, or any financial interest in, any such undertaking;

(b) assist in organising training schemes for employees of any registered insurer;

(c) appoint insurance agents.

(4) Where the Federal Executive Council is of opinion that it is in the public interest so to do, it may by order published in the Federal Gazette abridge or restrict the powers of the Corporation to any extent necessary; and when so abridged or restricted the powers of the Corporation shall be exercisable subject to and in accordance with the provisions of the order, and not otherwise.

(5) For the avoidance of doubt, it is hereby declared that the foregoing provisions of this Decree relate only to the capacity of the Corporation as a statutory corporation, and nothing in the said provisions shall be construed as authorising the disregard by the Corporation of any rule of law.

(6) In this section the expression "statutory corporation" means any body corporate (including a company in respect of which any government in Nigeria, federal or state, holds a majority of shares, but excluding any other company incorporated under the Companies Decree 1968 or any enactment thereby repealed) established directly by or under any law in force in the Federation

1968 No. 51.

Corporation not to be exempt from taxation etc.

5.—(1) It is hereby declared that, subject to subsection (2) below, the Corporation shall be liable for taxation of any description (including liability for any duty, rate, levy or other charge whatsoever whether general or local, properly levied and payable).

(2) Nothing in this section shall be construed to impose liability for company income tax upon the Corporation until such time as the amount in the general reserve fund of the Corporation is for the first time equal to twice the amount of the paid-up capital of the Corporation.

General directions.

6.—(1) The Commissioner may give to the Board directives of a general or of a special nature with regard to the exercise of the functions of the Corporation; and as the case may require, it shall be the duty of the Chairman, the Board and the Managing Director to comply with the directives unless matters of policy are in dispute and subsection (2) of this section applies.

(2) In the application of subsection (1) above, where the Commissioner intends to initiate a policy affecting the exercise of the functions of the Corporation, he must consult with the Chairman, and in the event of disagreement between the Commissioner and the Chairman over the implementation of that policy, the policy and any directive issued in that respect,

shall stand suspended, so however that if any part
of the policy so in dispute is severable from any other
aspects of the policy not in dispute, the policy or the
directive issued shall be suspended only in respect
of the part in dispute; and thereafter the policy, or
the part in dispute, so suspended shall, upon its being
referred by the Commissioner to the Federal Executive
Council, be affirmed, modified, or rejected by that
Council, and the Council may give such directions
thereon as it thinks fit.

7.—(1) Without prejudice to subsections (1) and
(2) of section 1 of this Decree, and subject as hereinafter
in this Decree provided, the Corporation shall be
deemed to be a company registered under the Insurance
Companies Act 1961.

> Corporation
> deemed to be
> a registered
> insurer. 1961
> No. 53.

(2) Accordingly, and in so far as the provisions
of the Insurance Companies Act 1961 are not inconsistent with those of this Decree, the Corporation
shall comply with the requirements of the Act of 1961
aforesaid as if the Corporation were a company so
registered, and that Act shall, in relation to the Corporation, have effect and be construed accordingly.

8.—(1) Subject to subsections (2) and (3) below,
a registered insurer shall, in respect of every insurance
policy issued or renewed by it on or after 1st October
1969, reinsure with the Corporation an amount equal
to 10 per centum of the sum insured in the policy,
upon and subject to the provisions in Schedule 2 to
this Decree; and the registered insurer shall forthwith
pay over to the Corporation an amount equal to 10
per centum of the premium received by the registered
insurer on the issue or, as the case may be, renewal
of the policy.

> Compulsory
> reinsurance
> with the
> Corporation
> by registered
> insurers.
> Schedule 2.

(2) The Corporation shall, in respect of any reinsurance
ceded to it pursuant to subsection (1) above by a
registered insurer, pay to such registered insurer
commission at such rate as the Corporation may determine after taking account of any applicable commercial

consideration; but no profit commission shall be payable on such cessions.

(3) The Corporation may in its discretion refuse to accept from any registered insurer any reinsurance accommodation relating to any particular risk, and upon such refusal the registered insurer shall, as respects that particular risk, not be required to comply with the requirements of subsection (1) above.

(4) The Federal Executive Council may, in respect of subsection (1) above, by order published in the Federal Gazette—

    (*a*) increase or reduce the percentage mentioned therein;

    (*b*) exempt any class, or part of a class, of insurance business therefrom;

    (*c*) exempt any registered insurer therefrom.

(5) Any registered insurer who contravenes or fails to comply with any requirement of subsection (1) above shall be guilty of an offence and shall be liable on conviction to a fine of not less than £100; and if the default is continued after the conviction, the registered insurer shall be liable to a further sum of £25 for each and every day during which the contravention to commence or default continues, the liability for such further sum from the day following the conviction, or from such day thereafter as the court may order.

Recovery of unpaid premium from registered insurer.

9.—(1) Without prejudice to the provisions of section 8 (5) of this Decree, where any registered insurer contravenes or fails to comply with any requirement of that section and thereby evades or fails to pay any amount of premium which is due from and payable by it under section 8 (1) of this Decree, the amount of the premium so unpaid shall—

    (*a*) notwithstanding any other enactment, be a first charge on the property of the registered insurer; and

    (*b*) be a debt due to the Corporation,

and the Corporation may sue for and recover that amount in any court of competent jurisdiction, with full costs, from the registered insurer.

(2) In any action brought under subsection (1) above, the production by the Corporation of a certificate signed by the Registrar of Insurance setting out the name of the defendant and the amount of premium due shall be sufficient evidence of the amount so due, and sufficient authority for the court to give judgment for the said amount.

10.—(1) It shall be the duty of every registered insurer to produce to any person authorised by the Registrar of Insurance, on production by that person, if so required, of a duly authenticated document showing his authority, such books of accounts, records and documents, and to supply copies of and extracts from such books, records and documents and to furnish such other information, as may reasonably be required for purposes of sections 8 and 9, or any other provisions, of this Decree.

Duty of registered insurer to furnish information.

(2) If any person fails to comply with the requirements of this section, he shall be guilty of an offence under this Decree.

General financial provisions

11.—(1) The share capital of the Corporation shall, subject to subsection (2) below, be one million pounds divided into twenty thousand shares of fifty pounds each, and the said shares shall on the commencement of this Decree be deemed to be subscribed for, issued, and called up in full; and payment in respect of such call up shall be made by the holder of the shares at such times and in such manner as the Federal Executive Council may direct.

Share capital of the Corporation etc.

(2) The Commissioner may, from time to time, with the approval of the Federal Executive Council; increase the share capital of the Corporation; and, as soon as may be after any such increase, the Board may make calls for the additional shares on such terms and conditions as the Board may determine.

(3) All the shares in the Corporation shall be taken up by the Federal Military Government, and subject to subsection (1) and (2) above, shall be paid for by that government.

(4) The Accountant-General of the Federation, when authorised under this subsection by the Commissioner for Finance, shall charge to and isssue out of the Consolidated Revenue Fund of the Federation (hereinafter in this Decree referred to as "the Consolidated Revenue Fund") any sum required for making payment for shares in the Corporation taken up by the Federal Military Government.

Liability of share-holder limited.

12. The liability of any holder of shares in the Corporation shall be limited to the amount, if any, unpaid on the shares held by the holder.

Declaration of dividend

13. No dividend shall be declared by the Board unless—
(a) at the time of the declaration the amount in the general reserve fund of the Corporation exceeds the amount of £500,000;
(b) such dividend has been earned and has been approved by the Commissioner.

Loan of £100,000 to the Corporation.

14.—(1) The initial expenses and working capital of the Corporation shall be provided out of a loan to be granted to the Corporation by the Federal Military Government; and for that uppose, where the Commissioner for Finance is satisfied as to the amount he may authorise an advance by way of loan not exceeding £100,000 from the Contingency Fund of the Federation or such other fund as the Commissioner aforesaid may direct, and the loan when so made shall bear interest at such rate as the Commissioner aforesaid may approve or require.

(2) The Accountant-General of the Federation shall, as directed by the Commissioner for Finance under this section, issue out of the relevant fund of the Federation sums necessary for making the loan of £100,000 to the Corporation under subsection (1) above.

15.—(1) The Corporation shall, at such times and in such manner as the Commissioner for Finance with the approval of the Federal Executive Council may direct, repay the loan made to the Corporation under section 14 of this Decree, together with interest at the rate prescribed.

(2) Any sums received by way of repayment of the said loan or of interest thereon shall be paid into the Consolidated Revenue Fund.

Repayment of loan of £100,000.

16. Subject to any restriction imposed by this Decree as to the amount thereof, the Corporation may, with the consent of the Commissioner given either generally or in any particular case, borrow by way of temporary accommodation from the Federal Military Government such sums as the Corporation may requiree in the exercise of its functions under this Decree.

Borrowing powers.

17.—(1) Subject to the following provisions of this section, the Commissioner may by order direct that the aggregate of the amount outstanding in respect of the principal of any moneys borrowed by the Corporation shall not at any time exceed £50,000; and while such an order is in force, that aggregate amount shall not, except with the approval of the Federal Executive Council, exceed the sum so specified.

(2) Nothing in this section shall prevent the Corporation from borrowing in excess of any limit (if any) imposed by virtue of subsection (1) above for the purpose of paying off any loan.

(3) A person lending money to the Corporation shall not be bound to enquire whether the borrowing is within the power of the Corporation.

Limit on borrowing.

18. Without prejudice to the provisions of any enactment requiring the establishment of technical reserves by a registered insurer, the Corporation shall establish and maintain a general reserve fund out of the profits of the Corporation for meeting contingencies, depreciation

General reserve fund

of assets, for the liquidation of any debt or liability of the Corporation and for such other purposes as the Board may consider necessary for the proper functioning of the Corporation under this Decree.

Application of profits.

19. The profits of the Corporation in any financial year shall be applied in such manner as the Board with the approval of the Commissioner may direct, and dividends on the shares of the Federal Military Government in the Corporation shall be paid into the Consolidated Revenue Fund.

Provisions relating to staff

Officers and servants of the Corporation etc.

20.—(1) Subject to sections 21 and 22 of this Decree, and to subsections (2) and (3) below, there shall be in the employ of the Corporation such number of officers and servants as may appear expedient and necessary to the Board for the proper and efficient conduct of the business and functions of the Corporation.

1968 No. 53.

(2) The Statutory Corporations Service Commission Decree 1968 shall apply to the Corporation and accordingly, in section 14 (3) of the said Decree after paragraph (*d*) there shall be added the following new paragraph—

"(*e*) the National Insurance Corporation of Nigeria."

(3) Accordingly, the officers and servants of the Corporation shall be appointed in accordance with the Decree of 1968 aforesaid.

(4) Unless otherwise precluded by this Decree, the Corporation may exercise any of the powers and perform any of the functions and duties conferred and imposed on the Corporation by this Decree through or by any of its officers and servants duly authorised by the Corporation in that behalf.

Managing Director of the Corporation.

21.—(1) There shall be an officer of the Corporation, to be known as the Managing Director who shall be appointed by the Statutory Corporations Service Commission and the person so appointed shall—

   (*a*) be the holder of a recognised qualification in the field of insurance and shall have at least ten years experience in insurance business;

   (*b*) not, while he is the holder of that office, hold any directorship in any corporation, company or concern other than the Corporation.

(2) The Managing Director shall be the chief executive officer of the Corporation and shall be responsible for the general administration of the Corporation, the execution of the policy of the Corporation and the transaction of its day to day business.

22.—(1) There shall be appointed by the Statutory Corporations Service Commission an officer of the Corporation to be known as the Secretary.

Secretary of the Corporation.

(2) The Secretary shall be responsible to the Managing Director, as the chief executive officer of the Corporation, and under his direction and control the Secretary shall carry out the day to day administration of the affairs of the Corporation; and without prejudice to the generality of the foregoing provisions of this subsection the Secretary shall be responsible for the following matters, that is to say,—

   (*a*) making arrangements for meetings of the Board;

   (*b*) preparing the agenda and the minutes of such meetings;

   (*c*) conveying decisions of the Board to members of the Board;

   (*d*) arranging for payment of fees and allowances, of meetings and all other matters affecting members of the Board;

      and he shall perform all other duties affecting the Corporation as may be specifically assigned to him by the Managing Director.

23.—(1) The Board shall make rules for the establishment and maintenance of a fund to be known as the "National Insurance Corporation of Nigeria Pension and Welfare Fund" for providing pensions

Retirement benefit fund for employees of the Corporation.

to empolyees of the Corporation, and in the case of injuries or death of such employees, for providing benefits to them or their dependants.

(2) Provision shall be made by the rules for the payment of contributions to the said fund by the Corporation or the employees of the Corporation or by both, as the Commissioner may direct or require.

(3) Rules made for the purpose of this section shall not have effect until approved by the Commissioner.

Accounts, Returns and Information

Accounts and audit.

24.—(1) The Corporation shall keep proper accounts and proper records in relation thereto and shall, in respect of each financial year, prepare a balance sheet, a profit and loss account, revenue accounts, and other statements and abstracts, in accordance with the requirements of the Insurance Companies Act 1961.

1961 No. 53.

(2) The accounts of the Corporation shall be audited by a firm of chartered accountants in Nigeria appointed annually and on such remuneration as may be fixed; by the Board with the approval of the Federal Executive Council; and no firm shall be qualified to be so appointed by the Board unless it is in the opinion of the said Council a reputable firm of chartered accountants and the firm has not less than three full-time partners.

(3) The auditors shall, on completion of the audits of the accounts of the Corporation for each financial year, prepare and submit to the Board the following two reports, that is to say,—

(a) a report (elsewhere in this Decree referred to as "the general report") which shall set out general observations and recommendations of the auditors on the financial affairs of the Corporation for that year and on any important matters which the auditors may consider necessary to bring to the knowledge of the general public; and

(b) a detailed report (elsewhere in this Decree

referred to as "the full report") which shall
set out detailed observations and recommendations of the auditors on all aspects of the
operations of the Corporation for that year.

25. The Federal Executive Council may, in respect
of any particular audit under this Decree, if of opinion
that it is in the public interest so to do, from time
to time give directions—

    (*a*) to the auditors of the Corporation requiring
them to carry out any examination which
would enable them to report to the Council
upon the adequacy of any measures taken
by the Corporation for the protection of the
interests of the shareholders, policy holders,
and other creditors, of the Corporation, or
upon the sufficiency of procedure in auditing
the financial affairs of the Corporation;

    (*b*) to the said auditors requiring them to enlarge,
within the requirements of their directions,
the scope of the audit of the financial affairs
of the Corporation or to adopt a different
procedure in the audit;

    (*c*) to the said auditors or any other persons requiring
them jointly or severally to carry out such other
examinations as may be mentioned in the
directions;

and it shall be the duty of the auditors or other
persons directed as aforesaid, to comply with
those directions and to report to the Council
accordingly.

26.—(1) The Corporation shall, within six months
after the close of each financial year, furnish to the
Commissioner and to the Registrar of Insurance,—

    (*a*) a copy of the audited accounts of the Corporation
and of the statements and abstracts, mentioned
in section 24 of this Decree;

    (*b*) a copy of the general report and of the full
report of the auditors mentioned in the said
section 24;

Power for Federal Executive Council to give directions to auditors etc.

Returns by the Corporation.

(c) a detailed report of the Board on the state of affairs of the Corporation for that financial year, including a statement of the amount out of the profits which the Board proposes to carry to the general reserve fund of the Corporation; and of the amount which the Board recommends should be paid by way of dividend;

and the Commissioner shall, as soon as may be after receipt thereof, lay before the Federal Executive Council a copy of each of the documents furnished to him under this subsection.

(2) As soon as may be after the Corporation has complied with the requirements of subsection (1) of this section, the Board shall cause the audited accounts of the Corporation and the general report aforesaid to be published in the Federal Gazette.

Power to call for information from the Corporation.

27 —(1) An officer of the Federal Ministry of Trade not below the rank of senior assistant secretary may, if authorised by the Commissioner in that behalf, give notice in writing under this section to the Corporation requiring the Corporation to provide the Commissioner with such information relating to the property, financial position, activities or proposed activities of the Corporation as may be required by the notice.

(2) The Corporation shall within a reasonable time after a notice is given to it under subsection (1) of this section provide the Commissioner with the information required thereby, but if a time is prescribed by the notice the Corporation shall provide the information within the time so prescribed.

Legal proceedings

Limitation of suits against the Corporation etc.

28.—(1) Notwithstanding anything in any other enactment, no suit against the Corporation, a director or any officer or servant of the Corporation for any act done in pursuance or execution or intended execution of any enactment or law, or of any public duties—

or authority, or in respect of any alleged neglect or default in the execution of such enactment or law, duties or authority, shall lie or be instituted in any court unless it is commenced within twelve months next after the act, neglect or default complained of or, in the case of a continuance of damage or injury, within twelve months next after the ceasing thereof.

(2) No suit shall be commenced against the Corporation before the expiration of a period of one month after written notice of intention to commence the suit shall have been served upon the Corporation by the intending plaintiff or his agent; and the notice shall clearly and explicitly state the cause of action, the particulars of the claim, the name and place of abode of the intending plaintiff and the relief which he claims.

29. The notice referred to in section 28 (2) above and any summons, notice or other document required or authorised to be served upon the Corporation under the provisions of this Decree or any other enactment or law may be served by delivering the same to the Chairman or the Managing Director of the Corporation or by sending it by registered post addressed to the Managing Director at the principal office of the Corporation. *Service of documents.*

30. In any action or suit against the Corporation no execution or attachment or process in the nature thereof shall be issued against the Corporation, but any sums of money which may by the judgment of the court be awarded against the Corporation shall, subject to any directions given by the court where notice of appeal has been given by the Corporation in respect of the said judgment, be paid by the Corporation from the general reserve fund of the Corporation. *Restriction on execution against the property of the Corporation.*

31. Every director, agent, auditor, secretary, and other officer or servant for the time being of the Corporation shall be indemnified out of the assets of the Corporation against any liability incurred by him *Indemnity for offices and servants of the Corporation.*

in defending any proceedings, whether civil or criminal in which judgment is given in his favour, or in which he is acquitted, if any such proceeding is brought against him in his capacity as such director, agent, auditor, secretary or other officer or servant as aforesaid.

Miscellaneous and General

False information.

32. If any person in giving any information for the purposes of this Decree or any regulation there-under , makes any statement which he knows to be false in a material particular, or recklessly makes any statement which is false in a material particular, he shall be guilty of an offence and liable on conviction to imprisonment for a term not exceeding five years or to a fine of £500 or to both such imprisonment and fine.

Offences by body corporate.

33.—(1) Where an offence under this Decree committed by any body corporate, including a registered insurer is proved to have been committed with the consent or connivance of, or to be attributable to any neglect on the part of, any director, manager, secretary or other similar officer of the body corporate, or any person who was purporting to . act in any such capacity, he, as well as the body corporate, shall be guilty of that offence and liable to be proceeded against and punished accordingly.

(2) Where the affairs of a body corporate established under any enactment are managed by its members, with or without directors, the expression "director" as used in subsection (1) above shall in proper case include any such member.

Penalty for offences for which no other penalty is provided.

34. Any person who is guilty of an offence under this Decree, or who contravenes or fails to comply with any provision of this Decree, for which no other penalty is specifically provided, shall be liable on conviction to a fine not exceeding £500 and, if the default in respect of which he is so convicted is continued

after the conviction he shall be liable to a further sum of twenty five pounds for each and every day during which the contravention or default continues and liability for such further sum shall commence from the day following the conviction, or from such day thereafter as the court may order.

35. The Commissioner may from time to time by order published in the Federal Gazette apply to the Corporation any of the provisions of the Companies Decree 1968 not inconsistent with this Decree, with any necessary modificatiions as he may prescribe, but otherwise nothing in the Companies Decree 1968 shall apply to the Corporation.

Application of Companies Decree 1968. 1968 No. 51.

36. The Corporation shall not be wound up except by or under the authority of a Decree.

Winding up of the Corporation.

37. Without prejudice to any other power of the Commissioner under this Decree to make regulations for any special purposes, regulations may be made by the Commissioner generally for the purposes of this Decree.

Regulations.

38.—(1) The Board may make rules or by-laws not inconsistent with this Decree or any regulations made thereunder, for the general and efficient conduct of the business of the Corporation as an insurer, and without prejudice to the generality of the power so conferred rules or by-laws may—

Power of Board to make rules and by-laws.

(a) prescribe the manner and conditions subject to which the Corporation may enter into reinsurance contracts;

(b) prescribe premium and commission rates, terms and conditions, to be offered by the Corporation in connection with insurance or reinsurance business.

(2) Where rules or by-laws are made pursuant to subsection (1) of this section, it shall not be necessary for their validity to cause them to be published in the

Federal Gazette but the Board shall bring them to the notice of such interested persons (including officers and servants of the Corporation) as the Board may, from time to time, determine.

Interpretation

39. In this Decree, except where the context otherwise requires, the following expressions have the meanings hereby respectively assigned to them, that is to say,

"the Board" has the meaning assigned to it in section 2 of this Decree;

"body corporate" includes an association of underwriters;

"the Chairman" means the Chairman of the Board;

"the Commissioner" has the meaning assigned to it in section 2 (2) of this Decree;

"the Commissioner for Finance" means the Federal Commissioner charged with responsibility for finance;

"the Consolidated Revenue Fund" means the Consolidated Revenue Fund of the Federation;

"the Corporation" means the National Insurance Corporation of Nigeria established under section 1 of this Decree;

"director", in relation to the Corporation, means a member of the Board;

"financial year", in relation to the Corporation, means the period of twelve months ending with 31st December in any year and, where appropriate, includes any lesser period ending with that date;

"the Managing Director" means the Managing Director of the Corporation;

"the general reserve fund of the Corporation" means the fund established and maintained by the Corporation pursuant to section 18 of this Decree;

"policy" in relation to insurance includes every writing whereby any contract of insurance is made or agreed to be made;

"the Registrar of Insurance" means the Registrar of Insurance under the Insurance Companies Act 1961;

"registered insurer' means, without prejudice to section 7 of this Decree, any person (other than the

1961 No. 53.

Corporation) registered as an insurer under the Insurance Companies Act 1961.

40.—(1) This Decree may be cited as the National Insurance Corporation of Nigeria Decree 1969 and shall come into force on 1st July 1969.

(2) This Decree shall apply throughout the Federation.

Citation, commencement and extent.

SCHEDULES

SCHEDULE 1   Section 3 (3)

SUPPLEMENTARY PROVISIONS AS TO THE CORPORATION AND THE BOARD

Tenure and Vacation of Office of Member of the Board

1.—(1) Subject as hereinafter provided a member of the Board appointed under section 3 (1) (e) of this Decree shall hold and vacate office as such in accordance with the terms of the instrument appointing him to be a member of the Board.

(2) A member of the Board holding office as aforesaid shall, unless he previously vacates it, vacate that office on the expiration of the period of three years beginning with the date of his appointment.

(3) A person ceasing to hold office as a member of the Board otherwise than by removal for misconduct shall be eligible for re-appointment as such a member.

(4) Before appointing a person to be a member of the Board under section 3 (1) (e) of this Decree, the Commissioner shall satisfy himself that the person will have no such financial or other interest as is likely to affect prejudicially the discharge by him of his functions as a member of the Board, and the Commissioner shall also satisfy himself from time to time with respect to every member of the Board that the member has no such interest; and any person who is, or whom the Commissioner proposes to appoint to be, a member of the Board shall, whenever requested

Tenure of office etc. of members of the Board.

by the Commissioner so to do, furnish to him such information as the Commissioner considers necessary for the performances by the Commissioner of his duties under this sub-paragraph.

(5) A person who is a member of any other statutory corporation shall not be eligible for appointment as the Managing Director or as a member of the Board under section 3 (1) (e) of this Decree.

(6) Nothing in sub-paragraph (5) above shall be construed as preventing any Permanent Secretary who is a member of the Board from being a member of any other statutory corporation.

Variation of terms of appointment of member of the Board.

2. Where a member of the Board (not being the Managing Director) becomes or ceases to be Chairman, the Commissioner may, with the approval of the Federal Executive Council, vary the terms of the instrument appointing him to be a member, so far as they relate to the date on which he is to vacate office as such or otherwise.

Member may resign from the Board.

3. A member of the Board holding office in pursuance of section 3 (1) (e) of this Decree may at any time resign his membership by notice in writing addressed to the Commissioner.

Power of Commissioner to remove member from the Board.

4. If the Commissioner is satisfied that a member of the Board appointed by him—

(a) absents himself from three consecutive meetings of the Board without the permission of the Chairman, or if that member is the Chairman, without the permission of the Commissioner; or

(b) holds any other office of profit under the Corporation; or

(c) enters into any contract with the Corporation or is concerned or participates in the sharing of the profits of any contract with the Corporation (not being a contract of insurance relating to his life or the lives of his dependants or relating to any property in which he has an insurable interest); or (*d*) is unable to pay his debts or has made arrangement with his creditors; or

(*e*) is incapacitated by physical or mental illness; or

(*f*) takes part in partisan political activities; or

(*g*) is convicted, or has at any time been convicted, in any court of law in Nigeria or elsewhere of any offence involving dishonesty or moral turpitude; or

(*h*) is otherwise guilty of any misconduct or is unable or unfit to discharge the functions of a member,

the Commissioner may, with the approval of the Federal Executive Council, declare his office as a member to be vacant and shall notify the fact in such manner as the Commissioner may think fit; and thererupon the office shall become vacant.

Tenure of office of Chairman

5.—(1) Subject as hereinafter provided, the Chairman shall hold and vacate office as such in accordance with the terms of the instrument appointing him Chairman.

(2) The Chairman may at any time resign his office as such by notice in writing addressed to the Commissioner.

(3) If the Chairman ceases to be a member of the Board he shall also cease to be Chairman.

Remuneration of Members of the Board

6.—(1) Subject to sub-paragraph (2) below, the Corporation shall pay to each member of the Board such remuneration as the Commissioner may, with the approval of the Federal Executive Council, determine; and if a person ceases to be member of the Board and it appears to the Commissioner that there are special circumstances which make it right that that person should receive compensation the Commissioner may, with the approval of the Federal Executive

Council, require the Corporation to pay to that person a sum of such amount as the Commissioner may, with the approval of the Federal Executive Council, determine.

(2) No remuneration except such allowance for expenses as may be expressly authorised by the Federal Executive Council shall be paid to any member of the Board holding office otherwise than in pursuance of section 3 (1) (*e*) of this Decree.

Proceedings of the Corporation

Meetings of
the Board.

7.—(1) The Board shall in each year hold a general meeting as its annual meeting, in addition to any other meetings in that year, and it shall specify the meeting as such.

(2) The annual general meeting shall be held within six months after the close of each financial year, so however that if any such meeting is held at any time after the commencement of this Decree and not later than 31st December 1969 it shall be deemed to have been held within the period hereinbefore prescribed.

(3) The Board shall ordinarily meet for the despatch of business at such times and places as the Chairman may from time to time appoint, but not less than three times in any financial year.

(4) The Chairman shall preside at all meetings of the Board when he is present; and when he is not present such other member of the Board present at the meeting as the members may appoint for that meeting shall preside at the meeting.

(5) Subject to paragraph 8 (3) of this Schedule, the quorum at any meeting of the Board shall be four.

(6) Where not less than five members of the Board request the Chairman, by notice in writing signed by them, to convene an extraordinary meeting of the Board for the purposes specified in the notice, the Chairman shall, upon receipt of notice convene an extraordinary meeting of the Board for those purposes at the earliest convenient date.

(7) Notwithstanding anything in the foregoing provisions of this paragraph the first ordinary meeting of the Board shall be summoned by the Commissioner, who may give such directions as he thinks fit as to procedure which shall be followed at that meeting.

8.—(1) All questions at a meeting of the Board shall be determined by a majority of votes of the members of the Board present and voting, being members who under this paragraph are entitled to vote at such meeting.

Voting at meetings.

(2) At any meeting of the Board each member thereof other than the Managing Director shall have a deliberative vote, and if there is equality of votes the Chairman at the meeting shall, if entitled to a deliberative vote, have a second or casting vote.

(3) The Managing Director shall have a right to be present at all or any meetings of the Board but he shall not have the right to vote at any such meeting, and he shall not count towards a quorum at any meeting of the Board.

9.—(1) If the Chairman considers that at any meeting of the Board a matter which, in his opinion, affects the public interest has been wrongly decided—

Power of Chairman to withhold implementation of certain decisions.

(a) he may cause the implementation of the decision to be suspended; and

(b) in such case he shall, within ten days after the date on which the decision was made, submit a statement of the decision together with his objections thereto and any representations which any other member of the Board may desire to make with regard to the decision (such statement, objections and representations being in writing) for determination by the Commissioner, and the decision aforementioned shall be implemented only if the Commissioner so determines and subject to any modifications which the Commissioner may direct.

(2) Without prejudice to the power conferred on the

Chairman by sub-paragraph (1) above, if the Chairman considers that at any meeting of the Board not attended by all the persons who, for the time being are members of the Board, a question which, in his opinion, is of sufficient importance to justify action being taken as provided in this sub-paragraph has been wrongly decided—

    (*a*) he may cause the implementation of the decision to be suspended for not more than one month after the date on which the decision was made; and

    (*b*) in such case he shall, within the said month, convene and hold another meeting of the Board at which the question aforesaid shall be again considered and determined,

    so, however, that he shall not exercise the power conferred by this sub-paragraph more than once in respect of the same question.

Standing orders etc.

10.—(1) Subject to the provisions of this Decree and of this Schedule, the Board may make standing orders with respect to the holding of meetings of the Board, the notices to be given of such meetings the proceedings thereat, the keeping of minutes of such proceedings and the custody or the production for inspection of such minutes.

(2) Subject as aforesaid and to any standing order made under sub-paragraph (1) above, the procedure of the Board with respect to holding of meetings shall be such as the Board may from time to time determine.

Disclosure of Interests by Members of the Board

Disclosure of interests by members of the Board.

11.—(1) A member of the Board who is in any way directly or indirectly interested in a transaction or project of the Corporation shall disclose the nature of his interest at a meeting of the Board, and the disclosure shall be recorded in the minutes book of the Corporation, and the member shall not take any part in any deliberation or decision of the Board with respect to that transaction or project.

(2) For the purposes of sub-paragraph (1) above a general notice given at a meeting of the Board by a member of the Board to the effect that he is associated with any trade or business or is a member of a specified company or firm and is to be regarded as interested in any transaction or project of the Corporation concerning that trade, business, company or firm shall be regarded as sufficient disclosure of his interest in relation to that transaction or project.

(3) A member of the Board need not attend in person at a meeting of the Board in order to make a disclosure which he is required to make under this paragraph if he takes reasonable steps to ensure that the disclosure is made by a notice which is brought up and read at the meeting.

Offices and Agency

12.—(1) The Corporation shall have its principal office in Lagos and may open branch offices in the Federation in accordance with the decision of the Board. *Offices and agency.*

(2) The Board may, with the approval of the Commissioner, open branch offices, or establish agencies, of the Corporation outside Nigeria.

The Common Seal

13.—(1) The seal of the Corporation shall be such as may be determined by the Board; and the affixing of the seal shall be authenticated by the signatures of the Chairman and of the Managing Director, or of some other members authorised generally or specifically by the Corporation to act for that purpose. *Common seal.*

(2) The Corporation may have for use in any territory or place not situate in Nigeria, an official seal which shall be a facsimile of the seal of the Corporation, and—

(a) such official seal may be affixed manually or may be engraved, lithographed, printed or mechanically reproduced upon any contract, instrument or other documents requiring the same;

(*b*) the provisions of this Schedule shall apply in respect of such official seal as they apply in respect of the seal of the Corporation.

Instruments of the Corporation

Execution of instruments.

14. Any contract or instrument which, if made, or executed by a person not being a body corporate, would not be required to be under seal may be made or executed on behalf of the Corporation by the Managing Director, or any other person generally or specially authorised by the Board to act for that purpose.

Presumption as to execution of documents.

15. Any document purporting to be a document executed under the seal of the Corporation authenticated as mentioned in paragraph 13 (1) above shall be received in evidence and shall, unless the contrary is proved, be deemed to be so executed.

Validity of Proceedings

Validity of proceedings.

16. The validity of any proceedings of the Board shall not be affected by any vacancy in the membership of the Board or by any defect in the appointment of a member of the Board, or by reason that a person not entitled to do so took part in the proceedings.

Miscellaneous

Membership of Board not office of emolument under any government in the Federation.

17. A person shall not by reason only of his membership of the Board be treated as holding an office of emolument under the Government of the Federation or the Government of any State therein.

SCHEDULE 2   *Section* 8 (1)

Provisions Governing Compulsory Reinsurance

1. The liability of the Corporation shall commence simultaneously with that of the registered insurer.

2. All loss settlements properly made by the registered insurer shall be binding on the Corporation.

3. The registered insurer shall furnish the Corporation, on such forms and at such times as may be prescribed by the Board, particulars of the cessions to be made and shall advise the Corporation of any material alteration affecting such cessions.

4. Accounts shall be rendered by the registered insurer to the Corporation at times to be prescribed by the Board and shall contain matters likewise to be so prescribed.

MADE at Lagos this 30th day of June 1969.

MAJOR-GENERAL Y. GOWON
Head of the Federal Military Government,
Commander-in-Chief of the Armed Forces,
Federal Republic of Nigeria

MARINE INSURANCE ACT, 1961

No. 54

AN ACT TO PROVIDE FOR MARINE INSURANCE AND TO PROHIBIT GAMBLING ON LOSS BY MARITIME PERILS

BE IT ENACTED by the legislature of the Federation of Nigeria in this present Parliament assembled and by the authority of the same as follows:-

1. (1) This Act may be cited as the Marine Insurance Act, 1961, and shall come into operation on a day to be appointed by the Governor-General by notice in the Gazette.

(2) This Act shall be of Federal application.

PRELIMINARY

2. (1) In this Act unless the context otherwise requires,— "action" includes counter-claim and set off; "freight" includes the profit derivable by a shipowner from the employment of his ship to carry his own goods or moveables, as well as freight payable by a third party, but does not include passage money; "moveables" means any moveable tangible property other than the ship and includes money, valuable securities and other documents;

"policy means a marine policy;

"prescribed form" means the form of Policy in the First Schedule.

(2) For the purposes of this Act, where there is a reference to—

(a) reasonable time, or

(b) reasonable premium, or

(c) reasonable diligence,

the question of what is reasonable shall be a question of fact.

(3) A contract of marine insurance is a contract whereby the insurer undertakes to indemnify the assured, in manner and to the extent

thereby agreed, against marine losses, that is to say, the losses incident to marine adventure.

4. (1) A contract of marine insurance may, by its express terms, or by usage of trade, be extended so as to protect the assured against losses on inland waters or on any land risk which may be incidental to any sea voyage.

(2) Where a ship in course of building, or the launch of a ship, or any adventure analogous to a marine adventure, is covered by a policy in the form of a marine policy, the provisions of this Act, in so far as applicable, shall apply thereto; but except as by this section provided, nothing in this Act shall alter or affect any rule of law applicable to any contract of insurance other than a contract of marine insurance as defined in section 3.

5. (1) Subject to the provisions of this Act, every lawful marine adventure may be the subject of a contract of marine insurance.

(2) In particular there is a marine adventure where—

(a)   any ship goods or other moveables are exposed to maritime perils, such property being referred to in this Act as insurable property;

(b)   the earning or acquisition of any freight, passage money, commission, profit, or other pecuniary benefit, or the security for any advances, loan, or disbursements, is endangered by the exposure of insurable property to maritime perils;

(c)   any liability to a third party may be incurred by the owner of, or other person interested in or responsible for, insurable property, by reason of maritime perils.

(3) For the purposes of this section, "maritime perils" means the perils consequent on, or incidental to, the navigation of the sea, that is to say, perils of the seas, fire, war perils, pirates, rovers, thieves, captures, seizures, restraints, and detainments of princes and peoples, jettisons, barratry, and any other perils, either of the like kind or which may be designated by the policy.

INSURABLE INTEREST

6. (1) Every contract of marine insurance by way of gaming or wagering is void.

(2) A contract of marine insurance shall be deemed to be a gaming or wagering contract—

(*a*) where the assured has not an insurable interest as defined by this Act, and the contract is entered into with no expectation. of acquiring such an interest; or

(*b*) Where the policy is made "interest or no interest", or "without further proof of interest than the policy itself", or "without benefit of salvage to the insurer", or subject to any other like term:

Provided that, where there is no possibility of salvage, a policy may be effected without benefit of salvage to the insurer.

7. (1) Subject to the provisions of this Act every person has an insurable interest who is interested in a marine adventure.

(2) In particular a person is interested in a marine adventure where he stands in any legal or equitable relation to the adventure or to any insurable property at risk therein, in consequent of which he may benefit by the safety or due arrival of insurable property, or may be prejudiced by its loss, or damage thereto, or by the detention thereof, or may incur liability in respect thereof.

8. (1) The assured must be interested in the subject-matter insured at the time of the loss, though he need not be interested when the insurance is effected:

Provided that where the subject-matter is insured "lost or not lost", the assured may recover although he may not have acquired his interest until after the loss, unless at the time of effecting the contract of insurance the assured was aware of the loss, and the insurer was not.

(2) Where the assured has no interest at the time of the loss, he cannot acquire interest by any act or election after he is aware of the loss.

9. (1) A defeasible interest shall be insurable, as also shall be a contingent interest.

(2) In particular, where the buyer of goods has insured them, he has an insurable interest, notwithstanding that he might, at his election, have rejected the goods, or have treated them as at the seller's risk, by reason of the latter's delay in making delivery or otherwise.

10. A partial interest of any nature shall be insurable.

11. The insurer under a contract of marine insurance has an insu-

rable interest in his risk, and may reinsure in respect of it; but unless the policy otherwise provides, the original assured shall have no right or interest in respect of such reinsurance.

12. The lender of money on bottomry or respondentia has an insurable interest in respect of the loan.

13. The master or any member of the crew of a ship has an insurable interest in respect of his wages.

14. In the case of advance freight, the person advancing the freight has an insurable interest, in so far as such freight is not repayable in case of loss.

15. The assured has an insurable interest in the charges of any insurance which he may effect.

16. (1) Where the subject-matter insured is mortgaged, the mortgagor has an insurable interest in the full value thereof, and the mortgagee has an insurable interest in respect of any sum due or to become due under the mortgage.

(2) A mortgagee, consignee, or other person having an interest in the subject-matter insured may insure on behalf and for the benefit of other persons interested as well as for his own benefit.

(3) The owner of insurable property has an insurable interest in respect of the full value thereof, notwithstanding that some third person may have agreed, or be liable, to indemnify him in case of loss.

17. (1) When the assured assigns or otherwise parts with his interest in the subject-matter insured, he shall not thereby transfer to the assignee his rights under the contract of insurance, unless there is an express or implied agreement with the assignee to that effect.

(2) Nothing in this section shall affect a transmission of interest by operation of law.

INSURABLE VALUE

18. Subject to the express provision or valuation in the policy, the insurable value of the subject-matter insured shall be ascertained as follows:—

(*a*) in insurance on ship, the insurable value which, in the case. of a steamship, includes also the machinery, boilers, and coals and engine stores if owned by the assured, and, in the case of a ship engaged in a special trade, the ordinary fittings requisite for that trade, is the value, at the commencement of the risk, of the ship, including her outfit, provisions and stores for the officers and crew, money advanced for seamen's wages, and other disbursements (if any) incurred to make the ship fit for the voyage or adventure contemplated by the policy plus the charges of insurance upon the whole:

(*b*) in insurance on freight, whether paid in advance or otherwise, the insurable value is the gross amount of the freight at the risk of the assured, plus the charges of insurance:

(*c*) in insurance on goods or merchandise, the insurable value is the prime cost of the property insured, plus the expenses of and incidental to shipping and the charges of insurance upon the whole;

(*d*) in insurance on any other subject-matter, the insurable value is the amount at the risk of the assured when the policy attaches, plus the charges of insurance.

DISCLOSURE AND REPRESENTATIONS

19. A contract of marine insurance is a contract based upon the utmost good faith, and, if the utmost good faith is not observed by either party, the contract may be avoided by the other party.

20. (1) Subject to the provision of this section, the assured shall disclose to the insurer, before the contract is concluded, every material circumstance which is known to the assured, and the assured shall be deemed to know every circumstance which, in the ordinary course of business, ought to be known by him. If the assured fails to make such disclosure, the insurer may avoid the contract.

(2) Every circumstance is material which would influence the judgment of a prudent insurer in fixing the premium, or determining whether he will take the risk.

(3) In the absence of inquiry the following circumstances need not be disclosed, namely:-

(*a*) any circumstance which diminishes the risk;

(*b*) any circumstance which is known or presumed to be known to the insurer, and for the purposes of this paragraph, the presumption shall extend and apply to matters of common notoriety or knowledge, and to matters which an insurer in the ordinary course of his business, as such, ought to know;

(c) any circumstance as to which information is waived by the insurer;

(d) any circumstance which it is superfluous to disclose by reason of any express or implied warranty.

(4) For the purposes of this section, "circumstance" includes any communication made to, or information received by, the assured; and whether any particular circumstance which is not disclosed, is material or not is, in each case a question of fact.

21. Subject to the provisions of section 20 (which refers to circumstances not requiring to be disclosed by an assured), where an insurance is effected for the assured by an agent, the agent shall disclose to the insurer—

(a) every material circumstance which is known to the agent, who shall be deemed to know every circumstance which, in the ordinary course of business, ought to be known by or to have been communicated to the agent; and

(b) every material circumstance which the assured is bound to disclose unless it comes to the knowledge of the assured too late to communicate it to the agent.

22. (1) Every material representation made by the assured or his agent to the insurer during the negotiations for the contract, and before the contract is concluded must be true; and if untrue the insurer may avoid the contract.

(2) A representation is material which would influence the judgment of a prudent insurer in fixing the premium, or determining whether he will take the risk.

(3) A representation may be either a representation as to a matter of fact, or as to a matter of expectation or belief.

(4) A representation as to matter of fact is true, if it is substantially correct, that is to say, if the difference between what is represented and what is actually correct would not be considered material by a prudent insurer.

(5) A representation as to a matter of expectation or belief is true

if it is made in good faith.

(6) A representation may be withdrawn or corrected **before** the contract is concluded.

(7) Whether a particular representation is material or not is, in each case, a question of fact.

23. A contract of marine insurance shall be deemed to be concluded when the proposal of the assured is accepted by the insurer, whether the policy is then issued or not; and, for the purpose of showing when the proposal was accepted, reference may be made to the slip or covering note or other customary memorandum of the contract.

THE POLICY

24. (1) Subject to the provisions of any statute, a contract of marine insurance shall not be admissible in evidence unless it is embodied in a marine policy in accordance with the form in the First Schedule to this Act or to the like effect. The policy may be executed and issued either at the time when the contract is concluded, or afterwards; and subject to the provisions of this Act and unless the context of the policy otherwise requires, the terms and expressions mentioned in the said First Schedule shall be construed as having the scope and meaning in that Schedule assigned to them.

(2) Nothing in this section shall affect the operation of a contract for such insurance as is mentioned in section 388 of the Merchant Shipping Act, 1961.

25. A marine policy shall specify the name of the insured, or of some person who effects the insurance on his behalf.

26. (1) A marine policy shall be signed by or on behalf of the insurer, or if the insurer is a corporation, the corporate seal may be sufficient.

(2) Where a policy is subscribed by or on behalf of two or more insurers, each subscription, unless the contrary is expressed, shall constitute a distinct contract with the assured.

(3) Nothing in this section shall be construed as requiring the subscription of a corporation to be under seal.

27. Where the contract is to insure the subject-matter "at and from", or from one place to another or others, the policy, is called a voyage policy; and where the contract is to insure the subject matter for a definite period of time the policy is called a time policy. A contract for both voyage and time may be included in the same policy.

28. (1) The subject-matter insured shall be designated in a marine policy with reasonable certainty; but the nature and extent of the interest of the assured the subject-matter insured need not be specified in the policy.

(2) Where the policy designates the subject-matter insured in general terms, it shall be construed to apply to the interest intended by the assured to be covered.

(3) In the application of this section, regard shall be had to any usage regulating the designation of the subject matter insured.

29. (1) A policy may be either valued or unvalued, and for the purposes of this section, a valued policy is a policy which specifies the agreed value of the subject-matter insured.

(2 Subject to the provisions of this Act, and in the absence of fraud, the value fixed by the policy is, as between the insurer and assured, conclusive of the insurable value of the subject intended to be insured, whether the loss is total or partial.

(3) Unless the policy otherwise provides, the value fixed by the policy is not conclusive for the purposes of determining whether there has been a constructive total loss.

30. An unvalued policy is a policy which does not specify the value of the subject-matter insured, but, subject to the limit of the sum insured, leaves the insurable value to be subsequently ascertained in the manner specified in section 18.

3. (1) A floating policy is a policy which describes the insurance in general terms, and leaves the name of the ship or ships and other particulars to be defined by subsequent declaration.

(2) The subsequent declaration or declarations may be made by indorsement on the policy, or in other customary manner.

Unless the policy otherwise provides, the declarations shall be made in the order of dispatch or shipment. In the case of goods, they shall comprise all consignments within the terms of the policy, and the value of the goods or other property shall be honestly stated, but any omission or erroneous declaration may be rectified even after loss or arrival, provided the omission or declaration was made in good faith.

(4) Unless the policy otherwise provides, where a declaration of value is not made until after notice of loss or arrival, the policy shall be treated as an unvalued policy as regards the subject-matter of that ·declaration.

32. (1) Where an insurance is effected at a premium to be arranged, and no arrangement is made, a reasonable premium shall be payable.

(2) Where an insurance is effected on the terms that an additional premium is to be arranged in a given event, and that event happens but no arrangement is made, then a reasonable additional premium shall be payable.

DOUBLE INSURANCE

33. (1) Where two or more policies are effected by or on behalf of the assured on the same adventure and interest or any part thereof, and the sums insured exceed the indemnity allowed by this Act, the assured is said to be over-insured by double insurance—

(2) Where the assured is over-insured by double insurance—

(a) the assured, unless the policy otherwise provides, may claim payment from the insurers in such order as he may think fit, provided that he shall not be entitled to receive any sum in excess of the indemnity allowed by this Act.

(b) where the policy under which the assured claims is a valued policy, the assured shall give credit as against the valuation for any sum received by him under any other policy without regard to the actual value of the subject-matter insured;

(c) where the policy under which the assured claims is an unvalued policy he shall give credit, as against the full insurable value, for any sum received by him under any other policy;

(d) where the assured receives any sum in excess of the indemnity allowed by this Act, he shall be deemed to hold such sum in trust for the insurers, according to their right of contribution among themselves.

WARRANTIES, ETC.

34. (1) For the purposes of this section and of sections 35 to 42

(which relate to warranties) a warranty means a promissory warranty, that is to say, a warranty by which the assured undertakes that some particular thing shall or shall not be done, or that some condition shall be fulfilled, or whereby he affirms or negatives the existence of a particular state of facts.

(2) A warranty within the meaning of this section may be express or implied, and is a condition which shall be exactly complied with, whether it is material to the risk or not. If it is not so complied with then, subject to any express provision in the policy, the insurer shall be discharged from liability as from the date of the breach of warranty, but without prejudice to any liability incurred by him before that date.

35. (1) Non-compliance with a warranty is excused when, by reason of a change of circumstances, the warranty ceases to be applicable to the circumstances of the contract, or when compliance with the warranty is rendered unlawful by any subsequent law.

(2) Where a warranty is broken, the fact that the breach has been remedied and the warranty complied with before loss shall be no defence to the assured; but a breach of warranty may be waived by the insurer.

36. (1) An express warranty may be in any form of words from which the intention to warrant is to be inferred.

(2) An express warranty shall be included in or written upon the policy, or be contained in some document incorporated by reference into the policy.

(3) An express warranty shall not exclude an implied warranty, unless it is inconsistent therewith.

37. (1) Where insurable property, whether ship or goods, is expressly warranted neutral, there is an implied condition that the property shall have a neutral character at the commencement of the risk, and that, so far as the assured can control the matter, its neutral character shall be preserved during the risk.

(2) Where a ship is expressly warranted "neutral" there is also an implied condition that, so far as the assured can control the matter, she shall be properly documented, that is to say, that she shall carry the necessary papers to establish her neutrality, and that she shall not falsify or suppress her papers, or use simulated papers. If any loss occurs through breach of this condition, the insurer may avoid the contract.

38. There is no implied warranty as to the nationality of a ship, or that her nationality shall not be changed during the risk.

39. Where the subject-matter insured is warranted "well" or "in good safety" on a particular day, it is sufficient if it be safe at any time during that day.

40. (1) In a voyage policy there is an implied warranty that at the commencement of the voyage the ship shall be sea-worthy for the purpose of the particular adventure insured.

(2) Where the policy attaches while the ship is in port, there is also an implied warranty that she shall, at the commencement of the risk, be reasonably fit to encounter the ordinary perils of the port.

(3) Where the policy relates to a voyage which is performed in different stages, during which the ship requires different kinds of or further preparation or equipment, there is an implied warranty that at the commencement of each stage the ship is seaworthy in respect of such preparation or equipment for the purposes of that stage.

(4) A ship is deemed to be seaworthy when she is reasonably fit in all respects to encounter the ordinary perils of the seas of the adventure insured.

(5) In a time policy there is no implied warranty that the ship shall be seaworthy at any stage of the adventure, but where with the privity of the assured, the ship is sent to sea in an unseaworthy state, the insurer is not liable for any loss attributable to unseaworthiness.

41. (1) In a policy on goods or other moveables there is no implied warranty that the goods or moveables are seaworthy.

(2) In a voyage policy on goods or other moveables there is an implied warranty that at the commencement of the voyage the ship is not only seaworthy as a ship, but also that she is reasonably fit to carry the goods or other moveables to the destination contemplated by the policy.

42. There is an implied warranty that the adventure insured is a lawful one, and that, so far as the assured can control the matter, the adventure shall be carried out in a lawful manner.

THE VOYAGE

43. (1) Where the subject-matter is insured by a voyage policy

"at and from" or "from" a particular place, it is not necessary that the ship should be at that place when the contract is concluded; but there is an implied condition that the adventure shall be commenced within a reasonable time, and that if the adventure is not so commenced the insurer may avoid the contract.

(2) The implied condition may be negatived by showing that the delay was caused by circumstances known to the insurer before the contract was concluded, or by showing that he waived the condition.

44. Where the place of departure is specified by the policy, and the ship instead of sailing from that place sails from any other place, the risk shall not attach.

45. Where the destination is specified in the policy and the ship instead of sailing for that destination, sails for any other destination, the risk shall not attach.

46. (1) Where, after the commencement of the risk, the destination of the ship is voluntarily changed from the destination contemplated by the policy, there is said to be a change of voyage.

(2) Unless the policy otherwise provides, where there is a change of voyage, the insurer is discharged from liability as from the time of change, that is to say, as from the time when the determination to change it is manifested; and it is immaterial that the ship may not in fact have left the course of voyage contemplated by the policy when the loss occurs.

47. (1) Where a ship, without lawful excuse, deviates from the voyage contemplated by the policy, the insurer is discharged from liability as from the time of deviation, and it is immaterial that the ship may have regained her route before any loss occurs.

 (2) There is a deviation from the voyage contemplated by the policy—

(a) where the course of the voyage is specifically designated by the policy, and that course is departed from; or
(b) where the course of the voyage is not specifically designated by the policy, but the usual and customary course is departed from.

(3) The intention to deviate is immaterial; and if there is a deviation a fact the insurer is discharged from his liability under the contract.

48. (1) Where several ports of discharge are specified by the policy, the ship may proceed to all or any of them, but, in the absence of any usage or sufficient cause to the contrary, she shall proceed to them or such of them as she goes to, in the order designated by the policy; and if she does not, there is a deviation.

(2) Where the policy is to "ports of discharge" within a given area and they are not named, the ship shall, in the absence of any usage or sufficient cause to the contrary, proceed to them or such of them as she goes to, in their geographical order; and if she does not, there is a deviation.

49. In the case of a voyage policy, the adventure insured shall be prosecuted throughout its course with reasonable dispatch, and, if without lawful excuse it is not so prosecuted, the insurer shall be discharged from liability as from the time when the delay became unreasonable.

50. (1) Deviation or delay in prosecuting the voyage contemplated oy the policy is excused—

(a)   where authorised by any special term in the policy; or
(b)   where caused by circumstances beyond the control of the master and his employer; or
(c)   where reasonably necessary in order to comply with an express or implied warranty; or
(d)   where reasonably necessary for the safety of the ship or subject-matter insured; or
(e)   for the purpose of saving human life, or aiding a ship in distress where human life may be in danger; or
(f). where reasonably necessary for the purpose of obtaining medical or surgical aid for any person on board the ship; or
(g)   ·where caused by the barratrous conduct of the master or crew, if barratry is one of the perils insured against.

(2) When the cause excusing the deviation or delay ceases to operate, the ship shall resume her course, and prosecute her voyage with reasonable dispatch.

ASSIGNMENT OF POLICY

51, (1) A marine policy shall be assignable unless it contains terms expressly prohibiting assignment; and a marine policy may be assigned either before or after loss.

(2) Where a marine policy has been assigned so as to pass the beneficial interest in such policy, the assignee of the policy shall be entitled to sue thereon in his own name; and the defendant shall be entitled to make any defence arising out of the contract which he would have been entitled to make if the action had been brought in the name of the person by or on behalf of whom the policy was effected.

(3) A marine policy may be assigned by indorsement thereon or in other customary manner.

52. (1) Where the assured has parted with or lost his interest in the subject-matter insured, and has not, before or at the time of so doing, expressly or impliedly agreed to assign the policy, any subsequent assignment of the policy shall be inoperative.

(2) Nothing in this section shall be construed so as to effect the assignment of a policy after loss.

THE PREMIUM

53. Unless otherwise agreed, the duty of the assured or his agent to pay the premium, and the duty of the insurer to issue the policy to the assured or his agent, are cuncurrent conditions; and the insurer shall not be bound to issue the policy until payment or tender of the premium.

54. (1) Unless otherwise agreed, where a marine policy is effected on behalf of the assured by a broker the broker is directly responsible to the insurer for the premium, and the insurer is directly responsible to the assured for the amount which may be payable in respect of losses, or in respect of returnable premium.

(2) Unless otherwise agreed, the broker has, as against the assured, a lien upon the policy for the amount of the premium and his charges in respect of effecting the policy; and, where he has dealt with the person who employs him as a principal, he has also a lien on the policy in respect of any balance on any insurance account which may be due to him from such person, unless when the debt was incurred he had reason to believe that such person was only an agent.

55. Where a marine policy effected on behalf of the assured by a

broker acknowledges the receipt of the premium, such acknowledgement is, in the absence of fraud, conclusive as between the insurer and the assured, but not as between the insurer and broker.

LOSS AND ABANDONMENT

56. (1) Subject to the provisions of this Act and unless the policy otherwise provides, the insurer shall be liable for any loss proximately caused by a peril insured against, but subject, as aforesaid, he shall not be liable for any loss which is not proximately caused by a peril insure against.

(2) In particular,—

(a) the insurer shall not be liable for any loss attributable to the wilful misconduct of the assured, but, unless the policy otherwise provides, he shall be liable for any loss proximately caused by a peril insured against, even though the loss would not have happened but for the misconduct or negligence of the master or crew;

(b) unless the policy otherwise provides, the insurer on ship or goods shall not be liable for any loss proximately caused by delay, although the delay be caused by a peril insured against;

(c) unless the policy otherwise provides, the insurer shall not be liable for ordinary wear and tear, ordinary leakage and breakage, inherent vice or nature of the subject-matter insured, or for any loss proximately caused by rats or vermin, or for any injury to machinery not proximately caused by maritime perils.

57. (1) A total loss may be either an actual total loss, or a constructive total loss; and any loss other than a total loss, is a partial loss.

(2) Unless a different intention appears from the terms of the policy, an insurance against total loss includes a constructive, as well as an actual total loss.

(3) Where the assured brings an action for a total loss and the evidence proves only a partial loss, he may, unless the policy otherwise provides, recover for a partial loss.

(4) Where goods reach their destination in specie, but by reason of obliteration of marks, or otherwise, they are incapable of identification, the loss, if any, is partial, and not total.

58. (1) Where the subject-matter insured is destroyed, or so damaged as to cease to be a thing of the kind insured, or where the assured is irretrievably deprived thereof, there is an actual total·loss.

(2) In the case of an actual total loss no notice of abandonment need be given.

59. Where the ship concerned in. the adventure is missing, at after the lapse of a reasonable time no news of her has been received, an actual total loss may be presumed.

60. Where, by a peril insured against, the voyage is interrupted and an intermediate port or place, under such circumstances as, apart from any special stipulation in the contract of affreightment to justify the master in landing and re-shipping the goods or other movables, or in transhipping them, and sending them on to their destination, the liability of the insurer continues, notwithstanding the landing or tranship-ment.

61. (1) Subject to any express provision in the policy, there is a constructive total loss where the subject-matter insured is reason-ably abandoned on account of its actual total loss appearing to be unavoidable, or because it could not be preserved from actual total loss without an expenditure which would exceed its value when the expenditure had been incurred.

(2) In particular, there is a constructive total loss—

(a)   where the assured is deprived of the possession of his ship or goods by a peril insured against and,

(i) It is unlikely that he can recover the ship or goods as the case may be,.or

(ii) the cost of recovering the ship or goods as the case may be would exceed their value when recovered; or

(b)   in the case of damage to a ship, where she is so damaged by a peril insured against that the cost of repairing the damage would exceed the value of the ship when repaired; and for the purposes of this paragraph, in estimating the cost of repairs, no deduction is to be made in respect of general average contributions to those repairs payable by other interests, but account is to be taken of the expense of future salvage opera-tions, and of any future general average contributions to which the ship would be liable if repaired; or

(c) In the case of damage to goods, where the cost of repairing the damage and forwarding the goods to their destination would exceed their value on arrival.

62. Where there is a constructive total loss the assured may either treat the loss as a partial loss, or abandon the subject-matter insured to the insurer and treat the loss as if it were an actual total loss.

63. (1) Subject to the provisions of this section, where the assured elects to abandon the subject-matter insured to the insurer, he shall give notice of abandonment; and if he fails to give notice of abandonment, the loss shall be treated as a partial loss.

(2) Notice of abandonment may be given in writing, or by word of mouth, or partly in writing and partly by word of mouth, and may be given in terms which indicate the intention of the assured to abandon his insured interest in the subject-matter insured unconditionally to the insurer.

(3) Notice of abandonment shall be given with reasonable diligence after the receipt of reliable information of the loss, but where the information is of a doubtful character the assured is entitled to a reasonable time to make inquiry.

(4) Where notice of abandonment is properly given, the rights of the assured shall not be prejudiced by the fact that the insurer refused to accept the abandonment.

(5) The acceptance of an abandonment may be either express or implied from the conduct of the insurer, but the mere silence of the insurer after notice shall not be construed as an acceptance.

(6) Where notice of abandonment is accepted the abandonment is irrevocable, and the acceptance of the notice shall be construed as conclusive admission of liability for the loss and the sufficiency of the notice.

(7) Notice of abandonment shall be unnecessary where, at the time when the assured receives the information of the loss, there would be no possibility of benefit to the insurer if notice were given to him.

(8) Notice of abandonment may be waived by the insurer.

(9) Where an insurer has re-insured his risk, no notice of abandonment need be given by him.

64. (1) Where there is a valid abandonment the insurer shall be

entitled to take over interest of the assured in whatever may remain
of the subject-matter insured, and all proprietary rights incidental
thereto.

(2) Upon the abandonment of a ship, the insurer thereof shall
be entitled to any freight in course of being earned, and which is
earned by her subsequent to the casualty causing the loss, less the
expenses of earning it incurred after the casualty; and, where the ship
is carrying the owner's goods, the insurer shall be entitled to a reasonable remuneration for the carriage of them subsequent to the casualty
causing the loss.

PARTIAL LOSSES (INCLUDING SALVAGE AND GENERAL AVERAGE AND PARTICULAR CHARGES)

65. (1) A particular average loss is a partial loss of the subject-
matter insured, caused by a peril insured against, and which is not
a general average loss.

(2) Expenses incurred by or on behalf of the assured for the safety
or preservation of the subject-matter insured, other than general
average and salvage charges, are called particular charges, and are
not included in particular average.

66. (1) Subject to any express provision in the policy, salvage charges
incurred in preventing a loss by perils insured against may be recovered as a loss by those perils.

(2) For the purposes of this section, "salvage charges" means
the charges recoverable under maritime law by a salvor independently of contract, but does not include expenses of services in the
nature of salvage which are recoverable, if properly incurred, as
particular charges or general average loss, as the case may be, where
rendered by the assured or his agents, or any person employed for
hire by them, for the purpose of averting a peril insured against.

67. (1) A general average loss is a loss caused by or directly consequential on a general average act, and includes a general average
expenditure as well as a general average sacrifice.

(2) There is a general average act where any extraordinary sacrifice
or expenditure is voluntarily and reasonably made or incurred in
time of peril for the purpose of preserving the property imperilled
in the common adventure.

(3) Where there is a general average loss, the party on whom it falls shall be entitled, subject to the conditions imposed by maritime law, to a ratable contribution, called a general average contribution, from the other parties interested.

(4) Subject to any express provision in the policy, where the assured has incurred a general average expenditure, he may recover from the insurer in respect of the proportion of the loss which falls upon him; and, in the case of a general average sacrifice, he may recover from the insurer in respect of the whole loss without having enforced his right of contribution from the other parties liable to contribute.

(5) Subject to any express provision in the policy, where the assured has paid, or is liable to pay, a general average contribution in respect of the subject insured, he may recover therefore from the insurer.

(6) In the absence of express stipulation, the insurer shall not be liable for any general average loss or contribution where the loss was not incurred for the purpose of avoiding, or in connection with the avoidance of, a peril insured against.

(7) Where ship, freight, and cargo, or any two of those interests, are owned by the same assured, the liability of the insurer in respect of general average losses or contributions is to be determined as those subjects were owned by different persons.

MEASURE OF INDEMNITY

68. (1) Where there is a loss recoverable under the policy, the insurer or each insurer if there are more insurers than one, shall be liable for such proportion of the measure of indemnity as the amount of his subscription bears to the value fixed by the policy in the case of a valued policy, or to the insurable value in the case of an unvalued policy.

(2) For the purposes of this section "measure of indemnity" means the sum which the assured may recover in respect of a loss on a policy by which he is insured, being in the case of a valued policy the full extent of the value fixed by the policy, and in the case of an unvalued policy, the full extent of the insurable value.

69. Subject to the provisions of this Act and to any express provision in the policy, where there is a total loss of the subject-matter insured,—
   (a) If the policy is a valued policy, the measure of indemnity shall be the sum fixed by the policy;
   (b) If the policy is an unvalued policy, the measure of indemnity

shall be the insurable value of the subject-matter insured.

70. Where a ship is damaged, but is not totally lost, the measure of indemnity, subject to any express provision in the policy, shall be as follows,—

(a) Where the ship has been repaired, the assured shall be entitled to the reasonable cost of the repairs, less the customary deductions, but not exceeding the sum insured in respect of any one casualty:

(b) Where the ship has been only partially repaired, the assured shall be entitled to the reasonable cost of such repairs, computed as above, and be indemnified for the reasonable depreciation, if any, arising from the unrepaired damage, provided that the aggregate amount shall not exceed the cost of repairing the whole damage, computed as above:

(c) where the ship has not been repaired, and has not been sold in her damaged state during the risk, the assured shall be entitled to be indemnified for the reasonable depriciation arising from the unrepaired damage, but not exceeding the reasonable cost of repairing such damage, computed as above.

71. Subject to any express provision in the policy, where there is a partial loss of freight, the measure of indemnity shall be such proportion of the sum fixed by the policy in the case of a valued policy, or of the insurable value in the case of an unvalued policy, as the proportion of freight lost by the assured bears to the whole freight at the risk of the assured under the policy.

72. (1) Where there is a partial loss of goods, merchandise or other moveables, the measure of indemnity, subject to any express provision in the policy, shall be as follows,—

(a) where part of the goods, merchandise or other moveables insured by a valued policy is totally lost, the measure of indemnity shall be such proportion of the sum fixed by the policy as the insurable value of the part lost bears to the insurable value of the whole, ascertained as in the case of an unvalued policy:

(b) where part of the goods, merchandise, or other moveables insured by an unvalued policy is totally lost, the measure of indemnity shall be the insurable value of the part lost, is liable, that amount shall be deducted from the insured value in order to ascertain what the insurer is liable to contribute.

(2) Where the insurer is liable for salvage charges the extent of his liability shall be determined on the like principle.

75. Where the assured has effected an insurance in express terms against any liability to a third party, the measure of indemnity, subject to any express provision in the policy, is the amount paid or payable by him to such third party in respect of such liability.

76. (1) Where there has been a loss in respect of any subject-matter not expressly provided for in the foregoing provision of this Act, the measure of indemnity shall be ascertained, as nearly as may be, in accordance with those provisions, in so far as applicable to the particular case.

(2) Nothing in this Act relating to the measure of indemnity shall affect the rules relating to double insurance, or prohibit the insurer from disproving interest wholly or in part, or from showing that at the time of the loss the whole or any part of the subject-matter insured was not at risk under the policy.

77. (1) Where the subject-matter insured is warranted free from particular average, the assured shall not recover for a loss of part other than a loss incurred by a general average sacrifice, unless the contract contained in the policy is apportionable; but, if the contract is apportionable, the assured may recover for a total loss of any apportionable part.

(2) Where the subject-matter insured is warranted free from particular average, either wholly or under a certain percentage, the insurer shall nevertheless be liable for salvage charges; and the insurer shall also be liable for particular charges for and other expenses of averting a loss insured against, where properly incurred pursuant to the provisions of a suing and labouring clause to the like effect as set out in the prescribed form, if contained in the policy.

(3) Unless the policy otherwise provides, where the subject-matter insured is warranted free from particular average under a specified percentage, a general average loss shall not be added to a particular average loss to make up the specified percentage.

(4) For the purpose of ascertaning whether the specified percentage has been reached, regard shall be had only to the actual loss suffered by

ascertained as in case of total loss:

(c)   where the whole or any part of the goods or merchandise insured has been delivered damaged at its destination, the measure of indemnity shall be such proportion of the sum fixed by the policy in the case of a valued policy, or of the insurable value in the case of an unvalued policy, as the difference between the gross sound and damaged values at the place of arrival bears to the gross sound value.

(2) For the purposes of this section—

"gross value" means the wholesale price or, if there is no such price, the estimated value with in either case, freight, landing charges, and duty paid before-hand, provided that, in the case of goods or merchandise customarily sold in bond, the bonded price shall be deemed to be the gross value;

"gross proceeds" means the actual price obtained at a sale where all charges on sale are paid by the sellers.

73. (1) Where different species of property are insured under a single valuation, the valuation shall be apportioned over the different species in proportion to their respective insurable values, as in the case of an unvalued policy; and for the purposes of this subsection, the insured value of any part of a species shall be such proportion of the total insured value of the same as the insurable value of the part bears to the insurable value of the whole, ascertained in both cases as provided by this Act.

(2) Where a valuation is to be apportioned, and particulars of the prime cost of each separate species, quality or description of goods are not ascertainable, the division of the valuation may be made over the net arrived sound values of the different species, qualities, or descriptions of goods.

74. (1) Subject to any express provision in the policy, where the assured has paid, or is liable for any general average contribution, the measure of indemnity is the full amount of such contribution, if the subject-matter liable to contribution is insured for its full contributory value. If the subject-matter is not insured for its full contributory value, or if only part of it is insured, the indemnity payable by the insurer shall be reduced in proportion to the under insurance; and where there has been a particular average loss which constitutes a deduction from the contributory value, and for which the insurer

the subject-matter insured, and particular charges and the expenses of and incidental to ascertaining and proving the loss shall be excluded.

78. (1) Unless the policy otherwise provides, and subject to the provisions of this Act, the insurer shall be liable for successive losses, even though the total amount of such losses may exceed the sum insured.

(2) Where, under the same policy, a partial loss, which has not been repaired or otherwise made good, is followed by a total loss, the assured may recover in respect only of the total loss.

(3) Nothing in this section shall affect the liability of an insurer under a suing and labouring clause in the prescribed form or to the like effect if contained in the policy.

79. (1) Where the policy contains a suing and labouring clause in the prescribed form or to the like effect, the agreement thereby entered into shall be deemed to be supplementary to the contract of insurance, and the assured may recover from the insurer any expenses properly incurred pursuant to the clause, notwithstanding that the insurer may have paid for a total loss, or that the subject-matter may have been warranted free from particular average, either wholly or under a certain percentage.

(2) General average losses and contributions and salvage charges, as defined by this Act, shall not be recoverable under the suing and labouring clause.

(3) Expenses incurred for the purpose of averting or diminishing any loss not covered by the policy shall not be recoverable under the suing and labouring clause.

(4) It shall be the duty of the assured and his agents, in all cases, to take such measures as may be reasonable for the purpose of averting or minimising a loss.

RIGHTS OF INSURER ON PAYMENT

80. (1) Where the insurer pays for a total loss, either of the whole or in the case of goods of any apportionable part, of the subject-matter, insured, he shall thereupon become entitled to take over the interest of the assured in whatever may remain of the subject-matter so paid for, and shall thereby be subrogated to all the rights and remedies of the assured in and in respect of that subject-matter as from the time of the casualty causing the loss.

(2) Subject to the foregoing provisions, where the insurer pays for a partial loss, he shall acquire no title to the subject-matter insured, or such part of it as may remain, but shall thereupon be subrogated to all rights and remedies of the assured in and in respect of the subject-matter insured as from the time of the casualty causing the loss, in so far as the assured has been indemnified, according to this Act, by such payment for the loss.

81. (1) Where the assured is over-insured by double insurance, each insurer shall be bound, as between himself and the other insurers, to contribute rateably to the loss in proportion to the amount for which he is liable under his contract.

(2) If any insurer pays more than his proportion of the loss, he shall be entitled to maintain an action for contribution against the other insurers, and be entitled to the like remedies as a surety who has paid more than his proportion of the debt.

82. Where the assured is insured for an amount less than the insurable value or, in the case of a valued policy, for an amount less than the policy valuation, he shall be deemed to be his own insurer in respect of the uninsured balance.

RETURN OF PREMIUM

83. Where the premium or a proportionate part thereof is, by this Act declared to be returnable,—

(a)   if already paid, it may be recovered by the assured from the insurer and

(b)   if unpaid, it may be retained by the assured or his agent.

84. Where the policy contains a stipulation for the return of the premium, or a proportionate part thereof, on the happening of a certain event, and that event happens, the premium, or, as the case may be, the proportionate part thereof, shall thereupon be returned to the assured.

85. (1) Where the consideration for the payment of the premium totally fails, and there has been no fraud or illegality on the part of the assured or his agents, the premium shall thereupon be returned to the assured.

(2) Where the consideration for the payment of the premium is apportionable and there is a total failure of any apportionable part of the consideration, a proportionate part of the premium shall, under the like conditions, be returned to the assured.

(3) In particular—

(a) Where a policy is void, or is avoided by the insurer as from the commencement of the risk, the premium shall be returnable, provided that there has been no fraud or illegality on the part of the assured; but if the risk is not apportionable, and has once attached, the premium shall not be returnable:

(b) Where the subject-matter insured, or part thereof, has never been imperilled, the premium or, as the case may be, a proportionate part thereof, shall be returnable; provided that where the subject matter has been insured "lost or not lost" and has arrived in safety at the time when the contract is concluded, the premium shall not be returnable unless, at such time, the insurer knew of the safe arrival:

(c) where the assured has no insurable interest throughout the currency of the risk, the premium shall be returnable, but nothing in this paragraph shall be construed to apply to a policy effected by way of gaming or wagering:

(d) where the assured has a defeasible interest which is terminated during the currency of the risk, the premium shall not be returnable:

(e) where the assured has over-insured under an unvalued policy, a proportionate part of the premium shall be returnable.

(4) Subject to the foregoing provisions of this section, where the assured has over-insured by double insurance, a proportionate part of the several premiums shall be returnable:

Provided that, if the policies are effected at different times, and any earlier policy has at any time borne the entire risk, or if a claim has been paid on the policy in respect of the full sum insured thereby, no premium shall be returnable in respect of that policy, and when the double insurance is effected knowingly by the assured no premium shall be returnable.

MUTUAL INSURANCE

86. (1) Where two or more persons mutually agree to insure each other against marine losses there is said to be a mutual insurance.

(2) The provision of this Act relating to the premium shall not apply to mutual insurance, but a guarantee, or such other arrangement as may be agreed upon, may be substituted for the premium.

(3) The provisions of this Act, in so far as they may be modified by the agreement of the parties, may in the case of mutual insurance be modified by the terms of the policies issued by the association, or by the rules and regulations of the association.

(4) Subject to the exceptions mentioned in this section the provisions of this Act apply to a mutual insurance.

SUPPLEMENTAL

87. Where a contract of marine insurance is in good faith effected by one person on behalf of another, the person on whose behalf it is effected may ratify the contract even after he is aware of a loss.

88. (1) Where any right, duty, or liability would arise under a contract of marine insurance by implication of law, it may be negatived or varied by express agreement, or by usage, if the usage is such as to bind both parties to the contract.

(2) The provisions of this section shall extend to any right, duty, or liability declared by this Act which may be lawfully modified by agreement.

89. Where there is a duly stamped policy, reference may be made to the slip or covering note, in any legal proceeding.

90. (1) If—

(a) any person effects a contract of marine insurance without having any bona fide interest, direct or indirect, either in the safe arrival of the ship in relation to which the contract is made or in the safety or preservation of the subject matter insured, or a bona fide expectation of acquiring such an interest; or

(b) any person in the employment of the owner of a ship, not being a part owner of the ship, effects a contract of marine insurance in relation to the ship and the contract is made "interest or no interest", or "without further proof of interest than the policy itself", or "without benefit of salvage to the insurer", or subject to any other like term,—

the contract shall be deemed to be a contract by way of gambling on loss by maritime perils, and the person effecting it shall be guilty of an offence, and liable, on summary conviction, to imprisonment for a term not exceeding six months or to a fine not exceeding one hundred pounds, and in either case to forfeit to the Crown any money he may have received under the contract.

(2) Any broker or other person through whom, and any insurer with whom any such contract is effected shall be guilty of an offence and liable on summary conviction to the like penalties, if he acted knowing that the contract was by way of gambling on loss by maritime perils within the meaning of this section.

(3) Proceedings under this section shall not be instituted without the consent of a Law Officer.

(4) Proceedings shall not be instituted under this section against a person, (other than a person in the employment of the owner of the ship in relation to which the contract was made) alleged to have effected a contract by way of gambling on loss by maritime perils until an opportunity has been afforded him of showing that the contract was not such a contract as aforesaid, and any information given by that person for that purpose shall not be admissible in evidence against him in any prosecution under this section.

(5) If proceedings under this section are taken against any person (other than a person in the employment of the owner of the ship in relation to which the contract was made) for effecting such a contract, and the contract was made "interest or no interest", or "without further proof of interest than the policy itself", or "without benefit of salvage to the insurer", or subject to any other like term, the contract shall be deemed to be a contract by way of gambling on loss by maritime perils unless the contrary is proved.

(6) For the purpose of giving jurisdiction under this section, every offence shall be deemed to have been committed either in the place in which the same actually was committed or in any place in which the offender may be.

(7) Any person aggrieved by an order or decision of a court of summary jurisdiction under this section may appeal to High Court.

(8) For the purposes of this section, the expression "owner" includes charterer.

91. (1) The enactments mentioned in the Second Schedule in

so far as they are in force in and form part of the laws of Nigeria, are hereby repealed to the extent specified in that Schedule.

(2) Nothing in this Act or in any repeal effected thereby, shall affect—

(*a*)   the provisions of the Stamp Duties Ordinance or any enactment for the time being in force relating to the revenue;

(*b*)   the provisions of the Companies Ordinance or any enactment amending or substituted for the same;

(*c*)   the provisions of any statute not expressly repealed by this Act.

(3) The rules of the common law of England, to the extent to which they are in force in Lagos under the Interpretation Ordinance shall, for the purposes of this Act, be in force in all Regions of Nigeria; and save in so far as they are inconsistent with the express provisions of this Act, shall continue to apply to contracts of marine insurance. To give effect to this subsection in any Region, the rules of the common law shall where necessary be deemed to have been duly revived; and for the removal of doubts, and subject to the provisions of this subsection, the usages of the law merchant in England shall be deemed to be part of the common law and be construed with and form part of this Act. For the purposes of this subsection, "Region".includes Lagos.

SCHEDULES

FIRST SCHEDULE

FORM OF POLICY

BE IT KNOWN THAT..as well in..own name as for and in the name and names of all and every other person or persons to whom the same doth, may, or shall appertain, in part or in all doth make assurance and cause..and them, and every of them, to be insured lost or not lost, at and from................................
....

Upon any kind of goods and merchandise, and also upon the body, tackle, apparel, ordinance, munition, artillery, boat, and other furniture, of and in the good ship or vessel called the................................
....whereof is master under God, for this present voyage,..................................or whosoever

else shall go for master in the said ship, or by whatsoever other name or names the said ship, or the master thereof, is or shall be named or called; beginning the adventure upon the said goods and merchandise from the loading thereof aboard the said ship,..
....upon the said ship, etc., and so shall continue and endure, during her abode there, upon the said ship, etc. And further, until the said ship with all her ordinance, tackle, apparel, etc, and goods and merchandises whatsoever shall be arrived at...upon the said ship, etc, until she hath moored at anchor twenty-four hours in good safety; .and upon the goods and merchandises, until the same be there discharged and safely landed. And it shall be lawful for the said ship, etc., in this voyage, to proceed and sail to and touch and stay at any ports or places whatsoever.. .... without prejudice to this insurance. The said ship, etc, goods and merchandises, etc, for so much as concerns the assured by agreement between the assured and assurers in this policy, are and shall be valued at...

Touching the adventures and perils which we the assurers are contended to bear and do take upon us in this voyage: they are of the seas, men of war, fire, enemies, pirates, rovers, thieves, jettisons, letters of mart and countermart, surprisals, takings at sea, arrests, restrains, and detainments of all kings, princes, and people, of what nation, condition, or quality soever, barratry of the master and mariners, and of all other perils, losses, and misfortunes, that have or shall come to the hurt, detriment, or damage of the said goods and merchandises, and ship, etc., or any part thereof. And in case of any loss or misfortune it shall be lawful to the assured, their factors, servants and assigns, to sue, labour, and travel for, in and about the defence, safeguards, and recovery of the said goods and merchandises, and ship, etc., or any part thereof, without prejudice to this insurance; to the charges whereof we, the assurers, will contribute each one according to the rate and quantity of his sum herein assured. And it is especially declared and agreed that no acts of insurers or insured in recovering, saving, or preserving the property insured shall be considered as a waiver, or acceptance of abandonment. And it is agreed by us, the insurers, that this writing or policy of assurance shall be of as much force and effect as the surest writing or policy of assurance heretofore made in any place in Nigeria. And so we, the assurers, are contended, and do hereby promise and bind ourselves each one for his own part, our heirs, executors, and goods to the assured, their executors, administrators, and assigns, for the true performance of the premises, confessing ourselves paid the consideration due unto us for this assurance by the assured, at and after the rate of.................

....

In Witness whereof we, the assurers, have subscribed our names and sums assured in..

N.B.—Corn, fish, salt, fruit, flour, and seed are warranted free from average, unless general, or the ship be stranded—sugar, tobacco, hemp, flax, hides and skins are warranted free from average, under five pounds per cent; and all other goods, also the ship and freight, are warranted free from average, under three pounds per cent unless general, or the ship be stranded.

RULES FOR CONSTRUCTION OF POLICY

(1) Where the subject-matter is insured "lost or not lost", and the loss has occurred before the contract is concluded, the risk attaches, unless at such time the assured was aware of the loss, and the insurer was not.

(2) Where the subject-matter is insured "from" a particular place, the risk does not attach until the ship starts on the voyage insured.

(3) (a) Where a ship is insured "at and from" a particular place, and she is at that place in good safety when the contract is concluded, the risk attaches immediately.

(b)   If she be not at that place when the contract is concluded, the risk attaches as soon as she arrives there in good safety, and, unless the policy otherwise provides, it is immaterial that she is covered by another policy for a specified time after arrival.

(c)   Where chartered freight is insured "at and from" a particular place, and the ship is at that place in good safety when the contract is concluded the risk attaches immediately. If she be not there when the contract is concluded, the risk attaches as soon as she arrives there in good safety.

(d)   Where freight, other than chartered freight, is payable without special conditions and is insured "at and from" a particular place, the risk attaches pro rata as the goods or merchandise are shipped; provided that if there be cargo in readiness which belongs to the shipowner, or which some other person has contracted with him to ship, the risk attaches as soon as the ship is ready to receive such cargo.

(4) Where goods or other moveables are insured "from the loading thereof", the risk does not attach until such goods or moveables are actually on board, and the insurer is not liable for them while in transit from the shore to ship.

(5) Where the risk on goods or other moveables continues until they are "safely landed," they must be landed in the customary manner and within a reasonable time after arrival at the port of discharge, and if they are not so landed the risk ceases.

(6) In the absence of any further license or usage, the liberty to touch and stay "at any port or place whatsoever" does not authorise the ship to depart from the course of her voyage from the port of departure to the port of destination.

(7) The term "perils of the seas" refers only to fortuitous accidents or casualties of the seas. It does not include the ordinary action of the winds and waves.

(8) The term "pirates" includes passengers who mutiny and riots who attack the ship from the shore.

(9) The term "thieves does not cover clandestine theft or a theft committed by any one of the ship's company, whether crew or passengers.

(10) The term "arrests, etc., of kings, princes, and people" refers to political or executive acts, and does not include a loss caused by riot or by ordinary judicial process.

(11) The term "barratry" includes every wrongful act wilfully committed by the master or crew to the prejudice of the owner, or, as the case may be, the charterer.

(12) The term "all other perils" includes only perils similar in kind to the perils specifically mentioned in the policy.

(13) The term "average unless general" means a partial loss of the subject-matter insured other than a general average loss, and does not include "particular charges".

(14) Where the ship has stranded, the insurer is liable for the excepted losses, although the loss is not attributable to the stranding, provided that when the stranding takes place the risk has attached and, if the policy be on goods, that the damaged goods are on board.

(15) The term "ship" includes the hull, materials and outfit, stores and provisions for the officers and crew, and in the case of vessels engaged in a special trade, the ordinary fittings requisite for the trade,

and also, in the case of a steamship, the machinery, boilers, and coals and engine stores, if owned by the assured.

(16) The term "freight" includes the profit derivable by a ship-owner from the employment of his ship to carry his own goods or moveables, as well as freight payable by a third party, both does not include passage money.

(17) The term "goods" means goods in the nature of merchandise, and does not include personal effects or provisions and stores for use on board.

In the absence of any usage to the contrary deck cargo and living animals must be insured specifically, and not under the general denomination of goods.

SECOND SCHEDULE   *Section* 91

ENACTMENTS REPEALED

Session and Chapter	Title or Short Title.	Extent of repeal.
19 Geo. 2. c. 37	An Act to regulate insurance on ships belonging to the subject of Great Britain and on the merchandizes of effects laden thereon.	The whole Act.
28 Geo. 3 c. 56.	An Act to repeal an Act made in the twenty-fifth year of the reign of his present majesty instituted "An Act for regulating Insurances on Ships and on goods. merchandizes or effects" and for substituting other provisions for the like purpose in lieu thereof.	The whole Act so far as it relates to marine insurance.
31 and 32 Vict. c. 86.	The Policies of Marine Assurance Act 1868.	The whole Act

CODE OF CONDUCT FOR MEMBERS OF THE INSURANCE INSTITUTE OF NIGERIA

1 We the members of the Insurance Institute of Nigeria believe that membership of the Institute is a special privilege which carries with it certain duties and a responsibility to maintain the highest standards of professional conduct, thereby upholding the reputation of the Institute and the good name of our industry and the business of insurance generally. Arising from this, this code of conduct has been devised by the Council of the Institute to regulate the conduct of members in their professional and business activities and in furtherance of the objectives of the Institute.

2 The business of insurance is founded on the principle of utmost good faith. This should be the dominant principle regulating the conduct of all members of the Institute in whatever branch or aspect of insurance in which they may be engaged. A professional insurance manager, underwriter, inspector or any other member of the Institute, must at all times, put service above self and should always endeavour to employ the most efficient and economical ways of doing his job and of achieving the legitimate objectives of his company or organisation.

3 All members should observe the general law of the land. In particular, they should observe, promote, and adhere to the customary practice relating to insurance and must ensure that their business is conducted on sound insurance principles. As regards their relationship with the general public, members must ensure that full information is given to the public and to each individual client as to the suitability, scope and limitations of any insurance contract under negotiation. In the settlement of insurance claims, members must ensure that all legitimate claims are settled promptly and that all claimants are given fair and equitable treatment at all times.

4   All members should always be transparently honest in all their professional dealings and should all times, refrain from unethical conduct and must not engage in any fraudulent or corrupt practice.

5   Members who hold the Institute's diplomas or degrees or other professional qualifications, should always ensure that advertisements and other public announcements with which their names or qualifications are associated are not such as might bring the Institute into disrepute. Members who are not diploma holders must not publicise their membership of the Institute in such a way as to imply the possession of a professional qualification.

6   A member shall not improperly ask for or accept any financial gain, property, inducement or benefits of any kind for himself on account of anything done or to be done by him in the normal discharge of his duties.

7   If a member fails to conform to proper standards of professional conduct, the Council of the Institute, on the advice of its disciplinary committee, may exercise its disciplinary powers as prescribed in the Institute's Constitution and Bye Laws and the member may be reprimanded or suspended or removed from membership of the Institute. The Council of the Institute, may further recommend that a member who has been thus disqualified from membership of the Institute, be barred from further employment in the insurance industry or by those companies that support the Institute's code of conduct.

8   On the understanding that every professional has a duty to support his profession and to encourage its growth and development, every member should do his best at all times to support his local Institute in all its activities Senior members of the Institute and holders of insurance degrees or diplomas have the added responsibility of helping to further insurance education and of encouraging others to attain their professional qualification. They should also encourage the young members to acquire higher academic and professional qualifications which would help to promote the business of insurance. Members should also support insurance education generally in all forms and should take every opportunity to promote insurance knowledge and education generally.

BIBLIOGRAPHY

General Principles
"General Insurance" by John H. Magee 6th Edition (1961 Richard D. Irwin).
"Elements of Insurance" by Dr. W. A. Dinsdale, 3rd Edition 1963 (Pitman).
'Teach Yourself Insurance" by H. A. L. Cockerell (1961) (English Universities Press).

Legal
"Insurance Law" by E. J. Macgillivray, 4th Edition (Sweet and Maxwell).
"The Law of Insurance" by Preston and Collinvaux (Sweet and Maxwell).
"Law of Motor Insurance" by C. N. Shawcross 2nd Edition (1949) (Butterworth Press).

Accident Insurance
"Third Party Insurance" by Batten and Dinsdale (Stone and Cox).
"Motor Insurance" by Batten and Dinsdale (Stone and Cox).
"Principles and Practice of Accident Insurance" by W. A. Dinsdale (Buckley Press Limited).
"Dictionary of Accident Insurance" by Welson (Pitman).

Fire Insurance
"The Law relating to Fire Insurance" (Welford and Otter-Barry) Published by Butterworth and Company (Publishers) Limited.
"Fire Insurance Theory and Practice" by T. R. Smith Published by Stone and Cox.
"Consequential Loss Insurances and Claims" by D. Riley. Published by Sweet and Maxwell.

Life Insurance
"The Principles and Practice of Life Assurance" by Young and Bacon published by Buckley Press Limited.

"Life Assurance from Proposal to Policy" by Freeman and New. Published by Sir Isaac Pitman and Sons Limited.

Marine Insurance
"Elements and Practice of Marine Insurance" by V. Dover Published by Witherby.

"The Law and Practice of Marine Insurance relating to Collision Damages, and Other Liabilities to Third Parties" by Murd. (Pitman).

Reinsurance
"Reinsurance Contracts" 4th Edition (1961) Compiled by the Directors of and Published by W. T. Greig Limited.
"Law and Practice of Reinsurance" (Golding) Published by Buckley Press Limited.

INDEX

Index